Idiot, Sojourning Soul

Idiot, Sojourning Soul

A Post-Secular Pilgrimage

BY

JUSTIN ROSOLINO

RESOURCE *Publications* · Eugene, Oregon

IDIOT, SOJOURNING SOUL
A Post-Secular Pilgrimage

Resource Publications
An Imprint of Wipf and Stock Publishers
199 W. 8th Ave., Suite 3
Eugene, OR 97401

www.wipfandstock.com

PAPERBACK ISBN: 978-1-5326-7482-2
HARDCOVER ISBN: 978-1-5326-7483-9
EBOOK ISBN: 978-1-5326-7484-6

Manufactured in the U.S.A.   01/16/20

Dedicated to Danny McGrath, whose voice I still hear
whenever I read my own name.

I am a fugitive and a vagabond, a sojourner seeking signs.
—ANNIE DILLARD, *PILGRIM AT TINKER CREEK*

It is always hard to see the purpose in wilderness wanderings until after they are over.
—JOHN BUNYAN, *THE PILGRIM'S PROGRESS*

Have done with your choosing. *Want* something.
—C. S. LEWIS, *THE PILGRIM'S REGRESS*

Contents

Pilgrim:

noun pil·grim \'pil-grəm\

1. an alien; a sojourner in a strange land
2. one who wanders
3. a religious know-it-all

Acknowledgements

THANK YOU, THANK YOU, thank you to Brooke for your infinite patience, to Adria Haley, Rhonda "Rockstar" Lowry, Nubia Echevarria, Caroline Martin, Wes Yoder, Becky Nesbitt, Derek(s), Jesse and Sarah, Kristin and Jeff, Scotty and TJ, Mom and Dad, Jenn and Aaron (and Vesper), Daniel Lanning, Matt Wimer, Devan and Will, Art Lindsley, Paul DeHart, John Thatamanil, Patout Burns, Robin Jensen, Paul Lim, my BA and LOCS families, and to Christ-haunted children of all ages. And, most importantly, to all who are left out (especially you).

Introduction

"In The Beginning . . ."

Nothing ages faster than relevance.

—JOHN MEIER[1]

I'm only good at being young.

—JOHN MAYER[2]

Speech! Speech!

THIS BOOK AROSE OUT of a speech I delivered a few years ago at the high school where I was teaching at the time. More specifically, it was the response to said speech that moved me to expound upon its contents. I was invited to give the baccalaureate address for the senior class. For those who don't know what a baccalaureate is, which would've included me until a couple years ago, it's a religiously themed ceremony honoring graduates from an academic institution. In New York, we just called it "graduation," and it certainly wasn't religious. Unless you call a compulsory gathering of hungover teenagers "religious."

I don't remember much about my high school graduation, but not because I was hungover. I'd already quit drinking by that point. Tenth grade, to be precise. This rather unconventional decision had nothing to do with any ethical or religious convictions on my part. It had everything to do with not wanting to be dead. By the ripe age of fourteen, I could already tell my relationship with alcohol was an unhealthy one. So I decided to take some steps towards temperance. Twelve, in fact.

1

I now teach history at a Christian prep school in the heart of the Bible Belt—a far cry from my alma mater, where evangelical Christianity was an almost unknown quantity.[3] Senior year, I remember seeing a yard sign promoting something called a Billy Graham Crusade (he was an "evangelist," I later learned). The sign was posted in front of a small chapel we not-so-affectionately called the White Church, mostly on account of its whitewashed exterior and comparably colorless clientele. To me and my friends, the word "White" meant "other," as in *not* Italian, Jewish, Black, or Puerto Rican. I literally knew no one who went to the White church. Homecoming week, some buddies of mine used said sign to make our senior float for the parade . . . meaning they stole it from lawn of the White Church. Our "float," if you could call it that, was a flat-decked clamming boat tied to a trailer hitch. Atop the deck was placed some hapless, nameless, helpless freshman conscript, hands zip tied behind his back, Billy Graham sign tucked squarely in his lap. Poor kid. We did not win the prize for best homecoming float.

Homeroom Class (We got spirit, how 'bout you?)

Later that year, I got to give the speech at graduation—my first foray into public speaking. It was predictably peppy: "Believe in yourself," "Follow your heart," etc. At the suggestion of my father, I concluded with the following lines, lifted from Rodney Dangerfield: "I've got just one thing to say to you: It's a jungle out there! You gotta look out for number one! Just don't step in number two."

That is not how I ended my more recent graduation address.

This time around, I thought I'd say something a little more substantive, what with me being a teacher and all. Not surprisingly, it was a lot less perky than the speech I gave as a wide-eyed eighteen-year-old. I figured I'd offer our graduating seniors a helpful snapshot of the world they were about to encounter.

I began by describing a contemporary culture that is more wary of religion than ever before. For better or worse, we are far less likely than our predecessors to look for solace or guidance in traditional religious texts or institutions. And while I had no intention of warning my audience of an ensuing "War on Christmas"—mostly because I don't think it's true (and am not terribly concerned, even if it is)—I did reference a broad swath of data suggesting that ours is an increasingly non-religious, a.k.a. "secular," culture.[4]

I first heard the term in college, when a devout, Kibbutz-bound Jewish friend called me a "secular guy." I demanded immediate explanation. He obliged: "No offense. I just mean you don't really base your daily decisions on religious beliefs, holy books or whatever." Defused, I admitted he was right . . . which remains one of my least favorite things to do.

Secular is an admittedly slippery word. In popular parlance, to be *secular* means to ground one's understanding of the world not on religion, but on what can be known through reason and observation, best exemplified by the vast accumulation of secular knowledge gleaned through modern science.[5] Until recently, most scholars assumed modernity and religion would be like opposing ends of a seesaw: the more scientifically advanced Western civilization became, the less we would care about religion.[6] But this has not been the case, especially not in America—and here's where it gets kind of confusing—because while *secular* means non-religious, it doesn't necessarily mean *anti*-religious.[7] You don't have to be an axe-grinding, high-voltage atheist to be secular. Lots of modern Americans remain interested in things spiritual, regardless of whether they attend Sunday services. Some even say they *want* to believe in God—and wanting to believe is particularly tricky in a culture where all gods are up for grabs and all truth claims equally suspect.[8]

Looking back on it, I think I was a "secular guy" by default. It certainly wasn't an informed decision on my part. Sure, I had my share of beefs with organized religion—who doesn't? But I was also pretty curious about spirituality. Lots of Americans find themselves in the same boat. We are "spiritual but not religious," genuinely curious about things mystical, yet highly distrustful of traditional religious organizations, including the Christian church. Just 44 percent of Americans today claim to have confidence in organized religion, compared to 66 percent in 1973.[9] One fifth of American

adults claim no religious affiliation, the highest percentage in the history of
Pew Research Center polling. And the largest demographic of religiously
"unaffiliated"? You guessed it: the eighteen to twenty-nine range, with a
growing number of Americans under thirty now falling into the unfortunately labeled category, "nones."[10] Almost a third of American millennials
are unaffiliated with any specific religion. In the U.S., the number of "nones"
has risen 10 percent since 2007,[11] with most saying they're not even looking
for a religion that's "right for them."[12]

Then there's the "dones," those Americans born and raised going
to church who've decided that, for a number of reasons, they're over it.[13]
Like the nones, the dones are a growing camp (#Exvangelical #Deconver-
sion #EmptyThePews), and their rise marks more than a casual drift towards indifference: in 2012, 15 percent of young Americans said they were
"hostile" towards the Bible, up a full 5 percent from the previous year.[14]
Not "apathetic" or "suspicious." *Hostile.* And while plenty of twenty- and
thirty-somethings are still interested in spirituality,[15] to most, the prospect
of converting to Christianity sounds about as appetizing as a raw chicken
smoothie topped with a generous dollop of room-temperature mayonnaise.

A H8ters' History

So why all the hate? To what do we owe this ever-expanding, culture-wide
hostility towards Christianity? With this question in mind, I reviewed the
last several centuries of church-sponsored oppression and colonial expansion.[16] I started back in 1492, when Columbus sailed the ocean blue, kicking off a new era of worldwide exploration, conquest, and fierce economic
competition between the colonial powers of Europe. Soon, a succession of
supposedly "Christian" empires were scouring the globe in search of new
land and resources. European colonizers carefully constructed a religious
foundation to support the subjugation of the "primitive" people groups they
encountered.[17] During the "Scramble for Africa," King Leopold of Belgium
made a personal fortune by plundering the Congo of its rubber and ivory,
resulting in the deaths of millions of displaced, and enslaved, inhabitants.
His justification? "What I do there is done as a Christian duty to the poor
African."[18] Things weren't much better in the Americas, where slave owners
interpreted the Bible as either defending or mandating involuntary servi-
tude.[19] On plantations, pastors were ordered to preach Bible passages that
encouraged submission—i.e., "Slaves obey your masters"—all while conveniently avoiding Jesus' more liberationist pronouncements, including this
one, from the Gospel of Luke: "He [God] has anointed me to proclaim good
news to the poor. He has sent me to proclaim freedom for the prisoners and

recovery of sight for the blind, to set the oppressed free."[20] Lest they stumble upon such sentiments and get any wacky insurrectionist ideas, slaves were forbidden from learning to read.[21] Clever, clever Christian colonizers. And not very Christian-y.

It wasn't only the newly colonized who bore the brunt of religious oppression. Women endured their fair share. Puritans were quick to build a new and improved patriarchy in America, based, in part, on the belief that evil and femininity were inextricably linked. From Jezebel to Bathsheba to Delilah, it was the infamous sirens of Scripture who were responsible for corrupting their male counterparts, just as their foremother, Eve, had done in the garden of Eden. Men were therefore justified in using coercion to keep their daughters and wives in check.[22] To this day, women report of being encouraged by their pastors to endure domestic mistreatment (i.e., "Wives, submit to your husbands").[23] In a #MeToo world where Black Lives Matter, no wonder we're not packing out the pews like we used to.

Science Friction

Keeping with the established theme of pessimism—always a winner at baccalaureate ceremonies—I turned my attention to some of the major philosophical and scientific critiques of Christianity that the college-bound are liable to hear. I tried to impress upon my students the merits of these insightful critiques: i.e., the tendency among American Christians to confuse the U.S. of A. with the kingdom of God;[24] the various, and valid, scientific criticisms of six-day creationism, especially when contrasted with the relatively weak counterarguments asserted by fundamentalists; modern Christianity's morbid fascination with the rapture, often to the neglect of the here-and-now; etc.[25] In other words, I tried to spell out the ways in which these criticisms of popular, contemporary Christianity are . . . what's the word I'm looking for . . . "correct."

To be clear: by "popular, contemporary Christianity," I mean something decidedly different than what Jesus' earlier followers were up to. In ancient Rome, Christians were known for their radical, counter-cultural concern for society's most vulnerable, including "orphans and widows," slaves, and exiles.[26] Even the most persecution-happy emperors were impressed by the "moral character" of their Jesus-following subjects: "[They] support not only their poor, but ours as well."[27] That's what being a "follower of the Way" used to mean (a moniker used far more frequently in the Bible than *Christian*).[28] But nowadays, not so much. For many a modern American, the word *Christian* has become decidedly derogatory, synonymous with "consumerist,"[29] "hypocritical," "sheltered," "angry," "judgmental," "anti-intellectual," "anti-science," and all sorts of similarly unflattering adjectives.[30]

Anti-science—a charge frequently leveled against American evangelicals, and it's not without warrant. Just a few years ago, one U.S. Representative condemned evolution and the big bang as "lies straight from the pit of Hell."[31] Sounds pretty anti-science to me. It seems the squabble between science and religion rages on, at least in some circles. And so, being a history teacher, I figured I'd cover some of the seminal figures in the development of said squabble.

Galileo! (Galileo) Galileo, Figaro!

First on my list came Galileo (1564–1642), that notorious natural philosopher who had the audacity to dissent from prevailing wisdom simply because it was wrong. Following in Aristotle's footsteps, most medievals pictured the cosmos as a series of concentric spheres, with earth at the center and "the heavens" at the periphery. Kinda like this:

Even among Europe's educated elites, most people assumed the sun circled round the earth.[32] And in their defense, it certainly looks that way to us. Hence the colloquial "sun*rise*" and "sun*set*," which even the Scriptures employ: "From sunrise to sunset, let the Lord's name be praised."[33] If taken too literally, these passages portray our planet as the immovable pivot point around which all else revolves—which is precisely what Galileo's colleagues believed.[34] They also assumed the farther from earth you traveled, the closer you'd get to "the heavens," which is where God was supposed to live. I guess people found it comforting to know God's celestial street address . . . until Galileo screwed it all up by proving the earth actually orbits the sun. This made a lot of people perturbed, and understandably so. It can be immensely satisfying to imagine oneself as the center of the universe.

But nudging humanity towards the cosmic margins wasn't Galileo's unforgivable sin. What really got him in hot water was crossing the Catholic Church, an institution already rocked by several ongoing crises of authority.

Long before Galileo ever peered through his first telescope, Catholic credibility had been already challenged by several instances of controversy and malfeasance (Spanish Inquisition, anyone?).[35] Then there was the Protestant Reformation of the sixteenth century, when priests like Martin Luther railed against Rome for hierarchical tyranny and selling "indulgences"—written guarantees of admittance into heaven, sold by the Church for a price.[36] Luther's criticisms caught on and, within a few decades, half of Europe had turned against the Catholic Church. Then along comes Galileo, whose discoveries were a direct challenge to Rome's already-diminished clout. Most Church leaders were on record as agreeing with Aristotle's ancient model of the cosmos, and Rome wasn't about to endure another scandal in the form of some uppity Italian (and I'm not talking about me).

Poor Galileo. It's not like he was trying to buck the religious establishment just for kicks. A churchgoing man, Galileo agreed with the traditional Christian view that, since Scripture is divinely inspired, it could never "lie or err."[37] Problem is, its interpreters can—and often do.[38] This wasn't a controversial claim at the time, nor should it be today: different people interpret the same scriptures differently. We've all got our little biases and blind spots.

Galileo's peers knew all of this. They knew biblical interpretation was tricky business. They were accustomed to reading the Bible with subtlety and patience. But for mostly political reasons, they sided against Galileo and put him on house arrest for the remainder of his days. And the rest, as we history teachers like to say, is history.

Marx, Darwin, and Nietzsche, Oh My!

Feeling I was on a roll—potentially downhill—I moved on to Karl Marx, founding father of modern communism. This was at a conservative Christian school, mind you, where the mere mention of Marx is liable to raise a few eyebrows. It probably doesn't help that he looked like an axe-wielding hybrid of Charles Manson and the creepy neighbor from *Home Alone*:

I mean, seriously, Karl . . . you couldn't've cleaned up a little for this pic? Maybe grab a shave? Watcha reachin' for in your pocket there . . . a pipe, perchance? Or maybe a meat cleaver?

With much trepidation, I explained Marx's diagnosis of religion as an "opiate" for the masses, a sort of spiritual anesthetic we use to make ourselves feel better.[39] According to Marx, we only need religion because we live in a sick society that reduces everything to a cruel competition between winners and losers, like some demented dodgeball game for grown-ups. The more we compete, the more we see one another only as adversaries, the more bitter and miserable we become. That's capitalism in a nutshell—at least, in Marx's view—which means religion isn't so much the cause of our problems as it is a symptom of the real disease: capitalism. Get rid of capitalism and you'll no longer need religion, the go-to drug of Western society.

And speaking of drugs, how could I leave out renowned cocaine enthusiast Sigmund Freud? It was Freud who dismissed religion as an "illusion" created to fulfill our own unsatisfied wishes. Life isn't fair, bad things happen to good people, etc. It's only natural that we'd want a benevolent deity to make everything right one day. We want to believe God will weed out society's rotten apples and create an afterlife where the rest of us can live happily ever after, forever freed from the annoyance of the world's insufferable jerks.[40] So we make it up. We wish divinity into existence. We conjure religious illusions like God and heaven, then choose to believe them. Case closed.

And what good baccalaureate address would be complete without covering Charles Darwin, the original Chuck D? Darwin went further than any of his predecessors in explaining the origins of life without recourse to divine intervention. Turns out, you don't really need God to make a world teeming with living organisms. All you really need is random mutation, natural selection, and a whole lotta time.[41] Organisms develop and diversify over the ages, almost as if by accident, and all without God having to get his heavenly hands dirty. After Darwin, we no longer needed Sunday school answers to questions like, "Why do peacocks have colorful tails?" Now we know: because primordial peacocks with big, colorful tails attracted more mates and spawned more offspring than their tiny-tailed, monochromatic counterparts, who eventually died out. It's that simple. Multicolored peacocks were thus "selected" to live on—not by divine providence, but by blind, pitiless indifference. The insentient forces of nature. Darwin freed us from the explanatory God of little children, and scientific consensus has long since confirmed his theory.

I figured I'd cap off our joyful jaunt down memory lane by reminding the audience of Nietzsche's controversial declaration: "God is dead."[42] Religion, said Nietzsche, is a crutch for the weak—life's losers who resent the world's winners. These unfortunate souls want to believe that they'll finish on top one day, when the beautiful people finally get their comeuppance and the meek inherit the earth.[43] So they invented a God who condemns strength, self-sufficiency, and success while rewarding the meek and mild with heavenly bliss (e.g., "blessed are the poor," etc.). Nietzsche figured modern society would smarten up eventually and realize religion was always just juvenile, self-soothing gibberish. Then we'd be free to move on and create a new, better, godless world in our own image. Some say we already have.

So how'd I wrap up my cheerful oration? Naturally, with a synopsis of Jesus' utter failure to address the above-mentioned criticisms.

Good News

If Jesus' goal was to explain the mysteries of the universe or explain away the problem of suffering, he didn't do a very good job of it. Neither do the

Gospel stories offer foolproof plans for taming the universe or making life more "fair." And as far as marking out a path for financial success or self-fulfillment, Jesus was even less effective, unworthy of untying the shoes of a Tony Robbins, Tim Ferriss, or Deepak Chopra.

If God is really real and Jesus is really God, it's reasonable to assume he could've proven himself through an overwhelming display of power. And why not? Why not hit us over the head with incontrovertible evidence? Isn't that what an all-powerful God *should* be like, shining forth in undeniable glory? Yet even after the resurrection, Jesus doesn't prove himself in the way that gravity proves itself to anyone who's ever taken middle school science, jumped off a cliff, or gotten a boob job.

"Christ's life was an absolute failure from every standpoint but God's."[44] A famous minister named Oswald Chambers wrote that. Strange words coming from a pastor, but he's got a point. Instead of an obvious, overpowering Messiah, we get a Christ who voluntarily embraces fragility, a Jesus who was easy to silence, even easier to kill. We get a fully human being who died a broke virgin with hardly a handful of (mostly female) followers. I wonder if he could even hold a steady job in today's world, fond as he was of speaking in poetic parables rather than cutting to the chase. It's not even clear that he was a very good carpenter. Couldn't somebody've bothered to keep a Jesus original for posterity's sake? A rocking chair or something? Or were the products of his craftsmanship that mundane? Some scholars say "carpenter" is too dignified a word; that he was more a day laborer than artisan, lower even than a peasant.[45] Would any of us really want to hire this guy, befriend him, date him, love him, let alone follow him? Yet *this* Jesus is supposed to be the source of some world-changing proclamation. "The Spirit of the Lord is on me," he declared, "because he has anointed me to proclaim good news . . ."[46]

When most of us hear the phrase "good news," we think of something that's supposed to feel . . . you know . . . *good.* "It's a girl!" "Down goes Frazier!" With all the desperation of a pre-2016 Cubs fan before they finally broke the series curse, good news is news we really, really want but aren't at all certain we'll receive.

But with Jesus, it's different. Because with Jesus, we get good news that's difficult to stomach—namely, that *this* is what heavenly love looks like when it lives in our world. According to the Bible, Jesus is "the image of the invisible God" and "the exact representation of his being."[47] This is what God looks like when he lives life on life's terms, surrendering himself to the slings and arrows of outrageous fortune. And make no mistake about this: Christianity means living in *this* world, as it is; not some idyllic, virtual reality, but the Real World in all its gory detail. So it was with Jesus, and I shudder at the possibility that *this* is what it looks like to be fully human, fully alive, and fully divine. In answering the perennial question, "What if God was one of us?" Jesus exposes our embarrassing need for emergency assistance, since we are all scared to death to live *that* kind of life, marked as it was by risk-taking, truth-telling, self-emptying, and suffering. Yet we sense that *this* is how we were intended to live among our neighbors, our friends, even—God forbid—our enemies; that *this* is how we are to love. But we can't. But we must. This is what he asks of us. This is what he asks of *me*. And the more merciful and patient he is, the more intolerable his implicit indictment becomes—so intolerable, in fact, that we crucify him.

In one of Scripture's most enigmatic moments, the apostle Paul calls the crucified Christ the "power of God."[48] Behold! God at God's best, nailed to a tree. On a raggedy cross, Jesus—a.k.a. the "Son of Man"—revealed the true power and purpose of God. "The Son of Man will be delivered into the hands of men, and they will kill him." Behold, the power of man pitted against the power of God.[49]

Power Struggles

What *is* divine power? Power to create, to love and endure, to bring life and hope, to heal what is broken, to overcome darkness and death. Sounds lovely, but if I'm being honest, that's not the kind of "power" I tend to revere. Neither did Napoleon, that diminutive, would-be emperor of everything. Nearing his final years, Napoleon pondered: "Alexander, Caesar, Charlemagne and I myself have founded great empires; but upon what did these creations of our genius depend? Upon force. Jesus alone founded His empire upon love, and to this very day millions will die for Him."[50] An empire of love, grounded on what theologians call *kenosis*, from the Greek *kenoō*, for "self-emptying."[51] A new kingdom unlike any humanly contrived empire, all of which rely on some force of coercion.[52] The revelation of this heavenly kingdom is supposed to be good news. More specifically, it's supposed to be news *from* God, for *us*. But to be *news*, it must be something that we didn't know already. It can't be something obvious, something that was already lying around. And to be *good* news, it must be something as welcome as it is surprising. Like a strange gift given in the nick of time and against all odds, it must be something miraculous.

The year my parents split up, when my dad went to rehab and moved into a one-room apartment by the train tracks, I thought it would be a Christmas with no laughter and no presents. I ended up getting the video game I asked for (Ms. Pac-Man, I think). Yippee. A year later, when I ask for Super Mario World and instead got my dad back—sober, employed, and remarried to my mom—that was good news.

And while we're on the subject of Christmas, remember that scene from the Charlie Brown special where Linus recites from the Gospel of Luke? What was it that the angels said to the shepherds near Bethlehem? "'Behold, I bring you good tidings of great joy, which shall be to all people ... On earth peace, and good will toward men.'" Glad tidings. Peace on earth. Good will toward everybody. Somewhere in the midst of this counterintuitive, crucified revelation called "Jesus," there's supposed to be something profoundly "good," some miraculous news to be delivered unto humanity by hosts of happy angels. *Something* ...

And that's where I left it. That was the glorious conclusion to my baccalaureate address. I left my students with an open question, because sometimes we need the space to chew on things before any answer can have real weight. Some truths need to happen *to* us, like when a child feels the cold ocean waves lapping at her feet for the very first time. Such encounters lift us out of ourselves until the world breaks open, becoming suddenly more wild and wondrous than mere moments before. And premature analysis, no matter how airtight, can empty such occasions of their evocative potency.

Also, I ran out of time. So there was that.

Conservative-on-Conservative Crime

I retreated from the podium and shuffled off stage. Fearing my imminent dismissal, I was both surprised and relieved by the audience's reaction. Immediately I received dozens of heartfelt expressions of gratitude from parents, students, colleagues; even members of the board of trustees. That night, my inbox was flooded by more of the same, all echoing the same sentiment: "Thanks for saying out loud what we've all been thinking."

This was not the response I expected. I guess I hadn't realized how many Christians are as troubled by the current state of American Christianity as I am. Like me, they are frustrated by how Christianity has been shaped by its own defensive response to the challenges of our times. Maybe you've noticed.

Over the last several decades in particular, Christianity has expanded its list of requirements to include a host of new and cumbersome conditions, including—but not limited to—fiscal conservatism, dispensational Zionism, neo-nationalist nativism, six-day creationism, and the wholesale rejection of climate science, all in a desperate attempt to fend off the threat of modern secularism. But by drawing deeper and evermore numerous lines in the sand, contemporary Christianity has only made it harder for the average American to make any real sense of Jesus, let alone cast their vote yea or nay. Even conservative Christians are left scratching their heads, questioning whether a Christ so confusingly construed can still be the bearer of any "good news."

Conservative—there's a provocative adjective for ya, especially these days. But if we can bracket clunky political connotations for a minute, I think it's fair to say that all Christians are "conservative" in that we try—however failingly—to stay true to what God has spoken into the world through Jesus, some two thousand years ago. Because Christians believe God accomplished something utterly unique in Jesus; something of cosmic, timeless, and transcultural significance.[53] We are therefore "conservative" by bent (from the Latin *conservare*, "preserving and faithfully observing"), more interested in orthodoxy than originality.[54] And something similar can be said of Jesus, a man whose mission was to reintroduce creation to its Creator, to reconcile a wounded and weary world to its own Origin, to gather what has been scattered and lost. So if by "progressive" you mean "a person who favors new or modern ideas,"[55] then Jesus might've been the least progressive, most conservative person in history.

But that's just the thing: because today, even the churchiest conservatives are beginning to suspect that something is amiss, that our current installment of "conservative" Christianity is anything but. And I'm not just talking about left-leaning, podcast-consuming, cosmopolitan Christians from the coasts. I'm talking Sunday school teachers, soccer moms, and Red State Republicans from flyover country.[56] Like me, they are bothered not so much by how Christianity has lost touch with the modern, "secular" world, but that Christianity has lost touch with itself, with its own story and essential identity. Instead of wondering how to convince the world to embrace Jesus, many Christians now wonder whether embracing Jesus might actually require renouncing—or at least radically reforming—contemporary Christianity as we know it.

A Branding Problem

Lots of people diagnose the above-described dilemma as a symptom of bad press. In Jeff Foxworthy's words, modern Christianity has a "branding problem."[57] It's not *what* Christianity is saying that's the issue; it's *how* Christianity has been saying it. It's a problem of style, not of substance; a crisis of marketing, not a problem with the product itself.

Two things: First, I just unironically quoted Jeff Foxworthy. Second, he may have a point. The squeaky wheel gets the grease, and let's face it: loud and proud fundamentalists usually get the lion's share of media attention

(Westboro Baptist Church comes to mind). Add to that evangelicalism's on-going animus towards secular science and you have a bit of a PR nightmare for modern Christianity.[58]

The solution? Put the fun back into fundamentalism! To that end, evangelical groups like Focus on the Family are attempting to rebrand themselves as more "conciliatory" and less "confrontational."[59] It's not a new tactic: for years now, churches have been busy employing all manner of marketing strategies in order to "soften" their message and broaden appeal: hipper music, tech-savvy churches, skinnier jeans, etc.[60] But with all due respect to the fantastic Mr. Foxworthy, I'd like to suggest Christianity's current crisis is not merely a matter of curb appeal (or lack thereof). But if not a problem of branding, then what?

Some claim Christianity is in decline because it's obsolete. Like chain-smoking while pregnant, it's just not a great idea and now we know better. Which is not to say religion played no positive role in contributing to human progress. The late Christopher Hitchens acknowledged religion as our first decent shot at making sense of the world, "a babyish attempt to meet our inescapable demand for knowledge."[61] And just like a baby's first poo, religion fails to represent the best we can do. But now, it's time to make better poo—and thanks to modern science, we can.

Science has allowed us to understand the world with far greater accuracy and insight than our ancestors.[62] Our cosmic origins and even life itself can all be explained as the result of what Darwin called "blind chance." No Intelligent Designer necessary. No Creator, no creation; no fall or redemption; no divine revelation (through the Bible or otherwise); no ultimate purpose; no God and, by extension, no Son of God. Which means Christianity is the real fossil . . . the landline of worldviews . . . destined to disappear faster than you can say "Blockbuster Video." So it's not that Christianity has gotten a bad rap; it's that it's a faulty product—which is another way of saying it isn't really true. This is the way of atheism, and it has its merits.

But for pestering little pilgrims like me, this answer won't do. Call me biased, but I think there are more interesting questions to be asked; questions that *should* be asked. And I am not alone.

In spite of everything—or maybe because of it—we remain a people haunted by the Big Why: What's our purpose? Why are we here? If we're honest, these are the questions that nag us when our heads hit the pillow at night. On we soldier, intrigued as ever by matters "spiritual," including angels, the afterlife, prayer,[63] and even that quirky carpenter from Galilee. That includes America's "nones," most of whom still believe in some sort of "higher power."[64] For a lot of us, something about Jesus rings capital-T true, even in the midst of our being burned out on religion, even in the thicket of doubt and disappointment.

The trick, of course, is figuring out what that "something" is.

So here's what I'm gonna do. I'm gonna spend some time talking about the God problem—and, more specifically, the Jesus problem. This will involve surveying our culture and getting a lay of the land. I'm also going to explain why it's a problem for all of us, whether "spiritual," secular, or something in between. Even if you're a contented churchgoer (#Blessed!) and could care less about the aforementioned critiques, even if religion doesn't have a bad rap amongst your circle of church friends, the fact is that your circle is shrinking . . . which is fine, assuming Christ's objective was more cliquey than cosmic. But if all those John 3:16 signs we see at football games are really true; if "God so loved *the world*" that he gave his only Son to save it; if, like Linus and Luke said, the "good news" is supposed to be that which brings joy to *all* people—then we might have a cosmic crisis on our hands.

But how'd we get here, so tangled and twisted in theological knots? What were the series of unfortunate events that led to Christianity's current, confounding state, and how has our understanding of Christ changed along the way? To answer these questions, I'm going to try and get at the real Jesus: who he was, and is, and—just as importantly—who he is not. Even more presumptuously, and at the risk of self-aggrandizement (memoir is the selfie stick of literature), I'm going to do all this by telling you my story, even though the point of the story is not really "mine." Because I am just another you, a fellow pilgrim doing my darnedest to navigate the zigs and zags of a perplexing terrain. Ours is an era in which Christians find themselves strange bedfellows with a swelling chorus of skeptics and seekers, "nones" and "dones," default secularists and the spiritually curious, who are together asking an unsettling question: Is Christianity as we now know it actually Christian?

1

From Thirty Thousand Feet

The single desire that dominated my search for delight was simply
to love and be loved.

—St. Augustine[65]

How grateful I was then to be part of the mystery, to love and to be loved.

—Conor Oberst[66]

Dysfunktional Families

When I was seventeen, my father did something extraordinary: he paid
me a compliment. It was after one of those excruciating, end-of-the-year
high school ceremonies with which today's parents have grown all too accustomed. I ended up winning the academic award for top history student
(yay for me). After all the obligatory pomp and circumstance, we drove
home in our old Volvo wagon and did what we always did—listened to the
radio—R & B, mostly. We may've been dysfunctional, but like Sly and the
Family Stone, we were funky. Paul Simon's "Slip Slidin' Away" came on and
my dad cranked it up, insisting I pay heed to Richard Tee's silky electric
piano, blurting out commentary, as he always did. "Man, listen to these lyrics!" he shouted: "I know a father who had a son, he longed to tell him all
the reasons for the things he had done . . ."[67] The song played on. The father
travels far to see his boy and give his reasons. The moment comes; the words

all but form on the tip of his tongue before gently receding; the moment goes, and so does the father. We listened, our eyes fixed forward. When it came time to turn onto our street, my father inched the volume down and ventured to speak, now in a muted key: "You know your teacher pulled me aside tonight and said, 'Jim, I've only ever had two really great history students in my life. One was my son. The other was yours.'" Thus concluded our little father-son moment, one of the few we had in the entirety of my childhood. I hope I've lived up to the compliment.

My parents never pushed me academically. Quite the opposite. By middle school, my dad already had me working at his bar part-time. Weekends and after school, mostly. Things went well until tenth grade, which was the first time my mom ever took issue with one of my report cards. This was back when you got those dreadful documents in the mail . . . meaning she usually got to 'em first. She circled the "Teacher Comments" column, which included phrases like, "Is a constant disruption in class" and "a negative influence on his peers." Then, at the bottom of the page, using terrifying blood-red ink, she wrote in all caps, "WHAT ARE WE GONNA DO ABOUT THIS?!" and left it on my bed. I found it a few hours later, circled the entire left column (which was straight A's) and wrote, "WHAT ARE *YOU* GONNA DO ABOUT *THIS*?" then left it on her desk. I thought it was a funny bit. It didn't go over as well as I'd hoped.

The bar was built in the 1880s atop an underground spring that meandered through the basement, where it would chill countless kegs of beer placed carefully in its path, all at a perfect 37 degrees. I liked working with my dad, seeing him in his element. The son of an absentee matriarch and a father who died too young, he made a living playing gigs and tending bar—not exactly vocational circles known for fostering healthy interpersonal habits. Not that he didn't love people. I suspect anyone who knows my father would agree that he wants nothing more than to love and be loved. But wanting to and knowing how are not the same thing.

The bar

My parents' friends all had names like Warts, Stork, Critter, and Patty O' Furniture. I'm not talking about "nicknames" here—as far as anybody knew, these were their full legal names. Misslehead was famous for taping a fishing pole to his bald skull and letting the baited hook dangle before his nose, all while downing shots of bottom-shelf whiskey. There was Carwash Eddie in his threadbare straw hat, wandering aimlessly through town, always pushing the same shopping cart. It took me years to figure out he was actually homeless. Eddie was a regular at my dad's bar, as were Billy Joel and Jackie "the Jokeman" Martling, of eventual Howard Stern infamy. Most were blue-collar working stiffs, the offspring of immigrants who scraped a living out of the earth with their hands. Many were terminal alcoholics. Several were dead by the time I was twenty, and my father still misses them. Oddly enough, some of these men were responsible for checking my father into rehab and guarding his newfound sobriety, simply because they loved him.

To me, this was all normal—The Way Things Are—and it had its perks. It's cool when your parents embrace a rock 'n' roll lifestyle. It isn't so cool when your dad shows up hammered to the father-son kickball game in middle school. Guess that's the trade-off.

Fats

After middle and high school came college, then the compulsory post-graduate interregnum of moving back in with my parents and waiting tables. After six months or so, I packed up my '87 Thunderbird and moved to Atlanta to play music. I played open-mic nights all over the city, desperate to find fellow musicians and put a band together. I even tried posting an ad in the "Musicians Wanted" section. The ad was a flop, but I did get a few interesting phone calls out of it. Like this: "What's up man, this is Fats . . . you know, like Fats Domino?" (I did). "Listen man, I read your ad. We should hook up. I dig a lot of the same stuff you do." Good to hear. "One thing though . . . what's with the Jesus thing? Are you, like, into bombing abortion clinics or somethin'? No offense."

"Ummm, yeah man . . . no problem," I answered, perjuring myself.

Maybe I should provide some more context: my ad referenced a jumble of creative and spiritual influences, including Marvin Gaye, Zeppelin, The Beatles, Dostoyevsky, and Jesus. And yes, I was trying too hard. But still, it surprised me that Fats associated the word "Jesus" with domestic terrorism. What's worse, Fats accused me of being a religious whack job. I was taken aback. Pissed is more like it. Dems' fightin' words.

Not that I was actually capable of administering a beatdown, what with me being 5'8" and all. Scrappy though.

Turns out, I didn't end up threatening Fats with violence. Why, you ask, other than the aforementioned lack of aptitude for thuggery? Mostly because I had become a Christian—a "born-again," a Jesus freak, a member of the God Squad, a "follower of the Way," or whichever you prefer.[68] I myself favor the term "disciple," from the Latin *discipulus*, for "learner." And given my newfound convictions, I figured the old go-to of verbal assault with the option to go physical was no longer appropriate.

Fats and I never ended up making beautiful music together, but for me, the long-term take away was this: somehow the life, death, message, and meaning of a brown-skinned pacifist from the wrong side of the Palestinian tracks had become synonymous with political coercion and ideological

bullying. Call me naïve, but at that point in my life, Fat's decidedly negative appraisal of evangelical Christianity was new to me, probably because
all of evangelical Christianity was new to me. We didn't have church camp
when I was a kid. We had A.A. meetings and guilt. Sure, I knew some of
the Christian basics: "Love your neighbor," etc. I just didn't know anybody
who took it that seriously. Certainly not in an "I'm going to orient my entire
life around Jesus" kind of way. To me, "Christian" was kinda like the word
"jousting": there were probably some harmless, twenty-sided die-slinging
Renaissance festival enthusiasts out there who were "really into" jousting,
but I'd never actually met one. Christianity was, at best, innocuous; at worst,
something associated with a brutish and uncivilized epoch.

My naiveté concerning evangelical Christianity was short-lived. Fats
has since become one of countless people I've met over the years who've
helped educate me about the public perception of popular Christianity. And
as previously mentioned, it ain't good.

Since the country's inception, American evangelicals have worked tirelessly to broadcast Jesus' message to the general public. The word is out. The
transmission has been sent. And while Christianity's PR campaign never
resonated with younger me, a decades-long onslaught of made-for-TV Jesus
movies and happy-clappy God-rock has been remarkably effective, at least
in informing the general public about the basics of the Christian story.[69]
Never before have copies of the Bible been more plentiful—in libraries,
bookstores, hotel rooms, online, etc. And there's the rub: most Americans
today have heard or read enough about Jesus to know that contemporary
Christianity doesn't bare much semblance to its namesake. Even younger,
secular me knew the gist of Jesus' teachings: "Do not resist an evil person.
If anyone slaps you on the right cheek, turn to them the other cheek also
. . . If anyone forces you to go one mile, go with them two miles . . . love
your enemies and pray for those who persecute you . . ." (Matt 5:39–41).[70]
Now compare Jesus' words with Donald Trump's oft-repeated motto of massive retaliation: "Get even with people. If they screw you, screw them back
ten times as hard."[71] It doesn't take a logician to see the contrast. Yet, for
a number of policy-related reasons, the majority of evangelicals voted for
Trump, if less than enthusiastically.[72] And it's not as though Republicans
have a corner on vindictive political rhetoric. Liberals have proven quite
capable of going toe to toe and tit for tat (see former Attorney General Eric
Holder's 2018 statement, "When they [Republicans] go low, we kick 'em.")[73]

Even before the 2016 election, Americans have tended to look askance
at religious organizations for being too focused on power, politics, and
money.[74] And it takes about 0.2 seconds to see the irony in associating
such an unholy trinity of attributes with a dead-broke day laborer born in

a Bethlehem feeding trough. More than ironic, Christianity has become a bit of a joke.

Which is not to say that people always took Christianity seriously in ages past. The ancient Romans scorned Christianity as a religion for losers and less-thans. What was a humble carpenter compared to mighty Caesar? What kind of Lord lets himself get crucified—in public, no less? Even the apostle Paul called the message of the cross "foolishness."[75] But the Romans scoffed at Christ's foolhardy followers for altogether different reasons than we do today.

Gimme Shelter

Most Americans today think Christians are a holy huddle of "sheltered" people, unwilling to deal with the "grit and grime of people's lives."[76] We see this sort of "safety first!" ethos in music, movies, and books targeted to church audiences (i.e., "safe for the whole family"). But were safety, security, or "family values" ever that Christian to be begin with? Wasn't it Jesus who warned his followers, "I am sending you out like lambs among wolves"?[77] What of Paul's talk of "foolishness"? Sometimes I wonder what fate would've befallen my father if, God forbid, his barfly buddies had all been cul-de-sac Christians.

Makes me think of Katy Perry (just go with it). While I'm probably not the intended demographic for *Women's Health* magazine, I happened upon an interesting article in the waiting room of my dentist's office a few years back. As I read, I was struck by her description of a highly insulated, suffocating, borderline creepy Christian childhood: "I had no idea there was a world outside."[78] *No idea.*

I played a gig opening for Perry once. Mercury Lounge in Manhattan, I think. This was before she blew up, back when she self-identified as contemporary Christian musician, Katy Hudson. It would now appear that the lovely Ms. Perry belongs to that growing class of Americans known as "post-Christian" (a.k.a. "dones").[79] It happens all the time: the minute they get a glimpse of the outside world, they make a break for it, and the Christian bubble bursts. And unlike previous generations, most don't return when they get married, have kids, and "settle down."[80]

But it's not always a case of the grass being greener on the other side of the Christian bubble. For a lot of ex-Christians, deconversion is more about disillusionment—the painful process of coming to grips with a dangerous, complicated world, often for the first time as adults. Somewhere along the way, the rug gets pulled from underneath, bringing down a whole framework of previously unexamined assumptions and ironclad absolutes.

In many ways, the dones are casualties of the culture war; the shell-shocked victims of their own sheltered childhoods. Take *HuffPost* contributor, Jessie Golem. Raised in a safe, stable, and loving environment, Golem "accepted Jesus into her heart" as a teenager. Then, after serving as an overseas missionary and seeing firsthand the miseries of extreme poverty, Golem grew to question, and ultimately renounce, her childhood faith. "Here I was," she recounts, "feeling like my church had failed me by keeping me sheltered and naive."[81] Reddit writer Kendall Hobbs has a similar deconversion story. As a young adult, Hobbs started wondering, "Why did God answer those prayers of mine [i.e. to help her ace a test, find her car keys, etc.] when he ignored the prayers of Christian parents whose children were suffering from chemotherapy treatments as they were dying of leukemia?"[82] Those selfsame questions drove former fundamentalist Bart Ehrman to leave the Christian fold: "If God is concerned to answer my little prayers about my daily life," Ehrman wondered, "why didn't he answer my and others' big prayers when millions were being slaughtered by the Khmer Rouge in Cambodia . . . ?"[83] Raised in a Christian home, John Green, author of *The Fault in Our Stars*, enrolled in seminary after college in hopes of becoming a pastor. After working with terminally ill children as a hospital chaplain, Green found himself "unfulfilled by the answers that are traditionally offered to questions of why some people suffer and why others suffer so little."[84] For similar reasons, musician Lisa Gungor grew evermore dissatisfied with religion's all-too-easy answers, especially after visiting Auschwitz as an adult and contemplating the horrors of the Holocaust: "In the tribe we were born into, these questions weren't really allowed. . .When you finally are able to ask them, it [faith] collapses . . ."[85]

Music and Other Odd Jobs

I played music professionally for the better part of ten years. I got to live my own lil' version of the alt-American dream. Here's proof:

Me playing a session in Nashvegas

Me looking significantly cooler than I am

Me sportin' the fro and double chin at Bonnaroo

Me melting peoples' faces off with sheer guitar-shredding wizardry

At various points in my almost-illustrious career, I shared stage and/or studio with Jars of Clay, Matt Nathanson, Take 6, Dave Barnes, Ian Fitchuk, Ed Cash, various members of the Zac Brown Band, and even India.Arie (once). I played gigs in over forty states, and in multiple countries. Sometimes I stayed in swanky hotels or pimped-out tour buses. Sometimes I slept on the floors of vans. After a while in the biz, I decided to explore some as-of-yet uncharted vocational territory involving consistent and predictable paychecks, health insurance, and a clearly delineated set of responsibilities for which I would be held accountable . . . I believe the appropriate vernacular is a "job."

As you might imagine, the transition to teaching has necessitated a substantial set of lifestyle adjustments. Waking before noon, for instance. One of the more challenging topics we cover in history class is the Jewish ghettos of the Holocaust. In the late 1930s and early 40s, the Nazis forced millions of Jews to relocate to enclosed, overcrowded communities with almost no access to medicine or running water. Those that survived were eventually sent to concentration camps.

When my students hear the word "ghetto," naturally, they think of American ghettos, which are a little different than Jewish ghettos during WWII, where residents were confined at gunpoint, prior to mass extermination.[86] I tell my students that "ghetto" can mean any environment where a high concentration of a particular people group live together, including America's "Christian ghetto." That's when they ask, "What's a *Christian* ghetto?" I then proceed to Google the term and read a few lines about insulated Christian communities whose residents shun mainstream culture, listen only to Christian music, and adorn their minivans with plastic fishes. At this point one of them says, "Oh yeah . . . that's totally my mom!"

No matter how you slice it, there's a serious disconnect between the Christ of popular Christian (sub-)culture and the Jesus of first-century Palestine, a man who we'd be hard pressed to describe as "out of touch." I'm not talking about the inevitable disconnect between our highest ideals and actual performance; anybody who's punted their New Year's resolutions by mid-January knows what it's like to fall short of well-intended goals. And if a "hypocrite" is one who falters on the road towards her highest aspirations, then all Christians—like all humans—are hypocrites by definition. What I'm talking about is the puzzling fissure between the Jesus of two thousand years ago and Jesus as depicted by popular contemporary Christianity. It's not that today's pop Christianity fails to live out the vision of its founder. It's that it fails to even try. More than that, it fails to even want.

Poverty: One Point of Disconnection

Take Jesus' stance on poverty. If Christ were an obnoxious Ohio State fan, his Buckeyes would've been the poor. It was, for him, a top priority, a non-negotiable. Same goes for his followers. They made a regular practice of selling their possessions and pooling their resources, caring for the sick, doing the sorts of outlandish things Jesus did—and often getting their clocks cleaned in the process.[87] To our modern eyes, they would've looked more like a hippie commune than a conservative coalition. And while it's an over-simplification to equate Jesus with the kale-eating tree hugger who sold you weed in college, it's equally problematic to imagine Christ eating shrimp-stuffed quail at a black-tie fundraiser for the newest corporate-sponsored candidate. The Gospels don't exactly read like a how-to manual for aspiring power brokers.

Plenty of Americans know about Jesus' special concern for the poor, even if they don't see this concern reflected in the lives of his followers. But many more have no clue Jesus made such a big deal out of it, nor that he expected his disciples to follow suit.

Case in point: in reaction to Pope Francis's encyclical on the "idolatry of money," Rush Limbaugh accused the pontiff of being a Marxist, mainly because he urged both Catholics and non-Catholics to rectify the "structural causes of inequality."[88] Elsewhere, the pope declared: "Working for a just distribution of the fruits of the earth and human labor is not mere philanthropy. It is a moral obligation."[89] The fourth-century Syrian saint John Chrysostom said something similar: "Not to share one's wealth with the poor is to steal from them and to take away their livelihood. It is not our own goods which we hold, but theirs."[90] Yet to Limbaugh, such talk smacks more of communism than historically orthodox Christianity.[91] I wonder what Rush thinks of Mother Theresa, who warned of the profound sense of spiritual alienation that accompanies excessive wealth: "Death is to be preferred."[92] The late Anglo-Catholic, G. K. Chesterton, offered a more stinging (and obnoxious) appraisal: "To be smart enough to get all that money you must be dull enough to want it."[93]

Okay, fine; that's all well and good for high church, Catholic types, with their incense and vestments and funny hats. But most American Christians are Protestant, including evangelicals, fundamentalists, and charismatics. What have ostensibly "conservative" Protestants thought about social justice through the ages?[94]

Let's look at John Calvin, a man whose very name evokes frightful images of frigid Puritans, Salem witch trials, and fumbling your way through *The Crucible* in tenth-grade English. Yet Calvin was much closer to what we'd now consider a social justice warrior than a stodgy conservative. It was Calvin who helped create a sophisticated welfare system in Switzerland for impoverished refugees.[95] Here's a guy who took seriously the biblical directive to be hospitable towards "aliens" and "foreigners," admonishing fellow Christians to do likewise.[96] To Calvin, this was what it meant to keep the "law of love."[97]

Evangelicals have been looking into this stuff lately, hoping to recover a more faithful, historically orthodox Christianity. Some are calling on contemporary Christians to rediscover what it really means to be a disciple—a "learner"—of Jesus. Evangelical books like *Not a Fan, Crazy Love*, and *Radical* all make a point of highlighting some of Jesus' often overlooked teachings on generosity and poverty.[98] *Purpose Driven Life* author Rick Warren even defended Pope Francis's stance on socioeconomic justice.[99] Twenty years ago, who'd have predicted a golf-shirt-wearing, baby boomer suburbanite like pastor Warren would one day be siding with the "liberals"?

Which raises another question: Where did Pope Francis, Ma Theresa, Rick Warren, and Calvin get all this hippy-dippy gobbledygook? From Jesus' own teachings, of course.

The New Testament gives us four biographical portraits of Jesus' life: Matthew, Mark, Luke, and John. While each of the Gospels has its own quirks, all four emphasize the importance of caring for the poor and loving one's neighbor: "The Spirit of the Lord is upon me," Jesus said, "because he has anointed me to bring good news to the poor."[100] And elsewhere: "It is easier for a camel to go through the eye of a needle than for someone who is rich to enter the kingdom of God . . . If you want to be perfect, go, sell what you have and give to the poor, and you will have treasure in heaven; and come, follow me."[101] No, Jesus and his cohorts weren't closet communists bent on violent revolution. But Christianly speaking, special concern for society's most vulnerable is about as "conservative" as you can get.[102] And yet, in twenty-first-century America, if you display too much enthusiasm for social justice, you're labeled a "liberal." Go figure.

Politics and Other Tricky Topics

I realize that a caveat is probably in order. Lest the reader presume I intend to dismantle conservative Christianity in favor of a more left-leaning Christ, let me assure you: I aim to do no such thing. In general, I'd agree with Jim Wallis's assessment that both political parties misunderstand Jesus. Republicans tend to glance over the "turn the other cheek" and "judge not lest you be judge" parts, while Democrats forget how the New Deal, abolitionism, and the civil rights movement were propelled by decidedly Christian visions of justice and mercy.[103] Moreover, the solution to the failures of both parties can't be as simple as constructing a more moderate Jesus, as if achieving "middle ground" were something inherently noble in itself. You can be "moderate" and still be dead wrong (e.g., "I'm only *moderately* in favor of cannibalism"). Honestly, I'm not sure following Jesus fits comfortably on any point of the American ideological spectrum. Political schemas rarely attempt to imagine, let alone incarnate, the kingdom of God about which Jesus spoke with such curious confidence.

It's also worth remembering that the ancient Christians were neither Republicans nor Democrats (nor American). They didn't vote in political elections, mostly because Caesar wasn't really interested in their input. Instead of a modern democratic republic, Jesus spoke of a kingdom—more specifically, *God's* kingdom—so foreign that it could only be envisaged in stories and similes. "The kingdom of heaven *is like*": a hidden treasure, the tiniest seed, a priceless pearl, all of the above. Even more strange, Jesus spoke of a kingdom that was both transcendent and immanent, already and not-yet: "My kingdom is not of this world," yet, "The kingdom of God is among you," sometimes translated as "in your midst," or even more audaciously, "*within* you."[104] And this is precisely what the disciples believed. To them, God's kingdom wasn't some postmortem retirement community in the clouds. It was something to be seen and tasted *today*, "on earth as it is in heaven."

Like Calvin, the pope, and Rick Warren, Jesus' disciples made a pretty big deal about the whole compassion thing. But they also believed being generous didn't give you a free pass to hate your enemies. You can't "love your neighbor" without *actually* loving your neighbor—which is inconvenient if you're a tatted-up ACLU intern and your neighbor's last name happens to be Limbaugh, Hannity, or Kavanaugh (or vice versa). You know that "love is patient, love is kind" passage from the Bible? The one you hear at weddings all the time? It's much less saccharine when you read it in context:

> If I give all I possess to the poor and give over my body to hardship that I may boast, but do not have love, I gain nothing. Love is patient, love is kind. It does not envy, it does not boast, it is not proud. It does not dishonor others, it is not self-seeking, it is not easily angered, it keeps no record of wrongs . . .[105]

In other words, being brave doesn't mean you are possessed of love. Neither does being an activist, or adopting a "cause." Our grandest, most public acts of compassion don't merit compensation in return. I don't win any extra Jesus points by out-philanthropizing my peers . . . or by having fewer material possessions than the Joneses next door. And no matter how many random acts of kindness I commit, I am never afforded the luxury of despising my neighbor. Jesus was just as interested in inward motives as externalized behavior. And to him and his merry band of followers, it was possible to be heroically charitable without ever really loving anybody.

This I find bothersome. I was naturally inclined towards minimalism long before it became "a thing," and it'd be nice to get some recognition for it. Shopping for iToys and following trends? Not for me. I don't hit the local Home Depot on Saturdays in search of renovation inspiration. Like, ever. But I get no extra credit for taking the monkish high road—at least, not according to the Bible. And this is one of the more vexing aspects of Christianity: not only does Jesus call me to let go of materialism and "worldly" superficiality; he doesn't even have the decency to let me bask in the self-satisfaction that accompanies such renunciation. It's like when I announced I was going vegan. Unimpressed, a friend observed, "Changing your diet is the easy part. It's the self-righteousness that takes practice."

Christ vs. Christianity

I was twenty when I first caught the Jesus bug. It took another two years before I even considered visiting a church. It's not that I'd given church some serious thought, weighed the pros and cons, and decided against it. On the contrary: *the thought never even entered my mind.* I just didn't associate Jesus with church, nor Christianity with Christ. Kind of like how I don't associate Amish communities in Idaho with authentic Cantonese cuisine. Just not a correlation I'd be inclined to make.

And I'm not alone in this. Untold scores of weary sojourners find themselves in a similar position, captivated by Christ, yet repelled by fundamentalist Christianity and its not-too-Jesus-y requirements. Take Anne Rice, authorial trendsetter of the sexy vampire genre. Rice experienced a dramatic conversion after decades of avowed atheism. Brimming with newborn fervor, she dedicated her talents to Jesus in works like *Christ the Lord: Out of Egypt*. In a vulnerable 2010 interview, Rice explained how she had grown progressively dissatisfied with living in a world cut off from God. But less than a year later, she posted the following on Facebook—much to the chagrin of her religious readers:

> Today I quit being a Christian. I'm out. I remain committed to Christ as always but not to being "Christian" or to being part of Christianity. It's simply impossible for me to "belong" to this quarrelsome, hostile, disputatious, and deservedly infamous

group . . . In the name of Christ, I quit Christianity and being
Christian. Amen.[106]

Rice's comments remind me of the late philosopher Simone Weil, pacifist, political activist, and sometimes socialist who kept company with the
likes of Trotsky and Camus. Weil had her own frustrations with mainstream
Christianity, especially in light of its troubling record of church-sponsored
colonialism: "It would be strange, indeed, that the word of Christ should
have produced such results if it had been properly understood" (her contemporary, C. S. Lewis, said something similar[107]). Again, there's this idea
that being faithful to Jesus Christ might require repudiating the modern
Christian establishment. While Weil experienced profound mystical encounters with Christ,[108] she declined baptism, saying: "I will remain with
all those things that cannot enter the Church." And she made this decision
because she believed the institutional church had taken to excluding the
very people whom Christ came to comfort and redeem: "I have not come to
call the righteous, but sinners."[109] Strange indeed. Like Dostoyevsky's fable
of the Grand Inquisitor, it's a curious thing when Christianity finds itself at
odds with its Christ.[110]

The Anti-Life Equation

Elsewhere in her online lament/letter of resignation, Rice accuses Christianity of being "anti-*life*." I think she means that, for whatever reasons, modern
Christianity stands in opposition to *culture*—its rich polyphony of creative
expression and intellectual, social, and aesthetic achievement; its unapologetic enjoyment of life itself. Kind of ironic, given Jesus' pronouncement, "I
came that they may have life, and have it abundantly."[111] But for countless
contemporary Christians, "life" is something to be tolerated, not treasured.
Which means this world is merely a disposable stage upon which the drama
of salvation takes place, nothing more.

It all started going south around two centuries ago, when Western
Christians grew increasingly fascinated by certain extrabiblical ideas about
"the rapture": an allegedly apocalyptic moment when true believers would
be beamed up to heaven, Star Trek style.[112] The implication is clear: Why
bother investing in culture, the arts, or civic life if it's all destined to be "left
behind"? Instead, focus on the after-life. Disengage. Keep yourself safe.
Numb yourself to delight. And above all, don't *want*—even if it means extinguishing every unsung longing in your own heart, through an endless
regiment of self-denial, self-hatred, life-hatred.

Long before Rice called it quits, Nietzsche offered a similarly unfavorable assessment:

> Christianity was from the beginning, essentially and fundamentally, life's nausea and disgust with life, merely concealed behind, masked by, dressed up as, faith in "another" or "better" life. Hatred of "the world," condemnation of the passions, fear of beauty and sensuality, a beyond invented the better to slander this life, at bottom a craving for nothing, for the end, for respite . . . and eventually, crushed by the weight of contempt and the eternal No, life must then be felt to be unworthy of desire and altogether worthless.[113]

Maybe that's what Rice was talking about. I don't know the lady, nor do I have any special insights into her motives. But I do know that not everything she writes is fiction.

Question Authority . . . or Else!

Then again, maybe Rice ain't that deep. Perhaps her public resignation from Christianity is more symptomatic of American individualism run rampant. Maybe Rice went rogue on religion because, like a lot of us, she's not comfortable submitting herself to any sort of communal structure—religious or otherwise.[114] We Americans are an individualistic breed: anti-authoritarian, anti-tradition, and (with the exception of some die-hard Jordan Peterson fans), anti-hierarchy—qualities not shared among all peoples in all times. "The right to think for oneself" is part of our national DNA, a trait we inherited from America's founders, who grew tired of taking orders from the British.[115] I'd go so far as to say that bucking tradition is one of America's greatest traditions. And it certainly has its advantages. We crank out rugged, risk-taking individualists like none other. P. T. Barnum, Elon Musk, the ShamWow guy . . . we love to hear the story of Random Go-Getter #41,938 who throws caution to the wind, moves to Hollywood, and makes the movie they've always dreamed of. Unfortunately for us, it was *Sharknado 6*.

I don't know about you, but "question authority" was one of my most cherished childhood mottos. I was raised on Rage Against the Machine, Public Enemy, and, thanks to my parents, the anti-authoritarian anthems of the 60s. My first year of college was about refuting everything that every adult had ever told me. Occasionally I was successful. Other times, not so much. I once set out to prove that it wasn't actually necessary to put wet laundry in the dryer. Water evaporates, which means everything dries *eventually*, right? So I left three soaking-wet loads of laundry in a petri dish pile on the floor, which soon started to smell like a corduroy-wearing wooly mammoth's undercarriage at high noon on the fourth of July. I'm pretty sure it sprouted its own DNA. I did laundry a grand total of six times that year. Yet another experiment in bucking authority gone horribly awry. By mid-April I was going to class commando, garbed only in tuxedo pants and a lime green rain jacket with a broken zipper, sans undershirt. If you are the adventurous, contrarian type and happen to have some spare time on your hands, I highly recommend never doing this.

Not much has changed since the heyday of Rage. Modern individualism is alive and well in America, only now we have less confidence in convention than ever before. Our faith in religious institutions and church leaders continues to decline. But in fairness, so has our trust in consumer products, public schools, TV news, and the political establishment (down with Washington insiders! Bring on Trump and Bernie![116]). Even scientific consensus is not without its detractors. Hence the rise of incredulous flat-earthers and anti-vaxxers who encourage a "decide for yourself" approach to science. As my old chemistry professor, Dr. Schitz, used to say, science is about "getting down to the facts," even when the facts fly in the face of commonsense. And yes, that was his real name: Schitz . . . as in, plural of "feces." High school must've been rough.

Irresistibly mockable names aside, Professor Schitz made an important point: science is supposed to help us uncover truth—the bare, unbiased facts—even when the truth is hard to stomach. But now, even science is held in suspicion. As Stephen Hawking observed, "We are witnessing a global revolt against experts, and that includes scientists."[117] True . . . but after all, it was celebrated scientist Richard Dawkins who, in his atheist's version of the Ten Commandments, included the injunction, "Question everything!" (including, presumably, the injunction to question everything).[118]

We may be living in a post-fact, "fake news" world, but anti-authoritarianism is nothing new. Generally speaking, "We the people" don't like to be told what to do, or what to believe—especially by traditional religious authorities.[119] Not coincidentally, we prefer private, spontaneous spiritual experience to things public, communal, and (especially) institutional.[120] We are "spiritual but not religious,"[121] favoring the "individual quest for meaning and direct experience" over religious rituals and Sunday services (Kanye's being the notable exception).[122] Same rule applies to America's most "conservative" Bible-thumpers, most of whom insist on the individual right to interpret Scripture for themselves. "Bible-only-ism," some call it.[123] So maybe Rice's public statement about abandoning Christianity is merely reflective of a deeply ingrained, anti-institutional bias. It's certainly convenient to dismiss it as such.

But perhaps we should examine Rice's comments more closely: "*In the name of Christ*, I quit Christianity." Not, "In the name of Satan," or "secular humanism," or "Charles Darwin." No, it was for Christ's sake and in his name that Rice opted out. And as I discovered after my baccalaureate address, growing numbers of committed Christians sympathize with Rice's predicament. They are unsure of how to square Christianity with Jesus Christ. I'm not talking about people who doubt God's existence or the Bible's relevance. I'm talking about sincere people of faith struggling to connect the dots between the Jesus of two thousand years ago and *our* Jesus, the Christ of contemporary American Christianity.

Most historians agree: Jesus was a real guy—a living, breathing human being who was crucified in the first century. Some even say we know more about Jesus than any other historical figure of his day. According to the Bible stories, it is *this* Jesus who loved the unlovely and broke bread with prostitutes and "sinners." And the main question I keep hearing among professing Christians is this: Is it even possible to reconcile *this* Jesus—the real guy from Nazareth—with the Christ of popular American Christianity? And why is such reconciliation even necessary?[124]

In his book, *Zealot*, Reza Aslan tells of how he became BFFs with Jesus at church camp. Echoing the stories of countless former evangelicals, Aslan had an intensely personal conversion experience in high school, only to grow disillusioned with the "detached" and "ethereal" Jesus of American evangelicalism.[125] Aslan realized that Jesus the "living man"[126] had somehow been severed from the collective imagination and lived response of his modern-day followers. And why not? If the whole point of Christianity is, as Galileo intimated, "how to get to heaven," why not streamline the transaction?

Aslan isn't the first to point out our propensity to frame Jesus in solely "spiritual" terms—as a conveniently pliable, disconnected divinity whom we're encouraged to invite into our hearts, assuming he can fit. Reminds me of a story a friend of mine told me. I'm not normally a sucker for "Guess what *my* kid did today?!" play-by-plays, but this one's worth repeating. One morning, my friend's son burst out of his Sunday school class and announced, "Guess what, mommy? I just prayed to accept Jesus into my heart!" A tender moment between a sweet Christian mom and her guileless child. A few days later, the same kid says, "Guess what, mommy? I just prayed to accept Spiderman into my heart!" How'd ya like to untangle that theological knot with your preschooler thirty minutes before bedtime?

Needless to say, unpacking the historical development of Christian theology is an overwhelming task, especially when you're tucking in your five-year-old. But since I'm a history teacher—and winner of the coveted

Oyster Bay High School History Award, no less—I figure I'll take a crack at it.

A Brief History of Boiling Things Down

When the Roman Empire fell in the fifth century, Europe descended into the "Dark Ages": an era of desolation, socioeconomic instability, and technological stagnation (think *Mad Max* meets a somehow-less-cheerful version of *Game of Thrones*).[127] Waves of Germanic invaders had reduced the empire's sprawling infrastructure to rubble, forever extinguishing the once great "light of Rome." In the absence of any secure civic institutions, the commoners came to rely on the Catholic Church for everything from health care to postal services and vocational training. Similarly, church leaders (popes, priests, etc.) assumed almost exclusive responsibility for interpreting and teaching the Bible.[128] Unfortunately—and predictably—as Rome consolidated more and more power, the church became evermore corrupt, with "official" interpretations of Scripture yielding increasingly bizarre, and self-serving, results.[129]

Take the doctrine of salvation, for example. By the Middle Ages, Christianity had all but morphed into a to-do list of rituals and rites. That meant participating in a labyrinth of laborious regimens, including—but not limited to—donating to the church, venerating relics, fasting, fighting on crusade, even self-flagellation. It was all about jumping through the right hoops. Wanna ticket on the train to glory? You'd best work off your sins before you die, else be doomed to pay off the remainder in purgatory—a sort of celestial waiting room between heaven and hell.[130] To the average, biblically illiterate churchgoer, this was the "good news" Jesus came to deliver.

Things went from bad to worse when a series of power-hungry, profligate popes encouraged Christians to buy "indulgences"—kind of like a note from your mom to get you out of detention—only "your mom" was your local parish priest and "detention" was purgatory.[131] Rome needed fast cash, and selling indulgences turned out to be one heck of a fundraiser. Some Christians probably found these kinds of mechanical conventions satisfying, maybe even comforting. Others, like Martin Luther, not so much.[132]

I don't mean to throw the whole Catholic Church under the proverbial popemobile. There've been some remarkably humble and inspiring pontiffs over the centuries. Take Gregory the Great, who defined his role as *servus servorum Dei*, "servant of the servants of God."[133] But among medieval pontiffs, this kind of humility was sorely lacking, and Martin Luther wasn't the first to notice. Others had come before, courageous clergymen who called out corrupt church leaders. Not surprisingly, they suffered from a range of unpleasant side effects . . . like being burned at the stake.[134]

But not young Luther. By luck or by providence, Luther defied both pope and king and lived to tell the tale. His success empowered the people to question authority, including even religious authority. Some say the Protestant Reformation was the beginning of the end of organized religion—at least in the Western world. Since, as Luther seemed to suggest,[135] you really didn't *need* churches, popes, or priests to get right with God, Christianity began a gradual slide towards "church optional."[136] Faith became less concerned with external religious rites and more about individual salvation and inner spiritual transformation. Thus Luther unleashed a new willingness to challenge time-honored hierarchies and institutions. And since medieval Christianity was mainly about (1) escaping eternal torment in hell and/or purgatory, and (2) not much else,[137] Protestantism made salvation a far more personalized, convenient affair.

Fast-forward a hundred years, when Protestantism crossed the pond and took root in American soil, where it gained fresh enthusiasm—especially during the religious revivals of the eighteenth and nineteenth centuries. It was the era of westward expansion, and Christian ministers did their best to keep up with wayfaring pioneers. Across an unfurling continent of prairies, plains, and untamed wilderness they went, propping up tents and holding revival meetings tailor-made for the transient traveler. No organs, pews, or church buildings out on the frontier.[138] It was in this context that Christian ministers adopted a decidedly practical approach to spreading Jesus' message: sing a few songs to set the tone, preach an impassioned sermon designed to stir the individual conscience and get people converted before they pulled up stakes and moved on. Remember, we're talking about the wild, wild West here—rugged frontiersmen with low life expectancies and highly uncertain futures. The idea was to cut to the chase and save wayward souls ASAP.

During the Second Great Awakening of the nineteenth century, preachers like Charles Finney kicked evangelical pragmatism into overdrive.[139] Revivalists embraced an increasingly efficient, results-driven approach to spreading the gospel message, urging individuals to pray the "Sinner's Prayer" and "accept Christ into their hearts."[140] Church services became even more focused on the efficient conversion of unbelievers. The formula was similar to that of the earlier Western revivalists: grab people's attention, preach a simple, emotionally appealing sermon, then urge individuals to open their hearts and make a personal decision to receive Christ.

Finney was the forefather of a Christian pragmatism still prevalent in American megachurches and evangelical youth groups today.[141] Since the age of frontier revivals, evangelical Christians have focused on broadcasting the gospel message as efficiently as possible. Of course, in order to compete for consideration in a highly distracted, ever-widening marketplace of ideas, "efficiency" usually means boiling things down. Trim the fat; highlight what's most appealing and accessible; leave all the mystery and ambiguity on the back burner. As pastor Kyle Idleman admitted in his best seller, *Not a Fan*, today's evangelicals go to great lengths to make Jesus look "as attractive as possible."[142]

Statistically speaking, these tactics have been wildly effective: 65 percent of Americans today claim to have made a "personal commitment to Jesus Christ" that is "still important" in their lives today.[143] There's even a Wikihow page with simple instructions on how to get "saved."[144] Problem is, none of us are all that sure what praying the "Sinner's Prayer" or making a "personal commitment to Christ" actually mean . . . or what they're supposed to mean (media mogul Ted Turner has been saved seven times—twice by Billy Graham—and he's still agnostic).[145]

Makes me think of a friend of mine, a drummer, who just finished touring with one of the biggest worship bands in the world. After spending months in the belly of the pop Christian beast, his already-simmering doubt finally boiled over into full-blown unbelief. Upon confessing his newfound atheism to his fundamentalist family, his father replied, "Okay, well . . . remember that time at Sunday school when you were a kid, when you prayed that special prayer and asked Jesus into your heart? You did that, right? You remember?" My friend nodded. "Well, then we're good. You're still saved. We're good."

What Is "It"?

What is Christianity, really? What do we mean when we talk about "getting saved" or "accepting Jesus into your heart"? Exactly who—or what—are we "accepting"? Christ the contrarian pacifist, or conservative culture warrior? The cynical ascetic, or staunch defender of family values? Is he high on capitalism, or down on Darwinism? Both/and? Neither/nor? In a world where Trump, Obama, Putin, Kanye West, and Lady Gaga all claim Christianity as their spiritual home, it's not an easy question to answer.

In a BuzzFeed post entitled "Why I Miss Being a Born Again Christian," Jessica Misener reflects upon her teenage experience as a member of a local church youth group. Misener attended the group's weekly gatherings of her own volition, driven by a deep desire for Jesus—or, in retrospect, what she "earnestly believed" was Jesus at the time. Maybe it was the spine-tingling worship music that drew her in and kept her hooked. Maybe it was the electric preaching or hospitable atmosphere. "Whatever 'it' was," she recounts, "it was powerful enough to bring a girl who grew up in a non-churchgoing family to a sweaty school gym for youth group every week."[146]

Former evangelicals Michael Shermer (now editor-in-chief of *Skeptic* magazine)[147] and John Jeremiah Sullivan[148] had similar experiences. Like Misener, they prayed to accept Jesus into their hearts, only to become disillusioned with the amorphous "it" to which they had clung so zealously in their youth. And defining the "it" is tricky: Is "it" the elusive feeling of self-transcendence, of being part of something bigger than yourself? The emotional high of something oceanic rushing over you, filling you with newfound purpose and wonder? Is "it" the comfort of being accepted into a welcoming, forgiving community? Or the satisfaction of being part of an exclusive clique, set apart from the irreligious "them"? Maybe "it" is the sense of security that comes with "getting saved," a feeling of certainty and confidence upon receiving your complimentary Get Out of Hell Free card?[149]

The problem with boiling Jesus down is the problem with boiling anything down: the finer details get burned off in the process of distillation. For this very reason, observant Christians—both "liberal" and "conservative"—have cautioned against oversimplifying Jesus. As early as the 1940s, evangelicals like A. W. Tozer were already wary of contemporary Christian "promotional methods," including the tendency to reduce "following the Way" to a momentary decision made in response to a stirring sermon: "Everything is made to center upon the initial act of 'accepting' Christ (a term, incidentally, which is not found in the Bible)."[150] A decade later, Yale intellectual Reinhold Niebuhr called this transaction an "artificial minute for our soul's salvation," echoing Tozer's concern: "It takes a whole Bible and a long life to tell me how simple yet how complicated that whole salvation is that has to be worked out ... it takes the whole 'world,' all life as well as death, the present and all the future unfold the meaning of great salvation . . ."[151] Like Tozer, Niebuhr worried that modern marketing methods would flatten the good news beyond all recognition.

What does it mean to streamline something multidimensional? Maybe Picasso can help. In his *Bull* series of lithographs, Picasso starts with a lifelike, fleshed-out image of a bull, then moves step by step through a sequence of abstractions in hopes of unearthing the inner "essence," or "spirit," of the bull:

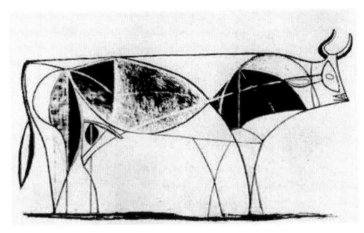

Frame by frame, Picasso simplifies the image, paring down the details to the bare bones. At last, by the final frame, he reveals the pure "essence" of bull. Behold:

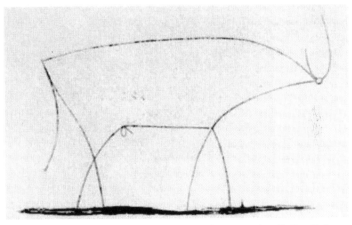

And I call bull schitz.

Because a black-and-white stick figure is not a bull, even if it is the handiwork of the great Picasso. At best, it's a wiry impression of a bull, a derivative of the genuine article. And it's definitely not *more* real than an *actual* bull (which would you rather have: the "essence" of a million dollars, or an actual ten-dollar bill?). Don't get me wrong: I'm a genuine Picasso fan. Especially his Blue Period. But if Picasso's intention in the *Bull* series was to substitute stripped-down abstractions for full-fledged reality, then here, Pablo honey, is where you and I part ways.

Which brings me to the point—or rather, the question: What do we actually mean when we say the name "Jesus"? In making Christ a more abstract, palatable commodity, Jesus has become a mere shadow of his former self. It's no longer clear how the "it" of popular Christian experience relates to Jesus the "living man"; the three-dimensional, historical human being. The more nebulous and compressed Christ becomes, the more easily he can be tailored to fit whatever preloaded ideological program(s) we happen to prefer.

Long before the birth of Christ, the philosopher Xenophanes speculated that if bulls knew how to draw, they'd adorn their stables with sketches of bull-shaped gods.[152] So it goes with human beings. "God made man in his image and we return the favor," Voltaire said.[153] It's what we do, even with Jesus, even if only unconsciously. We recreate Christ: as a divinized iteration of ourselves, or a projection of our deeply held values; as a scapegoat for our various (often valid) frustrations with faith; as a symbol of oppressive religiosity. We do it all the time. And we've gotten better at it. Or maybe it's just gotten easier to pull off: a boiled-down Jesus makes for a more malleable, user-friendly Jesus. To Fats, my "Musicians Wanted" friend, "Jesus" meant building fertilizer bombs in your basement and plotting the next attack on Planned Parenthood. To Reza Aslan, "Jesus" meant the diaphanous "Christ of faith," as opposed to the flesh-and-blood Jesus of history. To Katy Perry, "Jesus" meant being held hostage by a hermetically sealed religious community. Will the real Jesus please stand up?

2

The Pilgrim up Schitz Creek

God is dead.

—Nietzsche, 1887[154]

Is God Dead?

—*TIME* (magazine cover), early 1966

God is alive, magic is afoot.

—Leonard Cohen, late 1966[155]

Magic, Music, and Muggles

Tom Petty said music was the only real magic he'd ever encountered.[156] Makes sense. You hear "Beautiful Day," Pharrell Williams, or "Good Vibrations" and all of a sudden you're playing happy air drums on your steering wheel. Then "Everybody Hurts" comes on and, just as suddenly, you feel like an abandoned toddler at the mall. The ancient Greeks believed different scales could summon different emotions from within the listener.[157] Similarly, Calvin claimed music had a hidden and "incredible power" to move the human heart.[158] "Ah, music," smiled Dumbledore through a thicket of bearded grey, "A magic beyond all we do here!"[159]

Sounds nice, but ours is a world of real-life muggles, not made-up magicians. According to modern physics and physiology, music's apparently "magical" qualities are just that—apparent. Now we know what music really is: vibrations transmitted through a medium, received by the ear, and perceived by the brain. They may be "good vibrations" to you, but they're still just vibrations. Maybe you feel strangely inspired by the sound of concert A (or 440 hertz), but that doesn't mean concert A connects you to anything transcendent or "spiritual." Maybe you only like concert A because you're the beneficiary of complex evolutionary processes that disposed you to like it. Perhaps your prehistoric ancestors needed to be especially attuned to 440 hertz because that was the precise frequency of a Periwinkle-Billed Auklet's mating call. And maybe the Periwinkle-Billed Auklet was the best source of protein available to hunter-gatherers at that time—though that's highly unlikely, since a Periwinkle-Billed Auklet is something I just made up.

Sociologist Max Weber once described the unfolding twentieth century as the era of "disenchantment."[160] Most scholars since Weber have agreed: in "coming of age," the modern world has lost its earlier romance and simplicity. We used to invoke magic and superstition to make sense of things, especially things that moved us to wonder, like music. But now, thanks to people like Galileo, Newton, and Einstein, we have science to explain the universe. No magic required.

For all you history buffs, here's how it all went down.

Disenchanted: How God Lost His Gig

Galileo died in 1642, the same year Isaac Newton was born. And if Galileo was a certifiable genius, Newton was a spoon-bending, brain-pulsating mutant the likes of which the world has seldom seen. In less than two years, Newton figured out the laws of gravity and motion, including his famous Third Law: every action has an equal and opposite reaction; or, to put it in more ethical-philosophical terms, the principle of *karma*: what goes around comes around. Oh, and in his spare time, he invented calculus . . . all before turning twenty-five. When I was twenty-five, I'd barely figured out how to work a washer-dryer.

Like René Descartes before him, Newton saw the cosmos as an impeccably designed machine that runs according to divinely inscribed laws.[161] Once discovered, these laws could be applied to virtually every aspect of life.[162] Newton's discoveries helped lay the foundation for a period known as the Age of Enlightenment (circa 1600–1700), when Dark Aged ignorance finally gave way to the new light of modern knowledge. Irrespective of his intentions, Newton inspired future generations to reimagine God as a sort of celestial engineer whose supreme invention was the universe: a mechanism so efficient, so self-regulating that it needed a minimum of maintenance to keep it going. Some started to wonder whether divine intervention was ever even necessary.[163] Think about it: If God is all powerful and omniscient, why wouldn't he build a universe that runs by perpetual motion, correcting itself along the way? No tune-ups needed. Wouldn't such a feat make the Creator even more worthy of praise?[164]

In contrast, there was my old '87 Thunderbird, which leaked more oil than ExxonMobil. First car I ever bought. $300 cash. On the rare occasion it actually started, the broken seat belt dinger would chime relentlessly—*ding ding ding*—for the duration of the ride. Jet black, pleather interior, busted A/C, and power windows—which, of course, didn't work. And no radio. Not even AM. Multi-hour road trips were particularly intolerable. But for all the T-bird's failures, at least it prompted me to get to know my mechanic. He went from being some random guy at the gas station to being a man I actually counted on in a direct, palpable way. To invoke a pop Christian cliché, we developed a "personal relationship": I went from knowing *about* him to really knowing *him*.

I have since discovered that my relationship with my mechanic is inversely proportional to the relative crappyness of my car. I now drive an old Honda and have virtually no rapport with my mechanic. I'm not even that comfortable calling him "*my* mechanic," as I hardly ever see him—because I rarely ever need him. He is, for all intents and purposes, superfluous. Incidental. Unnecessary.

If the point of old-time religion was to get to know God like I knew my old mechanic, then Newton and company might've driven a permanent wedge between us and the Almighty. Even before Newton, men like Francis Bacon had begun insisting upon new standards for acquiring reliable knowledge. Instead of trusting traditional beliefs or gut-level feelings, Bacon called for "objectivity"—meaning that all truth claims were to be tested and verified before being believed. Reason thus replaced revelation. If the universe was indeed a mechanism, then science, not Scripture, would disclose its divinely authored laws.[165]

As an unintended consequence of all this "mechanistic universe" business, God became evermore separated from everyday life. Not coincidentally, a philosophical-religious trend known as deism enjoyed a brief period of popularity in the eighteenth century, especially among the educated classes of Europe and America. Jefferson, Franklin, Madison, Hamilton, and a number of other really smart guys with really White-sounding names—all basically deists.[166] Informed by the Enlightenment, they de-emphasized the supernatural in favor of a divine architect of reason and nature.[167] Some

By the 1960s, it seemed religion was on its last legs.[181] Sure, maybe some ultra-rational, anti-supernatural version of religion would survive, but certainly not the Christian orthodoxy of old. Jefferson went so far as to declare the imminent, and ineluctable, triumph of Unitarian deism over all other religions: "There is not a young man now living in the U.S. who will not die an Unitarian."[182]

Jefferson had a lot of great ideas. The swivel chair, for instance. But he was dead wrong about the future of religion in America. Jefferson didn't live to see the full effects of the Second Great Awakening, nor the rise of twentieth-century religious luminaries like Bonhoeffer, Billy Graham, Mother Theresa, and MLK, nor the inception of organizations like the Salvation Army, the Red Cross, Young Life, Kanakuk, World Vision, InterVarsity, FCA, YWAM, or the YMCA. Then came the 1970s, and 80s, and the emergence of the New Christian Right—a more militant, politicized adaptation of American evangelicalism that included the likes of Pat Robertson, Jerry Falwell, and the Moral Majority.[183] Some call it the "Fourth Great Awakening."[184] And regardless of whether you think the advent of a politically conservative Christian power bloc was a good thing, almost nobody saw it coming.

The Ebbs and Flows of Atheism

"God is on a winning streak," said CNN's Christiane Amanpour in 2007; "Religion is resurgent."[185] Around the same time, the famous philosopher and "methodological atheist" Jürgen Habermas acknowledged a worldwide "spiritual renewal," especially in Asia and Africa.[186] Even in "post-Christian" England, atheism has not enjoyed the absolute victory once predicted. Over half of today's Brits believe spiritual forces can influence human thoughts, actions, and circumstances. More startlingly, younger Brits believe in the supernatural more than their elder counterparts.[187] Ex-nun Karen Armstrong went so far as to describe Western Europe as "endearingly old fashioned" in its stubborn secularity.[188] Surprisingly, the dogmatic skepticism of twentieth-century Europe is starting to go stale.

What's really weird is the growing preponderance of unbelievers who, like Habermas, have grown wary of dogmatic atheism. Take the British conservative, Douglas Murray. In his article, "My Fellow Atheists, It's Time We Admitted that Religion Has Some Points in Its Favor," Murray argues that atheism has failed to address the deeper issues of life—the problems of tragedy and human suffering, the inevitability of death, the transformative power of reconciliation and forgiveness.[189] Murray's comments remind me of an interview I heard with Maurice Sendak, just a few months before he died. With characteristic candor, Sendak spoke of gratitude, growing old, losing loved ones, and awaiting death: "I'm not unhappy about what must be. It makes me cry only when I see my friends go before me and life is emptied. I don't believe in an afterlife, but I still fully expect to see my brother again."[190] *Fully expect?* On what basis? In spite of it all, we go on mumbling half-hearted phrases like "It's for the best," "She's in a better place," or "It was meant to be." Really? Meant by whom? What do we mean we when say such things? And what gives us the right to expect that they're true? We do not know. We appeal to presumably universal ideals like fate, love, goodness, destiny, and even human rights, but how can something be capital-T true if nothing is? Why do we talk about rights as if they were satellites with fixed orbits spinning round an unchanging ethical nucleus?[191] Don't get me wrong; I like rights—especially civil rights. I like what they've done for some of the world's most marginalized peoples. On a more selfish note, I like *my* rights, mostly because I like being able to do what I want. Philosophers call it "negative liberty": freedom *from* outside influence or interference.[192] Stay off my lawn. Mind your own business. But this kind of negative freedom only gets you so far. It's not that helpful in cultivating forgiveness or intimate reciprocity. Yes, you can make hate crimes illegal. You can force people to obey the law. You coerce them into altering their external behavior. But you can't legislate love from without. Because love is always an inside job. Always.

For whatever reason(s), and despite the inextricably knotted relationship between modernity and secularism, religion has proven surprisingly resilient.[193] There's even talk of a postmodern yearning for "re-enchantment," an implicit recognition that we've lost the magic; that in our rush towards a brave new world, something essential has been left behind.[194] Some scholars even describe our present age as "*post*-secular."[195]

And yet, at the same time, we're witnessing an upsurge of something called "scientism": the view that the universe is a closed, self-created box, outside of which is only nothingness. No "spiritual" realities or meddling deities; no "First Cause" to set things in motion. Everything that happens in the box is caused by something else in the box. And while poets, philosophers, and children prattle on about ineffable forces at work in the world, scientism is in the business of rendering the ineffable effable by ridding reality of all unnecessary ambiguity.[196]

The problem with scientism is that it seeks to explain, or explain away, even our most humanly vital concerns—suffering, love, longing—by reducing them to purely physical, chemical processes. But while science is exceedingly effective in addressing things like prostate inflammation, it's not that helpful in telling us why we are here, what "living" means, and why are we plagued by such unyielding desires to go on living, losing, loving, and being loved.

Sorry you're so sad, Mr. Sendak. I know you yearn for the impossible. You too, Dad. I know you miss your dearly departed drinking buddies from the bar oh so terribly. But take heart! That sunken feeling in your stomach is merely the result of neurochemicals being released by your brain, just little bits of dead matter moving to and fro. Actually, your dead friends were just dead matter moving to and fro, all reducible to unconscious particles buzzing along, doing their thing. Who knows? Maybe your tiny particles and their tiny particles will meet again one day, perhaps many more times over many billions of years, as they continue their insentient voyage through the universe, onward and outward, towards inevitable entropy and nothingness. From randomness we came and to randomness we shall return.

Some People Call Me Maurice

I've always loved Sendak. When I was little, I wanted to be Max from *Where the Wild Things Are*—half boy and half beast, utterly uncategorizable, fueled only by feral desire. On into high school, I resisted being identified with any one particular clique. Then I read Nietzsche in college, and my already overdeveloped sense of autonomy kicked into overdrive. It was me against the world. Trust no one. Question everything. All traditions and conventions were to be held in suspicion. If there was a devil, then surely his name was Certainty, and conformity his weapon of choice.

Eventually, I got really good at being *not* dogmatic—which meant not picking a side. To strongly disagree with any particular ideology was to give it too much credit. I preferred being pleasantly vague about all things ultimate. Why trouble myself by arguing against any one particular ideology, since all were equally ephemeral, like cloud formations that make pretty shapes before dissolving into nothingness? Besides, I liked being pleasantly vague. It worked for me.

Then, two things happened. First, I started studying political theory. My professor was a Platonist who believed in something called "objective" or "absolute" truth.[197] Dante was his name. He was unabashedly Catholic, openly gay, and even more openly quirky. Each class, he'd blurt out the most bizarre nuggets of unprovoked commentary, like: "John Locke didn't give a damn about love! Not one damn!!!" At which point I'd ask myself, "How's this gonna help me get into med school?" Professor Dante hated the idea of building any social or political system on a foundation of individual, negative freedom. And he hated it because he thought it sold us short on love. Because love always means lowering the drawbridge. It means binding your fate to someone outside yourself, which usually involves a whole lot of *not* doing whatever you want.

Dante wasn't a real fan of the Founding Fathers. I didn't even know that was an option. Once, in a momentary lapse of judgment, I dared disagree with him during class. I think I said something like, "Who's to say that what's true for you is, like, you know, true for me?" He responded, "Just because *you* haven't bothered to discover the truth doesn't mean it isn't there," at which point I briefly considered never speaking again.

Then, the next thing happened. I read Chuck Klosterman.

In reference to the much-maligned Left Behind series of the early aughts, Klosterman writes of having a "crisis of confidence." It's the rapture, in particular, that fills him with so much existential apprehension. Not that he's ever really believed in the rapture. Problem is, he doesn't *not* believe in it, either—hence the apprehension. It's a common and confounding condition, this ideological inbetweenness, even if it defies easy description. "'Nihilism' means you don't believe anything," Klosterman muses, "but I can't find a word that describes *partial belief in everything*."[198]

Here Klosterman encapsulates a fairly widespread postmodern phenomenon—namely, our generally fuzzy view of reality.[199] If all the surveys are correct, most Americans hold to a set of intuitive commitments that are, at least on the surface, mutually contradictory. Together, these intuitions offer little clarity about love, God, Jesus, meaning, and "truth," whatever that is. The one thing we're certain of is our absolute disdain for false certainty, a.k.a. *fundamentalism*: that oddly appealing, insidious notion that an individual can possess (and control) the whole truth. We know a fundamentalist when we see 'em. It's the self-assured Christian who's just a little too comfortable saying, "Because God told me so." It's the smug scientist who only trusts his interpretation of the data, because only *he* is free from bias. Most of us are as repelled by religious fundamentalism as we are scientism, both of which claim to enjoy direct, unfiltered access to infallible knowledge.[200] We don't really buy into either camp, though we suspect they're both partially true. And let's face it: atheism is too much of a commitment.[201] So we go on doubting the absolute claims of religion, even as we doubt our own doubts. This is our lot, we pilgrims of the twenty-first century, caught somewhere between the new and the old, in a world that's as post-Christian as it is post-secular.

Speaking for myself, Klosterman's words were as a mirror whose reflection brought unwelcome news: there I was, suspended in non-committal neutrality, where everything was kind of true and sort of important—which meant nothing was. And in this confusing, half-lit terrain, faith was but a whisper; a soft, green glow glimmering in the middle distance, out of reach, but not out of sight. Perhaps you've found yourself perched upon this same existential fence. Which is a polite way of saying you're up Schitz creek.

3

Always Bet on Black

How come you can hear a chord, and then another chord,
and then your heart breaks open?

—ANNE LAMOTT[202]

Like a Sore Thumb

I SANG IN AN a cappella group in college. You know, *Pitch Perfect*, Pentatonix, *Glee*? Yeah, that was me. And I was really, really into it. We wore starched white shirts and navy-blue blazers with Tucker Carlson bowties. This was actually a cool thing to do in college. And in agreement with the collective experience of countless recovering a cappella singers, I, too, can attest that it ceased being cool the minute I stepped off campus and into the Real World, where it's always better to hear the original versions of Bruno Mars, Van Morrison, or Imagine Dragons than some doo-wop facsimile. You should've heard our renditions of R &B. We could make Parliament-Funkadelic sound like Art Garfunkel.

After only a few months I started getting antsy about our homogenized Whiteness. We had not one person of Latino, Asian, or African-American descent. For an angsty Northeasterner with an overdeveloped sense of social justice, this would not do. Soon I was on a mission to convince every Black friend with even a hint of vocal aptitude to audition. I only had one taker, Sammy. But it came with strings attached: he'd audition for my singing group if I auditioned for his. Done and done.

Embrace the Whiteness . . .
Larry Mueller. Used by permission. All rights reserved.

It was a Tuesday evening when I made my debut. I showed up in the choir room at 7:00 p.m. sharp, as instructed by Sammy. There I found 250 African-Americans. And me. The group's name, Black Voices, probably should've tipped me off. I made my way into the overcrowded room and introduced myself to the first person I could. He responded with unmistakable sarcasm: "Wassup, my brother. My name's Malcolm."

"Nice to meet you," I replied.

Almost immediately, he corrected me, "Nah, I'm not Malcolm. My name's Jeff. There's only one Malcolm. You do know who Malcolm X is, right?"

Here we go. It's been less than five minutes and already I'm being grilled by the cultural competency police. And here I was, a hip New Yorker from a progressive family, the product of an ethnically diverse public school. I didn't deserve to be lumped together with the whitebread bourgeoisie. Instinctively, I parried, "Actually, my roommate's name is Malcolm. He's Black too. So I guess that's three Malcolms."

Several beats of uncomfortable silence.

"Alright, alright," smiled Jeff, "I'm just playin' with you man."

Just a few months prior, I'd had my first run-in with a no-holds-barred, loud and proud racist. I'm not talking about the sort of unexamined, arguably more deleterious racism that simmers below the surface. I'm talking a let's-have-a-talk-about-the-biological-inferiority-of-other-ethnic-groups-over-dinner racist. Her name was Becky. And, inconveniently for me, she was drop-dead gorgeous.

Bigoted Becky

We were on the same cruise ship over spring break. My singing group provided the musical entertainment; she and her friends were among the paying customers. Becky had incandescent emerald eyes, forever fixed in the sort of aloof expression one normally associates with mannequins, the catatonic, and the recently deceased. As far as I could determine, she had no hobbies or interests. None. Whenever I tried to spark up a conversation, I found myself fumbling for some legitimate reason to go on, other than her abundantly evident hotness. Let's see . . . we were both carbon-based life forms with opposable thumbs . . .

After a while I started losing hope. I felt like it would be shallow of me to blow her off purely on account of her tragically underdeveloped personality (a common and unfortunate side effect of being born beautiful, so I'm told). But the whole bigotry thing—that I couldn't overlook.

Except at first.

I didn't want to face the fact that beautiful Becky was a bigot. Sure, there were warning signs, little red flags indicating a certain mean girl elitism. "Some people are just losers," Becky announced. "I just don't like being around those people." *Those* people. But then, just then . . . I'd get lost in the glisten of her eyes and fall headlong back under her thrall. Finally, my buddy Derek staged an intervention:

"Dude . . . you know that Southern belle you've been hitting on all week? I'm not sure how to tell you this, but your Miss Alabama's a bigot."

"Whatever," I muttered.

"Seriously dude . . . she's, like, a total xenophobe."

"What?! No way! For real? Also, what's a xenophobe?"

Exasperated, Derek clarified, "Okay, think of it like this: it's like she's lactose intolerant, only with Black people."

I couldn't believe it. I wouldn't believe it. Not my beautiful Becky. It wasn't till later that night when I was forced to accept my friend's grim assessment.

We convened in the ship's main dining room, whereupon Bigoted Becky and her coterie of castmates from *The Help* informed me of the merits of eugenics, Jim Crowe, and social Darwinism. Some people were not *really* people, I was told; they are fashioned from inferior stuff, rightly relegated to the category of "less than." All the while, Becky sat there in silence, staring off into the void, nodding in occasional acquiescence. And for a little while I was needy enough, nineteen enough, and hormonal enough to go on with it. I scoured the boundaries of my moral imagination, desperate to find some way to rationalize my still-inflamed attraction. "Maybe she's only racist *some* of the time . . . like, when she's in public . . . around people she doesn't really know well . . ." Finally, reluctantly, I settled upon one basic and unremarkable thought: I don't think I can do this.

That was that. I would wrestle my libido into submission. I would make my objections known and shut it down. So that's what I did. I slid my chair away from the table and, with great fanfare, spouted off the kind of platitudes that resonate with infinite profundity when you're a college freshman: "Some of my closest friends are Black!" "Did I mention my roommate, Malcolm?" I said my piece and stormed out of the dining hall, my moral victory complete. It was hard to do, but also easy. More than that, it was gratifying, like cheering on Dwayne "The Rock" Johnson as he bazookas some nameless onscreen terrorist into oblivion. It felt good to be right, to have just cause for condemning someone so clearly in the wrong. I'd always prided myself on being brave and bold, a social justice warrior par excellence. Then again, I prided myself on a lot of things.

Fast-forward a few months and I'm being cross-examined by Jeff in Black Voices. Hadn't he gotten the memo? Didn't he know that I'd made such a heroic stand against Becky and her racist sorority sisters? Didn't this forever separate woke me from unenlightened "them"? Apparently not.

It was a rough start, but I stuck it out. Even Jeff became a friend after a while. But there was something about my participation in Black Voices that was far more distressing than the above-described process of initiation. What really made me uncomfortable was the overtly spiritual nature of the group. We sang songs about Jesus. Like, all the time. Jesus, God, the "joy of the Lord," Jesus, the Holy Spirit, still more Jesus, the "gospel." I guess that's why they called it a "gospel" choir. "We are a praying group," the organist would declare. "We are a group that prays." Okay, great. Well, I am a guy that doesn't know what you're talking about.

I liked Jesus enough, but I was by no means a Christian, and had zero interest in becoming one. Like Reza Aslan, I saw little connection between Jesus the "living man" and the contemporary Christian (sub)culture with which I was becoming acquainted. I detested the general notion of "sin" and the specific implication that I was a "sinner." But the s-word kept popping up in song after song, as did other alien terms like "repentance," "redemption," and "salvation." It was this kind of impassioned celebration of redemption that endeared Dietrich Bonhoeffer to the Black church in America.[203] But not me. Singing songs about sin and salvation was one of my least favorite things about Black Voices, second only to the practice of closing each rehearsals with prayer. All 250 of us would clasp sweaty hands, share our prayer requests, and petition the Lord for fifteen agonizingly awkward minutes.

Introducing Augustine

Making music was a nightly occurrence in college: rehearsals with my a cappella group, gigs with my cover band, singing with Black Voices. Days were another matter. I was studying philosophy and history, reading the likes of Locke, Plato, Nietzsche, and Marx. And if you're gonna give the history of Western political and social thought a go, you're gonna have to read some Augustine. Especially *Confessions* and *City of God*. In my case, I literally had to, since they were assigned in my poli-sci class. And since I still had that whole get-straight-As-or-collapse-into-an-abyss-of-despair thing going, there was no other option.

For some reason, I found this long-dead theologian captivating. His description of the individual as being organically connected to community was completely foreign to me, as was the notion of voluntary self-denial.[204] I was intrigued. And impressed. The guy was an intellectual gunslinger. But I couldn't get past the fact that he was a man of faith. How could someone so freakishly intelligent be a pedal-to-the-metal believer?

By this time, I'd already made some born-again Christian friends. They were likable, authentic people, comfortable in their own skin, clear-headed and composed when discussing even the most taboo topics. And in my view, they were often wrong. But there was no getting around the fact that they were kind, thoughtful people. And I resented the hell out of them.

Not that I didn't *like* my newfound evangelical friends. In fact, I rather enjoyed their quirks. I remember walking into my friend Jason's dorm room to find him reading a textbook on genetics while simultaneously listening to an audiobook by G. K. Chesterton. *The Simpsons* was on mute in the background. He was smoking a pipe. Occasionally, he'd glance at up the TV screen and giggle knowingly. This was a smart, weird, Christian dude. I respected him. I looked up to him. And I genuinely enjoyed his company. I just resented him.

I didn't like the fact that my Christian friends had landed on something solid. I didn't like that they were firm in their convictions and public about what they believed. I didn't like that, from the outside, they seemed to be on a far easier road than me. And I didn't like how transparent they were when speaking of their own personal failures. Like Augustine and Black Voices, they called it "confessing." And though they didn't preach at me, I imagined them conspiring against me, convening in some double-secret

Christian Batcave for hours on end, dissecting my spiritual status and plotting my ineluctable conversion.

My first religiously inclined friends at school weren't Christian. Freshman year, my roommate was a dreadlocked, guitar-playing Filipino who dabbled in Eastern mysticism. Every now and again, I'd find him leaning up against a tree near our dorm reading up on Zen and smoking hand-rolled cigarettes. That might've been the first time I ever considered "spirituality" or "belief" as something other than silly.

I hung out with a lot of Hindus, too. Fellow transplants from New York. Most were from well-to-do Indian families. Against the backdrop of an impenetrably alien, "The South's gonna rise again!" milieu, they might as well have been my siblings. I liked how unapologetic they were about their ethnic and religious heritage. My friend Romesh had posters of various deities on his walls—Vishnu, Ganesha, Durga—a hodgepodge of zoomorphic divinities, all of which I found fascinating. Over a period of months, I asked Romesh countless annoying questions about Hindu cosmology. He answered with an impressive level of commitment. While I never bought into the whole Hinduism scene, I was nevertheless intrigued by the possibility of believing in something. Anything, really.

Through the Looking Glass, Darkly

All those Black Voices rehearsals started doing a number on me. Gospel music can be dangerous that way. Wave after wave would wash over me, pulling me under, leaving me breathless. Sometimes, we'd be so deep in it for such a long time that I'd lose all sense of place. Then, when we'd finally come back down to earth, I'd regain my bearings and find myself slouching, shoulders bent forward towards the floor, as if I'd been ducking for cover.

One of our staples was called "He Is Alive." Set to the tune of Beethoven's Fifth, the words were simple and repetitious, bordering on the ridiculous. Over and over, we'd sing the song's only lyric—you guessed it—"He is alive." We shouted it as loud as we could, pushing the meter to the red. Toward the end of the song, we'd crescendo into a refrain so devastating it could peel paint off the wall: "He is alive! He lives in me!" In unison, we'd sing it, again and again and again: "He is alive! He lives in me!" It was mesmerizing, like music written in the tongues of angels. Also, I had no idea what we were singing about.

It was a song about Jesus, that much I knew. But Jesus was dead. Crucified. Or maybe "resurrected," living off in the clouds somewhere. Either way, how could Jesus live *inside* another human being, *today*? He was, after all, just a man. A special man of remarkable courage and compassion, no doubt, but still a man. How, pray tell, does one acquire Jesus? When you "get" Jesus "in" you, do you gain weight? And why were we praying to a human being, and a dead one at that?

The other thing that fried my brain was the idea of talking to Jesus in a personal way: as a friend, a partner in crime, a loved one. How can you know an intangible God—who is somehow also a crucified human being— like you know an actual *person*, much less a friend? And make no mistake, this is what Christians claim today, just as they did two thousand years ago: that it is possible to meet Jesus personally, right here, right now; just like the apostles met him in the first century; just like I met my pompadoured mechanic when I needed a new radiator. A relationship with Jesus. This is what we were singing about. This is what my Christian friends were telling me.

Gone Walkabout

I don't know exactly when it happened, but at some point my Marvin Gaye records started sounding different. I already knew every millisecond of *What's Going On* by heart. But now, it was like hearing them for the first time: "Oh, don't go and talk about my father. God is my friend." I played it over and over again, just like I kept showing up at Black Voices over and over again. I had no doubt the people with whom I gripped hands and sang "He is Alive" were sincere. But you can be sincere and sincerely wrong. In all likelihood, they were wrong. I was almost sure of it.

Another one of our standbys was called, "My Mind Is Made Up." I'd never heard it before, but to this day, it's one of the funkiest songs I've ever performed. We had an organist who'd kill it on her Hammond B-3, and a drummer who could groove for days. Sometimes we'd sing "My Mind Is Made Up" for twenty minutes or more, long after rehearsal was supposed to have ended. We just kept swaying and singing: "Nobody can hold me, nobody can mold me, Nobody can show me like You, Jesus!" Swaying and singing, clapping, holding hands, swaying and singing. Minutes became hours. Some of the bolder members of our company would stand up and sway on the folding chairs. I, on the other hand, remained anonymous, tucked away safely in the back row. But I was defenseless. And music—like love—is always dangerous, always threatening to carry you off and leave you stranded somewhere you hardly recognize.

The philosopher Paul Ricouer said poetry has the unique power to summon us into another "possible world." When we encounter poetry or a work of art, we are invited to partake of a new, broader reality that neither imposes itself upon us nor demands our submission.[205] Art is disarming precisely because it doesn't "tell" you anything. It issues no marching orders or directions to follow. Preachers talk *at* you, but not poems. As Kandinsky quipped, art invites us to "walkabout" freely and explore hitherto uncharted territories.[206] Most of us are familiar with this experience, even if we don't use highfalutin jargon to express it. We know what it's like to see a painting, or hear a song, and suddenly be taken out of ourselves, like a teenager who hears The Beatles for the first time and feels as if she, and she alone, has discovered the secret alchemy of the gods.

I think what really got me about Black Voices was the sheer immodesty of it all, the utter lack of pretense. For me, life had been a series of delicate negotiations between irony and feigned indifference. Like that headline from *The Onion*: "Report: 79% of Sincere Thoughts Played Off as Jokes." Eye-rolling and hole-poking were my specialties. They worked for me. And I certainly didn't want any unabashed earnestness throwing a wrench into the works.

But Black Voices knocked it all off balance. There were no Seth Myers moments, no tongue-in-cheek reprieves, nary a trace of the sort of snark afforded by detachment. It was all or nothing, sink or swim. This was new to me. It still is. Maybe I was most enthralled by the element of praise that ran through all the songs we sang: this idea that we were thanking someone or something for all the wonder and beauty of the world. But more than that, my possibly deluded friends in Black Voices were giving thanks for God's active involvement in their daily lives. That was always the most uncomfortable part of practice for me, because I had no one to thank.

After a while, my favorite song became, "My Mind Is Made Up." Which is ironic, since my mind was not made up. About anything.

Ambrose

In the first half of his autobiography, Augustine documents his struggle to come to grips with Christian truth claims. After prolonged periods of certainty, skepticism, and confusion, Augustine conceded that the idea of the Christian God was at least rationally defensible.[207] This didn't mean it was *true*. Just possible. But *possible* isn't the same as *probable*. "Possible" just means you can't eliminate it outright. Like so many unmarked bubbles on a Scantron sheet, where A, B, C, and All of the Above might be true, "possible" means feasible enough to be really, really aggravating.

What eventually nudged Augustine in Christianity's general direction was a friendly old man named Ambrose. He was like the father Augustine never had . . . except for the father he actually did have, who was kind of a jerk. Years after their first meeting, Augustine recalled how he'd taken a liking to the elderly Ambrose, "not as a teacher of the truth, for I had absolutely no confidence in your Church, but as a human being who was kind to me."[208]

I had an Ambrose. A semi-retired music professor named Ernest Mead. I met him during my first year at college. He'd heard I was a serious guitar player and asked me to come visit and talk music. A genteel Southerner in his early eighties, I had no idea what he expected of me, nor how I should act in his presence.

I remember the first time we met. He declared, "You and I are going to be great friends," and it became true. I'd show up at his house at all hours, beset by all manner of existential angst, unsure of whether he had any answers, but desperate for someone to listen. I always came with questions. Questions, questions, questions, questions. Mostly, he'd just listen, make tea and, on occasion, recite a bit of Psalm 46, "Be still and know that I am God . . ." He even let me call him by his nickname, Boots. I asked him once why he liked that name. He said he didn't, but it was better than his given name, Ernest. I agreed. Another time, he played a bit of Bach at his piano, which sounded to me as warm and ancient as the Atlantic. With the last note still lingering above our heads, he raised his index finger, slowly and gently, eyes still closed, and said, "Never forget that." I never did.

Eventually Mr. Mead gave me a house key. He said I could visit whenever I felt like I needed to come up for air, which was often. "You are welcome here," he would say. I wonder if that's how Augustine felt.

I don't know if Augustine sang or played an instrument. But I do know he was a remarkably honest man. I remember being struck by one of many candid prayers in his *Confessions*. It's the sort of thing you don't expect to hear from a certified saint: "Fearing a precipitate plunge, I kept my heart from giving you any assent."[209] I'd always assumed saints didn't talk about faith as if it were something tenuous. I already felt as if I were drowning in a maelstrom of half-truths and partial beliefs. I was looking for a firm foothold, not a precipitate plunge into still murkier waters.

Faith, Doubt, and Commitment

"It is wrong always, everywhere, and for anyone, to believe anything upon insufficient evidence."[210] So said mathematician William Clifford in 1877, thereby rebranding skepticism as an ethical duty. And Clifford wasn't the first to make such a claim.[211]

Since the Enlightenment, we Westerners have learned to view the world through a panoramic lens of skepticism.[212] "Question everything!" Before buying in, we stay suspended in suspicion till the item under consideration proves itself as undeniably true (the exceptions being fashion and technology, in which case whatever is "new" is automatically awesome).

Speaking personally, I'd always lived by the tenet, "When in doubt, doubt." It wasn't a conscious decision on my part. But it was there, this unspoken, implicit duty to disbelieve. I suspect the same of innumerable millennials who perpetually delay marriage, childbearing, and adulthood until these intimidating enterprises "prove" themselves to be safe and achievable, which they have an irritating way of never doing. When people ask me when I knew for sure the person I was about to marry was "the one," I usually tell them it was at the altar, when I said, "I do."

Skepticism can definitely be an asset. It's what drives us to question our assumptions. It's indispensable for problem solving. No skepticism, no modern science. It's also quite handy when purchasing a used car. But skepticism is not without pitfalls. For starters, it's not always possible to know something with absolute certainty prior to direct, personal experience.

Belief

In her book, *The Case for God*, Karen Armstrong explains how our understanding of belief has changed in the modern era. Nowadays, most of us think of belief as an act of cognition, i.e., something that takes place in the mind. If you "believe" something, it means you've thought it through. You've put on your skeptic's hat, examined the evidence, weighed the arguments, and made your decision yea or nay. But that's not how earlier cultures thought about belief. In the New Testament, the words "faith" and "belief" mean something more like heartfelt commitment than detached deliberation. "Credo," *I believe*, means *doing* something—engaging yourself, giving your loyalty, affection, and trust to something—and not merely acknowledging the veracity of certain creedal statements. Before the Enlightenment, it was generally understood that religion only made sense through participation and personal involvement. If you wanted to grasp the true meaning of a particular doctrine or spiritual teaching, you first had to put it into practice. We see this principle at work in the Gospels, as when Jesus declares, "Anyone who chooses to *do* the will of God *will* find out whether my teaching comes from God or whether I speak on my own."[213] It was only later on, in the seventeenth century, when our concept of knowledge became more "theoretical," that the word "belief" started to be used to describe "an intellectual assent to a hypothetical—and often dubious—proposition."[214] As a consequence, most people now assume you've got to decide whether you believe in God *first*. Only then do you put your religious/spiritual beliefs into practice. But that's precisely the opposite of what premodern people meant by belief, including the very people who penned the New Testament.

If Armstrong is correct in her analysis, then we're in a bit of a bind. For most of us, the suggestion that some things have to be believed to be seen makes about as much sense as the plot of *Inception* to a third-grader on NyQuil. But that's how the ancients rolled—and not because they were naïve nincompoops. To dismiss them as such is to be guilty of "chronological snobbery," which disregards the methods and insights of a people purely on the basis of when they lived.[215]

When the soon-to-be apostle Nathanael first crossed paths with Jesus of Nazareth, Nathanael wondered, "Nazareth!? Can anything good come from there?" His friend Philip's response was simple and, by modern standards, inadequate: "Come and see."[216] Likewise, the psalmist tells us, "Oh, taste and see that the Lord is good!" But how? How do I "taste" something without putting it my mouth? How do I know something as palpably real while maintaining a safe distance? How do I enter another "possible world" without *actually* entering?

Makes me think of the time my friends decided to start bringing food to the homeless downtown. This was right after college, when I was living in Atlanta. Late on Friday nights, we'd go to White Castle, buy a bunch of burgers, roll up and have an impromptu meal in the street. It wasn't till we actually bought the burgers and started driving south on 85 that we realized we had no idea what we were doing. So we decided to embrace Chesterton's maxim, "Anything worth doing is worth doing badly"—which is exactly what we did. We stank it up. Clueless White kids bumbling around downtown. The whole thing happened so sloppily, so clumsily; like a pile of luggage flopping open at the bottom of an escalator.

Pissin' Kitten

I remember meeting a wild-eyed man named Immanuel. He'd been living outdoors for years. The first time I met him, he called me out: "You don't know what you're doing." Then later, "You scared. You shakin' like a kitten pissin' out thumbtacks." These were not questions, mind you. They were statements of fact. The worst was when he'd shift into interrogation mode: "Do you even know who you are? Whatcha lookin' fo? *Why are you here*?" Once, I gathered the nerve to tell him he needed to get right with God and ask Jesus into his life. It seemed like something a competent Christian would say. "I already done that," he answered, both our eyes cast downward.

It took a few more Fridays for me to admit that I really didn't know why I was there or what I was doing, that I was frightened and embarrassed.

I told him I was there because I wanted to see if God and love were really real. He liked that. After a few months, Immanuel started reciting lyrics he thought I needed to hear. Otis Redding, Marvin Gaye, Curtis Mayfield: "People get ready, there's a train a comin' . . ." He knew every word of *Songs in the Key of Life*. Night after night he'd recite those words till they sank down deep into my bones, and I would thank him.

Later that year, when my father had the accident that forever tangled the wires in his brain, all those songs came back to me. Immanuel's songs, the spirituals we'd holler in Black Voices, all of it. Three weeks in the ICU and still my dad couldn't recognize me. He couldn't remember my mother, his wife of almost thirty years. He didn't even know his own name. *"Who am I? Why am I here?"* He wanted so badly to go home but didn't know what "home" was. He just kept murmuring, "I wanna get outta here. I wanna go home."

It was a random Thursday when he fell from the ladder. After that, my parents' collective grip on things began to give until, finally, they lost their jobs, their house, and the life they'd built together, brick by brick and dream by dream. Just a decade earlier, my father found the sobriety that had so long eluded him. And I remember those days, too.

I remember him going to rehab when I was in middle school. After he came home, he would slip out of the house each morning, I knew not where. My mother finally told me he was going to Mass, which the rest of us rarely did. I followed him there once and sat silently in the back pew, just to see what went on. I watched him kneel down, hands clenched together in silence. I watched his every movement, saying nothing and noticing everything, as children often do. I didn't understand it, but I didn't really need to. He was sober and that was enough.

Most days were bad days in the ICU. So I would talk about music. Sometimes I would sing Stevie Wonder, just like I did with Immanuel: "When you feel your life's too hard, just go have a talk with God . . ."

I never did figure out why we spent all those late nights downtown in Atlanta. I really don't know if I did it for the homeless or for me. Same with Black Voices: Did I show up just to win a bet and satisfy my promise to Sammy? Or because some part of me wanted to be recognized and applauded for doing something a lot of White people didn't do? And with Bigoted Becky: Did I spurn her affections out of a genuine desire to do the right thing, or because I wanted to be better than her, or to be perceived as being better than her?

Harder or Easier?

I never assumed religious faith would play a role in my life's trajectory. That's not to say I didn't find elements of Christianity admirable, even desirable. Sure, some of its practitioners were preachy and off-putting, but I figured that was more of a human condition thing than a religion-specific thing. I think my main issue with faith was that it was just not *possible*—certainly not for a scientifically literate urbanite, like me.[217] Walking on water? Turning it into wine? Maybe I could buy it if I'd been raised in a medieval monastery. But surely not now.

Some say it's impossible for modern folk to believe in miracles. That was the philosopher Hegel's position in the early 1800s. If Christianity were to survive, Hegel argued, it would have to grow up: "If this is not so, then it would be necessary to demand of men that they believe things which, after having attained a certain degree of education, they can no longer believe."[218] A century later, biblical scholar Rudolf Bultmann said something similar: "No one can or does seriously maintain the New Testament world picture."[219] By "New Testament world picture," Bultmann meant the primitive depiction of reality that prevailed among the Bible's authors, including the notion of a "three-story world" with heaven above, hell below, and the earth in the middle. The average well-informed person of today just can't take that stuff literally (neither did a lot of ancient Christians, by the way, including Augustine . . . but that's for another chapter).[220] Nor can we accept the idea of an invisible deity who intervenes in peoples' lives and hears their prayers—let alone an eternal God who somehow becomes his own son, dies, then comes back to life.[221] It's just not an option anymore. Not after Neil Armstrong and the Hubble telescope proved there were no "heavens above." Other than natural atmospheric contents, the only things "above" are planes, drones, smog, and satellites. And we know they're there because that's where we put 'em.

But then I read Augustine. He lived during the waning years of the Roman Empire, in a thought world fashioned after Plato. Most Greek philosophers presumed God was perfect and unchanging; immune to suffering—a.k.a. "passion"—and therefore incapable of compassion.[222] Of course, there were atheists even back then: Democritus and some of the Epicureans, among others.[223] Still, most of the ancients assumed there was some sort of eternal Creator behind it all, a First Cause or Primal Origin from which all reality was derived. Then along comes Jesus and shatters these assumptions to pieces.[224]

According to New Testament nerd Bruce Fisk, the idea that God would give voluntary consent to humiliation and crucifixion would have been

inconceivable to the average Roman subject. "Too much value was attached
to honor and status," says Fisk, "too many Roman institutions shielded the
elite from the masses; too many risks attended disruptions of the status
quo, for Christ's voluntary descent into slavery and death to make sense."[225]
Could a good man be crucified by a brutal imperial government? Sure. But
the idea that God would voluntarily embrace vulnerability? Nonsense. Even
if God had some strange reason for wanting to experience human suffering and humiliation—which is a stretch in itself—how could God actually
pull that off? How can infinite and eternal divinity suffer? Isn't "suffering"
synonymous with being *less* than divine? Could God, the Uncaused Cause
of time, space, matter, and reason, be capable of empathy? Impossible. Yet
this is what we are presented with in the biblical story of Jesus: a God who
plumbs the depths of humiliation and human weakness.[226]

The notion of a self-effacing God posed some serious philosophical
problems for Augustine. He just couldn't wrap his head around the idea of
divine humility. He struggled for years to make sense of God's self-efface-
ment in the person of Jesus. Could it be possible that *divine* being comes
closest to *human* being in the most unlikely of locations—the one place
most of us would never think to look—vulnerability?[227] And when it comes
to faith, did the ancients have it any easier than we do? Was it ever really
"possible" for anyone to have faith, even first-century simpletons?

Most of us assume we're too far removed from Jesus to ever find faith.
Too much time has passed, too much space between us. Everybody knows
the Gospels were written decades after Jesus' death.[228] "For all we know,
Jesus didn't even say that," we tell ourselves, as if exposing the temporal
distance between Jesus and the written testimonies about him were the real
source of the rift. But did humanity ever enjoy easy, immediate access to
Christ? Was the divinity of Jesus ever that obvious? His own family thought
he was "out of his mind" (Mark 3:21). Why shouldn't we? When Jesus asked
his friend Peter, "Who do *you* say I am?" the fisherman-turned-apostle
answered, "You are the Messiah, the Son of the living God." Jesus replied,
"Blessed are you, Simon son of Jonah, for this was not revealed to you by
flesh and blood, but by my Father in heaven."[229] Hasn't it always been that
hard for flesh and blood to believe?

Sometimes I wonder what it would've been like to meet Jesus the "living man"; to have spent days, weeks, even years in his company; to have
known firsthand the timbre of his voice, the distinct peel of his laughter. If
I'd had the opportunity to record our every moment together, to write it all
down and get it all on video—even if, like the apostle John, I'd rested my
head on Jesus' very shoulder and broken bread with him during the Last

Supper—would I have been any closer to faith, *real* faith? Søren Kierkeg-aard thought not.[230] Kierkegaard described faith as a "marvel," a miraculous occurrence, something that, by definition, exceeds the range of human possibility. But for that very reason, faith is open to everyone, since not a single one of us can "do" it. No one is excluded from it, because no one can pull it off in their own strength. It's the great equalizer because it's the great impossibility.

A Leap into the Void

There was no getting around it: the journey to God always requires what Augustine called a "leap."[231] Like Harrison Ford stepping out onto that invis-ible bridge thingy in *Indiana Jones and the Last Crusade*. A "leap of faith." I hated the thought of it, mainly because I didn't do a whole lot of "leaping." It's hard to make any kind of "leap" while maintaining a pose of detached indifference. I figured such reckless frivolity was reserved for those who took life seriously enough to not take themselves too seriously, that rare breed of human who needs neither irony nor guile to make her way in the world. But I was even more disturbed by what the verb "leap" implied: a leaping *into* something—into someone—which, in turn, suggests trusting that something or someone to catch you. It terrified me, even as it terrified Augustine.

Then I thought of Immanuel. I don't think I ever would've gone down-town if I'd waited for the courage to come first. It only came afterwards. Marriage is like that, too. It wasn't until my therapist suggested that I try be-ing an ordinary little husband who does his little best that marriage became possible . . . as in, possible *for me*. "Just show up and do the next little thing." Sometimes friendships are like that. Maybe beliefs were like that.

Over the course of a semester, the Augustine–Black Voices tag team convinced me of one solitary fact—namely, that there were smart, sensible, and sincere human beings out there who had made the leap. They believed in God. More than that, they loved and trusted him, even when they didn't. They had their reasons—sometimes, logically defensible ones—which meant I could no longer dismiss Christianity as something inherently anti-rational and outmoded. To me, the question of whether faith was a miracle beyond human capability had become irrelevant: I had met genuine people of faith, in the flesh, and there was no getting around it. Like the small-est slant of light peeking through a door, faith had become "possible" to me (though still highly improbable). Regardless of their intentions, Black Voices, Augustine, and my Christian friends had succeeded in interrupting the flow of my habitual skepticism. And maybe that's all they did.

I kept on singing with Black Voices, even as I kept on despising their talk of "sin." I wasn't sure that Jesus really healed the sick, calmed the waters, or rose from the dead, but neither could I reject those claims anymore. I had not become a Christian, nor could I sing, "He is alive, He lives in me!" with their conviction. But I was beginning to love their song.

4

In Search of Something Else

We must therefore recognize that if the historical Jesus were to walk
into the room . . . the first disturbing impression might be not so much his
greatness but his strangeness.

—DENNIS NINEHAM[232]

What would be the value of the passion for knowledge if it resulted only
in a certain knowingness . . . and not, in one way or another . . . in the knower's
straying afield from himself?

—MICHEL FOUCAULT[233]

"Love," and Other Mutant Superpowers

GROWING UP AS A nominal New York Catholic, the rules of religion were
simple: don't kill anybody or mock the disabled, make the requisite church
appearance on Christmas and Easter, and you've got a decent shot at making it through the pearl gates (which, presumably, was what religion was
all about). While Bible study was not part of our regular family routine, I
had at least a nodding acquaintance with the greatest hits of Holy Writ, e.g.,
"Love your neighbor as yourself." Sounded like a pretty good idea. I liked
hippy Jesus, especially his Golden Rule. Most people do. Laozi, Confucius,

the Beatles, even L. Ron Hubbard all had their own variations on a similar ethical theme. The problem, of course, is actually doing it.

"Love for the neighbor does not want to be sung about," wrote Kierkegaard, "it wants to be accomplished."[234] Those words hit me hard. I was, after all, a singer. I specialized in singing about love: in my a cappella group, in my various and sundry cover bands, even in Black Voices. I always had a romantic streak, and, in my early twenties, music was an opportunity to give it voice without being too vulnerable. "All You Need Is Love," "Let Love Rule," "Pride (In the Name of Love)." Singing other people's love songs on an elevated stage was a comfortable fit.

But *actually* loving people? *Actually* wanting the best for my enemies and forgiving those who've wronged me? These things I could not do. And I was becoming increasingly aware of my own inability, especially after reading Augustine's *City of God* and Martin Luther King's "Letter from a Birmingham City Jail." King used all sorts of audacious adjectives when describing love (*agape*): "spontaneous," "unmerited," "unconditional," and "gratuitous."[235] From where I was sitting, he might as well have said "masochistic," "moronic," "irrational," and/or "impossible." In 1963, when four Black children were killed in a Birmingham church bombing, King begged fellow activists to extend forgiveness: "We must not become bitter—we must not lose faith in our White brothers."[236] Wait . . . *what*? By what peculiar power was he able to utter such sentiments, much less act upon them?

Even more baffling, King exercised the same sort of restraint when his own home was bombed—*with his wife and baby inside.* I'm not sure I can imagine a situation in which retaliatory violence would be more justifiable. But not for Martin. He chose to "cut the chain of hate and evil."[237] This I found mystifying, mostly because I was accustomed to living in a linear world where predictable effects follow their associated causes like links on a chain. You heat water to 100°C and it boils. You bomb my house, I'll bomb yours. That's The Way Things Are. And revenge holds a perfectly legitimate place in the conventional order of cause and effect.

But King wouldn't have it. He wanted more than order. He wanted *agape*—which is another way of saying he wanted surprise. "Chaos is God's body," wrote Updike; "Order is the Devil's chains."[238] King wanted those chains cut. So that's what he did. He broke the cycle. And I knew nothing of the strange and convulsive well from which he drank.

"Might makes right" has been the motto of schoolyard bullies and oppressive oligarchs since time immemorial. That's usually what we mean when we use the word "power." He who has the strongest punch gets to call the shots. But King was interested in something else—an altogether different kind of power. So he willingly unclenched his fists, spread wide his fingers, and let his right to resent spill out like sand through a sieve.

I'm not saying King was an unsullied saint. I was already aware of King's alleged philandering. I had no illusions about him being a flawless moral exemplar. But I couldn't dismiss him purely on account of his failures. Part of me wanted to, but I couldn't. Even if King only managed to forgive his enemies *on occasion*, every once and a while—still this was incomprehensible to me. Could I ever do that, even once? Could I ever even *want* that? Was I even born with the organ from which such love sprang forth?

The medievals and early Protestants[239] talked about love as if it were "supernatural"—not like how we use the word, as a catchall for wizards, superheroes, and all things sci-fi, but as a means of describing the phenomenon whereby finite creatures are divinely empowered to exceed their natural capacities. In Latin, *super-* means "above," "beyond" or "in addition to."[240] So when Clark Kent ditches the horn-rimmed glasses and flies faster than a speeding bullet, we call him *Super*man—because he's doing something that transcends any natural human abilities. A mild-mannered reporter bench pressing an airplane? A boy playing Quidditch on a flying broomstick? A drunk saying "no" to a free drink, or MLK choosing to forgive the thugs who just tried to kill his kids? These are what earlier Christians would've called super-natural occurrences—not because they have anything to do with magic, but because they're things that journalists, kids, drunks, and dads don't do.[241] And they don't do those things because they can't.

Unmerited, unconditional, gratuitous. King's words kept buzzing around in my brain, towering over me like giants of apocalyptic judgment. I started to wonder whether some things were simply beyond me, things I couldn't muscle my way through by my own unaided willpower.

"Knowledge is power," they always say, and they're almost always wrong in saying it. In reality, power is power. You can know a whole lot about something without having the power to do anything about it. Just ask any well-educated addict who knows all the relevant medical data and still can't stop using.[242] The power just isn't there, even if all the pertinent information is. Something else is required to make it happen, some additional, otherworldly power.[243] "Christianity stands or falls with its power to change human nature," King said.[244] That's what he believed. That's what he was betting on.

Of Frats and St. Francis

At some point I stumbled upon St. Francis of Assisi, a spellbinding saint if there ever was one. As a young man, Francis abandoned his family's wealth and status, embraced lepers, sang songs to wild animals, and lived among the poorest of the poor. Self-giving and compassion were the signposts that marked his less-traveled road to joy. The way up was down. And he did it all while keeping his feet firmly planted in the soil of everyday life.

Nothing about Francis made sense. Far from being wooed by Francis's "relevance," it was precisely his *irrelevance*, his almost embarrassing out-of-placeness, that I found so alluring. Like a dwarf star thrown into the center of the Milky Way, he threw everything out of whack. There was nothing remotely practical about Francis of Assisi. Like Augustine and MLK, he spoke of "love" not as a fleeting feeling, but as *something else*, a way of being-in-the-world that, to me, seemed impossible. And I wanted it. Or, at least, I wanted to want it.

In direct violation of my comfort zone, Francis and company talked a lot about Jesus. It's not like I felt any particular disdain for Jesus, but he seemed to have a knack for knocking things off kilter. After all, it was Jesus who convinced King to renounce violence, and look where that got him. Even though I'd become a fan of Francis, MLK, and the rest of God's crazies, I kept doing my best to ignore the Jesus-shaped elephant in the room, losing myself in their ideas, but disregarding the essential subject to which their lives bore such strange and powerful witness. But eventually, and with much hesitation, I figured I'd better read what Jesus actually said . . . which would mean actually reading the Bible. And I had almost no inclination to do so.

I was living in my frat house at the time, an unlikely setting for Bible study. The whole place reeked of stale cigarettes, yesterday's beer, and someone else's vomit. My room was on the second floor, right next to the big double-hung window. Every Saturday night, a fellow frat daddy named Stooge would shatter said window by hurling an empty keg right through it, occasionally decimating some unsuspecting car in the lot below. He'd get this almost feral look about him, like a rabid wolf staring down its prey before going in for the kill. Stooge was an odd duck. He didn't like music. Not a specific genre of music, mind you; music, *period*. On one occasion, Stooge declared that if he could get rid of any crayon color, he'd pick whichever one was most unique, because—and I quote—"I hate when things stand out too much, things that are too different," at which point I thought to myself, "So, Stooge . . . any plans on invading Poland?"

I didn't get much sleep that year, for obvious reasons. On a positive note, my living situation had the unanticipated benefit of boosting my grades, as I was eager to spend as much time as possible anywhere else—including the library. Turns out they had Bibles. Who knew?

Painfully Untidy Stories

I didn't have a clue where to start. I didn't even know there were two main sections, called "testaments" or "covenants."[245] You've got the Old Testament, a.k.a. the Hebrew Bible, including the epics of Abraham, Moses, and the ancient Hebrews. Then there's the New Testament, including the four Gospels (Matthew, Mark, Luke, and John) and an assortment of letters—a.k.a. epistles—written by apostles like Paul, Peter, and John. Eventually somebody told me where to find all the Jesus parts. And so I began.

The first thing that struck me was how strange it all seemed. It's a bizarre book, the Bible, full of oddly unperformable stories. Take one of Jesus' well-known parables:

> Two men went up to the temple to pray, one a Pharisee and the other a tax collector. The Pharisee stood by himself and prayed: "God, I thank you that I am not like other people—robbers, evildoers, adulterers—or even like this tax collector. I fast twice a week and give a tenth of all I get." But the tax collector stood at a distance. He would not even look up to heaven, but beat his breast and said, "God, have mercy on me, a sinner." I tell you that this man, rather than the other, went home justified before God. For all those who exalt themselves will be humbled, and those who humble themselves will be exalted.[246]

How, exactly, does one "do" this parable? How do you perform it and check it off your to-do list? Option A: become a holier-than-thou perfectionist—in which case you're in danger of becoming the self-righteous Pharisee. Then there's Option B, which is to do your darndest to be like the humble tax collector whom God seems to favor. But what if you do an exceptionally good job of being humble and self-deprecating, and what if you know full well that you're doing an exceptionally good job of it?[247] Then you've fallen into another, more surreptitious form of self-exaltation. You've become an intolerably smug martyr and you're back at square one (which is square screwed). That's why you can't "do" the parable. It'll always undo you first.

Whatever else Jesus was up to, his words and deeds suggested something other than behavior modification or improved moral performance. A lot of people find this kind of unperformability frustrating. I found it fascinating.

I definitely wasn't hooked in by the Bible's aesthetics. Sure, Scripture has its share of silver-tongued verse. The ecstatic longings of Isaiah, Song of Songs, the Psalms: "As a deer longs for flowing streams, so my soul longs for you, O God . . . Deep calls to deep in the roar of your waterfalls; all your waves and breakers have swept over me."[248] Lovely stuff. But for every moment of beauty there were chunks of drab and cumbersome discourse. Exhibit A: "Phares begat Esrom; and Esrom begat Aram; and Aram begat Aminadab . . ."[249] And who could forget 1 Corinthians 1:16? "Beyond that, I don't remember if I baptized anyone else." Or my personal fave: "If a man's testicles are crushed or his penis is cut off, he may not be admitted to the assembly of the Lord."[250] Hard pass.

I was twenty when I started reading the Bible. By that point I'd already sampled the best of Blake, Coleridge, and Wordsworth. I knew how exquisitely well-ordered words could rend the heart and leave the reader ravished. Scripture didn't do that for me . . . at least not on a consistent basis. But I kept on reading. It was more about exploration than critical analysis. I wasn't trying to see behind the Bible's pages. I wasn't looking to uncover the presuppositions or prejudices of its authors. Nor was I asking questions about its literary influences or historical accuracy—not that those aren't important lines of inquiry. They're just different questions than the ones I was asking.

I don't think I ever made a conscious decision to suspend disbelief when reading the Bible. Neither did I try to part company with reason. I just wanted to try it on and see how it felt: angel and demons, miracles and prophecies, the underworld and afterlife. Truth is, it felt weird as hell. But I figured God was probably weird as hell . . . assuming God, heaven, and hell were even real. But the weirdness had a ring of truth to it. Or at least a ring of realness to it. Why shouldn't the Scriptures be strange? Why shouldn't a book about things transcendent take me aback? Life itself was strange enough, something to be contended with, even raged against. Jacob wrestled with God under cover of night. Maybe he was on to something.

It was the Bible's strangeness that kept me curious, like the strangeness of Jesus. The theologian Rowan Williams describes the Gospels as a cluster of "painfully untidy stories."[251] Reading them felt as if some anomalous world were unfolding before my feet, outrunning me at every turn. And I liked it. I even liked reading the parts I didn't like. I guess I was tired of being told things I already knew or already believed. The Bible was *other*, an as-of-yet uncharted Something Else. It was a refreshingly foreign book, a source of endless surprise. It still is.

When a Stranger Calls

They say there's only two ways you can meet God: as yourself, or as a stranger.[252] The first scenario involves projecting yourself outwardly, then engaging in an ongoing dialogue with your externally projected self. In so

doing, you come to see and appreciate yourself afresh. You become newly conscious of yourself. According to the philosopher Ludwig Feuerbach, Christianity is really all about this sort of self-projection and self-discovery. To be "self-conscious" is, for Feuerbach, to know yourself from a uniquely insider's perspective. And since "God" is merely a projection of yourself, disguised in the language of divinity, "prayer" is just ennobled self-talk—or more specifically, self-love. "In prayer," Feuerbach wrote, "man adores his own heart."[253] So when you pray, you're basically enjoying your own company, telling yourself things you want to hear. And in fairness, I think a lot of prayer is probably just that: wishful thinking. Talking to yourself . . . in which case I was already pretty good at it.

But it's that second scenario that I found more fascinating . . . and disturbing. For me, the thought of encountering a divine stranger was not a comforting one. "Praying is *not* listening to yourself speak," Kierkegaard said somewhere. But if not yourself, then who? "Who are you, Lord?" blurted Paul when he was blinded by divine light on the road to Damascus. And it wasn't like Paul was new to the religion game. He was already devout when he voiced those words. Yet somehow Paul knew that it was really *God* whom he'd encountered on that road . . . and because it was God, Paul knew that he didn't know: *"Who are you?"*

I'm a pretty sociable guy (Enneagram 7-wing, depending on which test you consult). Sometimes people tell me, "You've never met a stranger." But if that were really true, it would mean I've also never made a friend. Because all friends start off as strangers. Before I met my wife, she was an unknown quantity, a Someone Else. And that's the only way I could meet her—*really* meet her—by letting her be *her*, rather than a projection of me.

Is God really Someone Else? An "other," *not* fashioned in my likeness, an unfathomable ocean of dark divinity? Talk about stranger danger. If, as Augustine and Pascal intimated, God is "completely other,"[254] and if heaven is for real, would I really want to go there? Could I tolerate being exposed to God's full foreignness, even for a moment? I remember being dumbfounded by Annie Dillard's musings on divine otherness:

> Why do people in church seem like cheerful, brainless tourists on a packaged tour of the Absolute? . . . Does anyone have the foggiest idea what sort of power we blithely invoke? Or, as I suspect, does no one believe a word of it? The churches are children playing on the floor with their chemistry sets, mixing up a batch of TNT to kill a Sunday morning. It is madness to wear ladies' straw hats and velvet hats to church; we should all be wearing crash helmets. Ushers should issue life preservers and signal flares; they should lash us to our pews. For the sleeping god may

wake someday and take offense, or the waking god may draw us to where we can never return.[255]

Much appreciated, Annie. Thanks for sharpening the teeth of my already-overdeveloped existential anxiety.

This Time, It's Personal

Even less tolerable was the notion that God was somehow *personal*. An ethereal life-force, or metaphysical "ground of being"? That I could deal with. But a God who has desires and opinions? Who speaks and acts. . . and maybe even judges? First I scoffed, then quaked at the thought of an invisible, eternal Someone Else. And if Jesus really meant what he said in Matthew's Gospel, if hatred really is tantamount to murder, then surely I'd be incinerated the minute I met the Almighty. "My ears had heard of you, but now my eyes have seen you," said Job, "therefore I despise myself and repent in dust and ashes."[256]

Despite what you may've heard, God doesn't get much tamer in the New Testament. Just look at Luke's Gospel. After a long, thankless day of fishing, the apostle Peter comes up empty. Then Jesus shows up and tells him to give it one more go. Peter obliges, perhaps half-heartedly, only to haul in the catch of a lifetime, the fisherman's mother lode. And then Peter loses it. He realizes who Jesus really is. He falls to his knees and begs Jesus to leave: "Go away from me, Lord; I am a sinful man!"[257]

But there were promises there, too; promises great and precious. There were assurances of deep rest, love, hope, joy, and reconciliation. The same psalmist who pleaded, "Where can I go from your Spirit?" also said, "Taste and see that the Lord is good!" Driven by a similar yearning for the sacred, Augustine petitioned the Lord with prayer: "Bring to me a sweetness surpassing all the seductive delights which I pursued."[258] Like Augustine, Jean Pierre de Caussade was a priest who took the dreaded "leap of faith" and lived to tell the tale. And he thought it was worth the risk: "Let us run and fly to that love which calls us. Why are we waiting? Let us set out at once, lose ourselves in the very heart of God and become intoxicated with is love."[259] "Sober inebriation," Augustine called it.[260] Likewise, de Caussade spoke of knowing God as enjoying God, a profligate pleasure of the heart. So did the seventh-century saint, Isaac the Syrian: "The person who hungers and thirsts for God's sake, God will make drunk with his good things, with the wine whose inebriation never leaves those who drink it."[261] These crusty old saints talked about God like reckless teenage romantics.[262]

The Not-Me-Ness

At some point my internal dialogue took an unexpected turn. Something sneaked in while I wasn't looking—some invisible not-me-ness, interrupting the familiar flow of thoughts and feelings that had hitherto defined my experience. Something or Someone Else, roaming this way and that, gently impressing itself upon my innermost fears and wants. By what door had it entered? How long would it tarry?

Then the oddest thing happened: I started posing questions to the Someone Else. I hadn't noticed till I was already doing it, having these wordless tête-à-têtes with Someone Else about whether or not he existed. It was embarrassing. And also surprising. Turns out, the Someone Else was a good listener.

But again, that's the problem, isn't it? Being *listened to*? Being *watched*? "He sees you when you're sleeping, he knows when we're awake": an effective tool for terrifying toy-crazed toddlers into obedience, but it's also one of the creepiest lyrics of all time. For my part, the thought of being scrutinized by a Peeping Tom in the sky made me feel about as tranquil as a newborn ferret on Prednisone.

New questions flooded my mind: Why couldn't God mind his own business and stay out of mine? Was God codependent? An eavesdropping, hypercritical control freak? If even mere mortals like myself could scrounge up the decency to "live and let live," why couldn't God? 'Course, I routinely passed judgment on almost everybody I met, but that was beside the point. The idea of an all-knowing Absolute suggested moral absolutism—or, worse still, what Christopher Hitchens called "celestial despotism": involuntary subjugation to round-the-clock surveillance by a telepathic Judge capable of convicting me of thought crime.[263]

And yet Christians talk a lot about finding "peace." The Bible does, too. In the New Testament, Paul says the peace of God "transcends all understanding."[264] Paul seemed to think God's peace was made available to those who took the leap of faith: "May the God of hope fill you with all joy and peace as you trust in him."[265] *As* you trust, not before. There it is again: the element of risk. As Augustine prayed in his *Confessions*: "You are my true joy if I submit to you."[266]

That's a pretty big "if."

5

I Wanna Have Sex with the Devil

If I open the door, you will know I'm poor,
and my secrets are all that I own.
Oh Lord, I have made you a place in my heart,
and I hope that you leave it alone.

—Greg Brown, "Lord, I Have Made You
a Place in my Heart"[267]

How to Win Friends, Influence People,
and Resent Everybody

In tenth grade, I was an insufferable jackass. That's what they said anyway. Opinionated, judgmental, and obnoxious. That's one of the fringe benefits of attending public school in New York: you're gonna get your fair share of unfiltered feedback.

I liked high school, even after I quit drinking. I liked the structure it afforded, the clockwork rhythm of the day. Bell rings, report to homeroom, bring your no. 2 pencil, repeat. I even liked being graded on my performance, mainly because I was good at performing. It was, and is, an effective coping mechanism. My sister's drug of choice was more conventional: drugs. Mine was a bit more cryptic: perfectionism. Turns out, deep-seated insecurity and an unquenchable need for affirmation are outstanding motivators for success (academic, or otherwise). If you're looking for a way

76

to keep the world at arm's length while maintaining an illusory sense of control, I highly recommend it.

Eventually I realized that my generally crappy attitude was not winning me a lot of friends. So I made a conscious decision to adopt a new persona. I would become "nice." People liked nice people, and I liked the idea of being liked. So I resolved to be friendlier and more tolerant. I would become a student about whom teachers would say things like, "works well with others," and, "is a welcome addition to the class." And I pulled it off. How? Simple: mimicry. Performing. I watched older, more popular kids and imitated their behavior. It's the same strategy I used to learn guitar. Wanna play like Stevie Ray? Watch, listen, replicate. I figured the same could be done with social skills—and it can.

Months passed and the whole charade got easier. Inside, I had lots of unanswered questions about who I was and what life was all about. I still wanted to impose my will upon the world and blamed reality for being insufficiently malleable. But being nice seemed a better, more efficient way to get what I wanted. And my performance was working. My reputation improved and more people liked me. Lo and behold, I had succeeded in changing myself without really changing myself. And I enjoyed the new and improved me. The more kindly I treated others, the more intoxicated I became on my own bubbly, fermented self. Sure enough, by senior year I was voted "Most Friendly" by the graduating class . . . and, perhaps not coincidentally, "Most Likely to Wind Up on a Psychiatrist's Couch." True story. I have my high school yearbook to prove it. Come to think of it, I have *this* book to prove it.

Now that I'm an educator, I like to keep apprised of the hippest trends in education theory. A few years ago, "tiger mom" Amy Chua identified three key traits that have helped people groups achieve higher levels of success in the U.S.: (1) a superiority complex, (2) insecurity, and (3) impulse control.[268] Chua knows something about how to excel in a competitive marketplace. A Harvard grad, she now teaches at Yale and writes best-selling books in her spare time. I confess: there's a part of me that envies her achievements—especially the Harvard part. I was not so fortunate.

I remember when my dad drove me up to Boston for my interview. We spent an hour in a chalky-white echo chamber of a waiting room, no doubt designed to arouse terror in the hearts of aspiring applicants. There were about twenty other interviewees with us, parents in tow. Most donned coke-bottle glasses and navy-blue sport coats embroidered with family crests. My father and I were in denim jackets . . . and over our heads. About twenty minutes in, my dad leans over and whispers, "Alright, let's be honest: you're probably not gonna get in here. But hey, at least you could kick anybody's ass in this room."

Harvard never happened for me. But for the most part, the insatiable need to achieve served me well—at least, on the surface. Sure, I was a quivering gerbil of perfectionism, but a gerbil with a killer transcript. So maybe Chua is right. Or half-right. Either way, there remain some pretty troubling implications to her position. For one thing, feelings of superiority and insecurity may be effective drivers for vocational success, but that doesn't mean they're traits worth having. I don't know about you, but I haven't come across too many poems extolling the virtues of vainglory and hypertension.

I see some of these traits in my own students (not to mention their parents . . . #helicopter #lawnmower #snowploughparenting). Like me, they find themselves acting out some form of the following equation: insecurity + high-performance mentality = being loved. You win approval by performing, by being your "best self": the hardest worker or biggest slacker, the most multiculturally sensitive or least politically correct, by either amassing or renouncing more wealth than your peers, etc. That's the gig. That's how it works.

The great thing about performing all the time is that it can make people like you (assuming you're any good at it). It can earn you all sorts of cool points. But it can also make you a stranger in your own life. It can split you in half: there's the self you present to the world, and the secret self you presently are—the "false" self vs. the "authentic" self—and the two have a tendency to grow further and further apart, till you can hardly tell which is which.[269]

That's how I did life. I performed. When things went well, it meant I got what I wanted: adulation and acceptance. But my heart remained hidden, even from me. And no matter how much of an affirmation high I was on at any given moment, the same questions remained: Who am I, really? Why am I here? Is this all there is?

Getting to Know My Own M.O.

As far as I could tell, I only chose to do something if it satisfied one or more of the following criteria: (1) I felt like doing it; (2) it promised some desirable result that would be beneficial to me, e.g., fame, fortune, comfort; (3) I felt obligated to do it; or (4) was afraid not to. Take college, for instance. I wanted to be a doctor, probably because that's what I learned to want. It wasn't so much the actual practice of medicine that I found alluring. It was the prospect of being an important person: "Excuse me . . . that's *Doctor Rosolino*." The promised paycheck didn't hurt, either. So, I chose to go to college. And it would have to be a good college, since I wanted to make bank and dominate. But equally important, I was afraid *not* to go to college. So off I went, registered for Professor Schitz's Intro to Chemistry class, and prepared for conquest. I barely made it a semester.

Looking back on it, most of my decision-making had always boiled down to a kind of crude mathematics of maximizing pleasure, minimizing pain, and defending my inalienable right to do whatever I wanted—which put me on about the same ethical ground as a goldfish. Fear and self-interest determined my choices: be slightly funnier, friendlier, and smarter than the competition; try to look like you don't care; don't try things that you might be bad at; don't let them see your weakness. Results were mixed.

One day I read something startling in Augustine: "To hear You speak about oneself is to know oneself."[270] A thousand years later, Calvin made a similar claim: "Man never achieves a clear knowledge of himself unless he has first looked upon God's face."[271] According to these dead saints, self-analysis can only get you so far. They were clear on this point: to meet myself, I'd need to meet God. But what would God have to say? And would I want to hear it?

"Keep it real," people say. "To thine own self be true." A lofty credo, but not without problems. For one thing, how can you be true to your self if you don't know who you really are? And what if, upon reflection, you discover that you're an insufferable jackass?

The more I read the Bible, the more I noticed how much Jesus seemed to care about the inner condition of the human heart—not that lopsided, blood-pumping organ in your chest, but the "heart" (*kardia*) in the ancient sense: the core of the self, where our most visceral longings and desires live. *Kardia* is, as one contemporary philosopher writes, "Part compass and part internal guidance system." It both points us in a particular direction and propels us on towards it.[272] And *kardia* was a topic of particular interest to Jesus.

For me, this posed a problem. Like most adolescents, I didn't have a whole lot of experience with introspection. Nor did I want to. Like looking through your sketchy ex's old text messages, I was afraid of what I might find.

Things got really uncomfortable when I discovered the Sermon on the Mount—Jesus' first, and arguably most significant, sermon: "You have heard that it was said to the people long ago, 'You shall not murder, and anyone who murders will be subject to judgment.' But I tell you that anyone who is angry with a brother or sister will be subject to judgment."[273] These words gave me pause . . . *anyone* who's angry? I'd always loathed judgmentalism, but for some reason Jesus' spooky sentences shook me to the core. I think it was the whole idea of having my hidden motives and desires excavated. I wasn't even sure what my motives were, and I definitely wasn't thrilled about having them dissected by the spiritual power(s) that be. According to the late scholar, Jaroslav Pelikan, the Sermon on the Mount is an "intensification" of Old Testament commandments. Jesus ups the ante by addressing not only the "outward observance" of behavioral codes, but "the inward spirit and motivation of the heart."[274] But what were the real inner motivations of my *kardia*, my hidden heart?

Imperceptibly, and against my better judgment, Jesus' warnings began to worm their way into my conscience. Like little beads of condensation, they gathered on the walls of my mind, whispering new wants and new questions: Who am I? Why am I here? What's it all about? To paraphrase Augustine, I had become a question to myself. Some call it an "existentialist phase," and it's frequently associated with being nineteen, homesick, and a little lonely. But still, not all questions are meant to be outgrown.

What were the things that really drove me? Take writing this book: I write because I find it therapeutic, and because I'm genuinely interested in historical-theological ideas. But I'm also genuinely interested in getting attention. Then there's the whole Bigoted Becky episode: Would I really have made such a public display of disgust if the whole incident weren't so . . . public? Wasn't I guilty of sizing up human beings with the same sort of callousness as she?

Augustine showed me how little practice I had in soul-searching. *Confessions* is a shockingly transparent book. It is, after all, a memoir of a dead saint. I expected a spotless account of a steadily ascending spiritual life. Instead, I found the story of an ordinary man well acquainted with his own defects of character.

Even more surprising, Augustine *wanted* to uncover the hidden recesses of his heart, that he might be known and seen by God. I'd heard Christians talk about "knowing God," but the apostle Paul spoke of being known *by* God—"fully known"—to me, a terrible thought.[275] "My weakness is known to you," Augustine prayed; "You, Lord, know everything about the human person . . . to your eyes, the abyss of human consciousness is naked."[276] Nudity in the face of divine scrutiny? Sounds awful. I'd always related more to the psalmist: "Lord, you have searched me and you know me . . . you perceive my thoughts from afar . . . Where can I flee from your presence?"[277]

But not Augustine. To him, full exposure before the Most High God was as a healing balm. Page after page, he probed the darkest crevices of his heart, prying open his wants and holding them up to the light of inspection. I wondered why anyone would ever do that. Under any circumstances. Ever.

Things to Never Say Aloud

After a while, I started seeing a strange, paradoxical freedom among the dead saints, including the apostles and biblical authors. Instead of squirming under God's gaze, they embraced their powerlessness and welcomed the prospect of being fully known. So did my newfound Christian friends. They did all sorts of rash and outlandish things, like apologize. They forgave one another and made amends. They were a reconciled people; reconciled to life, to themselves, to each other and, apparently, to God. They were also disarmingly honest. Like this:

"I'm afraid I wanna have sex with the devil."

That's what a friend of mine used to tell her dad every day on the way to school. Her father, a round and tender man, would drive her up to her little country grammar school and say, "All right, honey. Love you. Have a great day." She'd respond with a subdued smile, "Okay, Daddy," and sling her bulky backpack over her shoulders. Never in a hurry to shut the car door, he'd ask, "Honey, is there anything else you feel like you need to tell me?" Slowly she'd gather the courage to say it, just like the day before: "Well, Daddy . . . I'm afraid I wanna have sex with the devil." Notice the sheer irrationality of it: "I'm afraid I wanna have sex with the devil"—as in, "*Maybe I really do want this, deep down inside . . . or maybe I'll want to want it one day, and I just don't know it yet*"—which, to your average OCD eleven-year-old, is tantamount to saying: "Maybe this is the worst possible thought that anybody in the world has ever had." Every day, same car ride to school, same routine. Patiently, he'd listen; patiently, he'd whisper: "Honey, I love you know matter what, and I know that's not what's really in your heart." For almost three years this went on, until it went away. Decades later, when she recounted the story to me, she wondered aloud: "Who knows? Maybe my dad was wrong; maybe it *was* down deep in my heart. Maybe it still is. But God . . . to be loved like that; to be seen and known and accepted like that, over and over and over again . . ."

Fully seen, fully known, fully loved. This is *agape* love—the kind of love that turns water into wine and shame into mist. This is love that wakes the dead. And as I sat there listening to her story, I felt like I'd glimpsed someone drinking from a freshwater fountain, only to find that I, too, was thirsty.

Power and Vulnerability

But there were other holdups along the pilgrim's path. Firstly, I didn't like how the dead saints talked about "submission." Augustine, Ma Theresa,

Tozer, Oswald Chambers,[278] St. Francis, Isaac the Syrian, George MacDonald, de Caussade, T. E. Eliot, even modern-day evangelicals like Billy Graham and Charles Stanley[279]—all use distasteful terms like "self-abandonment," "submit," and, worse still, "surrender." A.A. calls it Step 3: surrendering one's "rights."[280] To me, words like "surrender" implied impotence: the complete absence of power.

But did I even know what "power" was? I'm not talking about power as defined by the world's bullies, but power to love and long-suffer, to reconcile and forgive. "To have what we want is riches," wrote George MacDonald, "but to be able to do without is power."[281] Such power craves no attention. It is gentle, patient, and enduring, fathomless and free—free even to be misunderstood. The power of God is, according to the apostle Paul, "made perfect in weakness."[282] To me, the non-coercive power of St. Francis, MLK, and even my born-again buddies was utterly paradoxical. Feminist theologian Sarah Coakley calls it "power-in-vulnerability."[283] Could she be right? Is "power," when properly understood, more akin to humility?

For me, this is what made the leap so foreboding. It wasn't just fear of the unknown, though that was part of it. And it wasn't just the fear of being duped. At bottom, I wasn't afraid to believe because I thought God might not be there. I was afraid because I thought God would be. I knew taking the leap would mean opening up, bearing all, subjecting all to Someone Else—benevolent though he may be. It would mean creating space and relinquishing autonomy, even in the midst of uncertainty. What would become of me if I unclenched my fists and took that leap? Would there still be enough of "me" left over to live on?[284] Or would I disappear completely?

The Great Physician

Augustine spoke of salvation as soul-mending. Curative care for the spiritually ill: "Cast yourself upon him, do not be afraid . . . Make the leap without anxiety. He will catch you and heal you."[285] In *Confessions*, the words "salvation" and "healing" both come from the same Latin root, *salus*.[286] Likewise, the desert monk Evagrius Ponticus called God the "physician of souls."[287] So did my Christian friends. "The Great Physician," they said, capable of binding up the brokenhearted and making all things new. And in ways that weren't visible to me at the onset, that's what I was always after.

It happened on a Tuesday, I think. My lil' leap of conversion. I was walking to the library and ran into a friend who asked how I was doing. Almost involuntarily, I confessed, "I think I am becoming a Christian." And that was it. I wasn't planning on saying it, mostly because I wasn't sure it was true. Maybe it didn't become true until I said it, like the "I do" on my wedding day. No peeling thunder or parting of the skies. No angelic visions. It was still a Tuesday, and I was still me. I still pined after affirmation and applause. I still longed to plant my flag upon the world and hear my anthem sung. I still had doubts and questions. But I couldn't shake the sense that Jesus was really there, crucified and alive. Somehow, in all that wandering I had begun wondering; in the wondering I had begun wanting; in the wanting I had begun seeking; in the seeking I had begun believing; and in believing I was already loving.

6

In the Simplest Terms and the Most Convenient Definitions

"God is love," but get it in writing.

—GYPSY ROSE LEE

Religion, Abortion, and Other Icebreakers

I WENT TO MY first Bible study because of a girl. Not an atypical backstory, I now realize. Like me, she was a musician, and like Bigoted Becky, she was stunningly attractive . . . minus the racism part . . . which was definitely a bonus. Let's call her Biblicist Britney.

Britney's Bible study met every Wednesday night in what looked to be the living room of an American craftsman–style house–turned–church. They were an eager, hospitable group, almost awkwardly so: the Stepford smiles and appropriate side hugs; the knowing, compassionate looks . . . it was a bit overwhelming at times. I don't think I said a word for the first two months, for fear of being outed as insufficiently pious. Things went swimmingly until one fateful evening when, in what might've been the most ill-conceived conversation-starter of all time, I somehow managed to bring up abortion. I was ardently pro-choice at the time, though I wasn't sure exactly why; I guess I just preferred my artsy-fartsy abortion advocate friends over their more prudish, preppy political rivals. I also had some roots in second-wave feminism, thanks to a fiery New York matriarch, and the enduring influence of my Margaret Atwood–reading sister. None of this went over particularly well at Bible study.

Almost immediately, Biblicist Britney informed me that terminating a pregnancy was "morally wrong," because it says so in the Bible. And Britney weren't no airhead: a high-achieving pre–med student with articles already published in peer-reviewed journals, she knew her stuff, especially her Bible. So I asked her where the Bible explicitly condemns abortion. Reflexively, she directed me to Psalm 139: "For you created my inmost being; you knit me together in my mother's womb . . . My frame was not hidden from you when I was made in the secret place, when I was woven together in the depths of the earth. Your eyes saw my unformed body . . ."[288] It's a lovely psalm—a love song, really—traditionally ascribed to King David of Israel. And to my Bible study crush, Psalm 139 proved beyond a shadow of a doubt that life begins at conception. But I was not convinced.

For one thing, the Psalms seemed more lyrical than literal (a "psalm" is, by definition, a sacred song or hymn). It certainly didn't appear as though the psalmist was trying to offer in-depth medical analysis of conception or gestation. It's way too poetic for that. Just a few lines earlier, the same psalm reads: "If I rise on the wings of the dawn . . . even there your hand will guide me."[289] So, God has actual, physical hands, and the author has wings? Are we meant to believe human embryos are literally "knit" together like yarn into needleworks? Or is it possible the psalmist is saying something about divine omnipresence—that God is somehow everywhere, even in utero? Or perhaps it's about God's intimate knowledge of each person, from beginning to end? Or all of the above? Maybe Britney was right, and abortion was "morally wrong," but that couldn't be established solely on the basis of one poetic passage of Scripture, regardless of its perceived level of authority.

My views on abortion have since evolved, by the way. I no longer consider myself "pro-choice," though Biblicist Britney had little to do with my eventual flip flop. I still wouldn't call myself "pro-life," mostly because that's the dumbest designation ever (Is there really an absolute dichotomy between the values of *choice* and *life*? Do you actually know any pro-lifers who are fundamentally opposed to the concept of personal choice? And is it intellectually honest to reduce the entire "pro-choice" position to being "anti-life," and, by extension, "pro-death"?). As in other decisions of potentially devastating consequence, e.g., climate change, I favor the cautionary principle: when the stakes are high and you're in doubt, it's best to tread lightly. Since I'm not an accredited climatologist and am unwilling to risk the planet's future, I try to play my little conservationist part. I recycle. I drive my itsy-bitsy eco-friendly Hondas (the Thunderbird has long since gone home to glory). And since I have no idea when life begins, and would rather not play an active role in ending it, I feel obliged to err on the side of caution. But not because of Psalm 139.

Looking back on it, it was a gradual confluence of philosophical, ethical, and medical arguments, combined with ancient Christian insights, that slowly nudged me towards the "conservative" end of the abortion debate. By "conservative," I mean by today's labyrinthine political standards. Back in 1971, delegates of the Southern Baptist Convention actually supported legislation allowing for abortion in special cases—e.g,. rape, incest, "and carefully ascertained evidence of likelihood of emotional, mental, and physical health of the mother."[290] They reaffirmed that position on two separate occasions, both after the infamous *Roe vs. Wade* case that legalized abortion in America. Other prominent evangelicals made similar statements at the time.[291]

But enough about Southern Baptists and the swingin' seventies. Back to Biblicist Britney. Though our would-be romance never got off the ground, our conversations did spark in me a newfound curiosity about the Good Book. What was the Bible actually supposed to be? A compendium of moral lessons, or accurate historical accounts? Cautionary folktales, religious poetry, or superstitious propaganda? Was I being asked to emulate the lives of its main characters? And were they "characters," or actual historical figures?

Jets vs. Sharks

I soon became aware of two prevailing and radically dissimilar schools of thought on the big Bible question. In one corner, you've got the conservative Christian camp—which would include evangelicals like Biblicist Britney, "born-agains," holy rollers, and fundamentalists (though nobody really likes to be called a "fundamentalist" anymore . . . sounds too Taliban-ish). In America, conservative Christians see Scripture as more than a mere collection of inspiring stories.[292] It is the written revelation of God, entirely free from error or contradiction, clear and direct in what it teaches.[293] Some call this view of Scripture "biblicism." At the opposite end, there's the skeptical critics. Rather than revere Scripture as a uniquely reliable reservoir of spiritual truth, skeptical critics approach the Bible with deliberate suspicion, asking: Who really wrote it, and why? What was their agenda? Did its authors and/or editors tamper with the text in hopes of promoting certain values, or silencing certain voices? What were their prejudices? Influenced by modern biblical scholarship, skeptical critics scrutinize Scripture in order to dissect and deconstruct it, to discover where, and when, it came from.

These two camps are crosstown rivals; the Jets and Sharks of late-modern Christianity. There are exceptions, of course; inbetweeners who, for any number of reasons, locate themselves somewhere in the middle. You'll find some conservative Christians who claim to take the whole Bible literally . . . except when it comes to practicing the sort of radical simplicity exemplified by Jesus, maybe not so much with the literalism. Same goes for skeptical critics, many of whom dismiss the Scriptures as subpar fiction, yet find themselves inspired, challenged, even ethically bound by Jesus' teachings.

If, like me, you didn't grow up familiar with either camp, I should probably spell out some potentially confusing Christian lingo. And if you're kind of lazy about language or put off by the prospect of pursuing conceptual clarity, a word of caution: the more significant the subject matter, the more necessary it is to define relevant terms. Our fondness for slogans of 140 characters or less notwithstanding, we miss a whole lot by glossing over the finer syntactic details. There's a big difference between, "My professor, Schitz [proper noun]" and "My professor schitz [verb, present indicative]." Just ask my college chemistry teacher, Professor Schitz.

Biblicism: The Basics

Biblicists see Scripture as a unique document of unrivaled religious authority—which, historically speaking, isn't a particularly scandalous position for a Christian to take. Jesus himself quoted the Old Testament regularly and based his teaching on its authority. In like manner, his followers strove to live and preach "in accordance with the Scriptures,"[294] including the four Gospels and the apostles' writings—a.k.a. the New Testament, which they saw as an extension of the Old.[295] Like Christians today, the ancients based their beliefs, or "doctrine," on the Bible (e.g., God exists, created the universe, and became incarnate in Jesus, who suffered, died, and rose from the grave). As one historian observed, "It was everywhere taken for granted that, for any doctrine to win acceptance, it had first to establish its Scriptural basis."[296] The Bible has always functioned this way, as a required source and reliable referee in theological disagreements, the Supreme Court or final arbiter for deciding matters of doctrine.[297] So if someone in sixth-century Syria or twenty-first-century Toledo claimed that Jesus didn't *really* suffer, die, and rise from the grave, Christians would use the Bible to counter those claims.[298] Though most early Christians were illiterate, followers of the Way met together for frequent Bible study. When they couldn't, they were advised, "Let everyone at home take the Bible and read sufficiently in passages that he finds profitable."[299]

While Bible study is nothing new, biblicism is more of a modern development. As explained by the historian, David Bebbington, biblicists believe the Bible is completely free from error or discrepancies and should therefore be read as literally as possible.[300] The philosopher Christian Smith gets even more specific, defining biblicism as "a theory about the Bible that emphasizes together its exclusive authority, infallibility, perspicuity, self-sufficiency, internal consistency, self-evident meaning, and universal applicability."[301] Taken together, these assumptions lead to the popular "Handbook Model" of the Bible, according to which Scripture is supposed to serve as a "compendium of divine and therefore inerrant teachings on a full array of subjects."[302] That there's some intimidating verbiage, Professor "Smith" . . . if that is your real name. Let the deciphering begin . . .

First, there's "perspicuity," "internal consistency," and "self-evident meaning." Generally speaking, biblicists believe that as long as you're diligent in reading your Bible, sooner or later its singular, obvious, and intended meaning will jump right off the page. You read it the same way you read a how-to manual: follow the directions, use common sense, and achieve predictable results. So suggested Jerry Falwell in a 1981 interview with *Penthouse* magazine (which, I assume, included no full frontals).

For Falwell, theology is an "exact science," like engineering or chemistry: "You come to exact, simplistic answers if you follow the proper equations."[303] Since it's a "perspicuous" book of "self-evident meaning," the untrained reader needn't suffer through prolonged periods of confusion, nor should there be any real struggle to reconcile one passage with another. Some biblicists even see academic training as a negative rather than an asset: "The very fact that I did not study a prescribed course in theology made it possible for me, to approach the subject with an unprejudiced mind and to be concerned only with what the Bible actually teaches."[304] Thus spoke Lewis Sperry Chafer, former president of Dallas Theological Seminary—a pretty ironic admission for the head of an academic institution to make. The implication is clear: you don't need pastors, educated elites, or what Galileo called "wise expositors" to help you understand Scripture.[305] You need you and your Bible—hence the term, "Bible-only-ism."

Then there's that bit about "exclusive authority," "infallibility," and "universal applicability." As Smith explains, biblicists believe God gave the Bible as the definitive written authority on *all* subjects and areas of life.[306] It is, as stated by the influential nineteenth-century theologian, Charles Hodge, a "storehouse of facts."[307] Following Hodge, early fundamentalist B. B. Warfield declared Scripture to be "trustworthy in *all* its affirmations *of every kind*,"[308] including "matters of history and science."[309] Accordingly, biblical authority extends far beyond the scope of matters spiritual.[310] It is, according to one evangelical website, "totally accurate in matters of History, Prophecy, and every issue of life."[311] So if you wanna know the best way to lose weight, predict stock market trends, or determine the age of the earth, you'll find the most accessible, accurate instructions in the Good Book. Hence the current proliferation of Christian books espousing a "biblical" view of dating, dieting, coaching, cooking, fashion, fitness, finance, ad infinitum.

A recent article in *Faith and Fitness Magazine* (which is a real thing, BTW) exemplifies Smith's point. According to the article's author, "The Bible is designed by God to provide us a blueprint for living life."[312] That's the same basic terminology scholar Bart Ehrman uses when describing his erstwhile beliefs about Scripture. Now an outspoken agnostic and best-selling author of books like *Misquoting Jesus: The Story Behind Who Changed the Bible and Why*, Ehrman spent his younger evangelical years looking to Scripture as an "inerrant blueprint" for living, only to become disillusioned by biblicism later on.[313]

Most of my Christian friends in college were default biblicists. When speaking of Scripture, they used descriptors like "infallible," "literal," "sole authority," and "totally consistent." These seemed to be the Good Book's biggest selling points; the pillars of its purported reliability—especially the "infallible" part. I soon discovered countless evangelical books on the subject, all aimed at defending biblicism from its detractors.[314] Most warned against parsing out sections of Scripture that seemed more metaphorical than historical.[315] "The Bible ain't a buffet," I was told. "You can't pick out your favorite verses and forget the rest." You either take the whole thing at face value, or you leave it alone.

Of course, *saying* you take the Bible literally is a lot different than *actually* taking it literally—or actually knowing what it says. Lots of American evangelicals claim to read Scripture "literally," either because they feel obliged to do so, or because it's what they grew up hearing and tacitly accepting.[316] But even if you claim to take it all "literally," that doesn't tell us much about which sections you're actually reading and which you're blowing off.[317]

Sidebar: I've been taking an informal poll of my high school students over the last few years and, when asked directly, most confess an almost urgent belief in the Bible's authority. Funny thing is, they don't know much about what's in it. Many haven't even heard of the Sermon on the Mount, arguably Jesus' most celebrated collection of sayings. They're aghast when they learn about Jesus' injunction to "turn the other cheek" and love your enemies. Ironically, they learn about Jesus' teaching by learning about Gandhi—that humble Hindu who, during the Indian Independence Movement, based much of his non-violent resistance strategies on Jesus' sermons.[318] Most of my students were born and raised in church, mind you. They've sat through scores of sermons and Sunday school lessons. And apparently, the main lesson they've learned is this: what you say *about* God, Jesus, and the Bible is a lot more important than what God, Jesus, and the Bible actually have to say.

I don't want to imply that my students are all mindless automatons. Far from it. For them, biblicism was simply normal. Or neutral. It's how they grew up. From the earliest age, they learned to talk the talk—even when harboring their own hidden doubts. Sociologist Robert Wuthnow explains, "An orthodox belief about the Bible can be so familiar that it serves as a kind of litmus test of being a devout, conservative Christian."[319] If you're reared in the Bible Belt, it's simply a given that being a Christian means adopting a certain biblicist way of speaking about Scripture.[320] You pick it up by osmosis, like I did in college. I figured biblicism was just part of the program, something Christians have always believed. So I accepted it without much reflection, mostly because it was the only option with which I was presented—and honestly, I didn't require much convincing. I don't have any sad stories of being bullied, brainwashed, or force-fed by Bible-beaters. Truth be told, I was already well disposed towards literalism long before darkening the door of Britney's Bible study.

Literalism? Me Likey!

I am, by nature, a literalist. Always have been. I follow recipes to a T, enacting each directive line by line. Like Drax from *Guardians of the Galaxy*, I have an almost allergic reaction to ambiguous turns of phrase, which is why I lasted all of fifteen seconds in the one and only yoga class I've ever attended: "First, draw your thigh towards your heartbeat, letting your anger breathe out from behind the knee . . ." Umm, no. In contrast, there's my wife: a free-spirited dynamo without a literalist bone in her body. She's a threat to saunter into the kitchen at any moment and announce, "Let's add some cinnamon! Or pomegranate seeds!" to our almost-completed sausage pizza, miso soup, stewed sauerkraut, or whatever dish would most logically exclude either pomegranate seeds or cinnamon. As soon as she starts hovering around the oven with that cinnamon-and-pomegranate-eating grin on her face, you'd best cover your pots and pans. On the bright side, she makes pretty good eggs.

Literalism has its advantages. It works great with cooking. Yet when applied across the board, literalism can cause confusion, contradiction, and frustration . . . like when we took our first family vacation to the ocean when I was a kid. After weeks of my parents getting me all psyched about how we were going to stay "on the water," we finally arrived at our destination:

a beach house . . . several hundred yards removed from the water, in fact. What about the preposition "*on*" did my parents not understand? In what inconceivably boring adult universe does a house kinda sorta near the beach equal "*on* the water"? In my little literalist head, we were about to spend a week living in something akin to Sealab 2021: a transparent, dome-shaped vessel suspended atop undulating waves. I'd wake each morning to the sight of iridescent fish swimming under my feet. Instead, we got a beach house. One of a series of colossal disappointments, the most recent being "hoverboards." And don't even get me started on *The NeverEnding Story*.

So yeah, I liked biblicism. A lot. The prescription was simple enough: read your Bible faithfully and, sooner or later, its one true meaning will emerge. Then, just follow your marching orders. Like when Ephesians 4:26 says, "Do not let the sun go down on your anger," it means make sure to patch things up before going to bed. Easy peasy, lemon squeezy. I liked the notion of having God's shrink-wrapped, freeze-dried thoughts forever bound within a book. I liked having ostensibly immediate and objective access to divine knowledge. More than that, I liked being right. There's something seductive about religious fundamentalism and the confidence it breeds. Part of me thought that's what faith should be like, probably because I assumed that's what God should be like: functional. Useful. Predictable. *This* was a deity I could work with. *This* God would give me inflexible moral and practical parameters; rules to follow and taboos to avoid. *This* God would provide the principles I needed to best do life. Away with mystery! Away with uncertainty! On with steely eyed precision! And so, armed only with my Bible, my wits, and two-plus decades of total life experience, I fancied myself equipped to navigate a world newly cleansed of all ambiguity.

It was a good fit—at least for a while. But in an all-too-familiar script, my budding biblicism wasn't built to last.

The Breakup

Things went south when I started looking deeper into church history. I soon realized that the early Christians couldn't have been biblicists, even if they'd wanted to. For one thing, 90 percent of the Roman populace was illiterate,[321] which would've made it extremely difficult for your average follower of the Way to be a biblicist (how do you read Scripture literally if you literally can't read?). That's probably why ancient Christians placed such an emphasis on gathering together to hear Bible reading and the apostles' teaching.[322] On top of that, the New Testament wasn't fully written until late in the first century, and it wasn't compiled into one finalized unit, or "canon," till the late fourth century, which even conservative evangelical scholars will admit.[323]

So it's problematic to portray the earliest disciples as reading the Bible in its present, canonized form. And even if they knew how to read, the printing press wouldn't make Bibles abundant for another thousand years. Books were rare commodities in the ancient world, and the Bible was no exception.[324] So the idea that Jesus' first followers were thoroughgoing biblicists is a bit far-fetched.

Then there was the literalism—which, again, I kinda liked. But the more Scripture I read, the less I was able to make it work, mainly because the Bible contains so many metaphors . . . and a metaphor is, by definition, *literally untrue*.[325] Like, "love is a red, red rose"; which, of course, it isn't. But it's also not a lie. Because "figurative" doesn't mean fictitious. A statement can be true without being literally true. That's why metaphors can be so memorable, so moving; they help us see things in a different way by making the same old same old shine like new. The tricky thing is to figure out which parts are figurative and which parts aren't.

Sometimes it's easy, like when Jesus says, "First take the plank out of your own eye, and then you will see clearly to remove the speck from your brother's eye."[326] Christians have always interpreted this passage as an injunction against rushing to judgment rather than an absurdist statement about two-by-fours lodged in retinas.[327] Otherwise, Jesus' disciples probably would've spent a lot more time fishing lumber from their eyes . . . which, in case you're wondering, they didn't.

That leaves the third fatal flaw of fundamentalism: it leads to all sorts of crazy contradictions. Some are glaringly obvious, as when the prophet Amos declares, "I am not a prophet."[328] Others are more subtle, like when the Old Testament says God has wings, hands, arms, and feet, which Jesus further complicates by stating, "God is spirit."[329] Well, which one is it? Bird, bipedal primate, or bodiless phantom? The Bible doesn't get much better when it comes to geometry and earth science. Sometimes it references the "four corners of the earth."[330] Other times it says the earth is a sphere.[331] So unless you can think up some way to make a rectangle round, one of those descriptions *has* to be non-literal.

Galileo had the same basic problem with biblicism. He knew there were parts of Scripture that couldn't be taken literally, like, "The sun rises and the sun sets, and hurries back to where it rises"—which it clearly doesn't.[332] Like most churchmen of his day, Galileo thought the primary purpose of Scripture was to show human beings how to go to heaven, "not *how* the heavens go."[333] In other words, it isn't the most helpful resource for figuring out what makes the universe tick. And Galileo wasn't the first to notice: Augustine beat him to the punch a thousand years earlier.

Like it or not, the Bible doesn't make for a very good science book. You can search its pages for thorough expositions on gravity, space-time, or quantum mechanics, but you'll search in vain. Because the Bible was never intended to serve as an exhaustive authority on everything, especially matters of natural history and science. Since its purpose is spiritual rather than scientific, it talks about the natural world like we do—by using everyday language and figures of speech.[334] That's why it says "sunrise" instead of, "The natural phenomenon by which the rotation of the earth around the sun appears as if the sun emerges from the earth's eastern horizon from the distinct rotating reference frame of the human observer." Doesn't quite pop like "sunrise."

Look at the Old Testament book of Genesis. If you take the first chapter at face value, it means God created both day and night on the first day, then waited another three days to create the sun and moon. But how do you have day and night without a sun or moon? Already by the third century, leading Christians like Origen of Alexandria wondered: "What man of intelligence will believe that the first and the second and the third day, and the evening and the morning existed without the sun and moon and stars?"[335] Augustine was even more harsh:

> It is a disgraceful and dangerous thing for an infidel [a non-Christian] to hear a Christian, presumably giving the meaning of Holy Scripture, talking nonsense on these topics; and we should take all means to prevent such an embarrassing situation, in which people show up vast ignorance in a Christian and laugh it to scorn. The shame is not so much that an ignorant individual is derided, but that people outside the household of faith think our sacred writers held such opinions . . .[336]

And before you get all, "That's because they were God-hatin' heathens!" remember that Origen, the son of a Christian martyr, was almost martyred himself, and Augustine remains one of the most influential Christians of all time (no Augustine, no Aquinas, Luther, Calvin, etc.). Yet neither Augustine nor Origen felt bound to interpret the creation story literally.

On Baby Smashing and Other Bible Faves

Speaking of things that shouldn't be taken too literally, check out Psalm 137:9: "Happy is the one who seizes your infants and dashes them against the rocks" (NIV). Or the equally grotesque English Standard Version: "Blessed shall he be who takes your little ones and dashes them against the rock!" Go ahead. Look it up. One of my tenth-grade students did. Then she burst into my room in tears, wondering how she was supposed to make sense of all this baby-dashing business. If "understanding" Scripture means implementing every line as literally as possible, what's your average Bible-toting teenager supposed to do with the cursing psalms? I notice not too many soccer moms have Psalm 137 bumper stickers slapped on their mini-vans, and for good reason: it endorses infanticide. Accordingly, Gregory of Nyssa issued the following caution in the fourth century: "The immediately apparent meaning of the things said [in the Bible] in many instances causes us harm in the pursuit of the life of virtue"[337] (not to mention harm to the infant). Obviously, Jesus' early followers didn't interpret Psalm 137 literally—not in spite of their convictions, but because of them.[338] It's hard to "love your neighbor as yourself" while simultaneously smashing your neighbor's newborn.

So why's it in there? Maybe because it encapsulates the anguish of the ancient Israelites, who, after being conquered by the Babylonians, were forced to live as exiles in a hostile land. It's a furious psalm, blistering with ferocious honesty. Is it "true"? Sure, in a Tarantino sort of way. Transparent to the good news of Jesus? Not so much.[339]

With this in mind, Galileo offered the following insight:

> The Holy Bible can never speak untruth—whenever its true meaning is understood. But I believe nobody will deny that it is very often abstruse, and may say things which are quite different from what its bare words signify. Hence in expounding the Bible if one were always to confine oneself to the unadorned grammatical meaning, one might fall into error. Not only contradictions and propositions far from true might thus be made to appear in the Bible, but even grave heresies and follies.[340]

What kinds of "contradictions," "heresies and follies"? For starters, how about insisting that God created day and night before creating either the sun or the moon, which is what the "bare words" of Genesis suggest? Galileo knew that if Christians were blindly committed to line-by-line literalism, "It would be necessary to assign to God feet, hands, and eyes," because the Bible tells us so.[341] Lest Scripture collapse under the weight of its own inner tensions, Galileo urged Christians to consult "wise expositors" to help determine the "true meaning" of the text—which, as Gregory of Nyssa pointed out, isn't always "immediately apparent."

Augustine had his own share of struggles with literalism—especially when reading the Old Testament, what with its subscientific language, ultraviolent imagery, and morally questionable pronouncements.[342] Former God rocker Lisa Gungor knows that story. Reflecting upon her own painful process of deconversion, Gungor recounts: "I told Michael [her husband] that I don't know if I can read the Old Testament . . . I was like, 'I can't even read the Bible now anymore.'"[343] And can we really blame her? Or Augustine, for that matter? If you're a dyed-in-the-wool literalist, the Old Testament is a virtual non-starter—especially if you've got a weak stomach . . . or a strong moral compass . . . or a low threshold for baby smashing.

It was a "wise expositor" named Ambrose who helped Augustine move beyond the rigid literalism of his youth. Through Ambrose's influence, Augustine learned to read Scripture "spiritually" and "figuratively," rather than "literally"—which, in turn, enabled him to interpret those "difficult passages in the Old Testament" (e.g., Psalm 137) that previously seemed indefensible.[344] Unfortunately for many modern-day fundamentalists, including younger me (and, presumably, younger Gungor), the collective wisdom of Augustine, Ambrose, Galileo, and Gregory is all forgotten history.

All of this I found infuriating. Not only did Augustine and company challenge my right to read Scripture for myself, without any meddling middlemen or expert expositors getting in the way, they also made the Bible seem a lot more complicated—a.k.a. "abstruse," as in the opposite of "perspicuous." So did Martin Luther. While Luther relied on Scripture, not the pope, as the supreme authority on Christian doctrine, he also believed some sections of the Bible were more reliable than others. Take the Letter of James, which Luther called an "epistle of straw." In Luther's view, James contradicted the more general biblical message of grace (for similar reasons, Luther wanted Revelation "thrown into a river").[345] At the very least, Luther acknowledged the presence of paradoxes and points of tension in the Bible, reconcilable though they may be. But in so doing, he violated biblicism's claims about the clarity, internal consistency, and self-evident meaning of Scripture. If it's an easy-to-use handbook, why the need for "wise expositors," including even Luther, to help us make sense of it?

How to Make Things Worse

There was no more denying it: the Bible just didn't read like a handbook, much less a crystal-clear blueprint for knowing and navigating the world. Not with all that figurative imagery in there. It's doubtful the biblical authors ever intended it to be read that way. And if they did, they did a God-awful job. I have a hard enough time following the assembly instructions for my kid's Melissa & Doug train table. But at least Melissa & Doug try to make things user-friendly. The Bible offers no such courtesy.

As the previously impregnable walls of my biblicism continued to crack, I scrambled in search of reinforcement. And then I did something really, really stupid, something the more seasoned biblicist would consider tantamount to spiritual suicide: I took a graduate-level class in New Testament studies. This was at a "secular" university, mind you, meaning we'd be analyzing the Bible as a historical document, using the same techniques scholars use when examining any ordinary piece of literature. That's when I learned about modern scientific and historical studies of Scripture, a.k.a. "historical criticism." And in what has become a clichéd experience among young evangelicals, it was a New Testament class that drove the final nail in my fundamentalist's coffin.[346]

For the uninitiated, here's the skinny on "historical criticism."

Back in the seventeenth century, early Enlightenment philosophers like Spinoza and Thomas Hobbes began using new analytical methods to investigate the Bible. Others followed suit, deconstructing Scripture just as scholars had been doing with Shakespeare, Dante, and the like.[347] They noticed all the aforementioned problems and discrepancies . . . and then some.[348] Using the latest scientific and literary techniques, these scholars started asking new questions: How could Moses have written the Pentateuch, the first five books of the Old Testament, if it gives the details of his own death?[349] Moreover, the Pentateuch includes Genesis, which depicts the creation of the world. How could Moses have written an accurate, eyewitness account of the world's creation if he wasn't even around to see it? Genesis also includes two dissimilar (contradictory?) creation stories. In Genesis 1:1—2:3, God (called *Elohim*) creates man and woman simultaneously, after having previously created all other living things. But in Genesis 2:4-25, God (here called *Yahweh*) creates Eve by using one of Adam's ribs, then makes the rest of the animal kingdom afterward. Historical–critical scholars started to wonder: Maybe Genesis isn't really a "book" after all, but two (or more) separate creation stories smashed together?[350] Similar problems appeared in the New Testament. The three "Synoptic" Gospels—Matthew, Mark, and Luke—place the date of Jesus' crucifixion on the first day of Passover, while John puts it a day earlier.[351] Inevitably, the question had to be asked: Maybe the books of the Bible were compiled by a bunch of sloppy, superstitious schmucks who didn't know any better?[352]

Time went on and more serious criticisms of Scripture started to mount, especially in the nineteenth and twentieth centuries. As a result, both the Bible and the church lost some serious street cred. Skeptical critics felt freer to cross-examine the Scriptures without fear of being burned at the stake or wacked on the proverbial knuckles by the powers that be. This opened wide the gates for more controversial historical-critical scholars like D. Friedrich Strauss,[353] Herman Gunkel, Julius Wellhausen, and a bunch of other really smart dudes with really German-sounding names.

They concluded that Scripture is an undeniably *human* book, produced by human authors, whose various—and sometimes discordant—perspectives couldn't be whitewashed or wished away. The gloves were off, the curtain pulled back. As a result of these findings, growing numbers of people started wondering whether the Bible was ever that reliable in the first place. All this newfangled "historical criticism" business made conservative Christians super freaked. And not in a Rick James kinda way.

Defense! Defense! Defense!

Freaked: that's how I felt when I moved to the South. Defensive. Freaked out. An anxious Long Island fish out of water. Freshman year of college, they called me "Yankee." I'm not sure I even knew I was a Yankee until then. Truth is, I became *more* of a Yankee after moving to the South. Every New York inflection grew more nasal and hyperbolic, like an unpolished Joe Pesci parody. And why not? If you can't fit in, you might as well stick out. Plus, I liked playing the part of the exotic "other." But an even bigger part of me felt threatened by all the unfamiliar Southern mannerisms: "Bless your heart"? Tim McGraw? Debutantes? I'd heard of "coming out," but it definitely didn't involve heterosexuals dancing cotillion. Suddenly, instinctively, I underwent an almost involuntary transformation: more talking with my hands, more loud and proud of my northern roots, more conspicuously interested in Civil War history—especially that part where the Confederacy loses. It was fight or flight. A survival strategy.

Biblicism is kind of like that. A survival strategy. A way for Christians to cope in an increasingly skeptical world. To a large extent, the popular biblicism of today was birthed in reaction to the explosion of modern historical criticism. In the twentieth century especially, anxious evangelicals grew evermore adamant about the supremacy of Scripture. The Bible became Christianity's trump card, a one-size-fits-all conversation stopper. Why are open-carry laws, gender-ambiguous bathrooms, and [insert your preferred hot-button issue here] wrong? "Because the Bible says so!" How can you argue with that?

And That's How the Christian Cookie Crumbles

If, like me, you meet Jesus through popular evangelical channels, you're gonna go through a biblicist phase. It's almost a rite of passage. Then one day you learn about the Bible's complex origins and more controversial contents, how and when it was compiled, canonized, and eventually translated . . . and things start getting a little shaky. And in spite of the enormous efforts of evangelical apologists to resolve any apparent difficulties in Scripture,[354] the supposedly solid ground of Christianity gives way.

I've seen it before in my own students. The minute the average fundamentalist teen learns about the Bible's not-so-neat-and-tidy history of compilation—that it didn't fall from the sky as one coherent unit; that its various books reflect the personalities and cultures of its numerous and diverse authors from different times and locations;[355] that some books weren't even completed until the late first century at the earliest, decades after Jesus' crucifixion; that the biblical authors sometimes quoted sources from outside the canon of Scripture, including pagan philosophers;[356] that some of the original letters once revered as Scripture have since been lost (e.g., Third and Fourth Corinthians);[357] that the Bible wasn't assembled into a singular, unalterable unit until the late 300s CE; that it contains discrepancies and scientific inaccuracies, which even some of the early fundamentalists admitted,[358] it's all over.[359] The bedrock of belief breaks apart.

"A Very Human Book"

They say how something breaks can tell you a lot about what it was. Based on the candid comments of so many former evangelicals, the essential "it" of conservative Christianity is neither Christ, nor belief in Christ, but belief in the Bible—a book *about* Christ. And if the Bible can be shown to contain even a hint of ambiguity or inaccuracy, then Christ can't be the real deal. The stakes are that high. Influential evangelical Albert Mohler asks, "If we cannot trust the Bible, in *all* its parts, to reveal God with perfect truthfulness, how can we know him [God] at all?"[360] Herein lies the Achilles heel of biblicism. Just ask Reza Aslan:

> The bedrock of evangelical Christianity, at least as it was taught to me, is the unconditional belief that every word of the Bible is God-breathed and true, literal and inerrant. The sudden realization that this belief is patently and irrefutably false, that the Bible is replete with the most blatant and obvious errors and contradictions . . . left me confused and spiritually unmoored.[361]

Aslan's story is by no means unique. Lots of erstwhile evangelicals feel "unmoored" after learning about the Bible's difficulties. Take Bart Ehrman. When one of his seminary professors suggested that the author of Mark's Gospel might've made an error when quoting the Old Testament, Ehrman was floored. Soon Ehrman noticed other biblical boo-boos, like when Jesus says a mustard seed is the smallest of all seeds (which it isn't).[362] The "floodgates opened," prompting a "seismic shift" in Ehrman's understanding of the Bible, God, faith, Jesus . . . all of it.[363] Once he realized the Bible was a "very human book," he could no longer trust it as the "inerrant blueprint" it was supposed to be, and his evangelical faith quickly evaporated.[364]

John Jeremiah Sullivan calls it a "Jesus phase,"[365] and Americans aplenty have lived out their own version of the same script. Take BuzzFeed blogger, Jessica Misener. While studying religion in seminary, Misener began to notice incongruities in the Bible: "As I learned ancient Greek and Hebrew and pored over the biblical text in its original languages, and read it in larger quantities than I'd ever read it at church, its discrepancies began to shine a hot and uncomfortable spotlight on my personal religious views." Like Ehrman, Misener realized the Bible was a "deeply *human* book."[366] Soon "swelling doubt" arose and swallowed her faith whole—a faith which, in her words, "hinged almost solely on believing the Bible to be the literal, inspired word of God." Her biblicist buddies at Yale fared no better: "We evangelicals, with our infallible view of scripture ripped from our hands, were left gasping for air."[367]

More on Being Unmoored

I know that gig. Feeling like you've been duped. Cut adrift. The only thing I knew to do was to keep on reading—more books on church history, the Bible, and especially historical criticism. But this led to only greater disappointments. Because for all its conscious commitment to intellectual honesty, historical criticism offers no more clarity than conservative biblicism.

For starters, modern historians make a big deal about recovering the "Jesus of history"—the real-deal rabbi from the first-century. By relying on reason, evidence, and the best modern methodologies, historical-critical scholars try to depict Jesus as accurately and objectivity as possible. That means following Jefferson's lead by stripping the Gospels of any supernatural embellishments. No miraculous healings. No hocus-pocus. Clearly these must've been added to the text later on, since miracles are, by definition, impossible—and therefore inadmissible.[368] It also means peeling away any alterations to the original manuscripts in order to unearth the "historical Jesus." But herein lay the problem: nobody can ever agree on which parts are historically accurate and which sections need to go. To this day, historians keep coming up with various, often mutually exclusive versions of the "*real* historical Jesus" based on their own research.[369] There's Jesus the rebel, Jesus the great moral teacher, Jesus the cynic philosopher, Jesus the failed apocalyptic prophet . . . the list goes on.

Albert Schweitzer knew all this. After much historical-critical study of the Bible, Schweitzer admitted that scholarly renditions of Jesus inevitably reflect the scholar's own preferences and prejudices.[370] Each scholar reconstructs Jesus "in the image of his [or her] own personality"; meaning that if you want Jesus to be more of a self-help guru or feminist-socialist, you're probably going to figure out how to make it happen by arranging your evidence accordingly. That's what eventually drove Schweitzer to abandon his "quest for the historical Jesus." James Cone, the father of Black liberation theology, affirmed Schweitzer's decision: "Schweitzer demonstrated conclusively that the liberal search for the historical Jesus was a failure and only represented creations of the human mind . . . We are not free to make Jesus what we wish him to be at certain moments of existence. He is who he was . . ."[371]

That last part hit me hard: Jesus *is* who Jesus *was*—the "living man" we meet in the stories of the New Testament. Anything else amounts to a "creation of the human mind." A vain exercise in wish-fulfillment. Talking to yourself. Moreover, if Jesus were merely the mirrored image of his followers, why'd they abandon everything to follow him? Seriously: Why risk family and fortune to follow a yes man who's got nothing radical or revolutionary to say? Why submit yourself to the tutelage of some stooge who's only going to tell you what you already know? Would the Romans really prosecute a man like that, much less crucify him? For what, being too agreeable?

Now compare this saccharine Jesus with the earth-shattering Christ whose appearance blinded the apostle Paul: "Who are you, Lord?" *That* was Paul's question—something one asks of a stranger, not one's own reflection. For W. H. Auden, it was precisely the otherness of Jesus that came closest to proving his divinity: "I believe because he fulfills none of my dreams, because he is in every respect the opposite of what he would be if I could have made him in my own image." Auden's confession of faith flies in the face of wish fulfillment—and for that very reason, among all the world's great prophets, it was Jesus alone who inspired Auden to cry, "Crucify him!"[372]

So there I was, back at the beginning, wondering what the Bible was supposed to be. If not "conservative" fundamentalism or "liberal" historical criticism, then what? Do I keep the Bible and lose the biblicism? Or was it time to give the whole Bible the boot?

7

A Tale of Two Eltons

God is Christlike, and in him is no un-Christlikeness at all.

—MICHAEL RAMSAY[373]

Standing on Shoulders

G.K. CHESTERTON DEFINED "TRADITION" as extending democracy back through time.[374] He also chain-smoked cigars, refused all forms of physical exercise, and never went to the dentist. Like, ever. Fortunately, what Chesterton lacked in commonsense hygiene, he made up for in wisdom on the importance of tradition. "The democracy of the dead," he called it. *Tradition*, thus understood, means giving your dead ancestors a vote. It means soliciting input from those who've gone before. When it came to the big Bible question, that's what I needed: some new and informed voices in the conversation. A fresh perspective. Why not look for it among the dead?

This would mean a dramatic, perhaps irreparable break with Bible-only-ism, of course. But why not? Going it alone wasn't getting me real far. Besides, if part of Jesus' mission was, as Scripture suggests, to start an organically connected, social "body"[375]—a *family*, extending through centuries and continents—then I wanted to know what other members of that family thought about the Bible. As the late evangelical John Stott admonished, "To be disrespectful of tradition and of historical theology is to be disrespectful of the Holy Spirit who has been actively enlightening the church in every century."[376] Enlightenment. Wisdom. That's what I was looking for. So I decided to take a new approach: I invited the dead saints to Bible study.

Back to Augustine I went. Back to *Confessions* and *City of God*; on to Irenaeus, Ignatius of Antioch, Syncletica of Alexandria, and other ancient forerunners of the faith, sometimes called "church fathers" and "mothers" (kinda like America's Founding Fathers, minus the powdered wigs). Some, like Polycarp, had direct contact with Jesus' original disciples. Many were submerged in the earliest Christian communities. Most were brilliant, admirable people of remarkable conviction. But they were still just people. Fallible, finite creatures, like you and me. Even so, the more I questioned my take on the Bible, the more I wanted to know what the fathers thought—not because I prized their opinions as inerrant (they aren't), but because I valued their viewpoints, at least as much as my own. So did John Calvin, by the way. Even though he was one of Protestantism's original pathfinders, Calvin remained circumspect of any theological ideas that weren't already anticipated in the writings of the church fathers—which is why, in the preface to his *Institutes of the Christian Religion*, he tried to show how his ideas aligned with the fathers' established teachings.[377]

The Single Meaning Theory

Turns out the church fathers weren't cut from the cloth of modern biblicism. They didn't read Scripture like me and my fundamentalist friends did. To begin with, most modern biblicists subscribe to something called the "single meaning theory" of biblical interpretation.[378] The idea is that when you read a passage, you're supposed to zone in on its one, literal, and intended meaning, to the exclusion of all other possible meanings.[379] That's the reading lens recommended by evangelicals like John MacArthur: "Don't assume there are many interpretations of a biblical passage. There may be many applications, but there is only one true interpretation."[380] It's sort of like answering a middle school math question: "$2 + 2 = 4$" means "correct," while "$2 + 2 = 5$" means "summer school."

But the dead saints didn't talk about Scripture that way. Instead, they thought of the Bible as containing multiple "senses," or "layers of meaning."[381] To them, reading Scripture was more like examining a diamond, holding it up to the light and letting its facets dance under different aspects. A single passage of Scripture could therefore be faithfully interpreted in a number of "true" ways.[382]

Look at how Augustine approached Genesis 1. After spending a whole lotta time analyzing the six-day creation story, he still couldn't wrap his head around the word "day." The only thing he was sure of was that Genesis 1 couldn't be a literal historical account, because if God is eternal and exists *outside* of time, then God must've created the universe *before* time began, in one nontemporal moment. Incidentally, a lot of modern physicists think Augustine was on to something (there was no "time" before the big bang; like magnetism, time is a feature of the physical universe).[383] As for the meaning of "day" in Genesis 1, Augustine never closed the case on it: "I have worked out and presented the statements of the Book of Genesis in a variety of ways according to my ability; and, in interpreting words that have been written obscurely for the purpose of stimulating our thought, I have not rashly taken my stand on one side against a rival interpretation which might possibly be better."[384]

To be clear, Augustine was one of early Christianity's most confrontational and opinionated apologists, definitely not someone known for being loosey-goosey. Yet even the mighty Augustine allowed for multiple readings of Genesis 1 without ever insisting that one interpretation trump all others, "provided only that the interpretations are *true*."[385] Which is not to say that a particular verse can mean whatever you want it to mean; just that it can mean more than *only one* thing.

Maybe all this "multiple meanings" talk sounds suspiciously like a sellout, a gesture of submission to postmodern America's sacred cows of tolerance, relativism, and political correctness. Maybe you're like me and gravitate more naturally to MacArthur's laser-focused literalism. You wouldn't be alone: 28 percent of Americans today claim the Bible is "to be taken literally, word for word."[386] If, like most of my students, you were raised on biblicism, the "single meaning" lens probably seems natural, even necessary; an indispensable anchor of historic Christianity. But as popular as it is today, biblicism is more novelty than orthodoxy.[387] It wasn't even a thing until a few centuries ago, and it really didn't gain serious traction till the 1920s, just after the First World War (more on that later).[388] In other words, the "single meaning theory" was never that orthodox or conservative to begin with. And here's the greatest irony of it all: it's a bias modern Christianity picked up from its avowed nemesis, secular science.[389]

Correlation Does Not Imply Causation

What is *science*? In the modern sense, science is an organized, systematic effort to acquire facts about the universe through observation, experimentation, and reason. One of the main goals of science is to determine the exact cause of natural phenomena—e.g., if you heat water to 100°C at sea level, it'll boil every time. "Cold, hard facts," not, "It just *feels* that way to me." So when

Scientist Stacy conducts an experiment to determine what precise factor causes Lyme disease, he's trying to eliminate as many variables as possible in order to identify the single, solitary cause (and yes, Stacy is a dude . . . ever heard of skateboarding icon Stacy Peralta, or retired small forward Stacey Augmon?). No lazy correlations between two seemingly related things. No going with your gut or following your feelings. Because scientists like Stacy live by an important axiom: "correlation does not imply causation."

Let me illustrate by way of an anecdote.

A few years ago, a friend of mine and I were going to a wedding out of town. In an effort to minimize cost, we agreed to carpool with a married couple we'd never met. Fourteen hours. Each way. It was my friend's idea (for the sake of anonymity, I will refer to him only by the initials, "Heath Blackard"). Aside from being a pathological penny-pincher, Heath is legendary for giving awful directions. For example—and I quote: ". . . then you make a left a mile or so before that yard where the 'FOR RENT' sign used to be . . ."

The decision was almost instantly regrettable. What we saved in gas money we paid for in twenty-eight hours of humorless misery. Our traveling companions had very little to say, even to one another. On the rare occasion they ventured to speak, their comments circled around such titillating topics as yard work, linoleum tile, and the merits of fifteen-year-fixed mortgages. By hour nine we were getting desperate. So Heath decided to spice things up by bringing up his favorite subject, death: "Isn't it weird how old people live just long enough to reach some major milestone, something they feel obligated to be around for? Like how Johnny Cash died a few months after June Carter." Interesting observation, Heath. Thanks for sharing. Then the gal in the passenger seat says, "Yeah, that's so true. Like when my grandpa died right after my grandma. It's like, somehow, her being alive kept him alive, you know?" To which her husband responded, "Wait honey . . . that's different. Your grandfather was murdered."

Correlation doesn't imply causation. Just because all six of your country music–loving cousins vape doesn't mean listening to country *causes* you to vape (or vice versa). Just because Johnny died right after June Carter doesn't mean *all* elderly males die immediately after their wives. Two things can correlate without necessarily causing one or the other.

Thankfully, scientists don't think in sloppy generalities. They conduct countless experiments in an attempt to identify the one and only answer they're looking for. And because this method of inquiry has been so remarkably successful in science, it's influenced the way modern Westerners think about everything, including the Bible.[390]

But that's not necessarily the best way to approach every aspect of life. I don't have one single, objectively correct answer to the question, "Why do I love my wife?" Maybe it was her pixie haircut and impish smile that drew me in. Maybe it was her lack of pretense, or her almost effortless affection for life. Maybe all of the above. But just because I can't articulate the single, isolated reason for loving my wife doesn't mean I don't.

Let's get back to baby smashing for a sec. If Psalm 137:9 can have only one literal and correct meaning, then the Bible is an irredeemable horror show—especially if you consider yourself a follower of the Way, because Jesus' way doesn't include baby smashing. But if the literal sense of Psalm 137 is only one *possible* meaning, then we've got something to work with. Instead of taking it as a moral prescription, we can read it figuratively— which is exactly how the New Testament authors interpreted much of the Old. (Incidentally, a new appreciation for, and understanding of, the multiple meanings of Scripture might be helpful for modern Christians who struggle to locate *the* "one and only" biblical theory of atonement, to the exclusion of all other explanatory theories. Premodern Christians felt no such obligation.[391]) For example, in his letter to the Galatians, the apostle Paul interprets Jerusalem in at least three distinct ways: first, as the literal/ historical city of the Jews; second, as an allegory for the church; third, as a symbol of Jesus' coming kingdom—a.k.a. the "Holy City" of God.[392] Augustine used the same sort of technique when reading the Hebrew Bible. So did John Calvin.[393] Come to think of it, so did Jesus.

A Jesus-Shaped Lens: The Christological Key

You can learn a lot about Jesus from how he read the Old Testament. For one thing, Jesus thought it was all about him: "If you believed Moses, you would believe me, for he wrote about *me*."[394] That's how Jesus interpreted the Hebrew Bible—"christologically"—through the interpretive goggles of his own life and purpose. He thought *he* was the lens through which the entire Old Testament should be understood—Adam and Eve, Jonah and Noah, Abraham and Isaac, even the Psalms. Bold claims indeed. You may accuse Jesus of many things, but not false modesty. This was a man on a messianic mission. Most of us cringe at Kanye's supercilious self-appraisals: "I am Warhol . . . Shakespeare in the flesh!" But Kanye ain't got nothin' on Jesus: "*I* am the way, the truth and the life," and, "Before Abraham was born, *I* am."[395] And it's not like he toned down his message to accommodate the audience. In John 5:39, Jesus tells a group of predominantly Jewish onlookers: "You search the Scriptures [i.e., the Old Testament] because you think they give you eternal life. But the Scriptures testify of me." And he taught his disciples to read Scripture the same way. That's why the apostles, church fathers, Reformers, and even the New Testament authors all viewed the Hebrew Bible as pointing to Jesus—often indirectly and nonliterally, through parallels, allegories, "shadows", and "types."[396]

According to John Calvin, a "type" is a symbol representing something that's yet to come.[397] It gives you a taste of what's in store, and helps you make sense of it once it arrives—kind of like watching a teaser trailer for a movie you haven't seen yet. Much like his theological hero, Augustine, Calvin made a habit of interpreting the Old Testament stories as "types" pointing to Jesus.[398] And while he favored "simple and literal interpretation" whenever possible,[399] Calvin was unapologetic about reading the Old Testament christologically: "We ought to read the Scriptures with the express design [i.e., purpose] of finding Christ in them."[400]

Take Noah's ark. Like the church fathers before him, Calvin interpreted the ark as a "type" prefiguring the church Jesus would one day establish (which is why so many ancient churches were shaped like arks).[401] Likewise, Noah's quest to save his family from the flood foreshadowed Jesus' mission to save his "family" (a.k.a. the human race) from evil, dissolution, and death, and Jonah's three days in the belly of the whale parallel the crucified Christ's three days "in the heart of the earth" before rising from the grave (Matt 12:40).[402]

Then, there's the crucifixion. Hanging there in humiliation, Jesus quoted the Old Testament: "My God, my God, why have you forsaken me?" That's a direct lift from Psalm 22, written centuries before Jesus was even born. The original author was probably expressing his own personal anguish in the face of troubles many and bitter. But if Psalm 22 is supposed to have one—and *only* one—literal, intended, and original meaning, was Jesus guilty of ripping Bible verses out of context? Is Psalm 22 about the psalmist's life, or Jesus' death? Which "sense" or "layer of meaning" is *true*? Are we sure the psalmist knew his words would one day be evoked by the crucified Christ? Perhaps. Perhaps not. Maybe it doesn't matter. As C. S. Lewis once confessed: "An author doesn't necessarily understand the meaning of his own story better than anyone else."[403]

Elton + Elton

Now for a confession of my own: I am an Elton John fan. As in, currently . . . though he almost lost me at "Can You Feel the Love Tonight?" (the 80s and 90s were not kind to Sir Elton). But the early stuff, when he was more of a minstrel—*Tumbleweed Connection, Goodbye Yellow Brick Road*— sheer, analog magic. I remember seeing an interview with Elton's cowriter,

Bernie Taupin. Like C. S. Lewis, Taupin said writers don't always know the meaning(s) of what they're writing. Apparently Taupin has no clue what "Take Me to the Pilot" is about (that makes two of us). But at least I have an excuse. He *wrote* the thing. If anybody should know its literal and intended meaning, it's Taupin. But he doesn't. And maybe that's okay. Maybe the meaning(s) of Scripture are, like children, never really "yours"—even if, like the psalmist, you had a hand in bringing them into being.[404]

An altogether different Elton provided another helpful hint on how to think about Jesus—and, by extension, the Bible. Elton Trueblood was his name. A twentieth-century Quaker theologian, Elton #2 explained that Jesus' status as "Lord" is not merely an honorific title. Christians don't call Jesus "divine" simply because he was more moral or religious than other people. "It is far more radical than that," Trueblood clarified, "It means that *God* is like *Jesus*." In other words, the most authentic, accurate, penetrating way to think about God is to think *christologically*. Our truest God-thoughts are Jesus-thoughts. The "real" God isn't a grumpy old man hiding behind Jesus, ready to pull the ol' bait-and-switch just as soon as you pray the sinner's prayer and accept Christ into your heart.[405] Neither is Jesus God's smooth-talking face man, sent to give you a good impression so you'll skim the fine print and sign your life away. Rather, *God* is like *Jesus*, the visible embodiment of invisible divinity, a window into the heart and mind of the hidden God.

The dead saints followed the same christological strategy when reading the Bible. From the church fathers through the Reformers, Jesus was seen as the climax of the biblical story, the cipher for understanding everything about God.[406] Accordingly, every story of Scripture should direct the reader to Jesus, even if only indirectly, through "shadows," "types," and allegories. It's the key to unlocking even the most byzantine passages of the Old Testament. When you read it all christologically, through a Jesus-shaped lens, words like "God" and "Spirit" become less capricious and more concrete. The whole thing starts to cohere around the person of Jesus. And for me, this was welcome news, since it was Jesus to whom I'd been drawn.

Okay, but still . . . how the hell do you read hellish passages like Psalm 137 christologically?

One option would be to look for the "elevated," "spiritual," or "anagogical sense" of the passage.[407] From the Greek, *anagoge* means "ascent" or "upward movement."[408] To read a verse *anagogically* is to interpret it allegorically, as though it offered a glimpse of God's promised future. In the case of Psalm 137, this promised future would be the kingdom of God, where far-flung refugees and aliens—like the psalmist himself—will finally be free, at home, and at rest. The "anagogical sense" awakens anticipation by pointing the reader upward and onward towards a hope-filled future. And for enslaved exiles like the author of Psalm 137, hope was in short supply.

Of course, you could read it more plainly, as an uncensored expression of righteous rage, an imprecatory elegy for those who hunger for ultimate justice, like how prisoners in Nazi death camps prayed, "Arise, O Lord . . . let the nations be judged before you!" (Psalm 9:19)[409] I remember when I was a kid, watching my mom march her 4' 11" frame across the street to confront our coked-up neighbor, who'd just beaten his wife. I remember feeling a swell of satisfaction and pride, knowing my mom was about to be a lifeline for someone in desperate need and put our abusive neighbor in his place—which she did (fiery 4' 11" matriarch > 6' 1" woman beater). Maybe Psalm 137 is supposed to tap into that feeling, that almost primal yearning for restitution. Or maybe it's more about giving us permission to hate before we can learn to love—especially if *agape* means more than mere "coexistence" or "tolerance" between estranged enemies. Maybe it means all of the above. But for Jesus' followers, one thing is certain: Psalm 137 can never be taken in the "literal sense."[410]

I'll say this for biblicism: it's efficient. No need for interpretive subtlety. If, as young Reza Aslan was taught, every line of Scripture is "true, literal, and inerrant," it shouldn't be that hard to understand. No "types," "shadows," or messy allegories to work through. No interpretive goggles required. Not even christological ones. Just stick to the clear meaning of the text and do what it says. Sounds simple enough. But no matter how insightful, authoritative, or authentic a document may be, you've still gotta make sense of it. And once in a while, you're gonna blow it—especially if you're going it alone.

To paraphrase the Oxford evangelical, Alister McGrath, you may have an inerrant text, but you can still have an errant interpretation.[411] That was Galileo's point some five centuries ago, which Rick Warren echoed more recently: "I believe in the inerrancy of Scripture; I do not believe in the inerrancy of my interpretations."[412] When all is said and done, simply stating that the Bible is "inerrant" and "can never speak untruth" doesn't automatically solve everything. In fact, it might not solve much of anything.

Pride and Ambition

To a hammer, everything looks like a nail. We see what we want to see . . . or, at least, what we've learned to want to see—from family and friends, from heroes and mentors, from the culture at large, or whichever online echo chambers we inhabit. Reading the Bible can be like that. We've all got our biases and quirks. We highlight passages that seem important to us, because they seem important to us. In an achievement-driven, hyper-individualistic culture like ours, it's no coincidence that we hear lots of, "I can do all things through Christ who strengthens me!" in postgame interviews and Oscar acceptance speeches, but not so much, "Make it your ambition to lead a quiet life: You should mind your own business and work with your hands."[413]

Which brings me to the final flaw of fundamentalist biblicism: it encourages people to presume the purity of their own interpretive motives, all while holding other interpretations (and interpreters) in suspicion—maybe even contempt—which is exactly the kind of thing Augustine warned against. "Pride," he called it: "A distorted love of one's own excellence."[414] Think about it: If you can only trust *your* personal take on the text, if nobody is sufficiently qualified to challenge your interpretation, what does that say about your (inflated) opinion of yourself? About your willingness to listen, collaborate, empathize, and hold space for other human beings? To risk being misunderstood, or risk being wrong? How can you love your neighbor without ever trusting them?

There's an old story about a monk who was tempted by the devil. Disguised as an angel of light, Satan appeared to him in a vision, saying, "I am the archangel Gabriel, who gave insight and understanding to the prophet, Daniel; who heralded the birth of John the Baptizer; who visited Mary, the virgin, and revealed to her the coming of the Lord. And now, I have been sent to deliver unto you a message of the utmost importance, which you alone have been found worthy to receive." After a brief pause, the young monk replied, "I'm sorry that you've come all this way, but I think you must have me confused with someone else." And with that, the devil fled.

Different story, (possibly) same monk: once, in an effort to further his spiritual instruction, the monk joined a company of clergymen on pilgrimage to see an esteemed elder, Antony of Egypt. As soon as they arrived, Antony began reading Scripture passages aloud, asking his visitors to explain what he was reciting. One by one, they rattled off their interpretations, none to Antony's satisfaction. This went on for some time, until finally Antony read one last passage. Turning to our humble hero, who had yet to speak, Antony asked, "What do *you* think it means?" The young monk answered, "Father, I do not know." Then a smile came across Antony's face, and he said, "This one has found the true way, for he said, 'I do not know.'"[415]

What's the moral of the monk stories? Simple: he who presumes to have a corner on holy truth is usually the least qualified to speak on it. And the converse is also true: humility is usually a sign of spiritual depth and maturity. It's like the Scriptures say: "God opposes the proud but gives grace to the humble."[416] That's why the young monk is the hero: because he's humble. His greatest strength is his weakness. He knows that he doesn't know. It is this very attribute, this utter lack of pretense, that puts the devil to flight.

Secret Pride and Religious Mischief

Jesus never said, "Blessed are the self-confident." He said, "Blessed are the humble," and he meant it.[417] Better to be the young monk than the religious know-it-all who's just a little too sure of himself. John of the Cross called this kind of arrogant religiosity "secret pride." You know the type: ultra-confident, super-spiritual, high on zeal and low on humility, always wanting to teach rather than be taught, always wanting to talk about spiritual things . . . and we all know those kinds of people. In fact, some of us *are* those kinds of people.[418]

"I am the way and the truth and the life," Jesus said. As soon as any individual or institution claims to *possess* holy truth, it ceases to be holy, becoming something altogether different—an "it," sterile and stale, a *thing* among other things, a tool to be used at our discretion and for our own self-serving purposes (e.g,. as ammunition for an ideological argument, a bullet point on our religious resumes, or a medal to pin on our puffed-out chests). More than just obnoxious, "secret pride" can be downright dangerous. What is arrogant religiosity, if not a "distorted love" of one's own moral or theological excellence? It's an intoxicating feeling. Addictive, even. Nietzsche was right when he warned, "Those who feel 'I possess Truth'— how many possessions would they not abandon in order to save this feeling! What would they not throw overboard to stay 'on top'—which means, above the others who lack 'the Truth.'"[419]

Augustine addressed this very issue in his *Confessions*. Like Nietzsche, Augustine cringed at the notion of "possessing" the truth, as if it were a piece of "private property," amenable to human direction and control: "For your [God's] truth does not belong to me nor to anyone else." Augustine saw a real danger in arrogant interpreters who "love their own opinion," not because of its veracity or potential benefit to others, "but because it is their own." Karl Barth called it "religious mischief," and it's a temptation to which none of us is immune: "Experience becomes the enjoyment of itself, satisfaction it itself, and its own goal . . . The human has taken the divine into its possession. He has put it [God] under his management."[420] So take heed, fellow pilgrim, and beware the mischievous, arrogant interpreter—especially when that arrogant interpreter happens to be you.[421]

For my part, I was already adept at loving my own opinion long before I discovered biblicism. I knew how to cobble together arguments and muscle my judgments down other peoples' throats. But patience? Compassion? The freedom to be misunderstood? The freedom to be wrong? That's what I was after. I wanted *agape*, to love and be loved, which would mean being fully seen and fully known. But that would require honesty with self and others, coupled with the humility to acknowledge the plank in my own eye. I held out as long as I could, but eventually it became clear that my bald-faced brand of biblicism wasn't getting me any closer to *agape*. And to Jesus, this was a problem.

The more I read the Bible, especially the Jesus parts, the more I felt obligated to examine my own heart. And the closer I looked, the less I understood. Augustine felt the same way: "I have great fear of my subconscious impulses," he prayed, "which your eyes know *but mine do not*."[422] And how could he? How can any of us? No matter how much time you spend exploring the caverns of your own subconscious, you'll never be able to examine your own self *objectively*, as if from a critical distance. You can't extract yourself from your own deepest desires and untraceable intentions. You can't get outside your own life, your own field of vision. That was one of Wittgenstein's most arresting observations: just as it is impossible to see your own eye with your eye—the very organ you use to see—so it is impossible for the self to see itself.[423] "The self is more distant than any star," Chesterton wrote.[424] This is the great insight about which Marxists, mystics, modern physicists, philosophers, and neuroscientists all agree: we do not enjoy easy access to the churning depths of our own selves.[425]

Flying Solo vs. Sola Scriptura

Martin Luther is sometimes credited with creating the modern individual, the emancipated self.[426] It was Luther who, five centuries ago, lambasted the Catholic Church for the corrupt practice of selling indulgences.[427] Then, when the pope pushed back, Luther made his famous stand in the German city of Worms (yes, there's actually a city called Worms . . . and you thought Middelfart, Denmark was rough).

The year was 1521. The setting, a high-profile church court hearing, where Luther said something like this: "Unless I am convinced by the testimony of the Holy Scriptures or by evident reason—for I can believe neither pope nor councils alone, as it is clear that they have erred repeatedly and contradicted themselves—I consider myself convicted by the testimony of Holy Scripture, which is my basis; my conscience is captive to the Word of God."[428]

It's tempting to depict Luther as a one-man army whose victory signaled the triumph of individual conscience over "the collective." Captain Picard vs. the Borg. Self vs. society. Holden Caulfield vs. high school. If you squint your eyes, you can almost see Luther staring down a cadre of fearsome Inquisitors, his face painted *Braveheart* blue, culminating in a defiant cry: "*Freeeeeeedom!*"

While comparisons to William Wallace are a bit much, Luther really was a revolutionary of sorts. First, he went toe-to-toe with the medieval church and lived to tell the tale. Second, he put Scripture above the pope as the ultimate authority on Christian teaching and practice.[429] It was the Bible, not the pope, to which Luther's conscience was held captive. A bold idea . . . and an empowering one . . . especially for the marginalized medieval masses. It wasn't long before droves of disgruntled Catholics followed Luther's lead, leaving the medieval church behind.

Thus began Protestantism and its doctrine of *Sola Scriptura*: reliance upon Scripture as the sole and sufficient authority on Christian doctrine. Since, as Luther argued, church leaders were capable of error, where else could the faithful look? The Bible was the last leg to stand on, the only sure footing in a swirling sea of uncertainty.[430]

Ever since Luther, most Protestants have adopted some version of *Sola Scriptura*. No more high-flown hierarchies, "wise expositors," or ecclesiastical elites. Read it for yourself, just like Luther did. So suggested the early American fundamentalist, George Frederick Wright, back in 1885: "The ground upon which the Protestant pulpit is permitted to speak with its present authority is the general belief that the Bible is the word of God, and that it is not a sealed book even to ordinary readers . . ."[431]

Evangelicals like Wright "democratized" the Bible by leveling the playing field. Sounds good to me. Like any red-blooded American, I like democracy. I like the idea of equal access. Problem is, the Bible isn't exactly an easy read.[432] It can be hard to understand, and even harder to come to any lasting consensus about it—hence the almost constant proliferation of Christian denominations and sects since Luther, each with its own interpretive spin. That was Abe Lincoln's unwelcome discovery during the American slavery debate, with the abolitionists on one side and plantation owners on the other. "Both read the same Bible," Lincoln lamented, "and pray to the same God."[433] There you have it; the problem of interpretation in a nutshell. No matter how highly you esteem the Bible, you've still got to make sense of it, and we all have our own interpretive slants.

Regardless of their intentions, the Protestant Reformers unleashed a new willingness to throw off the shackles of tradition. Now take that new-found willingness, coupled with the doctrine of *Sola Scriptura,* and give it easy access to an abundance of affordable Bibles—courtesy of Gutenberg's printing press. Next, add a pinch or two of modern democratic Enlightenment principles, especially the "right to think for oneself,"[434] plus the conviction that each of us sees the world pretty much as it is;[435] then top it all off with a few sprinkles of rugged individualism, and voilà: the basic recipe for what eventually became American biblicism, a.k.a. Bible-only-ism.[436]

But to guys like Luther, basing your beliefs on the Bible alone didn't mean *reading* it alone.[437] Neither Luther nor Calvin were big on the idea of DIY Bible study. Both were wary of spiritual lone rangers who interpreted Scripture any way they liked.[438] Both supported traditional "high church" hierarchies and the established aristocracy.[439] By our standards, guys like Calvin, Luther, and even free-spirited St. Francis were more like stuffy conformists than rebels.[440] Sure, Luther caused a ruckus back in 1521 . . . but Han Solo he was not.

Christology and Community

Sola Scriptura never meant flying solo. Not even to Luther.[441] For the early Protestants, biblical interpretation was a public, church-wide endeavor. Calvin was adamant about it.[442] Divine truth was to be learned and lived in community. We see hints of this principle in Jesus' dealings with the disciples. In John's Gospel, when Jesus says the Spirit of God will "guide *you* into all the truth," he was talking to the apostles as a group, all gathered together.[443] The "you" is plural, not singular.[444] It was to be a joint effort, a family affair. And the "Spirit" of which Jesus spoke was *his* Spirit, the "Spirit of Christ."[445]

Remember: God is like Jesus. There's nothing in God that is un-Christlike. What Christians call the Trinity—Father, Son, and Holy Spirit—is fundamentally *christological*, just as it is fundamentally communal. But in the world of human affairs, community means interdependence. It means risk. Trusting one another. What could be *less* safe than relying on other people? But the disciples did it anyway. So did the church fathers—real human beings in real human communities. The whole thing was bound up in humanness from the beginning.

Maybe that's always been Christianity's main problem: it's just too human to be true.

8

Trust Issues

In God We Trust:
All Others Pay Cash.

—JEAN SHEPHERD[446]

There Is No Dana, Only Zuul

AND NOW FOR A pop quiz. Don't worry, it's only one question long. So don't
screw it up:

#1. Of the authors listed below, which one made the following state-
ment about the Bible? "The human qualities of the raw materials show
through. Naiveté, error, contradiction, even (as in the cursing Psalms) wickedness is not removed."[447]

A. Mark Twain, *Memoranda*

B. Charles Darwin, *On the Origin of Species*

C. Thomas Jefferson, *Notes on the State of Virginia*

D. C. S. Lewis, *Reflections on the Psalms*

E. Zuul, gatekeeper of Gozer, *Ghostbusters*

The answer is . . . drumroll please . . . D. Yes, celebrated Christian
author C. S. Lewis, the same Lewis who called Scripture the "Word of God,"
"holy" and "inspired"; the same Lewis who penned over a dozen books in

defense of Christianity (not including his *Chronicles of Narnia* series). Yet Lewis saw fit to apply words like "error," "contradiction," even "wickedness" to the Bible, e.g., the infamously infanticidal Psalm 137.[448]

Most biblicists find this kind of admission unnerving, if not traitorous. That's because biblicists operate under what's called the "divine dictation" assumption: in order for a document to qualify as "divinely inspired," God has to possess its author like a *Ghostbusters* poltergeist does a human host, overpowering the writer's brain and personality, effectively transforming a person into a pencil.[449] Though "divine dictation" is more of an Islamic concept than a historically Christian one (*Qur'an* means "recitation"), it's gained a lot of currency among modern evangelicals. As of 2004, less than 1 percent of American evangelicals think humans had anything to do with the writing, compilation, or transmission of the Bible.[450] The implication is clear: Scripture can only have genuine spiritual authority if it circumvents human involvement altogether. How else could it be the "Word of God"?

A couple problems with this assumption. First, "divine dictation" makes it hard to understand those pesky baby bashing passages we visited earlier. Then there's verses like 1 Corinthians 1:16, where Paul writes: "I also baptized the household of Stephanas; beyond that, I don't remember if I baptized anyone else."[451] Don't remember? Apparently, Paul baptized a whole lot of people and, like most of us, was prone to the occasional lapse in memory. But this didn't seem to bother him. Neither was it a source of embarrassment for the early Christians, who could've easily left 1 Corinthians 1:16 on the cutting room floor. But they didn't. So if God's voice—and *only* God's voice—is supposed to be doing the talking here, are we to assume God has a shoddy memory?[452]

Scholar Peter Enns thinks modern Christians are far too influenced by the "divine dictation" theory. Though the signs of human authorship are, Enns explains, "integrated into the nature of Scripture itself," most biblicists feel compelled to explain away any trace of humanness, lest Scripture appear less "Bible-like."[453] If it didn't arrive instantaneously via divine lightning bolt, it can't be a trustworthy depository of truth.[454]

But the Christians of old didn't talk about the Bible that way. They knew it was a "very human book"—indeed, a *fully* human book, "divinely inspired," but a divine-human product whose human authors wrote at different times and from different situations, each according to his individual style and personality.[455] Erudite evangelicals have long acknowledged this, including early fundamentalists like B. B. Warfield.[456] And with good reason: Christians have never insisted on an absolute, either-or dichotomy between divine and human activity. Neither did they divide the world into two distinct, non-overlapping domains, one "spiritual" and the other physical/material. At least, not until recently.

In order to further elucidate this important historical/theological point, allow me to reference a time-honored scholarly resource. I mean, of course, Star Wars.

How to (Almost) Kill a Franchise

At the turn of the last century, America's geeks endured what must've felt like a cinematic catastrophe. The year was 1999. The sky was all purple, there were people runnin' everywhere. As opening night of *The Phantom Menace* drew to a disappointing close, throngs of furious fanboys evacuated the nation's theatres, retreated to their parents' basements, and took to the Web. Soon, sci-fi forums were inundated with a deluge of anti–George Lucas vitriol, courtesy of the nation's nerds, who'd turned on their beloved patron saint of space operas like a pack of patricidal cannibals. Why so angry? Reason 1: Jar Jar Binks, a perhaps unintentionally racist CGI character about whom nothing more should be said. Reason two: midichlorians.

In case you missed *The Phantom Menace*, midichlorians are (or were) fictional microorganisms that inhabit the cells of every living creature in the Lucasverse. The more of 'em you got, the better your chances of controlling "the Force."[457] And for space opera aficionados, this was precisely the problem. They hated the idea of reducing the Force to something physical, something you could examine under a microscope. The Force was supposed to be "spiritual": an energy field that transcends matter and binds everything together in mystical oneness. Then Lucas ruined it all by boiling it down to a bunch of microbes. Lame.

Star Wars buffs aren't alone in this sort of anti-materialism. It bubbles up now and again under different guises and in varying degrees: there's Docetism,[458] Cartesianism, Yogācāra Buddhism, dispensational premillennialism, gnosticism, radical postmodern gender criticism, Origenism, logical positivism, the transcendentalism of Emerson and Thoreau, deontological libertarianism . . . the list goes on. We see it in movies like *The Matrix*. We read about it in books like *The Alchemist* and (hopefully not) *The Secret*. We blame our physical forms for holding us back and keeping us down. Mind over (and against) matter. Anytime some overzealous personal trainer screams, "Your body will achieve it if your mind will believe it!" they're unwittingly perpetuating a hidden bias against embodiment. (They're also lying: amputees don't sprout new limbs just by *thinking* about it. The Buddha acknowledged the mind's limitations when he challenged a famously unattractive philosopher to *think* himself into becoming handsome. Spoiler alert: it didn't work.[459])

Anti-Matter

Americans are often accused of being a superficial people—all about bling, botox, and boobs. Materialism run amuck . . . and maybe so. But somehow, we're equally fervent in our *anti*-materialism. Sure, we're "body obsessed" when perusing porn or flipping through fitness and fashion mags, but it's almost always an obsession with *someone else's body*, i.e., Nicki Minaj's trunk, Channing Tatum's abs, or your perfectly fit (and always out of reach) "future self." We're cool with mysticism and "spirituality," just as long as you don't mix the mystical with the material. We modern Westerners prefer a strict separation between spiritual and physical things, including microscopic things, like atoms . . . or DNA . . . or midichlorians. Somehow, the material world seems too mundane to matter.

But that's the funny thing about Christianity: the whole deal rests on the conviction that God, though Spirit, isn't opposed to matter. "God saw all that he had made, and it was very good,"[460] which means God and nature aren't natural enemies. The Almighty isn't afraid of getting cooties from creation. In fact, the opposite's true: God seems to take special delight in working through his creatures, including human beings.[461]

Early on in his letter to the Corinthians, Paul thanks God for all the followers of the Way in the city. But if you think about it, it was *Paul* who brought the gospel message to Corinth, preaching to anybody who'd listen.[462] It was *Paul* who did all the schlepping around, just as it was *Paul* who got his apostolic arse kicked all over the Peloponnesian peninsula. Why thank God for it? I used to ask the same question at Thanksgiving when compelled to say grace before dinner. Why thank God for a meal that my mom worked all day to make from scratch?

The reason is simple: Christians believe God is present and at work in the Real World, in and through the lives of human beings. And not just superstars like Paul, but ordinary people, like my mom, me, and you. The Christian God doesn't need to sidestep human involvement in order to get things done. It's not a cosmic tug-of-war between humanity and divinity.[463] Something can be "fully human" without precluding God's presence or direct participation.[464]

Like Jesus, for instance.

The Peculiar Logic of Incarnation

Anne Lamott calls Jesus "God with skin on."[465] The New Testament uses slightly loftier language, calling Jesus "the Word made flesh,"[466] the "image of the invisible God,"[467] "the radiance of God's glory" and "exact representation of his being."[468] In John's Gospel, Jesus tells his friends, "If you really know me, you will know my Father as well," and even more presumptuously, "From now on, you do know him and have seen him . . . Anyone who has seen me has seen the Father."[469] And his followers bought it hook, line, and sinker. To them, he was "fully God" *and* "fully man,"[470] the eternal Son of God[471] *and* a real human being who suffered, died, and was buried.[472] It's a both-and, not an either-or. Christians call it "the incarnation," and it has some revolutionary implications.

For one thing, the incarnation means matter isn't fundamentally flawed, as if evil were the unavoidable byproduct of embodied existence. It is Satan, we are told, who is both pure spirit and pure evil.[473] So if the world's great religious are right—if all is not right with the world—then it's not a problem we can blame on our bodies.[474] Which means it's not, as some mystics and mathematicians suggest, a predicament from which we can extricate ourselves by becoming ever more abstracted, detached, or "spiritual."

In *Mysticism and Logic,* philosopher Bertrand Russell praised mathematics precisely because of its steely reliance upon "pure" reason, "without appeal to any part of our weaker nature, without the gorgeous trappings of painting or music." No tugging at the heartstrings. No feeling your feels. Mathematics, wrote Russell, is "cold and austere," "sublimely pure," unfettered by the messiness of the material world:

> Real life is, to most men, a long second-best . . . The world of pure reason knows no compromise, no practical limitations, no barrier to the creative activity. Remote from human passions, remote even from the pitiful facts of nature, the generations have gradually created an ordered cosmos, where pure thought can dwell as in its natural home, and where one, at least, of our nobler impulses can escape from the dreary exile of the actual world.[475]

There you have it, the gospel according to Russell. "Real life" is a "dreary exile" from which we must "escape," while the world of "pure reason" is our "natural home," a paradise purged of all worldly passion, impurity, and material limitation.

This leads me to the second, arguably more important thing about the incarnation: it spells the ultimate validation of embodied existence, of "real life" in the Real World. Theologians call it the "glorification of matter," the exaltation of creation.[476] By becoming human, God affirms and ennobles the world. More than this, the incarnation tells us that God has chosen to entwine his own story with ours and bind his fate to our own. That's what we discover in Jesus: a God who leads us not into faraway fantasies or angelic orbits, but ever more deeply into the world, a God to whom "nothing human is alien."[477] And for this reason, among others, being a follower of the Way means loving the world more, not less.

Christianity is surprisingly "worldly" in this regard. Indeed it must be, if hopes to be authentically Christian. With this in mind, Dietrich Bonhoeffer issued the following warning: "Every attempt to portray a Christianity of 'pure' love purged of worldly 'impurities' is a false purism and perfectionism that scorns God's becoming human . . . God was not too pure to enter the world."[478] That's what the incarnation means. It's an entering in, not a bailing out. It tells us that the world is neither a prison to be escaped, nor an illusion to be dismissed. It's the real deal. The whole thing matters; the stakes really are that high. And God will not be put to flight by the impurities of the world.

Hard to imagine, let alone believe. By my reckoning, the world seemed an always-already fractured place, full of gauzy things that flicker and sputter, like dying lamps against a blackened landscape. Could the incarnation make reality more solid? Could it reveal a world pregnant with possibility and purpose? Simone Weil thought so. "The beauty of the world is Christ's tender smile coming to us through matter," she wrote. "The longing to love the beauty of the world in a human being is essentially longing for the Incarnation."[479] A late-life convert and contemporary of Russell, Weil believed creation stood as a monument to God's grace, an invitation to drink deep from the cup of divine goodness and beauty. Which means music might be magic, after all, but only because the world is.

Behold, the peculiar logic of incarnation. And it's got nothing to do with escapist spirituality, or *angelism*, the "excessive abstraction of the self from itself."[480] Quite the opposite: the incarnation calls us to be fully present and immersed in reality. This is what Francis of Assisi personified by living among lepers and treating even the tiniest animals with tenderness. I think this is what Leonard Cohen was getting at in his poetic description of the saintly man: "Something in him so loves the world that he gives himself to the laws of gravity and chance. Far from flying with the angels, he traces with the fidelity of a seismograph needle the state of the solid bloody landscape."[481]

Francis didn't love the lowliest creatures in an abstract sense. He didn't love them "in spirit," whatever that means, and he certainly not for the sake of a "cause." He loved them for real. Nitty-gritty, full-blooded, flesh-and-bone love. As Chesterton said, Francis reillumined the reality of the incarnation by "bringing God back to earth."[482] And Christians believe Francis pulled it off not by tenacity of will, but by the indwelling fires of the living God.

Has Anybody Here Seen My Old Friend John?

They say "God don't make no junk." Just because the Bible is "fully human" doesn't mean it's full of crap. Jesus' early followers certainly didn't think so. Nor did they think less of Jesus because he was "fully human." Church fathers like Ignatius of Antioch and Polycarp of Smyrna knew the Bible was written by human authors . . . because they were there. Both Polycarp and Iggy were alive and kicking while the New Testament was being completed. Both were mentored by John—as in the *apostle* John, dinner guest at the Last Supper and key player in the New Testament.[483] Since John was a fallible human being, we can assume his friends were familiar with his shortcomings . . . and he had his fair share.

Seems John was a bit of a glory hound. Power hungry, even. On one occasion, he had the audacity to ask Jesus for a VIP seat in the kingdom of heaven. When the other apostles heard about it, they were none too pleased.[484] I'm assuming Polycarp and Ignatius heard about it, too. They knew John well enough to know his failures. They knew he wasn't an inerrant megaphone for the Almighty, but a fully human being, just like the rest of us. But that didn't stop Iggy and Polycarp from trusting the apostles' letters as the "Word of God"—even their old friend, John's.

Speaking of things finite, aren't all means of communication that way—inherently limited? Bounded by finitude? Whether you're receiving a transmission from the Associated Press or from an apostle's mouth, the content you're getting is always *mediated,* always carried along and conveyed by finite things. Even poetry and pictures are finite; even music. Songs, like sonnets, have an end. A picture may be worth a thousand words, but not a thousand-and-one words. Nature, too, is finite—every soft-sighing tree and lapping wave; all lovely, but limited, like sermons spoken or words written on a page. The same goes for our unconscious fancies and innermost thoughts, even our most ecstatic emotional experiences: all naturally explicable phenomena, all reducible to a limited number of neurons, synapses, and electrical impulses. The Bible is finite, too, testifying to its own finitude: "Jesus did many other things as well. If every one of them were written down . . . the whole world would not have room for the books that would be written."[485]

When you get right down to it, the real question isn't whether God can speak through the Bible, or a song, or a sunrise. It's whether God can speak *at all.* If God has to bypass all things creaturely in order to make himself known, can he ever get a word in edgewise?

Short Circuit

The humanness of Scripture only makes sense because of the humanness of God. Jesus, the fully human "living man" of history, is the incarnation of the eternal God. This same Jesus is also the lens for understanding the whole story of Scripture. And that's how you read it, by the way—as a *story*, a narrative whole. But most of us don't. We're more accustomed to analyzing and applying it than taking it in. For their part, historical-critical scholars focus almost exclusively on what's *behind* the Bible: Who wrote it? Why? What were their priorities and prejudices? In the name of scientific objectivity, historical-critical scholars don't engage the text on a personal level, lest they fall into the trap of adopting a particular "slant."

But "objectivity" is a "slant," too. It requires its own, often unacknowledged, interpretive goggles. It reinforces its own distinct assumptions—for instance, that it's even possible to read anything "objectively," including raw data from an experiment. It glosses over things like "confirmation bias" and "motivated learning," to which even the best scientists fall prey. We scrounge around looking for data to confirm conclusions we already believe. We look for evidence to support what we think we already know.[486] We do it all the time. Some of us spend years trying to become "objective" readers, utterly unbiased and disinterested. A useful practice for combing through real estate contracts and marketing research data? Undoubtedly. But that's not how I read my wife's first love letter. I didn't try to remove myself from it. I just started reading and let it crash over me, leaving me in love-struck ruin.

When it comes to Bible reading, historical-critical scholars and fundamentalists are two wings on the same bird of prey. Both read the Bible in isolated slivers, in order to extract something from it. When successful, they say they "got something out of it": an applicable principle, an example to follow (or avoid), a tidbit of practical or moral instruction, support for or against a particular position, etc. It's more about extraction than encounter. Fundamentalists read Scripture step by step, as if following a recipe in order to achieve a desired, predictable result. Historical-critical scholars read it like detectives, looking behind every corner in search of any sign of tampering, discrepancy, historical inaccuracy, and the like. Either way, most modern Bible readers habitually short-circuit the whole reading event. Which makes it kinda hard to encounter Scripture as a Something Else.

But what if reading the Bible was supposed to be more like encountering a piece of art, or enjoying a good meal? When you're hungry and somebody gives you a ripe, juicy pear, you don't pull out the lab kit and commence dissection. You don't analyze the constituent parts—the fiber, fructose, water, etc.—before consuming each ingredient, one at a time. You sink your teeth into it. You dive in. The same goes for a work of art: you don't "get" a Picasso, a Sendak story, a symphony, or a love letter by looking *behind* it, i.e., reading penetrating psychological profiles or historical biographies on the artist/author/composer, speculating about his or her hidden agenda, etc. You don't "get" it by stripping away the exterior in order to uncover its "inner meaning." A story—like a sculpture, a painting, or a pear—only "happens" to you when it hits you as a whole and you're swallowed up in its fullness.[487]

That's how it happens, if it happens at all. That's how you confront Something Else. Then, later on, when you recover, you can reflect on it critically. You can do what I did the first time I heard Led Zeppelin when I was a kid: pull it apart and see how it works. How did Jimmy Page get that sludgy tone on "Immigrant Song"? Is that a single coil pickup, or a humbucker? Is he playing through a Vox, flat-out, or maybe with a fuzz box? What came first: the riff, the groove, or the melody? This is all good stuff. Important stuff. And it all comes later. But first, the song has to drag you around in its undertow for a while. Only then can you dust yourself off, recover your wits, and try to make sense of what just happened.

Of course, the Jesus story is different in that it places a much heavier demand on you, the listener/reader. Jesus' message is as obnoxiously binary as it is personal: "Who do *you* say that I am?" he asks. Whether or not you "buy it" is between you and him. But there are no spectators here. No "objective" readers or casual listeners. It's addressed to *you*, which means you've got to read it "subjectively," for yourself.[488] Only then do you start trying to figure things out. Only then do you confer with your fellow pilgrims, compare notes, and start walking.

9

Creed Rules!

Writing is nothing but the representation of speech.

—JEAN-JACQUES ROUSSEAU[489]

Back to School

IN FIRST GRADE, OUR teacher challenged us to memorize all fifty states. A daunting task for a bunch of six-year-olds. Our method was simple: we would memorize an infuriatingly catchy song entitled—you guessed it— "The Fifty States Song." Week after week we sang it, over and over and over again. Then, finally, the big spring recital, where our strategy of endless repetition bore triumphant fruit. I must admit, I was impressed with my six-year-old self.

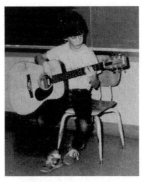

My six-year-old self

Nailing "The Fifty States Song" is probably my most vivid first-grade memory, other than the time Petey Paladini peed himself during the spelling bee . . . which was just wonderful to witness. This is the same Petey who, years later, would ask me on an almost daily basis if I wanted to get stoned. He had this way of slurring every syllable into one, barely intelligible utterance: "Heyman . . . youwunnagehssstone?" Every morning before school, same thing: "Yo. Youwunnagehssstone?" I was never quite sure how to respond: "Um, Petey, I have biology in like ten minutes. Also, it's like 7:15 in the morning, and I'm thirteen." Then we'd repeat the whole routine twenty-four hours later, and Petey would look just as befuddled by my early-morning abstinence as he'd been the day before.

Most people learn by repetition (including Petey, when he wasn't waking and baking). Learning by rote is the oldest trick in the book. Several thousand years old, in fact. It's how the rabbis of antiquity memorized massive portions of the Torah. Since most of the earliest Christians were Jews, they borrowed rabbinical memorization techniques to learn Jesus' teachings. They recited brief, memorable statements, or "formulaic summaries," in order to retain and pass on the basics of Christian doctrine.[490] One of these formulas is known as the "Jesus Tradition."[491] And unlike "The Fifty States Song," this one's short and sweet: "suffered, died and was buried." The second-century African bishop Tertullian included this formula in one of his most influential writings: "We believe Him to have suffered, died, and been buried, according to the Scriptures."[492] The same basic formula is repeated multiple times in the New Testament.[493] Formulaic summaries were a handy teaching tool in the ancient world.

Early followers of the Way had other tricks up their sleeves, too. Sometimes they learned Christian teaching by putting words to music and singing the same thing over and over again—like we did with the fifty states. Eventually, some of these songs showed up in the New Testament, like when the apostle Paul quotes a hymn about Jesus:

> Though he was in the form of God,
> did not count equality with God a thing to be grasped,
> but emptied himself, by taking the form of a servant,
> being born in the likeness of men.[494]

That's how they rolled in antiquity, when Bibles were in short supply and the printing press wasn't yet a twinkle in Gutenberg's eye. It was all about oral tradition. And while it might seem foreign to modern-day churchgoers, the original gospel message was "nonliterary"—meaning it was primarily preached, practiced, and sung rather than read.[495]

The ancients also used images to recount the gospel, including icons, mosaics, and other visual aids. A thousand years before European Christians settled North American, Syrian Christians travelled all the way from the Arabian Peninsula to share the Good News with the people of mainland China.[496] Impressed, Emperor T'ai-Tsung issued the following edict:

> Bishop Alopen of the Kingdom of Ta-ch'in [Syria], bringing with him the Sutras [Scriptures] and Images, has come from afar and presented them at our Capital. Having carefully examined the scope of his teaching, we find it to be mysteriously spiritual, and of silent operation. Having observed its principal and most essential points, we reached the conclusion that they cover all that is most important in life, and that this Teaching is helpful to all creatures and beneficial to all men.[497]

So it was *images* as much as *texts* (sutras) that made a "mysteriously spiritual" impression on the emperor and his subjects.[498]

A Christian wall painting, possibly of the three wise men on Palm Sunday. Gāochāng, China, circa seventh-eighth century.

It took me a while to learn all this stuff. It took a lot of reading, and a lot of asking questions. But to my eventual surprise, I started seeing evidence of an orally transmitted gospel from within the pages of Scripture itself.

Take Paul's letter to the Romans, wherein Paul urges Christians in Rome to stick to the "pattern of teaching" they received from the apostles, especially when it comes to the death and resurrection of Jesus.[499] Likewise, Paul reminds the church in Thessalonica: "When you received the word of God, which you heard from us, you accepted it not as a human word, but as it actually is, the word of God, which is indeed at work in you who believe."[500] Most modern scholars believe 1 Thessalonians was the first letter Paul actually wrote—probably dating around 50 CE—which means the Thessalonians were following Jesus long before the rest of the New Testament was even finished.[501] And Paul's second letter to the Thessalonians reiterates his previous point: "Stand firm and hold fast to the teachings we passed on to you, whether by word of mouth or by letter."[502] For the ancients, the "Word of God" referred as much to oral tradition as it did to written Scripture.

From the Middle East to Asia Minor to Europe, Paul's letters were already in wide circulation by the end of the first century.[503] Early Christians had at least *some* access to *some* of what would eventually become the New Testament. But it took a long time for the New Testament to be completed, and an even longer time for literacy to become commonplace. Which is why Irenaeus wrote, "We have learned from none others the plan of our salvation, than from those through whom the gospel has come down to us, which they did at one time proclaim in public, and, at a later period, by the will of God, handed down to us in the Scriptures, to be the ground and pillar of our faith."[504]

What was once preached in public was later written down in the Bible—meaning the early church was not entirely dependent upon the written words of Scripture for understanding and disseminating the good news.[505] Instead, it was "passed on" orally, in memorable, bite-sized fragments. But if that was the case, what guarantee do we have that the ancient Christians conveyed and interpreted the apostles' teachings accurately? How can we trust what's been "passed on"?

For one thing, followers of the Way didn't interpret the gospel like my wife interprets recipes, all footloose and fancy-free. On the contrary: Jesus' disciples strove to read Scripture according to what some scholars call the "rule of faith"—the established "pattern of teaching" and communal practice that had prevailed in the churches since the time of Jesus and the apostles.[506]

The Rule of Faith

A few decades after Jesus' crucifixion, bishop Clement of Rome told Christians to rely on the "holy rule of our tradition" as the main guide for Christian living, preaching, and even biblical interpretation.[507] This "rule" encapsulated the rudiments of Christian teaching and reflected the common consensus of belief among Jesus' ancient followers. So if some sect started to deny an essential doctrine that the rest of the churches believed, they'd get called on it. Take the divinity of Jesus, for instance. Since praying to Jesus Christ (the "Word" or "*Logos*"[508]) was an "unavoidable element of Christian worship," early Christians were in the habit of professing Jesus' divinity. Deviations from this tradition were seen as heterodox, or alien to the rule of faith.[509] And yes, the rule of faith came before the Bible. Actually, if somebody suggested that a certain book or letter should be accepted into the canon of Scripture, it first had to meet the standard of the rule of faith.[510] If it didn't (e.g., 1 Clement), it didn't make the cut.

By the second century, Christian leaders like Tertullian and Irenaeus believed the rule of faith had been accurately preserved through the teaching and practice of the various Christian churches. Tertullian presumed that even if the Bible had never been copied or circulated, the teaching and oral tradition of the apostles would still be found among Christian communities and recognized as authentic by Jesus' followers.[511] Simply put, the church's oral tradition *was* the rule of faith.[512] In the 300s, Athanasius of Alexandria exhorted fellow Jesus followers to trust oral tradition alongside the sayings of Scripture: "Beyond these sayings, let us look at the very tradition, teaching and faith of the catholic church from the beginning, which the Lord gave, the apostles preached, and the fathers kept."[513] The ancients didn't seem to suffer from a prejudicial suspicion of oral tradition. In a mostly illiterate world, they couldn't afford to.

I confess: learning about the rule of faith freaked me out at first. I think a lot of us are partial to written forms of communication. Evangelicals are no exception. The written word just seems more trustworthy. Scholars call this bias "textualism."[514] I can't speak for you, but when I hear the phrase, "oral tradition," I usually picture a couple kids playing telephone with Dixie cups and a string, dropping every other word, mangling the original message beyond recognition.

But the telephone game isn't really a fair analogy. Ancient practitioners of rabbinical memorization techniques were a bit more painstaking than the average first-grader. Most civilizations throughout history have used oral tradition as a primary means of passing down their formative values, stories, and symbols. Of the over four thousand languages spoken today, less than one hundred have any form of written literature. Homer relied on oral tradition when composing the *Iliad* and the *Odyssey*.[515] And in all likelihood, the four Gospels of the New Testament were biographies that emerged out of ancient oral traditions. But unless you're a hardcore textualist, who cares?

Creed

Out of the public, oral traditions of the ancient church came the early Christian creeds: bullet-point reminders of who Jesus was and what his life, death, and resurrection really meant. In religious-speak, a "creed" is a basic statement of faith rather than a comprehensive explanation of the good news in all its intricate detail. Creeds provide a short, skeletal framework of doctrine within which a certain amount of interpretive diversity takes place. Put another way, a creed is kind of like the bumpers in bumper bowling: they're there to prevent our ideas from drifting too far off the reservation.[516] That's what Christians mean by the term "creed." Not to be confused with this:

or this:

or this:

CREED

The oldest known Christian creed is the Old Roman Creed, dating back as early as the second century.[517] It's a whopping thirteen lines long:

- I believe in God the Father almighty;
- and in Christ Jesus His only Son, our Lord,
- Who was born from the Holy Spirit and the Virgin Mary,
- Who under Pontius Pilate was crucified and buried,
- on the third day rose again from the dead,
- ascended to heaven,
- sits at the right hand of the Father,
- whence He will come to judge the living and the dead;
- and in the Holy Spirit,
- the holy Church,
- the remission of sins,
- the resurrection of the flesh
- the life everlasting.[518]

Thirteen basic points on which all orthodox Christians agree, whether Roman Catholic, Byzantine, Anglican, or fundamentalist.[519] As you can see, the ancient creeds don't come close to fleshing out the whole of Christianity theology. They certainly don't replace the Bible or render it unnecessary. Nor do they anticipate all relevant philosophical questions (e.g., if God is "almighty," can God create a stone so heavy that even God can't move it?). Instead, they summarize the common core of what Jesus' early followers believed. They serve as an outline of what Clement of Alexandria called the "most important points" of the Christian faith,[520] or what contemporary scholar N. T. Wright calls "central Christian belief about God."[521] So if you find yourself in a church that teaches Jesus wasn't actually crucified, you're probably in a "non-creedal" church. And if your church depicts Jesus as an intergalactic hero whose mission is to shuttle the faithful to Alpha Centauri in exchange for their personal fortunes, I'd start getting suspicious. Also, if offered, I'd probably pass on the Kool-Aid.

Mere Christianity

Implicit here is the idea that there actually was—and *is*—something called "mere," or essential, Christianity, a phrase popularized by C. S. Lewis, but first introduced by seventeenth-century Puritan Richard Baxter, who resisted the temptation to associate Jesus with any one nation or political party: "I am against all Sects and dividing Parties," said Baxter, "but if any will call Mere Christian by the name of a Party . . . I am of that Party which is so against Parties . . . I am a CHRISTIAN, a MERE CHRISTIAN, of no other religion."[522]

Notice there's nothing in the Old Roman Creed about the authority or inerrancy of Scripture (the Bible wasn't even canonized until much later). Neither does the creed mandate any particular political or economic agenda. It doesn't even say much about Jesus' social teachings—probably because the whole "love your neighbor as yourself" thing so permeated early Christian practice that it required no further reinforcement. When the plague swept through Rome in the third century, Dionysius of Alexandria testified, "Most of our brother-Christians showed unbounded love and loyalty . . . they took charge of the sick, attending to their every need and ministering to them in Christ, and with them departed this life serenely happy; for they were infected by others with the disease . . ."[523] Even persecution-happy emperors were impressed by the generosity of their Jesus-loving subjects.[524] Some scholars think Christianity blossomed for this very reason: it extended radical compassion to a bullied and beleaguered population.[525] In an empire where peasants frequently starved to death, Christianity offered an egalitarian and inclusive alternative to the Roman social order,[526] a welcome glimpse into a "possible world"—i.e., the kingdom of God—where empathy and lovingkindness are the norm, not the exception.[527] Christ's conspicuous concern for the poor stood in stark relief to the brutality of ancient Rome. You couldn't get much more countercultural than "Blessed are the poor . . . the meek . . . the merciful . . ."[528]

While most early Christians agreed on Jesus' social teachings, they did have some serious theological questions to work through—some of which weren't answered by the Bible: e.g., if God is eternal and unchanging, and if Jesus is "fully God," how could he become a human being and experience things like hunger, pain, humiliation, even death? If there's only one God, how can Jesus be God, too?[529] And what about the Holy Spirit? Though triadic language does appear in the New Testament and other early Christian writings,[530] the word "Trinity" isn't actually in the Bible . . . which means early Christians had to wrestle with this stuff. In fact, the creeds arose out of a need to clarify Christian teaching and settle these kinds of debates—and this is key: the fact that the Jesus' early followers found it necessary to formulate creeds and recite them on a regular basis should tell us something about modern Bible-only-ism.[531] If, as modern biblicists insist, the Bible has only one crystal-clear meaning, why the need for creeds? Shouldn't everyone, everywhere come up with the same interpretation?

But they don't. And I'm not talking here about the extreme cases, e.g. Nazi theologians who used Scripture to support the Third Reich.[532] I'm talking about normal, decent people who'd swear on a Bible that theirs is *the* correct interpretation (the Nazis considered themselves normal and decent, by the way . . . but that's another story[533]). If you're even remotely clever, you can twist Scripture to suit whatever preexisting purposes you have in mind, just like the Nazis did as part of Hitler's well-oiled propaganda machine.[534] Biblically savvy slave owners pulled a similar trick in the antebellum South.[535] That's why the American slavery debate was so confusing during the Civil War: both sides claimed to be Christian; both believed in their own objectivity; both appealed to the same set of Scriptures.[536] Sixteen hundred years earlier, Tertullian had already realized that some issues couldn't be settled by relying on Scripture alone: "We must not appeal to Scripture and we must not contend on ground where victory is impossible or uncertain enough."[537] In other words, pointing to a Bible verse and shouting "Because it says so!" doesn't always cut it.

Thank God for Dead Saints

Learning some church history made me feel better about leaving biblicism behind. The rule of faith, the creeds, and especially the church fathers and mothers gave me permission to struggle with the Scriptures, mainly because *they* struggled with the Scriptures.[538] Even the great and powerful Augustine had a hard time with it, and he was an intellectual juggernaut.[539] I figured if the great saints of old couldn't turn the Bible into a user-friendly handbook, maybe I wasn't supposed to, either. And it wasn't just the dead saints who failed to meet the exacting standards of fundamentalist biblicism. Plenty of modern-day followers of the Way have had their own wrestling matches with the Bible; people like C. S. Lewis, J. I. Packer, Greg Boyd, Tony Campolo, and N. T. Wright, who together reminded me that there was something called "mere" Christianity, that it was possible to be "simply Christian" without insisting upon the sort of line-by-line literalism that leads only to confusion, contradiction, and disenchantment.[540] "Simply Christian." I liked that. Keep it simple.

But "simple" doesn't always mean "easy."

10

Apocalypse Now and Then

Nothing in your life is arbitrary. It's all for a purpose.

—Rick Warren, *The Purpose Driven Life*[541]

Nobody exists on purpose. Nobody belongs anywhere. We're all going to die. Come watch TV.

—Morty, *Rick and Morty*

The Great Darwinian Disaster

One hundred and fifty years ago, Charles Darwin unleashed his earth-shattering theory of evolution upon a naïve and unready world. Never before had anyone publicly challenged the notion that God created the world in six literal, twenty-four-hour days, just like it says in Genesis.[542] By contradicting the clear teaching of Scripture, Darwin threatened to undermine the exclusive authority of the Bible, the very foundation of Western civilization.[543] Panicked Christians sounded the alarm and rallied the troops, anxious to counter the new "evolution problem." Almost overnight, Darwin's ideas galvanized evangelicals and engendered a new, angrier, more literalist fundamentalism that swept the nation, forever pitting Bible-believing creationists against secular liberals. Any churchgoer suspected of accepting even a smidgeon of Darwin's ideas was summarily expelled . . . and with good reason: once people started doubting the exclusive reliability of Scripture, they'd stop believing in God, Jesus, traditional American values, inalienable rights, even morality. Mere anarchy would ensue. Despite the best efforts of concerned Christians, their warnings fell on deaf ears. Soon creationism was banned from public schools, and the rest is history. Darwin won the day, and your weird Uncle Ned—you know, the one who stockpiles canned goods and posts pics of all twelve of his MAGA hat–wearing homeschooled kids every time they visit the Creation Museum? Yeah, he lost.

You get all that?

It's a familiar script: God was in his heaven and all was right with the world, then Darwin showed up and spoiled the party for everybody. It's got everything a good story needs: heroes, a villain, a crisis in need of resolution. If it had three chords and a tractor, it'd be a country song. Problem is, it isn't true.

First of all, religion didn't die after Darwin. That much should be obvious. Second, Darwin wasn't the first to argue that biological change happens gradually, though he was first to argue persuasively that evolution is, at least in part, a result of random chance.[544] Third, I'm probably being a bit hard on Uncle Ned. And finally, the biggest hole in the story: plenty of Bible-believing Christians had no problem with Darwinism when it was first introduced.[545] According to a leading Christian publication in the 1880s, less than half of all evangelical pastors in the U.S. interpreted Genesis 1–3 literally.[546] They didn't necessarily believe God created Adam "from the dust of the ground," or Eve from Adam's rib. Some even affirmed evolution—which means "young earth creationism" was never that "conservative" to begin with.

Not that Darwin was uncontroversial in his day. Some Christians were wary of the broader theological implications of his ideas. Others, like Charles Hodge, rejected him outright.[547] An influential evangelical theologian, Hodge dismissed Darwin as a hack, his worldview as "tantamount to atheism," and his theory of evolution as "utterly inconsistent with the Scriptures."[548] Inspired and informed by Hodge, fellow evangelical B. B. Warfield responded to the rise of secular science by giving the Bible a promotion: what was once the written record of divine revelation now became the final authority on all manner of subjects, including science and natural history.[549] By the late 1800s, Warfield and co. had effectively elevated the status and scope of Scripture. The stakes were that high and the choice that simple: it's either Scripture or science, Darwin or Jesus. Take your pick.

The Humbling of Humanity

Ain't no denying it: Darwin definitely ruffled some feathers and bruised some egos in his day. Taken in tandem with Galileo's discoveries, modern science had dealt humanity a doubly humiliating blow: first, by removing our planet from the center of the universe; second, by tracing our lineage back to lowly, ape-like ancestors. Humbling indeed. But still, I doubt such humiliation would've been sufficient to provoke the modern fundamentalist movement. Humility is a Christian virtue, after all: "God opposes the proud but gives grace to the humble," Scripture says.[550] Sure, maybe my knuckle-dragging predecessors swung from trees and slept in the dirt. But as far as origins go, is that any less dignified than being fashioned from dust?[551]

Well, yeah . . . assuming God is like a Christianized Odin, fickle and detached. In that kind of scenario, then sure, Adam would've enjoyed a uniquely awesome and privileged position, purely on the basis of physical proximity to God's "hand." Thus implied Michelangelo in his famous fresco, *The Creation of Adam*:

There he is, "the Man Upstairs," a mere hairsbreadth from Adam, who was alone called into being by a special, direct, and immediate act of creation.

Perhaps.

But if Augustine, Aquinas, Karl Barth, and the apostle Paul were right—if God really is "closer to us than we are to ourselves"[552]—then Michelangelo's rather risqué rendering of creation is a little misleading. Because God isn't a "Big Guy in the sky." And he's definitely not surrounded by throngs of scantily clad angel-babies (it's also highly unlikely Adam had CrossFit abs). Because God is *everywhere*. Thus sayeth the psalmist:[553]

> Where can I go from your Spirit?
> Where can I flee from your presence?
> If I go up to the heavens, you are there;
> if I make my bed in the depths, you are there.[554]

It's like the medieval monks used to say: "God is an infinite sphere, whose center is everywhere and circumference nowhere."[555] Long before modern science launched satellites into space, before the Wright brothers dared dream of one day scaling the skies, Christians knew you couldn't find God by looking up, no matter how powerful your telescope. "God is *Spirit*,"[556] said Jesus, not some bearded guy in a loose fit blouse, floating in the clouds. That's partly why American Christians didn't rally against evolution en masse till the Scopes "Monkey" Trial, that infamous showdown between fundamentalist Christians and secular science.[557] It wasn't till 1925—a full sixty years after Darwin dropped his *Origin of Species*—that evangelicalism *became* "fundamentalism," a religion defined by biblicism, anti-intellectualism, and anxious opposition to modern science (more on that in the next chapter).[558] Before then, plenty of evangelicals were fine with evolution.[559] To them, Darwinism didn't require a solution because it wasn't really a problem.

Take the Harvard botanist, Asa Gray. A longtime friend and collaborator of Darwin, Gray helped popularize his theory in America. And Gray was an outspoken, evangelical Christian—which, to our twenty-first-century ears, sounds oxymoronic (if not regular moronic). Nowadays, pairing the words "Harvard botanist" with "evangelical Christian" makes about as much sense as "Amish Cantonese," "sexy skin tags," or "the Honorable Sir Blake Shelton." But not for Gray. His commitment to rigorous scientific inquiry was matched only by his commitment to Christ. Gray didn't see evolution as a threat to faith. Neither did Darwin, for that matter, though he did find it hard to believe in a benevolent Designer. In a candid letter to Gray, Darwin confessed, "With respect to the theological view of the question; this is always painful to me. I am bewildered. I had no intention to write atheistically. But I own that I cannot see, as plainly as others do, and as I should wish to do, evidence of design and beneficence on all sides of us. There seems to me too much misery in the world . . ."[560]

I don't have a clue what Darwin's real motives were. I'm not even sure what *my* motives are half the time. Regardless, Gray saw nothing inherently atheistic about his friend's hypothesis. Quite the contrary: Gray believed Darwinism actually *supported* the Christian conviction that all human beings are created in the image of God (see Genesis 1:27). This was in the mid-1800s, mind you, when America's slavery debate was boiling over into full-blown civil war. On the pro-slavery side, you had a cabal of racist creationists who argued that God must've created Blacks and Whites separately—and definitely not equally.[561] Against these assertions, Gray used Darwin's findings to support the traditional Judeo-Christian view that all people share a common ancestral origin and are endowed with the same God-given dignity.[562] Rather than an existential threat, Gray saw Darwinism as a resource for faith. And he wasn't the only one.

More on Early Christian Darwinism (and Other Oxymorons)

In 1886, the famous abolitionist pastor Henry Ward Beecher (brother of Harriet Beecher Stowe, author of *Uncle Tom's Cabin*) argued that evolution, "instead of obliterating the evidence of divine design, has lifted it to a higher plane, and made it more sublime than it ever was contemplated to be under the old reasonings."[563] Theologian James Woodrow took a similar position. A contemporary of Beecher, Woodrow argued that while Scripture was "inspired" by God and "inerrant" in "every expression which it contains," it teaches *that* God created the world, not *how* he created it (Aquinas and Galileo made comparable cases[564]). "The doctrine of evolution," wrote Woodrow, "is not and cannot be either Christian or anti-Christian, religious or irreligious, theistic or atheistic."[565] To him, the question of how to interpret Genesis 1–3 was entirely secondary: "What difference can it make with regard to any relation between ourselves and our fellow-men, or between ourselves and the Lord Jesus Christ, whether the earth came into existence six thousand years or six million years ago . . . whether the species of organic beings now on the earth were created mediately or immediately?"[566]

Look at it this way: if all effects have some prior cause, and if God is the creator (a.k.a. "First Cause") of all that exists, then everything in the universe is ultimately the result, or "effect," of God.[567] These "effects" can, in turn, cause other "effects," like my mom with Thanksgiving dinner. She did most of the shopping, chopping, slicing and dicing, etc. No mom, no meal. In Aquinas-speak, she was the "mediate" or "intermediary cause" of our yearly holiday feast. But she didn't cause herself to exist. Neither did she cause our finely tuned universe to exist, nor the earth, nor its soil for the bearing of fruit, nor those fruits for the sustaining and nourishing of life (including her own), etc. All these links in the causal chain are vitally important. All of them matter.

Sure, an omnipotent God could create a full-blown, fully functioning universe "immediately," and in one fell swoop, without recourse to any "mediate causes", including my mom. But as Aquinas argued—and I'm inclined to agree—God takes greater delight in creating through his creatures, his "co-creators." By bringing the world into being through various intermediary causes, God yields more aggregate goodness and beauty than would any direct, divine dictatorship: "It is a greater perfection for a thing to be good in itself and also the cause of goodness in others, than only to be good in itself."[568]

Let's get back to Woodrow. An accomplished biologist and theologian, the guy knew his stuff, including the philosophical complexities of causality. Like Aquinas before him, Woodrow figured an all-powerful God could've used whatever methods or means he wanted when making the world, including microbes, moms, or mutated genes; including quantum fluctuations in an unstructured vacuum, before the big bang;[569] including even the painfully slow, often counterintuitive processes of natural evolution.

And it's not like Woodrow came to these conclusions on his own, in some lame, last-ditch effort to thwart the Darwinian menace. From time immemorial, followers of the Way have been accustomed to interpreting Genesis 1–3 figuratively.[570] Even William Jennings Bryan—that notorious Scopes Trial litigator who opposed teaching Darwinism in public schools—embraced evolution earlier in his career.[571] So did some of the first Christian "fundamentalists," like B. B. Warfield, who considered himself a Darwinist in his younger years.[572]

Warfield was a key contributor to *The Fundamentals: A Testimony to the Truth*, a collection of highly influential essays published in the 1910s and intended to clarify core Christian beliefs (it's where we get the term "fundamentalist," BTW[573]). The son of a cattle breeder, he grew up knowing a thing or two about natural selection. He'd also read plenty of Calvin, who himself taught a "gradualist" version of creationism (incidentally, Calvin believed God's creation of the world was a matter of *faith*, not something that could be proven by historical or scientific evidence).[574] While championing the modern doctrine of "biblical inerrancy," young Warfield believed God might've intervened in natural history to bring humanity forth from primitive ancestors.[575]

Figurative ≠ Fictitious

Figurative doesn't necessarily mean fictitious. Something can be *true* without being *literally* true, like the creation stories in the Bible. The main message of Genesis 1–3 is that God created the world, "and it was *good*"—a much different story than we find in either Greek mythology or ancient Eastern philosophy, where strife is woven into the very fabric of existence from the start.[576] Not so in Genesis. Here we find a universe forged in original goodness, a world created freely and superfluously, out of love, not necessity. Nobody *made* God do it. Every galaxy and grain of sand—all of it "good," all of it gift.

In the final analysis, the creationism-vs.-evolution debate skirts the real issue. Neither option serves as a satisfying, stand-alone solution to our most pressing human problems: Now that we're here, what's the way forward? Where are we going? What's the meaning of life? And from whence do such abiding curiosities spring?

That last part is particularly important: Why is it that we're able to question our own existence? Of what possible evolutionary advantage is our uncanny capacity to wonder, to reflect upon anything and everything, including our own selves? Sure, I can see how curiosity would've rendered our species more fit for survival. I doubt our prehistoric ancestors would've discovered fire or invented the wheel unless they were more inquisitive and resourceful than the competition. With varying degrees of success, über-smart atheists like Sam Harris and Steven Pinker have tried using a similar Darwinian logic to explain the emergence of things like morality, altruism, cooperation, and community; e.g., prehistoric hunting bands would've fared better in the wild than isolated, uncooperative individuals.[577] "Strength in numbers," etc. But still, why the nagging hunger for things sacred and transcendent, even today? Why are we still so interested in the Big Why? Is it just an embarrassing evolutionary leftover, a vestigial trait, like nipples on dudes? Can we really reduce all of our religious impulses and deepest longings to Darwinian survival strategies? What then of "Love your enemy"? What of *kenosis*, the "self-emptying" of Jesus, which Christians are called to emulate? It was a despairing Christ who, fearing imminent arrest and crucifixion, prayed, "My Father, if it be possible, let this cup pass from me; nevertheless, not as I will, but as you will."[578] I'm not an evolutionary biologist, but that doesn't sound like much of a winning survival strategy to me.

Skin in the Game

I remember one time when my wife gave me multiple second-degree burns. It was an "accident," of course (or so she maintains). I'd just gotten home from a cold and rainy soccer practice. Almost immediately, I made a beeline for the restroom, drew a hot bath, and plopped myself into the rapidly rising water. Unfortunately for me, it was also rapidly cooling water.

Turns out, my wife had just finished showering and used up most of the hot water. So in a combination of frustration, laziness, and inspired idiocy, I asked her to boil a pot on the stove and pour it into the tub . . . with me in it. Tragically, she obliged.

Try as I might, I'll never forget the sight of my own peeled skin floating around me in the water, like little translucent lily pads of thinly sliced turkey. It took ten weeks for my burned leg to heal. *Ten weeks*. On the plus side, it gave me some serious marital leverage. Now, whenever she wants to rent a chick flick, I remind her, "Sure, I guess we could Netflix that new Anne Hathaway movie . . . is that the one where she pours boiling water all over her husband's leg? Or am I thinking of something else?"

And this has always been Christianity's main issue with Darwinism. Accidents, that is. Not Anne Hathaway (though *Ocean's 8* was a bit of a misfire). For followers of the Way, the word "accident" poses a problem, mainly because we don't believe God makes any. Certainly not the God of whom Jesus spoke, a God who seemed dead set on rescuing the world and bringing about a new, heavenly kingdom.

Blind Chance, Accidents, and Apocatastasis

Darwinian evolution consists of two main aspects: (1) *natural selection,* the process by which living organisms better adapted to their natural environments tend to survive and thrive (e.g., peacocks with colorful tails); (2) *random variation,* as when an animal with a specific genetic code morphs into something else, purely by chance. If this variation allows said animal to better compete for survival, it'll live long and prosper . . . and probably procreate, resulting in offspring that are also more suited for survival—i.e., peacocks with big, bright tails were able to scare off more predators, attract more mates, and make more babies than their colorless counterparts. No Intelligent Designer necessary. Just the slightest tweaking of an organism's genetic encryption, all thanks to what Darwin called "blind chance"—meaning there's no overarching purpose, no divine providence at work.[579] It's all a happy accident.

Actually, "accident" is the wrong term, since it implies things like purpose and intention. "Once you know that there are no *purposes,*" wrote Nietzsche, "you also know that there is no *accident;* for it is only beside a world of purpose that the word 'accident' has any meaning."[580] And when it comes to the origin and development of species, strict Darwinians don't believe in any grand "purpose" behind it all.[581] Nobody pulling the strings. Just energy, physical laws, and matter, all banging around inside a closed box called "the universe." Call it naturalism, or scientism, or reductive physicalism, or eliminative materialism. All say the same basic thing—namely, that there's nothing *above, outside,* or *behind* the natural universe, and certainly nothing capable of affecting things *in* the universe. Which means genetic mutation must happen *only* at random, to the exclusion of any "supernatural" direction or interference.[582]

Natural selection was never really a problem for Christians in ages past. Jesus' earliest disciples were shepherds, so it's safe to assume they knew the basics of sheep breeding (like B. B. Warfield). It's the *random* part that's always been a problem for Jesus followers, mostly because it presupposes an impenetrable barricade between Creator and creation, with God sealed in one box and the universe in another, and never the twain shall meet.[583] If, as some strict Darwinian naturalists insist, every historical instance of genetic mutation *must* be "random"—as in, *not* divinely ordained or influenced in any way—it means God has to keep his holy hands off the whole historical process of biodiversification. And for followers of the Way, this is an issue.

For starters, most Christians are reluctant to say God *can't* do something. The word "God" implies at least some capacity to affect change, some ability to bear upon the Real World. Whatever else we mean by "God," we don't mean an impotent, idle spirit.[584] Even the laziest person is more than a mere spectator in the unfolding drama of human history—even your pathologically indecisive, chronically inactive college roommate, with his gas-guzzling stoner van. Even he made *some* kind of impression upon the world, if only a carbon footprint.

So here's the real heart of the impasse: if you're a strict Darwinian naturalist, then you're at odds with one of Christianity's central claims—namely, that the kingdom of God is coming, *no matter what*. That's certainly what the Christian creeds propose, as do Jesus' parables.[585] It's hard to think of "God" *as* GOD while relegating him to the celestial sidelines, especially since so much of what Jesus said and did presupposed a God who was actively involved in the Real World, whose coming kingdom wasn't a bona fide certainty, not a matter of chance: "He *will* come to judge the living and the dead," the creed says, "and his kingdom *will* have no end."[586] Since the God revealed in Jesus promises *apocatastasis*, the ultimate "renewal of all things" at the end of time, then God must be at least *capable* of bringing this renewal about.[587] So if words like "accident," "random," and "chance" mean God is somehow incapable of influencing history towards its ordained end, then the Christian is loath to use them.

This is usually where the Christian/naturalist conversation peters out, assuming it ever even gets going. Christians can't offer any conclusive evidence that God guided (or even influenced) the evolutionary process, and atheists can't prove God didn't. "God is outside the entire order of the universe," wrote Aquinas.[588] How do you prove that an utterly transcendent deity has been tinkering with our DNA? How do you verify whether something *outside* the universe is (or isn't) affecting things *inside* the universe?

God and Nothing

"God is no-thing," said St. John of the Cross. Put more provocatively, "God does not exist."[589] At least, not in the way other *things* exist. And please, make no mistake about this: when followers of the Way speak of God, we do not mean a mere "thing" among other things.[590] And we definitely don't mean a bigger, better version of ourselves (i.e., Michelangelo's "Man Upstairs").

Let me illustrate by way of *Raiders of the Lost Ark*, the first movie I ever saw in the theatre. My dad took me when I was a little kid. While I've never actually smoked crack cocaine, I suspect it'd be similar to how I felt that day, half-drunk on adrenaline, Milk Duds, and popcorn, feet fidgeting against the sticky theatre floor. Long after the end credits rolled, I just sat there, transfixed, rendered incapable of speech. "Wanna watch it again?" my father asked. I did—as in, immediately. And in one of the coolest parental decisions of all time, he let me. Same seat, three additional viewings.

I'll never forget when the bad guys opened the Ark of the Covenant, the apple of Indy's eye. This is the same ark where Moses' Ten Commandments had been preserved for millennia—or so Indy and his Nazi adversaries believed. Driven by greed, the Nazis wrenched the ark open, only to have their collective faces melted off by the sacred fires seething within. Horrifying stuff. I don't think I slept for a month.

If you've never seen *Raiders*, my condolences for what must have been an endlessly dreary childhood in the Peruvian Andes, or the outer rings of Saturn, or whatever cultural vacuum you have the misfortune of calling "home." But if, like most sentient beings, you've seen *Raiders*, you might recall what the Ark of the Covenant looked like: a gilt-edged wooden chest plated with gold veneer. Kinda like this:

Atop the chest stood two angelic figures carved of gold, perched on opposing sides. And between the two angels, empty space. Nothing. But a very special kind of nothing—a nothing intended to represent God, the God who is not a thing. Theologian Rowan Williams explains, "The cherubim flanking the ark defines a space where God would be, *if God were anywhere.*"[591] But of course, God isn't anywhere. Because God is not "in" the world. "In him we live and move and have our being," not the other way round.

Like St. John of the Cross, Christians from Augustine to Dionysius to Aquinas have all emphasized the no-thing-ness of God.[592] Which is not to say they were atheists. We call these men "saints" because they were people of faith . . . meaning they believed God was, in fact, real; just not the way other *things* are real—things like peacocks, popcorn, quantum-scale particles, Bigoted Becky, or even the Bible.[593] Galileo was right to remind his inquisitors of divine immateriality: God has no "hands"; no arms, no body, no DNA profile; no size, weight, shape, or dimensions. He exists prior to, and apart from, time and space. He is neither a function, nor a process, nor a property of something else. "God is spirit"; an infinite sphere, fully present at all points; an endless, non-spatial expanse; no-thing and nowhere, with the notable exception of everywhere.[594]

Agnosticism 101

Much to the consternation of Christianity's modern critics, there is simply no way to subject God to the same kind of scientific scrutiny as other objects or persons in the world.[595] You can't dust for God's fingerprints. No controlled experiment can either prove or disprove God's existence. For this very reason, the biologist Thomas Huxley coined the term "agnostic." A feisty proponent of Darwinian evolution, Huxley nevertheless acknowledged the limits of science: "I neither deny nor affirm the immortality of man. I see no reason for believing it, but, on the other hand, I have no means of disproving it."[596]

Some people dismiss Jesus for just this reason: If God and his kingdom aren't falsifiable—meaning you can't *disprove* the existence of God—then does God really matter?[597] If something can neither be verified nor falsified, it's usually irrelevant. I can't prove whether Bigoted Becky is the world's greatest poet if she keeps it a secret. But if it's *really* a secret, if she literally never talks about it; if no one ever sees, let alone reads, a single line of her work; if she destroys every copy of every poem she's ever written, taking her secret with her to the grave, then who cares if it's true? And if God is like that—an inconsequential, irrelevant add-on to the universe, affecting nothing and relating to no one—then are we really saying anything when we invoke God's name?

Unless, of course, God actually does something.

This Is the End

Followers of the Way use a variety of deferential handles when speaking of Jesus: Messiah, Light of the World, Lord of Lords, Lamb of God, Christ (which isn't Jesus' last name, but a title, meaning "anointed"). Perhaps the oddest of these cognomina is Alpha and Omega, the beginning and end— and not just the "end" of a suspenseful story, but the "end" (*telos*) in the ancient sense of the word: the goal and purpose of history.[598] There'd be no upsets in this story, no surprise endings or "oopsy" moments where God drops the ball and lets the whole thing unravel. Jesus wasn't giving it his best shot or leaving it to chance. He was both *proclaiming* a new reality and *accomplishing* it—bringing it into being—which is why he and his followers talked about history as if it were an unfurling story whose conclusion had already been written.[599]

If we imagine the arrow of history as a line moving forward, Jesus is the end (*telos*) of that line, bursting forth from within history's middle.[600] And so, with an almost eerie certainty, the book of Revelation reads, "'He *will* wipe every tear from their eyes. There *will* be no more death or mourning or crying or pain, for the old order of things has passed away.'"[601] In Black Voices, we said it a bit differently: "No more weepin' and a'wailin.' I'm goin' to live with God!" Not *maybe*, if we get lucky. "There *will* be no more death," period. Luck's got nothing to do with it.[602]

This is what Martin Luther King Jr. spoke of so eloquently and often, even as he foresaw his own impending death. And he did more than just speak of it. For MLK, the kingdom of God was more than one possibility among others. It was a *promise*:

> I just want to do God's will. And He's allowed me to go up to the mountain. And I've looked over, and I've seen the Promised Land. I may not get there with you. But I want you to know tonight, that we, as a people, *will* get to the Promised Land. So I'm happy, tonight. I'm not worried about anything. I'm not fearing any man. Mine eyes have seen the glory of the coming of the Lord.[603]

King's perspective was the polar opposite of movies like *The Terminator*, where a select few are cursed with foreknowledge of a dark and looming dystopia. In contrast, King's vision was stubbornly hopeful, even in the midst of his relatively crappy circumstances. Likewise, the apostle Paul professed, "I consider that our present sufferings are not worth comparing with the glory that will be revealed in us."[604] *Will* be revealed. Like MLK, Paul read the story of history backwards, interpreting each preceding page according to its already revealed conclusion. This is not a story of gradual social progress, fraught with "maybes" and "sort ofs." It's the story of a kingdom that has already been unleashed from within the world.

Room to Be Ourselves

Maybe the notion of an inevitable kingdom of God sounds too fatalistic. If history is predetermined, why not hit the snooze button and sit this whole "life" thing out? Well, for starters, personal responsibility is a pretty Christian concept (it's also quite helpful for maintaining relationships, avoiding incarceration, securing and retaining employment, etc.). And as much as I'd love to have another excuse for sleeping in, most Christians would agree that we're each endowed with some semblance of "free will." As one theologian put it, God creates and sustains a world where we have room to be ourselves. Which means we're free to make our own choices, including poor ones.[605]

The whole predestination-vs.-"free will" debate can get pretty knotty, and not just for theologians. Philosophers, physicists, and neuroscientists have long since joined the confusing fray.[606] Suffice to say, Christians hold to a variety of opinions on issues like determinism, chance, and choice. And with the exception of some exceedingly enthusiastic Calvinists, most followers of the way don't think of God as an overpowering puppeteer who micromanages every atom of the universe, thereby eliminating any hint of human freedom.[607] Just because history is headed towards a divinely appointed end doesn't mean we're all a bunch of remote-controlled automatons. For one thing, that would mean God *made* my wife burn my leg—which, for a variety of theological (not to mention marital) reasons, would be highly problematic.

Maybe we should consider a more uplifting case of free will in action: when MLK chose to forgive the bigots who bombed his home, almost killing his family, it really was King making that conscious, free decision, just as it really was God, willing and enabling the same. Remember King's prayer, "I just want to do God's will." God has a will, each of us has a will. God makes choices, we make choices. Sometimes, through prayer and supplication, those choices overlap. Theologians call it "double agency"—not in a 007/ Severus Snape kind of way, but in the sense that two free-willed agents (i.e., you and God) can both will the same thing at the same time.[608] Remember: God is no-thing and nowhere—not even "in" spacetime, and certainly not "in" your finite, physical brain. If you choose X and God chooses X, the result is a single effect, without compromising each other's personal freedom. It's not a zero sum game between two competing wills, as if one has to box out the other. Which means God doesn't need to wait his turn before tagging back into the course of human history—at least, not the God in whom Paul and MLK placed their hope. Theirs was a God on the move, a God of power and purpose, at work in the Real World.

This is strange stuff. It certainly sounded strange to me when I first got wind of it in college. My Christian friends talked about Jesus' kingdom as if it were in the next room. So did Jesus, by the way. And he talked about the kingdom as if he were the key to its coming. It was his task to bring it about—and in this charge he would not fail.

According to Jesus, God had world-changing plans for his life, death, and resurrection. "The Son of Man is going to be betrayed into the hands of men," Jesus said, speaking in always-awkward illeisms, "They will kill him, and after three days he will rise."[609] Jesus did third person–speak better than Zlatan Ibrahimović, better than Bob Dole at the New Hampshire primary. There's no getting around it: Jesus was convinced of his messianic uniqueness, just as he was convinced of God's sovereignty in directing the arrow of history toward its final fulfillment. To him, the kingdom was a locked and loaded eventuality.

Of course, confidence alone does not a messiah make.

The Power of Now . . . and Later

Frederick Buechner once described Jesus as an "explosion of a man," the eruption of Life itself into life.[610] That's what the disciples encountered when they met Jesus. It certainly helps explain why they threw caution to the wind in order to follow a thirty-three-year-old virgin with questionable career prospects. Again, I think of when Peter first realized it was God-in-flesh with whom he was speaking: "Go away from me, Lord . . ."[611] A surprising exclamation perhaps, but put yourself in poor Pete's shoes: when looking at Jesus, he saw what divine love looks like when it confronts and remakes the world. Not only that, Peter saw what a human being looks like who has not been conformed to this world's splintered image.

There he is—"light unapproachable," eternity breaking into the ephemeral present. And there he goes—healing the sick, feeding the hungry, loving the unlovable, reconciling, mending, making new. This is what Peter and the apostles witnessed: the present presence of eternity. God's coming kingdom of life clothed in flesh, unveiled before their very eyes, made manifest in the now.

Let's be clear on something: Jesus wasn't interested in a pie-in-the-sky, "in the sweet by and by" kind of spirituality. According to Jesus, the kingdom of God was—and *is*—already among us, breaking out "in our midst."[612] And while it awaits final completion in the yet-to-come, God's kingdom can be tasted today, in the now. As one theologian puts it, the kingdom has been "inaugurated," though not "fully consummated."[613] Launched, but not landed. Accomplished, but not fulfilled. Richard Rohr calls it the "now and not-yet Reign of God."[614] It implies an ongoing existential tension between time and eternity, the finite and the infinite. And it can definitely take some getting used to.

Humpty Dumpty Philosophy, or People of the Future?

There's a lot to be learned by looking backwards. As a history teacher, I should know: the past is a treasure trove of lessons to be learned and wisdom to be gleaned. According to Plato, all learning is actually a form of remembering. "The doctrine of recollection," philosophers call it—meaning life isn't about learning anything new, but recalling that which we already know.[615] For different reasons, modern psychoanalysis shares a similar enthusiasm for history—more specifically, *your* history, as well as mine. The hope is that, by probing into our personal histories and identifying our early, formative traumas, we can (re)discover and restore our "true selves," before we picked up the various and sundry (and often harmful) habits we now rely upon to cope with the turbulent present.

The aforementioned retrospective approaches all share a single, underlying presupposition: namely, that the answers to life's big questions lay neither in the present nor the future, but the past. Call it "Humpty Dumpty philosophy," and one of its main assumptions is that all would be well (or, at least, better) if we could hit the undo button and return to some long-lost, precorrupted yesteryear, when all was still good in the cosmic hood; a pristine "state of nature," where we could pick up the pieces and put ourselves back together again.[616]

As a person who makes his living teaching history, I have no interest in discouraging retrospection. There is indeed much to be gained by delving into the past—especially one's own. And as the direct beneficiary of therapy aplenty, far be it from me to disparage the benefits of counseling. But there's only so much learning, growing, and healing that can happen by revisiting, or even repairing, the past. And there's only so much healing we can do for ourselves.

The late Dominican priest, Herbert McCabe, described Christians as "people who proclaim that they belong to the future."[617] From the beginning,

followers of Jesus were a future-oriented people—a people on the move—
"ever singing, march we onward." It's all over the Scriptures, and in the writings of the church mothers and fathers. And of all the Bible's outlandish
claims, perhaps none is more striking than the following, from the New
Testament book of Colossians: "When Christ, who is your life, appears, then
you also will appear with him in glory."[618]

First, there's the idea that Jesus is going to appear again, no matter
what. Not *probably*, not if you think positively enough, do enough good, or
connive and cajole enough. The biblical authors were sure of it: Jesus would
reappear "in glory."[619] And that kind of certainty doesn't come easy these
days.

Equally strange is the notion that Jesus is "Life"—*your* life, and mine;
the goal, author, and ground of existence. All sorts of bizarre Bible verses
make the same basic point, i.e., Colossians 1:16: "For in him all things
were created: things in heaven and on earth, visible and invisible, whether
thrones or powers or rulers or authorities; all things have been created
through him and for him." The implication is that Jesus of Nazareth, the son
of Mary, is also Jesus the eternal Christ, the cosmic Source—and End—of
the universe.[620]

But what about appearing with Jesus "in glory"? Specifically, Scripture
says *you* will appear with Jesus in glory. According to Paul (the probable
writer of Colossians), Jesus isn't preoccupied with the past. Call Christ many
things, but nostalgic he was not. No sentimental pining after the "good old
days." Same goes for Paul: "When Christ appears, *then* you will appear with
him in glory." The "then" isn't referring to an idyllic, unspoiled past, but a
kingdom come, a "new heaven and new earth."[621] And in this coming kingdom, we will discover many things—not least of which will be ourselves.

There Is No "I" in Y-O-U

But first, some bad news: you don't exist. More precisely, you don't have a
"self." At least, not the way we usually think of the "self"—as an autonomous, unchanging "soul pilot" that you inherit at birth and carry with you
through life, a "ghost in the machine" steering your body and directing your
thoughts, determining who you really are.[622] Just ask the neuroscientists.
They've been looking. And despite the best available brain scanning technology, nobody's been able to find the self yet. Because there is no "I" in Y-
O-U, no disembodied consciousness hovering inside that three-pound ball
of neuron spaghetti lodged between your ears. Neither did your self exist as
an intact, immaterial entity before being paired with a body.[623] Because you
are always *becoming* yourself.

Two of Buddhism's main tenets are *anicca* ("impermanence") and *anatta* ("non-self"). Taken together, they offer an invaluable window into human nature—namely, that "self" is a *verb*.[624] We are ever-changing creatures; fluid, not fixed. You don't have to swallow Buddhism wholesale to appreciate this fundamental insight. To be a human being is to be "in process." Our moods, wants, even our opinions can change, sometimes by the minute (especially if you're in middle school).[625] Same goes for our habits, those deeply ingrained patterns of thinking, behaving, and perceiving the world. As modern neuroscience has corroborated, our brains remain "plastic," even into adulthood.[626] Which means the self is always *becoming*—always adapting, reacting, growing, and responding.[627] Even now. Even tomorrow. That's why you'll never "find yourself" by retracing your steps or mapping out your personality, no matter how many Enneagram assessments or StrengthsFinder tests you take. Because there is no "real you," no immutable "true self" waiting to be found.

This can be a tough pill to swallow, especially if you fancy yourself a "self-made man."[628] For Americans in particular, there's something attractive about the idea of a fully independent, sovereign self, impervious to extrinsic influence—including, presumably, divine influence. "I am the master of my fate: I am the captain of my soul," the poem reads, and like any good poem, it's got a kernel of truth to it: we *are*, in fact, responsible agents capable of making decisions of real consequence. We *do* have the power to choose. That includes even your stoner roommate from college, who freely chose to avoid making choices. But none of us is *absolutely* free (especially not him . . . though I hear he's eligible for parole in six months). Think about it: you didn't get to pick your ethnic background, your genome, or your gender before you were born. Nobody asked you which privileges and/or liabilities you'd like to inherit. If you're born into an inner-city food desert, where supermarkets and fresh produce are in short supply, you'll probably grow up on a steady diet of processed, sugary foods, which means you'll be much more likely to develop obesity, diabetes, and/or heart disease, any one of which can have permanent, lifelong consequences.[629] Maybe you'll grow to resent your upbringing. Maybe you'll romanticize it. Maybe it'll help make you more resilient in the long run, or more cynical, or more enthusiastic about becoming a nutrition advocate. Whatever the outcome, these kinds of factors play into who you'll eventually become. Which means you may not be as free and self-determining as you think you are. Nobody is. And while it's a reductive oversimplification to say we're all just "products of our environment," neither are we the products of ourselves.

To be a human is to be "under the influence"—of friends, family, instincts, role models, the weather, economic constraints, maybe even the will of God. Even when making the most sober-minded and "objective" deci-sions, you don't choose to choose what you choose. And you definitely don't choose to want what you want. This is one of the governing assumptions of classical education, going all the way back to Aristotle: we *learn* to value what we value and see the way we see. We're impressionable by nature, born with an innate talent for mimicry. It's how we learn new skills and adapt to new environments. It's essential to our survival. Of course, we're also born with an array of instinctual urges and biologically driven desires, e.g.., to eat, sleep, avoid danger, copulate, etc. But a good portion of our personal preferences are "acquired tastes," learned through observation and imitation (a.k.a. mimesis).[630] They may seem "natural" to you, as if birthed spontane-ously from within, but most are not. Eleven-year-old girls aren't born hating themselves for having cankles and muffin tops. You have to *learn* that kind of self-loathing. Only then, when you're older, can you "freely choose" to devote yourself to a ceaseless regimen of dieting and exercise, so you can finally have "the body you always wanted" (which you didn't).

Being Is Becoming

To *be* is to *become*. On this point, modern neuroscience and philosophy agree with what Christian theologians have been saying for centuries.[631] Now if, like me, you are a recovering perfectionist, the word "becoming" sounds a little too much like "performing"—a.k.a. living a life of shame-based striving in hopes of one day becoming [fill in the shame-based blank]. Thankfully, the good news of Jesus promises the exact opposite: it is *God* who is the author and perfecter of our "becoming." So proclaimed Paul: "And we all, who with unveiled faces contemplate the Lord's glory, are be-ing transformed into his image with ever-increasing glory," or in another translation, "from one degree of glory to another."[632] "Sanctification," theo-logians call it, ultimately culminating in "glorification."[633] In the East, they prefer the term *theosis*: the pilgrim's process of growing in God's likeness, into closer representation of the divine image.[634] And this process is bound up with what Christians call "grace": the unmerited, transformative power of God, at work in the lives of ordinary people. In the end, it is *God* who awakens, empowers, and transforms pilgrims along the Way, just as it is *God* who gives us our new "selves."[635]

"And now, with God's help, I shall become myself," Kierkegaard de-clared.[636] It's a dramatically different way of depicting selfhood. Peculiar, even. And it rubs pretty hard against the American ideal of the "rugged in-dividual." But even more alien is the idea of living life by leaning forward—or, more accurately, by living in the present presence of eternity.

Allow me to unpack this idea by telling a brief story. And unlike the "Darwin ruined religion" tale, this one's actually true.

The Present Presence of Eternity

I have a friend who's a professional photographer. A couple times a year he invites fellow paparazzi to volunteer their time and take professional-quality portraits of the homeless. Most of their subjects have never had their hair done, never worn lipstick, mascara, or a necktie. Most have never had their picture taken. It's nothing fancy, just your standard "smile for the camera" Sears portrait. A few years ago, he organized an event for a group of prostitutes in L.A. No preaching, no conditions, no demanding that participants swear off licentious living. Just a chance to give people the opportunity to have a nice self-portrait, maybe something they could frame or give to their families.

Months later, my friend found out one of the women he photographed in L.A. had a young son. One night, she came home early and found him lying awake in bed, staring at that portrait of his mom as if it were a window into another possible world. He didn't say a word. He didn't explain what he was looking for, or why he was gazing so intently at the picture. Maybe he didn't even know. But she did. The portrait enthralled him because it encapsulated who and what his mother could be, what she was meant to be. And this realization haunted her. Nobody told her, "Listen, lady, you need to get it together. Become that woman in the photograph, if only for your son's sake. It's the right thing to do. Figure it out." But for some reason, she started wanting to. And slowly, sloppily, she did.

To be a follower of the Way is to be a conditioned by the future, not determined by the past.[637] The kingdom of God is this future; the revealed *telos* and irrevocable end of all history—including our own, personal histories. It towers above and shines a redemptive light upon all moments leading up to it, thereby changing the meaning of all moments. The Christian is peculiar in that she locates her self in God's kingdom, the Eternal Now: a forthcoming, redeemed, and eternal reality that has been made present to her, even today.[638] She basks in, and sees by, its light. She knows her true identity is "hidden in God," where she will discover and become—for the first time— her fullest and truest self.[639] Only then will she learn her Real Name, the name God has kept hidden from before the foundation of the world.[640]

Eternity, thus described, is not merely *quantitative* (i.e., an endless quantity of successive years), but *qualitative*: an immeasurably higher quality, or caliber, of life. Existence redefined. That's how Jesus talked about it: "I have come that they may have life, and have it to the full," or "abundantly," from the Greek *perissos*, for "over and above . . . superior, extraordinary, surpassing, uncommon . . ."[641] And he wasn't talking about some fanciful, faraway future, but life in the now: "On earth, as it is in heaven . . ."

The Christian is a little like that woman in L.A. who, being gripped by a vision of her future and eternal self, becomes what she sees. Eternity has been made present to her, though it remains yet to come. She trusts in the faithfulness of God to build this future for her, just as she trusts God's kingdom cannot be derailed by cruel fate or blind chance. This is the focus of her highest hopes. More than that, she stakes her very life on it—and as a consequence, she lives in constant tension with the way things are, the now that is fallen and finite. She is always on the move, always becoming, always leaning forward, living into God's kingdom.[642] Though her hands remain dirty with the ordinary labors of life, she has the look of someone standing on the tips of toes, caught up in eternity. And if, O skeptic, she is a bit too heavenly-minded for your liking, perhaps you can forgive her for that.

To *be* is to *become*—there's nothing inherently un-Christian about that phrase. God is complete; we are in process. God is eternal; we are in time. God *is*; we *become* . . . or, if you prefer, we "evolve." Theologians call it "soul making"[643] or "identity building," that messy, meandering sojourn by which we grow up and become ourselves.[644]

F-Words

In the end, the real bone of contention between creationism and evolution is *chance*, not *change*. Christians have no real problem with change. In fact, we're counting on it: "He [God] who began a good work in you *will* carry it on to completion until the day of Christ Jesus," Paul promises.[645] This is our hope. This is what we're after. We want to be "transformed" by the renewing of our minds.[646] We want to be changed, healed, and renewed, even as we long for *apocatastasis*, the "renewal of all things." And this is what God has promised—not as one of many possible outcomes, contingent upon "blind chance," but as the inexorable end of history.

Unfortunately, most modern-day conversations about evolution and religion never get this far. The average biblicist simply assumes that accepting Darwinism means rejecting the Bible—and, by extension, Jesus. That's been the party line ever since the Fundamentalist-Modernist Controversy of the 1920s, when evangelicals started adding all sorts of new and cumbersome conditions for membership, e.g., "Though shalt reject science."[647] But in refitting Christ with these updates, something essential has been lost—or, more accurately, *added to*—"mere" Christianity. And that's the great irony of it all: in an attempt to safeguard Christian orthodoxy from the threat of modern skepticism and secular science, Christianity itself evolved, becoming something new and different: fundamentalism, America's favorite F-word.

11

Jesus, Darwin, and the (Unintended) Evolution of Christianity

Right now I'm having amnesia and déjà vu at the same time. I think I've forgotten this before.

—STEVEN WRIGHT

How Evangelicalism Became Fundamentalism

THEY SAY THE CHIEF cause of problems is solutions. Some call it the "law of unintended consequences," and it's one of the more maddeningly ubiquitous aspects of the human condition. Remember how social media was supposed to make us feel *more* connected, not less? And credit cards were supposed to *relieve* financial stress, not create opportunities for more of it? Then there's the mechanical clock, invented by monks who wanted to maintain a more regular regimen of scheduled, spiritual activities. Little did they know their invention would one day make our ultra-fast-paced consumer culture possible. Without clocks, there'd be no factories, no deadlines or output quotas, no perpetual rush to "beat the clock."[648]

Even Christianity can't escape the law of unintended consequences. Christianity is, after all, a human endeavor, a "cultural system" of integrated rituals, symbols, and communally shared beliefs.[649] And, like participants in any other cultural system, Christians are more than capable of screwing things up.

In the Roaring Twenties, American evangelicals became even more suspicious of modern secularism, especially in the natural sciences. For a variety of reasons—some sensible, even noble—they perceived modernity as a problem needing to be solved. So while flappers were flapping and jazz cats were swingin,' evangelicals were busy preparing for an ensuing culture war against secular society. That's when the aforementioned Fundamentalist-Modernist Controversy boiled over onto the national stage.[650] It's also when denying science became a requirement for being a bona fide Christian—in twentieth-century America, at least (the jury's still out on the twenty-first).

As previously shown, it wasn't so much Darwinism that fomented fundamentalist fervor.[651] It was a particular interpretation of Darwin's ideas that struck fear in the hearts of evangelicals. More specifically, it was *social* Darwinism, a.k.a. "scientific racism," that made Christians like William Jennings Bryan ever more antsy about evolution. And I for one don't blame them. Not entirely, anyway.

Social Darwinism and the Scopes "Monkey" Trial

The year was 1925, just six years after WWI's bloody beginning. A Tennessee court found public schoolteacher John Scopes guilty of teaching evolution. Defense attorney Clarence Darrow represented Scopes, with William Jennings Bryan representing the fundamentalist/creationist camp. Despite winning the case, Bryan lost the hearts and minds of mainstream Americans, most of whom turned against fundamentalist Christianity. Darrow kicked Bryan's butt all over the courtroom, exposing Bryan's ignorance of science and inability to navigate complex questions about the historical accuracy of Scripture. 'Twas not his best day.

Like B. B. Warfield before him, Bryan was open to Darwinism during his younger years.[652] Then, around the turn of the century, things started to change. Bryan grew more concerned about how Darwinism was being (mis) used to justify racism, classism, economic exploitation, even genocide.[653] By the mid-1910s, WWI had claimed ten million lives—all in the name of nationalism and ethnic strife. Bryan worried Darwinism would ultimately reduce all of human history to a brutal contest of "survival of the fittest," which he called, "The law of hate . . . by which the strong crowd out and kill off the weak."[654] And Bryan had reason for concern, especially after reading Vernon Kellogg's *Headquarters Nights*, a written collection of conversations between Kellogg and German officers of Kaiser Wilhelm's military command.

Kellogg was an American humanitarian and accomplished scientist who served as a medical relief worker in Belgium during WWI. In 1916,

Kellogg had some disturbing exchanges with German officers and intellectuals who subscribed to a twisted interpretation of Darwinism.[655] To them, the whole story of history boiled down to a cruel competition between rival societies, where only the strong survive. Only through such struggle would humanity progress unto perfection: "This struggle not only must go on, for that is the natural law, but it *should* go on."[656] According to the logic of social Darwinism, the vanquishing of lesser peoples was a moral obligation, a.k.a. "The White Man's Burden." By conquering those less fit for survival, the Germans believed they would be providing humanity with a much-needed service. They'd accelerate the evolutionary process by weeding out the weak. How thoughtful of them. Sure, they wiped out half of Belgium and Northern France during WWI, but it was all for the best, "for the sake of the species." To Bryan, a life-long defender of the defenseless, the societal implications of Darwinism made evolution seem irredeemably dangerous. And in Bryan's defense, WWI-era literature like *The Passing of the Great Race* and *The Rising Tide of Color Against White World-Supremacy* makes *Atlas Shrugged* look like *The Giving Tree*.

Bryan's plan for stemming the tide of social Darwinism was simple: evolution would have to be banned from public schools and erased from the national consciousness. Unfortunately for everyone, it totally backfired.

The Scopes Trial got huge press coverage, with much of the media siding against Bryan.[657] Popular journalists like H. L. Mencken lampooned Bryan as a "buffoon"[658] and Bible-believing Christians as "morons."[659] With similar scorn, Darrow characterized Christianity as a "fool religion"[660] and, by trial's end, made his intentions clear: "We have the purpose of preventing bigots and ignoramuses from controlling the education of the United States."[661]

The trial was later reinterpreted in the play *Inherit the Wind* and its subsequent cinematic adaptations, all of which depicted Bryan as a backward, Bible-beating bully. In reality, Bryan was a three-time Democratic presidential nominee with a heroic record on humanitarian issues. Like many other evangelicals of his day, he was a champion of America's most vulnerable, a progressive social activist who fought tirelessly for the little guy.[662] And yeah, I just said that last part: while evangelicals have always been socially conscious activists, it wasn't until recently that "evangelical" became synonymous with Republican. Like many Democrats before the 1980s, including President Jimmy Carter (a born-again Southern Baptist), William Jennings Bryan was socially progressive and religiously conservative—and, therefore, almost unrecognizable to our twenty-first-century eyes. It was only after the "Monkey" Trial and ensuing Fundamentalist-Modernist Controversy that firm lines were drawn in the sand, forever dividing "conservative" evangelicals from "liberal" modernists.[663] The two estranged camps headed for opposing corners faster than a gym full of seventh-graders at a Sadie Hawkins dance. Evangelicalism's conversion to fundamentalism was all but complete.[664]

Disco, the Culture Wars, and the New Christian Right

Speaking of Jimmy Carter, the 1970s was a tumultuous time in American cultural history. That's when God finally got his own party, the Republican Christian Right.[665] Meanwhile, another groovy party was goin' down, courtesy of an almost inexhaustible outpouring of Bee Gees–inspired disco (I'll leave it to you to decide which was the better party). Throughout the 70s and into the 80s, conservative Christians grew increasingly suspicious of a new secular "consensus" that seemed to imperil America's moral fabric.[666] As a consequence, popular evangelicalism moved in an even more fundamentalist, biblicist direction. Soon, *secular* became a taboo term; like *Voldemort*, never to be uttered aloud. As throngs of fundamentalists retreated to the 'burbs, a small but vocal minority went on the political offensive, rebranding Jesus as commander-in-chief of a new crusade to legislate God's kingdom on earth.[667] It was a must-win culture war. And like most wars, victory would be achieved by whatever methods proved most "effective."

Not that winning is a bad thing, per se (unless it's 2011 and you're Charlie Sheen). To endorse *any* view wholeheartedly—be it democratic socialism or zone defense—means you think your view should prevail, perhaps peacefully, over other, competing views. Christians are no exception: "We Shall Overcome" was a gospel song long before it became a civil rights anthem. The New Testament says Jesus "disarmed the rulers and authorities" of this world "by *triumphing* over them . . ."[668] Hence the historically Christian motto, "Jesus is victor."

But Jesus' victory was won through longsuffering and love, not political coercion or executive order. His was a triumph "from below," not a theocratic decree "from above."[669] He was, as the Scriptures say, "despised and rejected . . . a man of sorrows, and acquainted with grief. . . and we esteemed him not."[670] Yet it was *this* man, we are told, who overcame the world.

But hey, a lot has changed since the first century. In an ultra-competitive modern marketplace of ideas, only the strong survive. So in the 1970s, the New Christian Right took a more pragmatic approach by consolidating political power. Jerry Falwell founded the Moral Majority and Pat Robertson the Christian Coalition in order to foil the forces of "secular science" and moral relativism.[671] Soon the Republican Party became mission control for conservative Christian political activism.

Meanwhile, evangelical theologians came together to try and buttress the Bible against modern criticism. In 1978, they issued a document called the "Chicago Statement on Biblical Inerrancy." Reverberating Warfield, it reads, "Scripture is without error or fault in *all* its teaching, no less in what it states about God's acts in creation, about the events of world history."[672] And that's been the biblicist party line ever since. Recently, prominent evangelical Albert Mohler echoed the Chicago Statement's position: "I do not allow *any* line of evidence from outside the Bible to nullify to the slightest degree the truthfulness of *any* text in *all* that the text asserts and claims."[673] So if, for example, paleontologists dig up evidence suggesting that humans have been around a lot longer than six thousand years, such extra-biblical evidence would be, by definition, inadmissible.

Pastor John MacArthur takes a similar stance, even when interpreting the creation stories in Genesis. Against other "ostensibly evangelical" theologians with "scientific and academic credentials," MacArthur, a bestselling evangelical author, argues that Christians are obligated to dismiss modern science and believe the earth was created in six literal, twenty-four-hour days. To him, it's a black-and-white issue. Not only are "old earth" evolutionists (e.g., most scientists) wrong, so are "old earth creationists," "theistic evolutionists," and other Christians who follow what MacArthur calls a "new trend" in trying to harmonize Scripture with science.[674] That would include Christians like Francis Collins (former director of the Human Genome Project), theologians N. T. Wright and Alister McGrath, Simon Conway Morris (Chair of Evolutionary Palaeobiology at Cambridge University), theoretical physicist John Polkinghorne, and Oxford philosopher Richard Swinburne, all of whom affirm some form of evolution.

MacArthur isn't alone in issuing these kinds of indictments. An online series called *Wretched* dedicated a whole webisode to explaining why real Christians can't possibly reconcile the Bible with evolution.[675] And their message hasn't fallen on deaf ears: when asked directly, roughly a third of Americans today reject evolution.[676]

John MacArthur is a smart guy. Studious. He knows his Bible forward and backward, and he's dead serious about devotion to Jesus.[677] But when it comes to the finer historical details of the creationism-vs.-evolutionism debate, MacArthur is incorrect.

First of all, it's MacArthur's literalism-or-else! approach that's the "new trend," not figurative interpretations of Genesis. Christians from Augustine to Galileo knew the difference between figurative and fictitious. They were fine with interpreting parts of the creation story non-literally. So was William Jennings Bryan, even in the midst of the Scopes Trial. Harkening to Woodrow's earlier question, "What difference can it make?" Bryan testified:

> I do not see that there is any necessity for construing the words, "the evening and the morning," as meaning necessarily a 24-hour day . . . I think it would be just as easy for the kind of God we believe in to make the earth in 6 days as in 6 years or in 6 million years or in 600 million years. I do not think it important whether we believe one or the other.[678]

Billy Graham said something similar in the 1960s:

> I think we have made a mistake by thinking the Bible is a scientific book . . . I believe that God created man, and whether it came by an evolutionary process and at a certain point He took this person or being and made him a living soul or not, does not change the fact that God did create man . . . whichever way God did it makes no difference as to what man is and man's relationship to God.[679]

Maybe MacArthur doesn't realize it, but creationism vs. evolution is a markedly modern, "American-specific" debate. Just ask N. T. Wright: "In

England, very few people have anything like the same hang ups about creation and evolution as you do in America, except where certain movements
in education have come across from America and got into our subculture as
well."[680] Since Darwin, scientists from virtually all fields have endeavored to
challenge and refine his basic ideas. The result has been a nearly universal
consensus in Darwin's favor.[681] Even among Christian believers, Darwinian
evolution is no longer considered a theory, but established fact.[682]

But fear not, fundamentalists: just because evolution is true doesn't
mean the Bible isn't. Darwin's triumph doesn't require us to subject the
Scriptures to the Thomas Jefferson redaction treatment. For one thing,
that would mean rejecting the biblical miracles (as Jefferson did), which
would also mean rejecting the creeds and the rule of faith, not to mention
multiple tenets of historic Christian orthodoxy, including Jesus' resurrection—which, in Paul's view, was essential to "mere" Christianity.[683] No resurrection, no overcoming the powers of evil and death, no redemption, no
kingdom of God.

But the doctrine of creation is different. "Incidental," Aquinas called
it. And since six-day creationism was never essential to Christian orthodoxy anyway, churchmen from Chesterton to MLK never felt obligated to
die on the creationist hill.[684] Neither did they look to Scripture as an all-
encompassing, infallible encyclopedia, let alone an "infallible blueprint" or
how-to manual. Instead, they relied upon Scripture as the unique, written
account of God's saving relationship with humanity: creation, fall, salvation,
and restoration. Even early fundamentalists like George Frederick Wright
suggested as much: "The utterances of the Bible are *not* infallible *except*
as pertaining to things 'necessary to be known, believed and observed for
salvation.'"[685] Aquinas made similar statements, centuries earlier:

> Other things are only incidental to faith insofar as they are treat-
> ed in Scripture, which faith holds to be promulgated under the
> dictation of the Holy Spirit, but which can be ignored by those
> who are not held to know scripture, such as many of the histori-
> cal works. On such matters even the saints disagree, explaining
> scripture in different ways. Thus with respect to the beginning of
> the world something pertains to the substance of faith, namely
> that the world began to be by creation, and all the saints agree in
> this. But *how* and in what order this was done pertains to faith
> only incidentally . . .[686]

Many of the orthodox "confessions of faith" make analogous assertions, effectively limiting the scope and authority of Scripture.[687] Yet here we are, and
the standoff between science and Scripture continues. Call it an ideological

hangover; the lingering effects of the Scopes Trial, when evangelicalism became fundamentalism, and biblicism became a bottom-line requirement for membership.

But most Americans have forgotten all this stuff. . . assuming we ever learned it in the first place. Evangelicals too. We're historical amnesiacs, the victims of "broken memory."[688] And since we don't know our own history, we can hardly imagine a pre-biblicist Christianity, before religion and reason became the bitterest of enemies.

How to Cause Problems

Heaping my freshly washed clothes in a pile on the floor was supposed to solve the how-can-I-dry-my-clothes-without-exerting-even-the-slightest-smidgen-of-effort? problem. Instead, my little laundry experiment created new, unforeseen problems (and possibly new DNA). Fundamentalism was supposed to bolster the faith and keep skepticism at bay. But in keeping with the ever operative, always irritating law of unintended consequences, the fundamentalist solution created new problems. And we are its direct beneficiaries.

That's partly why so many fundamentalists end up punting after a while. The more you learn about human and natural history, the less you can swallow the handbook model of Scripture. And that's a big, big problem for American Christianity. Maybe an insurmountable one.

Unless the Bible was never intended to be an "inerrant blueprint" in the first place.

12

The Gratuitous God
(Or, Why I Am Not Bertrand Russell)

Theologians they don't know nothing about my soul.

—Wilco[689]

The one who prays is a theologian, and the one who is a theologian, prays.

—Evagrius Ponticus[690]

Of Gods and God

In his book, *The Power of God's Names*, pastor Tony Evans concedes, "The word 'god' can be somewhat vague."[691] True, if understated. *Somewhat* vague? Which "god" are we talking about? The Cosmic Clockmaker of deism, who winds up the universe and lets it run its course? A "God of the gaps" to fill the holes in our scientific knowledge? Or maybe a wish-fulfilling Santa-God who bestows presents upon deserving little girls and boys? We tell him what goodies we want, cross our fingers, and hope we've been good enough to get 'em. Conveniently, we need only visit Santa-God once a year, at your local mall, somewhere between Nordstrom and that somehow-still-in-business phone accessory kiosk. Or perhaps God is more like what Ricky Gervais calls an "invisible, free babysitter," someone whom overwhelmed mothers can call upon before hurrying off to work and leaving their children to the fates.[692] This deity functions as a readily accessible good luck charm, a much-needed source of consolation for the credulous. And don't forget about Guardian Angel God: a divine benefactor who's there to whisper you hints, help you find your keys, and guide you to that ever-elusive parking space. Like Athena to her human devotees in one of Homer's epics, a god to grant you favor.

If the aforementioned alternatives sound too superstitious for your liking, you might want to go with the Divine Moralist option: the cold, impersonal God of stuffy schoolmasters and bossy busybodies. The good thing about this God is that he's easily pleased: be polite, say no to drugs, don't mock the disabled or cuss in public, and you're pretty much good to go—in which case, Jesus' real purpose was to clarify a checklist of dos and don'ts. You can get a lot of mileage out of this kind of God. He/she/it can infuse your life with some much-needed structure. But if the divine moralist stops working for you, as he/she/it surely will, there's always pantheism's God: the God who is everything.

To paraphrase Marcus Aurelius: everything is interwoven, and the web is holy. That's pretty much pantheism in a tweet-friendly nutshell. Pantheists conceive of God as the sum total of all that exists. Call it "Nature" with a capital N, or "Reason" with an uppercase R. The advantage to this kind of deity is that he/she/it is amenable to commonsense observation: just open your eyes, pay attention, and you can find God in everything. So if you want to know what Everything God is like, you need to learn about what the universe is like. And if you don't like what the universe is like, with its millions of dying stars and dying children—you're not going to be thrilled about Everything God.

But fear not: you can always go with Gut-Level God, the God of your intuition (a.k.a. theosophy). Unlike the rigid religious systems of grumpy old men, you don't have to learn about Gut-Level-God, since he/she/it is already baked into your being at birth. Maybe you experience Gut-Level God when you look up at the stars at night. The sensation wells up within you, like a warm and rising tide, until you feel heavier and yet somehow lighter, all at once.

But if you really think about it, do such experiences require the existence of an actual deity, or even a belief in one? Atheist Diana Nyad thinks not.[693] In a conversation with Oprah, the famous swimmer explained, "I can stand at the beach's edge with the most devout Christian, Jew, Buddhist, and weep with the beauty of this universe . . ." at which point Winfrey interrupted: "Well I don't call you an atheist then . . . I think if you believe in the awe and the wonder and the mystery then *that* is what God *is*." But Nyad prefers not to use the word "God," since it implies a "presence . . . a creator or an overseer."[694]

First point: for an atheist, Nyad has a pretty good grasp on what the Abrahamic faiths (Muslims, Jews, and Christians) believe, which is that God is a *presence*, divine and distinct, and not merely an attribute of the universe, like gravity or grief. Second, their conversation offers an informative glimpse into Oprah's concept of God—namely, that experiencing awe is tantamount to encountering the divine. God, thus imagined, is not a Someone Else, but something that emerges from inside, an overpowering emotional experience. Much like the aforementioned versions of divinity, this God requires no supernatural revelation from on high; no good news, nor "news" of any kind.[695] Which is kinda nice, if you don't like surprises.

But here, the Christian is naggingly unique. Unlike pantheists, naturalists, and deists, Christians think of God as having revealed something otherwise inscrutable in the person of Jesus, something so counterintuitive that it compels us to rethink what we mean by the word "God." That's why Christians call Jesus the *final* revelation of God, the ultimate and definitive disclosure of the Uncreated Creator.[696] What's more, this disclosure is supposed to be good news—and not just "good" in an abstract or impersonal sense, but good *for us*. And Christians believe Jesus still reveals himself to ordinary human beings, just as he did to his disciples on the dusty roads of Palestine, all those centuries ago.[697]

But what, exactly, is this "news," and what, if anything, is so good about it?

"Getting" God

The good news of Jesus is, first and foremost, more than words (references to 80s power ballads unintended). This news is more than mere information *about* God and closer to what evangelicals rightly call a "personal encounter"—like how I got to know my old mechanic on a personal level. Which is not to say knowing *about* someone isn't important. Part of why I feel qualified to say, "I know my wife," is that I know specific things about her: her affinity to Gerbera daisies and early morning runs, her disdain for TV violence and love of laughter, her almost pathological inability to follow recipes, etc. This is meaningful information. Good stuff. But it neither implies nor necessitates an intimate, reciprocal relationship between persons. With a little effort, any competent stalker can acquire the same data.

You can know a whole lot about someone without ever knowing them as a person—a "thou," an unfathomably deep "other."[698] You can read up on Augustine all you want. You can load up your iPad with his complete works, memorize all the pertinent biographical info about his life, why he did what he did and wrote what he wrote, how he influenced Western culture, etc. But you'll never really *know* Augustine the way his friends did. It's hard to imagine ever having a dynamic, interpersonal relationship with something you can access on your iPad. Just ask anybody who downloaded the iPal—a.k.a. "Your Best Virtual Friend"—which is both a real thing and a sure sign of the apocalypse.

Evangelicals are known for stressing the importance of right belief. "Knowing God" necessitates knowing important things *about* God—that he exists, created the world, is holy, just, and good; that he loves us, cares about how we live our lives, is willing and able to forgive; that he sent his only Son to establish his kingdom and reconcile the world to himself. To "get saved" means to "realize and confess in earnest that Jesus died for your sins, and he'll return the favor with eternal life."[699] In contemporary Christianese, this is the "Sinner's Prayer," the basic flow chart you need to follow to complete the transaction and yield the desired results (e.g., entry into heaven).[700] It's about believing the right things in the right order.

But our evangelical ancestors had a much more nuanced understanding of faith. According to John Wesley, orthodox opinions are but a "very slender part" of "true religion."[701] And Wesley weren't no watered-down liberal. It was he who inspired the great American revivalists of the eighteenth and nineteenth centuries. Conservative Christians still regard him as a hero, one of the great pioneers of modern evangelicalism. Yet, Wesley realized that "right opinions" about God only got you so far. Because real, transformative intimacy always involves more than downloading data. You don't "get" God by performing a series of intellectual maneuvers in your head. The God revealed in Jesus is neither a conclusion to be drawn, nor the result of right thinking—because the Uncreated Creator isn't the result of anything.

Every Man a Liar!

Like Augustine, Aquinas, and Wesley before him, A. W. Tozer believed the Bible to be divinely inspired. But when it came to communicating holy mysteries, Tozer acknowledged the limits of language, including even biblical language: "The effort of inspired men to express the ineffable has placed a great strain upon both thought and language in the Holy Scriptures."[702] Simply put, God is beyond words, incapable of being adequately translated, "ineffable." Some saints go as far as to say that the more you know God, the less you can encapsulate him in speech.[703] With this in mind, Gregory of Nyssa warned, "Any man who entrusts to language the task of presenting the ineffable Light is really and truly a liar; not because of any hatred on his part of the truth, but because of the feebleness of his instrument for expressing the thing thought of."[704]

Language is a "feeble instrument," ill-suited to the task. But speak we must—which is why Jesus-lovers often resort to metaphor, as did our apostolic ancestors, who authored the Bible. Hence, God is a "rock," solid and enduring,[705] yet also tender: "As a mother comforts her child, so I will comfort you."[706] Words, allegories, images, gestures . . . that's all we got. God is both "king" and "servant," "fortress" and "fire," "breath" and "bread."[707] To speak of God is to speak in symbols, songs, poetry, and parables; and sometimes, even silence.

Reminds me of Black Moses. Not the Isaac Hayes record (which still holds up, by the way). I mean the brawny, bellicose fourth-century saint, not known for being particularly soft-spoken:

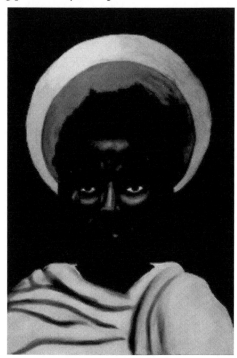

"Moses the Black," they called him. The Morpheus of monasticism, the Mace Windu of Christian mysticism. An intimidating Ethiopian of ill repute, Black Moses spent his younger years looting, brawling, and beating up on the locals. At some point he came across a group of hospitable monks who lived by the Nile. Impressed by their kindness and conviction, he left his life of crime and went to live among them. Eventually, Moses became known as the "apostle of non-violence," mostly because he refused to retaliate when some desert marauders beat him to the point of death (even though he probably could've kicked their collective asses). As the last bit of breath was leaving his lips, a fellow monk asked Moses one final question: "Moses, what do you see?" Caught up in a vision, Moses responded with a question of his own: "Is it better to say nothing?" His friend answered, "Yes, my child, it is better to say nothing."[708] And with that, Moses the Black passed unceremoniously from life into silence.

Science and Silence

We're like that, we humans. Our words fail us. So much the more when speaking of God. In a well-known Christmas sermon, Bonhoeffer preached:

> It is only with stammering tongues that we can speak his name or seek to describe what is embraced by this name. Words limp and stumble when they attempt to say who this child is. Yes, when human lips try to express the name of this child, strange word-pictures emerge, which we do not know: "Wonderful Counselor," "Mighty God," "Prince of Peace."[709]

That's what theology *is*, by the way: the fallible quest to understand and articulate what God has revealed in Jesus.[710] Theology is the study of God (*theos*), just as biology is the study of life (from the Greek, *bios*). Biologists want to know what organic life is actually like, not what they wish it were like. That's why they're called scientists, not science-fictionists. They observe, theorize, experiment, draw conclusions. Same goes for anthropology, the study of *anthropos* (Greek for "human"). Anthropologists aren't in the speculation business. Their goal is to understand human cultures as they actually are. Likewise, criminology is the study of crime, cosmology is the study of the origin of the cosmos, and *Vibeology* is a rather regrettable Paula Abdul album from the early 90s. Zing!

I realize most people don't compare science and theology these days. But in terms of their respective histories, goals, and methods, they actually have a lot in common. The biologist Thomas Huxley put it nicely: "Science seems to me to teach in the highest and strongest manner the great truth which is embodied in the Christian conception of entire surrender to the will of God. Sit down before the facts as a little child . . ."[711]

Honest theologians, like honest scientists, are not in the business of speculation. They're not trying to impose wish-fulfilling fantasies upon the object under investigation (God).[712] Instead, the theologian observes, re-flects upon, and interprets what God has said and done. She sits before the data, "as a little child," then tries to make sense of it—which means bending her thought and language to accommodate newfound, divine realities. This is the theologian's proper task (and we're all theologians, by the way).

All this means that doctrine—even orthodox doctrine—doesn't lead to divine encounter. Faith seeks understanding, not the other way around. You don't *think* God into existence by memorizing or accepting certain theo-logical concepts. The opposite's true: Christian doctrine has always taken time to develop and crystallize. In the ancient world, for any doctrine to be considered orthodox, it first had to "win acceptance" among the practicing communities of faith.[713] And that makes a lot of modern fundamentalists uneasy—especially those who frame "faith" as the result of right thinking. If *p* then *q*. That's how you "get" God.

But that's not really true to the history or lived experience of Jesus' early followers. The whole thing was a lot messier and more organic than that. As evangelical luminaries like John Stott have conceded, a full-blown doctrine of atonement (reparation for human sin) took years to develop.[714] Which is not to say the apostles were casual in their approach to theology. These were highly dedicated and attentive folk. They knew full well that Jesus was the Christ. They knew he would die "in our place," to reconcile the world to God, by doing something we couldn't do for ourselves. But *how* that mysterious transaction took place was a brain-bending, time-con-suming puzzle, even for the earliest disciples (a.k.a. "learners"). *How* Jesus' crucifixion "atoned" or made up for humanity's failures took a long time to think through. And so it remains unto this day, as Christians continue to unpack and debate the doctrine of atonement.[715] Faith seeks understanding, not the other way round.

It Starts with God

"We love," the Bible says, "because he first loved us."[716] God makes the first move. Only then do theologians scurry around and try to figure out what happened. God speaks first, as he loves first, as he *is* first.[717] Only then do we acclimatize our ideas to what God has revealed, that we might better understand divinity—and, in the process, ourselves. Some call it "kneeling theology." It's an enterprise fueled not by speculation or projection, but by humility, openness, and reflection. It requires a voluntary decision to relin-quish control and hold space for God to be God.[718] This means listening, learning, pondering, and praying.

God is known for many things, but not conformity. God speaks; we listen. And if we listen intently, our preconceived notions, priorities, even our deeply held desires will change. "Do not conform to the pattern of this world," Paul implored, "but be transformed by the renewing of your mind."[719] Maybe we *thought* we knew what words like "love" and "power" meant. Then, we encounter Jesus and see how *he* loved, what *he* meant by "power," and suddenly . . . or slowly . . . our worldview gets turned on its head.[720] Only then do we begin questioning our lifelong values and hidden assumptions. Only then do we consider the possibility of refining, maybe even repudiating, those habits of thought and behavior that, to us, have always seemed normal. As Flannery O'Connor promised, "You shall know the truth, and the truth shall make you odd."[721]

Sounds unpleasant. It can be. But there's no getting around it: honest theology involves a whole lot of squirming, since hearing God "speak" means encountering Someone Else. More dauntingly, it means being fully seen and fully known.[722] What does "intimate knowledge" mean, if it not something more than mere recognition, i.e., "I know what *that* is . . ."? That's not how we talk when speaking of someone we know in the deepest possible way. And make no mistake: whatever else the Christian means by "God," she means a *Person*—a unique Person, no doubt, divine and eternal, but a Person, nonetheless; Someone to be known—not like a historian knows Augustine, but like a blind mother knows her child.

I recently had a child of my own. A little boy named Grey.

Once, in a fit of cute aggression, I briefly considered eating him.

Fear not: Grey got the last laugh by evacuating his bowels all over our Navajo white carpet.

As the months rolled by, Grey got progressively cuter and less lizard-like:

But in the beginning he was a tiny tyke, so small that he didn't even it into a size zero (which raises some serious metaphysical questions: How can you be too small to be *zero*? So, if he was never born, would there be *more* space occupied in the universe?). Grey's skin felt like the molted coat of a komodo dragon. But to me, none of that mattered. Every day I'd hurry home to see him. I'd burst through the front door and make a beeline for little Grey. Then I plop him down on the couch and lie down next to him, and we just sit there and smile at each another.

Funny thing is, Grey was really bad at almost everything he did: peeing, sleeping, pooping, all of it. Actually, he was always pretty good at pooping. Prolific, you might say. But the rest of it, just awful. Every time we'd put him down, he'd put up a fight (and who decided the appropriate nomenclature for getting a child to sleep was to "put him down"? What is he, a Clydesdale?). Grey fussed at bedtime, just as he fussed whenever it was time to feed, whether by bottle or breast. All of this I found baffling. I can't remember a time in my life when I would've willingly refused food, sleep, or teat. But not baby Grey. He wouldn't have it. And honestly, I could care less. Because I love and enjoy him, and that's pretty much it.

Friends and Books

An Eastern Orthodox theologian named Kallistos Ware tells the story of a mystic who spent hours a day in silent prayer. His friends couldn't make any sense of it: Was there really that much to talk to God about? Finally, one of his friends asked him what he was doing in all that silence. The mystic answered, "I just sit and look at God and God sits and looks at me."[723] No agendas, no to-do lists, no quid pro quo. Just sitting there like two old friends, taking each other in. Fully known, fully loved.

In one of Scripture's more peculiar passages, Jesus has the audacity to call the disciples "friends"—*his* friends, the friends of God.[724] As anyone who's ever had a friend can tell you, friendship means a lot more than being a faithful servant or attentive follower. Friendship means knowing and being known. It means mutual enjoyment—loving and being loved. "Greater love has no one than this," Jesus said, "to lay down one's life for one's friend."[725]

I never read a line about divine friendship in Aristotle, Locke, Plotinus, or Hegel. They never talked about enjoying a personal, loving relationship with Reason, Nature, Nous, or Geist[726] That's not to say philosophy is fruitless, or that mathematics and formal logic are trivial pursuits. Far from it. There are remarkable insights to be found in Plato and the *Principia Mathematica*, just as there are moments sublime in Persian poetry. But to paraphrase Bertrand Russell, no matter how much you love mathematics, it'll never love you back.[727] It'll never drink you in, or weep with you in solidarity. Maybe you're moved by the sheer magnificence of nature, but the feeling will never be mutual. You'll never inspire Planck's constant to dance, or a painted canvas to rejoice over you with singing. They'll never really know you, or love you—and they certainly won't forgive you.

But, in fairness, neither will the Bible.

Putting the F.U.N. Back in Fundamentalism

I don't mean to dis the Good Book, but it is, after all, a *book*—an "it," a *thing*. A very special thing, no doubt: the unique, written record of God's revelation to humanity; but a thing, nonetheless.[728] As A. W. Tozer explained, Scripture is a means to an end, not the end itself: "It is not mere words that nourish the soul, but *God Himself* . . . and until the hearers find God in personal experience they are not the better for having heard the truth."[729] Likewise, the great Punjabi saint, Sadhu Sundar Singh, wrote, "His [Christ's] words are spirit and life . . . life can be infused only into life, not into the pages of a book."[730]

You can know the whole Bible by heart without ever having any heartfelt knowledge of God. Just ask my old New Testament professor, who started our first class with the following memorable admission: "I've always been fascinated by the Bible. I'm a lifelong fan. But I don't have faith. Maybe faith is an illusion. Maybe it's a gift. I see it sometimes in other people, and sometimes I admire it. But it's not mine." This lady is a gem: kindhearted, generous, sharp as a tack. She knows the Bible better than most Christians. But she's not a person of faith (her assessment, not mine). Maybe she's an atheist. Maybe she's agnostic. She might even be a closet theist. But affirming the existence of God isn't the same as knowing and loving God—or knowing that God loved you first. Besides, you don't "think" your way into experiencing *anybody's* love for you, much less the love of God, who is "light unapproachable."[731]

In an online post entitled "You Can Prove the Bible's Authority!," pastor David C. Pack asks, "What God would write an Instruction Book on how to live, command it be followed as His Word, and then offer no *proof* that it is?"[732] A fair question, especially if that's what the Bible is supposed to be: a compendium of divine directives. There's something appealing about that kind of holy book, and by implication, that kind of God: functional, undeniable, and necessary—or "F.U.N.," for short—a God you can *prove*. A F.U.N. God makes the world seem smaller, more manageable. I think that's why I took such a shine to fundamentalism in my early twenties. I liked the feeling of being in control—and, more importantly, in the right. Part of me still does. But compare pastor Pack's perspective with John Calvin's: "Those who wish to *prove* to unbelievers that Scripture is the Word of God are acting foolishly, for only by *faith* can this be known."[733] And it's not like Calvin held the Bible in low regard. He called it the "Word of God" about a zillion times in his *Institutes*. But Calvin didn't think of Scripture or its contents as something self-evident.[734] Instead, he believed the Bible only "seriously affects us" through the "inner persuasion" of the Holy Spirit.[735] Otherwise, it's just a book on a shelf, an inert text whose true spiritual significance remains undiscovered.[736]

Love and Art

Love, like art, makes the world bigger. It stretches the boundaries of our hearts and awakens new hungers and hopes. Moral rigidity doesn't do that. "Right opinions" don't do that. Neither do half-hearted clichés, like, "Things happen for a reason." At the end of the day, believing in a Creator doesn't do all that much, even if said Creator is rationally defensible and/or logically necessary; a First Domino to set all other dominos in motion, a.k.a. "the god of the philosophers."[737] As anyone who's familiar with Greek tragedies can attest, the mere existence of a Creator doesn't tell you all that much about said Creator; whether he/she/it cares about anyone or anything—let alone *you*. Maybe you're not even a blip on God's radar. Or maybe God thinks of you often, but only in frustration and disappointment, like how I think about Comcast. So you believe in God. Good for you. "Even the demons believe," Scripture says.[738] But does God believe in you?

Sure, I guess if you're sufficiently creative and optimistic, you can dream up a construct and call it "Love." But that's not the same as *being* loved, or knowing how God feels about you. It's not the same as encountering the God who wants to heal you, nourish you, and make you clean. Nor is it the same as recognizing that you could use a good cleaning.[739]

I Hold These Truths to Be Obscure

And now for an unpopular admission, especially for a history teacher: I have some serious issues with America's Founding Fathers —and, more specifically, with the documents they penned. So where's the beef? Let's start at the very beginning, a very good place to start:

> We hold these truths to be self-evident, that all men are created equal, that they are endowed by their Creator with certain

unalienable Rights, that among these are Life, Liberty and the pursuit of Happiness.

First of all, that's a run-on sentence, Mr. Jefferson. Second, does "men" include women, slaves, non-Whites, etc.? (it would take another two-plus centuries for America to answer that question). Finally, I don't think *any* of Jefferson's truths are self-evident. Certainly not by twenty-first-century standards.

Were it up to me, I would've kicked off the Declaration of Independence like this:

> We hold these truths to be self-evident: the existence of a personal, rational, benevolent God who guarantees our unalienable rights is anything but obvious. It's not even clear that there *is* a Creator, much less a series of rights said Creator has bestowed upon each individual.

And that's probably when Franklin, Jefferson, and Co. would've kicked my bony butt out of the Continental Congress. But honestly, when I look out at the world, "through a glass darkly," I don't see irrefutable evidence for a beneficent God whose main purpose is to safeguard our individual rights. I see rampant injustice, ambivalence, and ambiguity. Like the prophet Jeremiah, I see the "wicked prosper," even as the helpless suffer.[740] I see as much evidence for a world ruled by what Darwin called "cruel and malignant spirits"[741] as I do Jefferson's egalitarian Creator. And I'm not alone in this.

God of the Gaps

Ever since the Fundamentalist-Modernist Controversy of the 1920s, Christian conservatives have taken to depicting "faith" in a number of novel ways: as an emotional experience to be replicated, or the "therefore" at the conclusion of a logical argument (at which point you "get it"); as an unwavering commitment to "family values", or confidence in the inerrancy of Scripture, etc. The operating assumption is that, for God to be *real*, God's got to be F.U.N.—functional, undeniable, and necessary. We *need* God to fill gaps in our knowledge and explain how we got here: the origins of life, the big bang, the fine-tuning of the universe, etc. We *need* God to give us a firm basis for things like morality, democracy, objective truth, etc.[742] We *need* God to ensure the basic premises of existence, lest we lose ourselves in a quagmire of ethical relativism and existential ambiguity. To summarize, God exists because we need him to exist. God begins where science and reason end— and his main (and only?) job is to provide solid ground for us to stand on.

Seventy years ago, the Cambridge chemist, Charles A. Coulson, warned, "There is no 'God of the gaps' to take over at those strategic places where science fails; and the reason is that gaps of this sort have the unpreventable habit of shrinking"[743] (Galileo issued a similar caution, centuries earlier). And it's not as though Coulson wanted to forward the atheist cause. He wasn't saying that science had somehow supplanted religion, or that it was on the cusp of doing so. Coulson was a devout churchman and man of faith, so it's not like he didn't believe in God. Just not the "God of the gaps."

Despite Coulson's warnings, the scramble to find "gaps" for God to fill goes on, even today. Creationists keep debating evolutionists, usually culminating in Neil deGrasse Tyson or Bill Nye the Science Guy cleaning some unfortunate Christian's clock. And honestly, I kinda sympathize with the creationists here—and not just because I like rooting for the underdog. Truth is, I envy the biblicist's single-mindedness. The sense of certainty and confidence. I like it when my beliefs are held up as self-evident to anyone with half a brain who's willing to look. It gives me permission to be annoyed by those who deny what I affirm. But like most ego-feeding propositions, it's a dead end.

The main problem with the "God of the gaps" is that it relegates God to a supporting role. A F.U.N. God is, primarily, a practical God. Useful. Expedient for our human purposes. Divinity, thus defined, becomes predictable and utilitarian; a necessary cog in the grand mechanism of the cosmos, like gravity. No disrespect intended: gravity is, after all, a vital force of the universe. Is gravity *functional*? Quite. *Necessary* for my way of life? Absolutely. *Undeniable*? Yes, thanks to Newton and the consensus of modern science. But like other physical forces in the universe, I have no meaningful or transformative relationship with gravity. It doesn't empower me to love my neighbor, and certainly not my enemy. *Gravity* doesn't even inspire me . . . but in fairness, neither have most of Bullock's films since *Miss Congeniality 2: Armed and Fabulous*. Zing!

Some Other Stuff We Don't Need God For

I'll say this for humanity: we know how to forge order out of chaos. We are pattern-seeking primates. Meaning-making machines. Subconsciously, almost compulsively, we construct coherent systems of symbols to help us make sense of the world and get our bearings.[744] We create governments, ideologies, rituals, worldviews, and kingdoms.[745] And we're really, really good at it.

Early Christians called Jesus "the Way," but surely, he's not the *only* way to get by in the world. You don't really *need* Jesus if you want to organize

people and get things done. A little vision, some charisma, and an Instagram account should do the trick. Do we really need God's help here? Is
that really what Jesus came to reveal—an ethos? A worldview among other
worldviews? There were already plenty of worldviews around before Jesus
came, and we've come up with an impressive list of new ones since. There's
fascism, feudalism, scientism, individualism, communism, nationalism,
even pathological optimism (more on that in the coming chapters). Lots of
"kingdoms" to choose from, lots of functional "-isms" available, each with
its own inner logic. And some do a decent job of making sense of things.

Given humanity's outstanding capacity for kingdom building, it
doesn't seem like we really need Jesus to give us his—especially when you
consider what his kingdom really entails: loving and forgiving your enemies.
Christopher Hitchens thought this was one of Christianity's most deranged
aspects: "Nothing, nothing could be more suicidal and immoral than that
. . . We have to survive our enemies. We have to learn to *destroy* them!"[746]
And if we take life at all seriously, didn't Hitch have a point? Why should
MLK have forgiven his assailants? Did he even have the right to? Can any
of us honestly accept such an imbalanced, unjust resolution to things?[747] Is
there any better reason to reject Jesus and his kingdom than this?

The Gratuitous God

Several years ago, Richard Dawkins interviewed Father George Coyne, an
accomplished scientist in his own right. As expected, Dawkins questioned
Coyne on whether God was still necessary. Has not modern science rendered God "increasingly superfluous"? Pushing further, Dawkins asked,
"What's the point of believing in God at all?" Father Coyne's response was
surprising, especially for a man of the cloth: "The God in whom I believe is
a God who gave himself superfluously, *whether I 'needed' him or not* . . . He
gave himself superfluously, gratuitously. I didn't reason my way to God. I
didn't work my way to God. I didn't earn this faith in God. And this faith is
nothing other than *God himself.*"[748]

"Superfluous"? As in, *unnecessary*? Coyne seems oddly uninterested
in the F.U.N. deity of modern-day fundamentalism. Is it really possible that
God gave himself to a world where he might be overlooked, deemed unnecessary, or even rejected? Isn't being indispensable the highest possible
virtue, the goal to which we should all aspire—including God? Apparently
not. At least, not for Coyne. Nor for Dietrich Bonhoeffer, who was well
aware of the declining status of religion in the modern world. Like Coyne,
Bonhoeffer didn't think the shrinking of the "gaps" was such a bad thing—
and not because he'd abandoned his faith (which he surely did not). Rather,

Bonhoeffer believed the God who functions as a logical, practical footing for our lives is *not* the God whom Jesus came to reveal—which may be why Jesus spent so little time explaining the inner workings of the cosmos, and even less time explaining himself.

During his exchange with Dawkins, Coyne stumbled upon a possibility to which Bonhoeffer had alluded, decades earlier—namely, that in Jesus, God comes to us as something other than a functional, explanatory deity whose purpose is to answer questions like, "Where'd we come from?" Not that these are bad questions, per se. They're just not the sorts of questions Jesus was interested in addressing. And this is something most modern atheists don't seem to understand . . . with the possible exception of Terry Eagleton. Ever the contrarian, Eagleton takes an almost impish delight in reminding his unbelieving comrades: "Christianity was never meant to be an *explanation* of anything in the first place."[749]

Sounds strange coming from an avowed Marxist/atheist, but when it comes to Christian orthodoxy, Eagleton hits the nail on the head. Because faith isn't something we "need" in order to explain or navigate the world. Far from practical, faith is rife with paradox. It transcends the boundaries of human thought, which is precisely why it must be *given*.[750] "It is by grace you have been saved, through faith," the Bible says, "and this is not from yourselves, it is the gift of God— not by works, so that no one can boast."[751] You don't earn faith through behavior modification or rule following (a.k.a. moralism). You don't "get" it through cognitive gymnastics (what Bonhoeffer called "intellectual works righteousness").[752] There's no seamless transition from unbelief to belief, no "proof" whose conclusion is God.[753]

I'm not trying to depict Christianity as utterly opposed to reason. There are some extremely clever, even compelling arguments for God's existence.[754] But deducing the existence of a bottle of 1787 Chateau Lafite is a lot different than tasting it.

Which leads me to Coyne's second, more important point: namely, that the main thing God gives us in Jesus is not information about the universe, nor even information about himself, but *himself*.

Karl Barth: Mall Cop

In the Roaring Twenties, when William Jennings Bryan was getting his Scopes Trial on and the Fundamentalist-Modernist Controversy was heating to a boil, a feisty theologian named Karl Barth was making an altogether different commotion across the Atlantic. Barth kicked over a theological anthill by reminding the modern world of the real "content" of Christian revelation. And what is that mysterious content? It's neither a set of instructions to be followed, nor evidence for God's existence, nor even "right opinions" *about* God, but *God himself*—God in God's fullness, the God who is not an idea.[755] That's why premodern Christians were so adamant about reading Scripture christologically: because Jesus is the point of the whole story, the full and final revelation to which both testaments point. And if the atheists and agnostics are right, if God really is more mysterious than obvious, then we need God to *reveal* himself to us.[756] More than that, we need God to *give* himself to us. And that divine self-gift is Jesus of Nazareth, the Eternal Word "made flesh," the "supreme revelation" of God.[757]

The Bible calls Jesus "Emmanuel," meaning, "God with us." That's the gift. That's the primary "content" of revelation, the point of it all, the good news to which the Bible bears witness. And in the final analysis, that's what we're really after: not proof of God's existence, but experience of God's presence. We want to know, in the deepest, most personal way, that God loves us and is with us, here and now, in the Real World. And that's precisely what we get. That's the gift, given freely and gratuitously, received only by faith (*sola fide*). And the pilgrim's greatest temptation is to change "faith" into what Kierkegaard called "another kind of certainty"—something we can *think* ourselves into.[758] Because faith is a *miracle*: something that can never, ever happen, under any imaginable circumstances—even a little bit—ever.

Except when it does.

13

Bottom's Up!

Bury me on my face . . . Because, in a little while,
everything will be turned upside down.

—Diogenes the Cynic[759]

Any scene such as a landscape can sometimes be more clearly
and freshly seen if it is seen upside down.

—G. K. Chesterton.[760]

The way up is the way down.

—Richard Rohr[761]

When in Doubt, Ask a Fictional Hindu

In *Life of Pi*, a young Hindu boy named Piscine is propelled by an insatiable spiritual curiosity. Upon learning of the Christian doctrine of the incarnation, Piscine—or "Pi," for short—finds himself frustrated and yet fascinated, all at the same time. His ruminations are worth quoting in full:

> That a god should put up with adversity, I could understand. The gods of Hinduism face their fair share of thieves, bullies, kidnappers and usurpers . . . Adversity, yes. Reversals of fortune, yes.

179

Treachery, yes. But *humiliation? Death?* I couldn't imagine Lord Krishna consenting to be stripped naked, whipped, mocked, dragged through the streets and, to top it off, crucified—and at the hands of mere humans, to boot. I'd never heard of a Hindu god dying . . . It was wrong of this Christian God to let His avatar die. That is tantamount to letting a part of Himself die. For if the Son is to die, it cannot be fake. If God on the Cross is God shamming a human tragedy, it turns the Passion of Christ into the Farce of Christ. The death of the Son must be real . . . But once a dead God, always a dead God, even resurrected. The Son must have the taste of death forever in His mouth . . . Why would God wish that upon Himself? Why not leave death to the mortals?[762]

A reasonable question. What kind of deity would willingly endure such abject humiliation? "At the hands of mere humans," no less? What could be more upside down, more theologically absurd? In the Greek pantheon, Hephaestus dishonored his mother, Hera, by binding her to her golden throne. But at least that was god-on-god crime. At least Hera suffered humiliation by a fellow divinity, not some lowly human henchmen.[763] Only in the Christian story do we find a God who allows himself to be disgraced by mere mortals, the work of his own hands, and all without lifting a holy finger in retaliation. No angry threats hurled down from the cross. Not a single "You'll pay for this!" or "My dad can beat up your dad!" to those who disparaged and denied him. Instead, Jesus prayed the unthinkable, the unprayable: "Father, forgive them, for they know not what they do."[764]

Self-Emptying Divinity

The great Japanese author, Shusaku Endo, offered the following reflections on Christ's self-sacrificial love:

Regarding those who deserted him, those who betrayed him, not a word of resentment came to his lips. No matter what happened, he was the man of sorrows, and he prayed for nothing but their salvation. That's the whole life of Jesus . . . It was so clean and simple that no one could make sense of it, and not one could produce its like.[765]

Behold: non-retaliatory divinity, utterly devoid of resentment. Who could conceive of such a God? Who could produce its like? I'll see your "There's no such thing as God" and raise you an "especially not a God who submits himself to public degradation by his own creatures."

"Among the world religions," wrote Updike, "Christianity is unique in presenting a suffering God, a God who took human suffering upon Himself and in His agony gave birth to mankind's salvation."[766] You are free to dislike this aspect of Christianity, or even to deny it for this very reason, but don't kid yourself: the proclamation of a fully human, suffering savior is central to its message. It's shot through the creeds, the rule of faith, and the New Testament: Jesus "suffered, died, and was buried." Unlike Buddha, the God of Jesus does not detach himself from the troubles of the world. Unlike the fickle and aloof deities of Greek mythology, the God of Jesus does not make casual sport of human misery. Unlike the gods of Hinduism, Jesus endured unspeakable humiliation, "even death on a cross," like the commonest of criminals. And unlike the pragmatic gods of Enlightenment deism and modern-day fundamentalism, the God revealed in Jesus doesn't function to ensure our way of life, or to fill the gaps in our knowledge. In Jesus, God comes to us as someone we are free to deny, a God we can write off as irrelevant, impractical, or even unnecessary, if we so choose. The humiliation of the incarnate God is the essence of the aforementioned Philippians hymn: "Though he was in the form of God, did not count equality with God a thing to be grasped, but emptied himself, by taking the form of a servant." This is Christianity, its starting block and foundation. And if, upon reflection, you find these ideas scandalous, irreverent, or better yet, unbelievable, it means you are currently awake.

A Rabbi, Two Drunks, and an Abolitionist Walk into a Bar

Returning now to Pi's question: What kind of God lets himself be humiliated by the work of his own hands, and why? To which any semi-serious Christian can provide a sufficient answer: "For God so loved the world . . ." It is *love*—and nothing else—that compelled God to enter the human situation; to live, love, suffer, and die, that he might bring about his kingdom, "on earth, as it is in heaven." That's the one and only why, the sole motivation for God's voluntary submission to humanity.

Reminds of a story about an old rabbi. After decades of formal theological education, the rabbi finally learned the true meaning of love by eavesdropping on a couple of sloshed serfs named Ivan and Peter. Long-time drinking buddies, the plastered pair prattled on about how much they loved each other. "Bottoms up!" Peter would yell, then they'd pound another round. Finally, after much drinking and jabbering, Ivan looked his friend square in the eye, and asked, "Peter, can you tell me what hurts me?" "How should I know?" Peter replied. Ivan answered with another question: "If you don't know what hurts me, how can you say you love me?"[767]

"Accept Jesus Christ as your personal Lord and Savior," they say. That, plus "Jesus loves me, this I know" are two of the main pillars of evangelical Christianity, as well they should be. But even if Jesus *is* Lord, the one and only Savior of humanity; even if Jesus loves me in some abstract, esoteric sense, how can Jesus save me without really knowing me—including, or maybe especially, what hurts me? Remember: salvation (*salus*) always implies healing, the restoration of human beings from the inside out. How can God tend to my wounds if he doesn't know anything about them? How can God heal me if my subjective, inner life remains alien to him, if he's never shared my hardships firsthand? Can God really save me if he skips over those aspects of my humanness that are, to quote Sarah Coakley, "most in need of salvation"?[768]

Like any self-respecting Yankee, I like to think slavery, segregation, and Jim Crowe were all Southern problems. But I'm lying. Truth is, even in New York, even after the Civil War, much of American life remained segregated. On New York ferries, only White passengers were allowed to sleep in the comfy cabins below deck. If, like Frederick Douglass, you were Black, you had to sleep up top, exposed to the elements, no matter how cold or rainy it was. Sometimes Douglass rode the ferryboat with his White friends, which was particularly humiliating. Sooner or later, he'd find himself in the awkward position of having to convince them to sleep inside. Most took him up on it, and Douglass never thought the less of them for it: "I saw no reason why they should be miserable because I was." But still, in his heart of hearts, Douglass confessed, "I always felt a little nearer to those who did not take my advice, and persisted in sharing my hardships with me."[769]

The word *empathy* suggests shared experience. It means participating in another person's "inside view" of their own life. More than just "feeling sorry" for someone—e.g., offering your condolences via sympathy card—empathy involves bearing another's emotional burdens. It means vicariously experiencing their thoughts and feelings, as if, somehow, you *were* that other person, if only in flashes. But can God really do that? Can infinite, transcendent divinity ever know what it's like to be one of us? To suffer as we suffer, and fear as we fear? How can God empathize with us unless he's capable of experiencing what we experience, in all our fragility and finitude?

The Same Difficulty

It's one of life's immutable axioms: we feel closest to those who've walked a mile in our shoes; who know what hurts us, because it hurts them, too.

These kinds of relationships can be life changing. Liberating, even. And that's precisely what the early alcoholics discovered. They'd already tried every available remedy—the best doctors, specialists, and treatment centers—but to no avail. Even the most renowned psychiatrists could barely get the average alcoholic to talk openly about their addiction, let alone provide any real relief. Friends and family had even less success. But for some strange reason, within the relational networks of A.A., things were different:

> The ex-problem drinker who has found this [A.A.'s] solution, who is properly armed with facts about himself, can generally win the entire confidence of another alcoholic in a few hours. Until such an understanding is reached, little or nothing can be accomplished. That the man who is making the approach has had *the same difficulty* . . . these are the conditions we have found most effective. After such an approach many take up their beds and walk again.[770]

Eureka! At last, the miracle cure! The long-sought-after solution to the problem of alcoholism—and in the one place nobody bothered to look. Who'd of thought the best treatment for a hopeless drunk would be another drunk?

This is what the incarnation is all about: vicarious experience. Empathy. Shared hardship—or "coinherence," to use a more theological term.[771] The incarnation means God has entered our situation, sharing in our self-same human difficulties: "For we do not have a high priest who is unable to empathize with our weaknesses," the Bible says, "but we have one [Jesus] who has been tempted in every way, just as we are . . ."[772] And because Jesus was fully human, knowing our weaknesses "in every way," he is open to all, because no one is beyond the reach of a humiliated God. I don't care how far gone you think you are: you can't sink below the grasp of a God who's always already on the bottom. It's this strange self-emptying of Jesus that's the key to his universality (it's also why some of Europe's most prominent Marxist, postmodern, and atheist philosophers are revisiting Christian theology as a resource for reimagining what real "universality" might actually mean).[773]

Universality

Universal is a scary world, especially to our fundamentalist friends. For clarity's sake, by "universal," I'm not talking about "all dogs go to heaven," or some similarly sentimental schlock. I mean "universal" in the contemporary philosophical sense, i.e., something truly comprehensive in scope, capable of including every single human being, regardless of social, historical, psychological, linguistic, or cultural distinctions. And that's what

God's kingdom is: an "open universal."[774] Everybody's welcome. It's neither a sect, nor an ethnicity, nor even a nation-state (not even the U.S. of A.). All classes and cultures are invited. All tribes and tongues. This is what Martin Luther King and St. Francis were talking about. This is the otherworldly, all-encompassing love described by Kierkegaard:

> Erotic love is determined by the object [e.g., who or what one desires]; friendship is determined by the object; only love to one's neighbor is determined by love. Since one's neighbor is every man, unconditionally every man, all distinctions are indeed removed from the object . . . Is not this the highest perfection?[775]

All distinctions are removed. "There is neither Jew nor Gentile, neither slave nor free, nor is there male and female," the New Testament reads, "For you are all one in Christ Jesus."[776] There is neither liberal nor conservative, biblicist nor skeptic, alt-right nor Antifa. There's not even secular vs. religious, because in God's kingdom, there is no temple—and, therefore, no religion.[777]

As should be clear by now, the kingdom of God means much, much more than mere "coexistence"—an uninspiring feat that even the most pugnacious of Cold War politicians could achieve. Likewise, God's kingdom means more than "tolerance," a word often associated with Martin Luther King, despite the fact that he never used it. Seriously, what could be less radical, less liberating than "tolerating" your neighbor?[778] Tolerance may be a necessary condition and vital ingredient for the building and maintenance of loving relationships, and it's certainly preferable to the sort of odious intolerance that kept Frederick Douglass segregated from his friends, but ultimately, tolerance is insufficient. As Charles Williams observed, "Tolerance was, and remains, a noble virtue—yet a virtue which serves best as a guide to something greater than itself"—namely, *agape*.[779] Unconditional love. So congratulations, all you tolerant coexisters. You've now joined the esteemed ranks of Nixon and Khrushchev—and in fairness, maybe that's the best we can muster by sheer force of will. But in God's kingdom, and by God's empowering grace, "all things are possible" (Matt 19:26). Grieving mothers really do forgive the self-radicalized psychos who gunned down their children. In God's kingdom, the lion really does lie down with the lamb.[780]

Whatever your perspective on the afterlife, make no mistake: the kingdom of God is a community whose circumference stretches just far enough to include your bitterest rival, the very person you're powerless to love in your own strength. Unlike any earthly institution, tribe, government, or denomination, the kingdom of God is open to everyone—for, in emptying himself, the incarnate God has made room for all. This is the "highest perfection," the *agape* love of Jesus. It's the "beloved community" MLK dreamt of, an utterly non-sectarian, non-tribal universal. It's the why behind St. Francis' prayer, *Vi Voglio tutti in paradisio!* "I want you all with me in paradise!" This is hungry, omnivorous love. And it's given only in weakness.

The One and Only Stumbling Block

I once heard a megachurch pastor say he couldn't worship a Messiah he could beat up. I'm assuming he meant the peace sign–waving, diaper-wearing hippie Jesus of our post-60s imaginations. Either way, the pastor's comment completely misses the real scandal of Jesus—namely, his vulnerability. *That* was Christ's unforgivable sin, his truly crucifiable offense: he dared to manifest divinity in weakness. Young Pi was right, as much as that megachurch pastor was wrong. The God revealed in Jesus is a God who knows firsthand the "taste of death," a God to whom nothing human is alien.

Jesus' followers weren't scandalous because they believed in only one God. The Jews were already monotheists and had long been accepted as a valid religious sect by Roman authorities. Neither were Christians persecuted because of their belief in absolute, eternal truth. Plato and a slew of Greek philosophers believed the same thing, and the Romans were fine with it. What was really so offensive about Jesus and his disciples was that they associated vulnerability and humiliation with divinity.[781] To the Romans, this was the epitome of foolishness, the complete subversion of all worldly wisdom, and the apostles knew it: "We preach Christ crucified: a stumbling block to Jews and foolishness to Gentiles, but to those whom God has called, both Jews and Greeks, Christ the power of God and the wisdom of God."[782] That was—and is—the real "scandal" of the cross, the main "stumbling block" along the pilgrim's path.

Remember: God is like Jesus. So if you want to know what God is really like, in all his power and magnificence, you've got to look at Jesus Christ—specifically, "Christ *crucified.*" This God doesn't impose order by coercive imperial decree. He's not a sword-wielding despot, bent on building kingdoms upon the bones of vanquished enemies. Nor is God a feudal lord who creates through uncreation—a.k.a. conquest. Instead, God comes to us "from below," from a position of poverty and weakness: "He was despised and rejected . . . and we held him in low esteem."[783] This is the why and the how of Jesus' universality. This is the key to the cross-cultural applicability and timeliness of his message. Only a humiliated, self-emptying God can issue a universal appeal to all of humanity, from bottom to top. Only a God who's been rejected by the kingdoms and powers of this world can bring good news of a world to come. Only a crucified God can be the God of the resurrection, capable of turning the world upside down and setting all the wrongs right. "For the foolishness of God is wiser than human wisdom, and the weakness of God is stronger than human strength."[784]

I've always been a sucker for inclusivism. Blame it on my progressive parents, or growing up on umpteen hours of Sesame Street in syndication. If, for some reason, I were compelled to deconstruct and discredit my own Christian conversion, I would probably say something like this: "I became a Christian because I longed to belong." And not just to a clique or special interest group. Something in me always yearned for what Bonhoeffer called the "recapitulation of all things": the healing of humanity as a whole (a.k.a. apocatastasis), an ultimate, cosmic reconciliation—something that both requires worldwide repentance, and brings about what it requires.[785] I wanted ultimate reconciliation so bad that I could no longer stand aligning myself with any particular faction—even the winning side. I guess that's why I've always resonated so deeply with stories of unlikely friendships: Bird and Magic, Maher and Coulter, Scalia and RBG, Legolas and Gimli. Maybe that's why I joined Black Voices in the first place—to give the Real World and its petty tribalism the middle finger.

It was the Christian community who, for me, helped flesh out the abstract idea of the kingdom of God. They put skin on *agape*. They loved, forgave, dropped the ball, repented, and forgave again. And this, I learned, was the kind of kingdom Jesus intended to build.

Equal Opportunity Annoyer

Far be it from me to dissuade a fellow pilgrim, but if you're looking for a good reason to reject the good news of Jesus Christ, I can think of none better than this: his universality. Full acceptance and forgiveness for all who desire it, whether Jew or Greek, slave or free, male or female, "for you are all one in Christ Jesus." Such is the kingdom of God. Of course, this means the end of all tribalism, the ultimate supersession of any and all identity groups—and you might want to consider the implications of such a scenario. For one thing, it means reconciliation with the very people who annoy you the most: your enemies. And in this sense, the good news is also terrible news, because *agape* means *rooting* for your enemies; praying for their full and final flourishing. And for most of us, that's hard to imagine . . . let alone desire.

There's this famous (if indirect) quote from the new age novel, *The Alchemist*: "The universe is always conspiring in your favor." It's all over Instagram and Pinterest. Personally, I like it because it's poetic and concise, and because it throws into stark relief the absolute radicality of Jesus' message: "Love your enemies and pray for those who persecute you."[786] To rephrase, following Jesus means wanting the universe to conspire in your *enemy's* favor—or, at the very least, it means wanting to want that. Even after being beaten, scorned, and betrayed, Jesus prayed for nothing but the salvation of those who condemned him. This is what Jesus, "the living man," was really like, which means this is what God is really like: "While we were God's enemies, we were reconciled to him through the death of his Son."[787] Those are the apostle Paul's words, the same Paul who said he'd willingly endure damnation and be "cut off from Christ" if it meant that his people, his "kinsmen," could know the love of Jesus firsthand.[788]

Agape love and forgiveness are the keystones of God's kingdom. No forgiveness, no kingdom. It's a non-negotiable, an absolute dictatorial requirement: "If you do not forgive others their sins, your Father will not forgive your sins" (Matt 6:15). That's what Jesus taught. That's what he lived, that's how he died, and that's what his followers seek to emulate, however failingly—and not just for the sake of maintaining one's own inner serenity—e.g., "Anger is heavy, let it go . . ."—but for the genuine benefit of the other. That includes those who've hurt you the most, who are, as Dickens put it, "fellow-passengers to the grave, and not another race of creatures bound on other journeys."[789] Just as the grave lays claim to us all, so much the more does the jealous love of God.

Fair warning: if you're an Ayn Rand–worshipping individualist, the kingdom of God might just drive you crazy, since it's a kingdom built upon *agape* and forgiveness. It's banner reads, "I want you all with me in paradise!" not, "Get off my lawn!" The same warning applies to those who are high on identity politics, who believe the most important thing about a person is their group identity—a.k.a. their "tribe," over against other, competing tribes (e.g., male vs. female, Black vs. White, abled vs. disabled, Christian conservative vs. secular liberal, neoliberal establishment Democrat vs. progressive socialist Democrat, LGBT vs. LGBTQQIAPP+, Northern Conservative Baptist Great Lakes Region Council of 1879 vs. Northern Conservative Baptist Great Lakes Region Council of 1912, etc.[790]). In this regard, Jesus is an equal opportunity annoyer. He expects the same of all of us: love and forgive everybody, always and forever, period.

And it's not like you get a pass for being a churchgoing, "family values" enthusiast. Just because you're pro-family doesn't mean you're any closer to the kingdom of God—especially since "family first" often means "to the exclusion of all other people/families." You don't have to be a particularly holy or compassionate person to prioritize your familial tribe above others. Just ask Walter White from *Breaking Bad*, or the current boss of the Gambino family, or your average MS-13 member. They're all about "the family." Just not *your* family.[791]

Here's the bottom line: if you're looking to Jesus to help you achieve an irrevocable victory over your ideological opponents, you're going to be sorely disappointed. Neither is Jesus an effective weapon for the waging of culture wars. He doesn't make for a very good sledgehammer, especially if your goal is to eradicate those factions that happen to differ from your own. And if you're looking to Jesus for answers to your questions about planetary motion, personal finance, time management, or how to brand your startup, he's going to let you down. Sure, maybe the New Testament can give you a framework for interpreting reality, or even some decent principles for running your business. But in the final analysis, the God revealed in Jesus isn't primarily interested in solving these sorts of practical problems.

Not that God doesn't help us with *anything*. Speaking personally, the pilgrim's path led me to one inescapable conclusion: I needed God. Still do. Not as a practical explanation, but as a healing, transformative power. I was suffering from soul sickness and needed treatment. Ongoing treatment. "He is able!" we used to sing in Black Voices; able to change lives and heal human hearts, *for real*, in this life. The "god of the philosophers" makes no such promises. Neither do the gods of our gut-level hunches, nor the detached divinities of esoteric religion. They offer no ultimate reconciliation, nor any newfound power to love and forgive.

At the end of the day, it's not that hard to believe in God. But to believe God can change people, including you and me? That the dead will rise, and the sick take up their beds and walk again? This is the stuff of faith.

But here I am getting ahead of myself.

14

The Way Things Are

Mother is the name for God in the lips and hearts of little children.

—WILLIAM MAKEPEACE THACKERAY[792]

THEY SAY ADULTS HAVE no direct access to childhood memories, colored as they are by time and distance. Maybe so. But still, there are things I remember, things ancient and new.

My mother and I were sitting at the table on top of the world. We were eating peanuts. I liked the salty taste. I asked her if anything else tasted like them. She said cashews and sunflower seeds. The seeds stuck out to me for some reason. I'd tried them once before and thought the whole process was too labor intensive and time consuming. "Uncle Bobby eats those a lot," I said. She laughed and said, "Yeah, I know. He's addicted." "What's '*addicted*'?" I asked. Eyes cast down, she fiddled with the peanuts, spinning each one like a lopsided top: "It means you can't stop doing it," she answered. Just then, I felt as if I'd done something terribly wrong. I hadn't—at least, not at that particular moment—but there was no mistaking it: something had changed. Some silent and encompassing Something Wrong had been whispered into the world, and the whisper became the world.

Years later, I realized that what I'd once thought of as "the world" was really just the front room of a cramped one-story apartment. But so it goes with children.

I used to spend hours a day in that little apartment, drawing and coloring in my room, alone. I had this little plastic table that I'd covered with doodles of spaceships, superheroes, and monsters. I remember when my father brought a few friends over from the bar. He went out of his way to show them my drawings. Surely this was what it felt like to be on top of the world.

Light

Another day in the apartment. My mother brought home a present for me: a Superman nightlight. Being a mature, independent seven-year-old, I scolded her for giving me such a juvenile gift. "This is a stupid! I don't want it!" I yelled. "Okay, fine, it's not a big deal. I just thought you'd like it." I remember her voice trembling when she said those words, though I can scarcely stand to think about it, even now.

The nightlight incident stayed with me for a long, long time. Too long, like an ambient, low-grade pain. It wasn't my mother's reaction that I found so distressing. It was how badly I felt about rejecting her gift. Somehow, I knew my mother was making herself small by giving me something I hadn't asked for. I think this was the moment I first discovered I had power, *real* power; that if I could not alter the external world to suit my needs, I could, at the very least, destroy the lovely, and ruin whatever was doing its little best to break through. No one taught me how to do this. It was all too intuitive. And it was easy. Satisfying, even. Behold, I had discovered The Way Things Are.

I think the worst part was when I realized I couldn't take that moment back. I cried and cried; I begged my mother for forgiveness, I tossed and turned in my Star Wars sheets, as if writhing on the Inquisitor's rack. Still I couldn't inch back the clock or remove what I'd done from the tread of history. And there it remains, unto this day.

Dark

When you're born into a hemorrhaging home and you watch your parents flailing and clutching and barely hanging on, it's as if the ordinary events of the day begin to whisper: *It's not working . . . you know it, and they know it.* As a child who's all too familiar with that refrain, there's nothing worse than realizing you're the one who's just kicked them when they were already down. Here's how it works: every once in a while, you'll catch them mustering the courage to try, try again. You can almost hear them telling themselves, "Maybe this time will be different." And so they try. They wake up extra early to make you breakfast. They get you a comic book, just because they thought you'd like it. They buy you a nightlight. As a child, to be the one who tells them "You're not cutting it" is a horrible thing. Somehow, I had become the calloused fingers that would extinguish my mother's flame. Poof! Out you go.

Updike was right: "Life, just as we first thought, is playing grown-up."[793] The word "adult" doesn't necessarily mean "qualified." That's what I learned from my Superman nightlight: there were no real "grown-ups," only ordinary people, like my parents, trying to figure it out as they went along, all while dodging the same landmines as me. And they sometimes failed. "This is it," I realized. "This is *life*. This is The Way Things Are." And somehow, I was both its origin and victim, its source and symptom. And I had only just begun.

15

Optimism, Schmoptimism

Amid these tribulations must not man be most miserable, since, but half alive in life, he weakly draws his anxious and languid breath, as if he had a sword perpetually hanging over his neck?

—CALVIN[794]

The life of man, solitary, poor, nasty, brutish, and short.

—HOBBES[795]

In Praise of Pessimism

UPON RETURNING FROM A long day's pre-K, my niece made the following announcement: "Guess what, Mommy? I made a new friend today!"

"That's great, honey," my sister replied. "Is he friendly?"

"Yes, but he's scary too."

Through a thick haze of exhaustion and concern that only working mothers know, my sister summoned the energy to probe further: "Hmm . . . is he from nearby? Where does he live?"

"Everywhere. And also, he's invisible."

Officially weirded out, my sister asked, "Okay . . . well, maybe I know him. What's his name?"

My niece responded, "*Life.*"

The Problem of Life

"Life is suffering," sighed Buddha, and Nietzsche shouted, "Amen!" It can be said that religion is an attempt to fix this problem—the Problem of Life— and if there isn't really a problem, it's hard to imagine why anyone would bother with religion, especially since it can be really time consuming. If you're even remotely interested in things spiritual, it probably means you're intrigued by the possibility of making things better, which means you're already aware that there's Something Wrong.

Of all the major world religions, Hinduism was probably the first to take shape. The oldest Hindu texts, the Vedas, suggest the possibility of an eventual reunion with *Brahman*, the fundamental source of all reality. If each of us is a drop of water, *Brahman* is the primordial ocean from which we sprang. Here, the prescribed remedy for the Something Wrong is a return to essential oneness.

The Hindus also introduced the concept of *karma*—"What goes around comes around"—an axiom that even the peppiest yoga moms can chant by heart. The ancient Greeks stumbled upon a similar principle: every choice we make sets in motion a chain of events that ripples through time and space, eventually turning back on us like pitiless boomerangs.[796] It all started because of some fatal, prehistoric decision to steal fire from the gods or open Pandora's box, a choice that sealed our fate as collectively screwed.

Buddha developed a different strategy for dealing with the Something Wrong. Since suffering (*dukkha*) seems to be our main problem, the simplest solution is to get rid of the suffering.[797] And the best way to do that is by doing away with desire. No desire, no disappointment; no feeling bad after getting dumped, losing the game, or getting passed up for the big promotion. Buddha probably borrowed the idea from the Bhagavad-Gita, wherein Krishna observes, "Brooding about sensuous objects makes attachment to them grow; from attachment desire arises, from desire anger is born . . ."[798] So the trick is to detach. Let go of all earthly desire—which is precisely what some of our Buddhist brethren do best.[799] They learn to let go. That's Buddhism's basic strategy: accept the fact that the world is an illusion. Embrace the nonsensical nursery rhyme logic of reality—"life is but a dream"—else be doomed to relive your sufferings in an infinite series of lifetimes (*saṃsāra*) from which there is no exit.[800]

The Abrahamic faiths are noticeably less optimistic about our innate human capacity for self-remediation. Judaism, Christianity, and Islam all depict the world as concretely real and humanity as authentically culpable. Thus spoke Muhammad: "The self is inclined to evil."[801] Similarly, the Hebrew Bible declares, "Surely there is no one on earth so righteous as to do good without ever sinning."[802] Going further, the New Testament describes humanity as "fallen," "accursed," and, worse still, "dead."[803]

This is a hard sell, especially these days. Pessimism isn't a particularly winsome PR strategy. And barring the occasional, brooding anti-hero, it definitely isn't sexy. Nevertheless, pessimism remains a pervasive theme that runs through most serious religious writing, Abrahamic or otherwise. When it comes to Christianity in particular, none did defeatism better than John Calvin: "Corruption of nature drives all peoples as well as each one individually." The result? "Great madness."[804] Wonderful. Thanks for sharing.

Okay, fine. Maybe religious gloom and doom made sense in ages past, but this is the twenty-first century. Haven't we moved past all this medieval nonsense? Are things really that bad? Even if they are, why wallow in the doldrums with the winy emo kids?

American Optimism

"The American, by nature, is optimistic," JFK said. It's in our DNA, woven into the very fabric of our national identity. Historian Gordon Wood identifies optimism as one of the defining characteristics of our culture.[805] And it's been that way since the beginning. When America was a wee young lad and the United States barely an idea, John Winthrop offered the following words to his fellow Massachusetts Bay colonists:

> We shall find the God of Israel is among us, when ten of us shall be able to resist a thousand of our enemies . . . that men shall say of our plantations: 'The Lord make it like that of New England.' For we must consider that we shall be as a city on a hill, the eyes of the people are upon us.[806]

I'm sure Winthrop never dreamed he'd be quoted for generations to come. Even now, presidents from Reagan to Obama give obligatory shout-outs to Winthrop's "city on a hill" when reminding us of our national uniqueness. "American exceptionalism," they call it—and in many ways, I'd agree: from the get-go, America has stood out as an exception to the historical tendency towards tyranny, offering its citizens more freedom and opportunity than any other nation on earth. Pilgrims and Puritans like Winthrop believed it was their destiny to Christianize the New World and establish a "New Israel" on its fertile soil, where "true Christians" would find refuge and religious freedom. We would, in one historian's words, be the "center stage of God's unfolding drama on earth," a beacon to inspire the rest of the world unto repentance, conversion, and liberty.[807] Needless to say, the Native Americans and imported slaves didn't share such a sunny outlook.[808]

The Tyranny of Positivity

Several years ago, Oprah scandalized her audience by admitting, "The world is a mess."[809] Five little words that set the blogosphere ablaze. She was probably referring to what she'd witnessed over the course of her many philanthropic visits to Africa. I thought it was refreshingly honest comment. Not everyone agreed. One online influencer wondered, "Is Oprah Losing Faith??" Maybe so . . . but "faith" in what?

One of our most cherished national assumptions is that things are getting better; that someday soon, through sheer grit and determination, we'll bring the promised land to fruition. Any suggestion to the contrary is, as Oprah learned, liable to provoke backlash.

Most people prefer a low-res version of reality, wherein the world's problems fade harmlessly into the background. "Irrational optimism," some call it.[810] And it can make life seem a lot more manageable . . . if it doesn't make you crazy first.[811]

I'm not trying to hate on all you stargazing dreamers out there, nor disparage the power of positive thinking. I like optimists. I married one. I even like the irrational types. Gimme the corny dad from *Modern Family* over Eeyore any day. It was the optimists who first inspired me to dream big. They were the ones I wanted to be like: glass-half-full go-getters. Then, predictably, something changed.

You know the drill: wide-eyed boy enters college, only to become disgruntled upon entering adulthood. Blame it on getting my heart broken at nineteen, those first bitter tastes of vocational defeat in my mid-twenties, my father's brain injury and the resultant financial and familial collapse. Maybe it was studying the slouching spirals of history. Or maybe it was all of the above. At bottom, I think what really soured my opinion of the world was actually getting to know it.

The more I examined humanity's assorted attempts at making the world a better place, the more it seemed we were banging our collective heads against the wall. From Marxism to monarchism, no system of social organization has yet rendered us immune to corruption; no form of government has proven itself infallible. Not even democracy.

Winston Churchill said the only thing worse than democracy is everything else. He had a point. For one thing, the "will of the people" is often dead wrong. Take the formerly fashionable institution of slavery, for instance. Or mumble rap. Or the inexplicably profitable *Transformers* movie franchise. Or my cheesy college cover band.

Democracy Delimited

We were a shamelessly strategic group. Our goal? Frat-wide domination. We'd take the party scene by storm and make lots of money doing it. Our secret weapon? A carefully selected setlist of irresistibly frat-friendly cover songs: "Don't Stop Believing," "Jessie's Girl" . . . you name it, we covered it. And we didn't even have the decency to cover them well. Not that we lacked talent. We had that in spades. We just didn't rehearse . . . or show up on time . . . or possess even a modicum of interest in honing our craft. And to any audience member with a critical ear, it showed. Fortunately for us, most of our listeners weren't really that critical, mainly because they weren't really listening. And they *loved* us.

Here's a flyer we came up with to promote our shows. As you can see, we put at least a solid ten minutes of work into it:

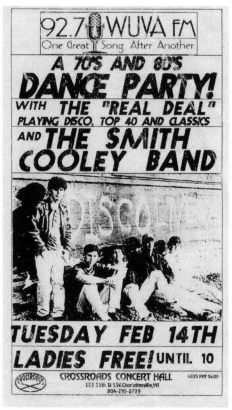

At first, it was all very satisfying, as applause usually is. But after a while, the whole thing got stale. There's only so many times you can have some random, blue-eyed, plastered Pi Phi stumble onto the stage and say,

"Okay . . . so, like, can you guys play 'Brown-Eyed Girl' again? But this time, can you, like, sing '*Blue*-Eyed Girl'?" without losing any remaining shred of musical integrity. With each passing gig, we got increasingly hungry for any semblance of critical pushback from the crowd. And we never got it. Not once. Our rhythm guitar player started farting into the microphone, in tempo, right on two and four. More applause. Sometimes I'd intentionally play the wrong chord, my amp cranked as loud as it could go, guitar jangling in unbearable discordance. And we never got fired . . . or even called on it. In fact, the sloppier we played, the more affirmation we'd receive: "OMG, you guys rule!" Or my personal favorite: "This was literally the best night of my life!" Really? So, *not* the night when the doctors finally found a compatible donor for your mom's desperately needed, not-a-minute-to-spare liver transplant, but the night we butchered Hootie's "Hold My Hand"? It wouldn't be a stretch to equate my college musical career with one prolonged, public plea for accountability. And I never got it. Not once. The public had exercised its democratic right to prefer my cover band over the nameless, faceless folk singer playing his heart out at the empty coffeehouse across town.

A well-orchestrated democracy does a lot of things better than anything else. It does a great job of insisting upon a bare minimum of individual rights. It expresses and safeguards the voices of the people. But democracy doesn't always disclose the true, good, or beautiful. It doesn't show me how to love my neighbor, nor does it give me the power to do so. It doesn't do a whole lot to reconcile human beings to one another. Nor can it reconcile me to myself.

If Churchill was right, then there's no perfect government out there waiting to be found, no legislative means of righting all the world's wrongs. The Problem is much, much deeper than that. But for many of us, that's a tough pill to swallow. It's hard enough to admit there's actually Something Wrong, much less something we can't fix.

Like Oprah, most of our modern-day role models are variations of *The Little Engine That Could*. Dream big, don't doubt yourself, live in possibility, etc. "Thou shalt be positive!" is our first and greatest commandment, and the second is like it: "Thou shalt believe in oneself!" So we are told in an endless onslaught of songs, cartoons, and shoe commercials, all while forgetting G. K. Chesterton's eerie observation that the world's asylums are full of people brimming with self-belief.[812]

Ain't Just a River in Egypt

The main problem with irrational optimism is not that it's *bad*, but that it's *untrue*. And untruth can lead to all manner of delusion and disappointment.

I see this in my own students sometimes. According to research, to-day's high schoolers are much more likely to assume they'll be awesome parents, spouses, and employees than did their teenage counterparts in the 1970s. They're also more likely to self-identify as A students with high IQs, even when they're not . . . which can make for some pretty awkward parent-teacher conferences.[813]

Of course, irrational optimism can be a lot more serious than that. Take the Hungarian Jews in the 1930s. Auschwitz survivor Elie Wiesel recalls how his neighbors were almost incapable of taking the nascent Nazi threat seriously. "Annihilate an entire people? Wipe out a population dispersed throughout so many nations?" It just seemed so unimaginable, so primitive. Even as the Nazis advanced upon his hometown, "The Jews of Sighet were still smiling."[814] They *wanted* to believe they wouldn't be rounded up like cattle and shipped off to death camps. They *wanted* to believe such madness was no longer possible in a modern, enlightened world cleansed of primi-tive barbarity. Surely, Europe had learned its lesson after the First World War, with its tens of millions of meaningless casualties. Mind you, they didn't call it the *First* World War while it was happening; it was "The War to End All Wars," until one day, it wasn't. Just two decades later, there was Hitler, the Holocaust, Pearl Harbor, Hiroshima.

Three percent of the human race was wiped out during WWII.[815] Think about that: three out of every hundred. Surely *this* would be the last straw. In its aftermath, world leaders resolved to ensure that no such catastrophe would ever again be visited upon humankind. In 1948, the U.N. passed its Universal Declaration of Human Rights, an unprecedented, international ban on torture, forced labor, and genocide. This declaration would mark the end of such senseless and encompassing violence. We would create a new world where such evil was no longer possible. But then came Stalin's purges, Korea, the killing fields of Cambodia, Chile, Rwanda, Darfur, Syria . . .

I don't mean to suggest that nothing ever gets better. In the last few de-cades alone, communist Russia collapsed, the Berlin Wall came down, new AIDS treatments have saved millions of lives, and the world's major powers have reduced nuclear armaments. Starvation among children has decreased and global life expectancy has reached a new high,[816] with the most drastic improvements occurring in impoverished regions of East Africa.[817] These are all remarkable triumphs, worthy of celebrating. But it's difficult for a serious person to survey the arc of history and declare it an unambiguous success. It's hard to sustain irrational optimism once you realize that some-where, some child whose name won't soon be forgotten is being sold into sex slavery, even as you read this very sentence.

From the Other Side

Eventually I came to see the world as a sort of self-enclosed snow globe, not unlike Buddhism's *saṃsāra*. "The door is locked," Bonhoeffer said, "and can only be opened from the outside."[818] And he said this long before the Nazis locked him up in the German concentration camp where he would live out his last days.

The Jewish philosopher Jacob Taubes took a keen interest in this kind of existential pessimism. Taubes devoted much of his life to studying the New Testament, particularly the writings of Paul. He was equally enthralled by some of Paul's influential interpreters, including Karl Barth, in whom Taubes saw a curious amalgam of cynicism and hope. To men like Taubes, Bonhoeffer, and Barth, the world was closed off to the divine, and no amount of positive thinking or self-will could pry the door open: "One can take the elevators up to the high-rises of spirituality—it won't help . . . You have to be told *from the other side* that you're liberated . . . *then* we see, when our eyes are pierced open. Otherwise we see nothing."[819]

Of course, we *do* see something. Lots of things, actually. We see love and loss, the passing of time, the wonders of nature, and the glories of human achievement. But we also see starvation, self-harm, slavery, and suicide. The one thing we *don't* see, at least not with crystal clarity, is the kingdom of God. Neither do we see the King of said kingdom. Because the God of Jesus comes to us only "from the other side." Like a thief in the night, God breaks into our world, an unwelcome stranger, "and the world knew him not."[820] Thomas Merton put it thus: "Into this world, this demented inn, in which there is absolutely no room for Him at all, Christ has come uninvited."[821] Merry Christmas, Charlie Brown.

It takes *faith* to see the God of Jesus Christ, and faith itself is a God-given miracle. But some things are as plain as day. You don't need faith to believe there's Something Wrong. You need Wikipedia and the History Channel. You need a decent attention span and the willingness to look at the unmitigated dementedness of life. If "all the world's a stage," it's pitched precipitously downward. Power corrupts, revolutions overthrow, new powers emerge, the good die young. Lather, rinse, repeat. And if, after carefully surveying the Real World, you're still holding onto the illusion that everything's fine and sanity reigns, consider *Rubik, the Amazing Cube*, an 80s-era Saturday morning cartoon based on the heartfelt story of—you guessed it—a Rubik's Cube, complete with a theme song by Menudo (the Latino predecessors to One Direction). Seriously, some studio actually green-lit that. Go ahead. Google it. YouTube to your heart's content. I dare you to try and get through one episode without succumbing to the temptation to swallow your own tongue till you pass out.

If we dare join the ranks of the pessimists (and my niece) by admitting that "Life" is a problem, are we not violating America's greatest commandment? Perhaps. But even if you won't acknowledge the Problem, even if you focus all your energy and attention on the mantra "Be positive!," you're still tacitly admitting that there's Something Wrong: a problem to be solved or struggle to overcome, if only your own negative thinking habits. Why remind yourself to look on the sunny side if, as the Legos say, "everything is awesome"? Why read books on how to "live your best life now" if you're already living the best life possible? No one has to tell you to "make the best" of filet mignon.

Palo

I used to work as a live-in counselor at a halfway house for teenage boys coming out of juvie. Most resembled a brawnier version of 50 Cent. In contrast, I looked like a somehow-less-intimidating version of Frodo Baggins (still do). My favorite kid was Palo. He had a Hendrix perm and wanted to learn to play guitar. I obliged. Palo's parents abandoned him when he was twelve, at which point he was surrendered to the state, given over to the foster care system. One day, when we were sitting out on the porch, Palo got real honest: "I'm ain't stupid, you know? I know nothin' gonna work out for me. I know how this gonna end. I'll always be a foster kid. I'll get my GED, maybe go to junior college if I'm lucky. But I ain't never gonna be normal. And the whole world is gonna pass me by and keep on goin'. The whole world is a war zone, and nobody gonna worry about me. This gonna be my life, and that's it."

I could've said something soothing and substaneless, like, "Everything will be all right." I could've told him that he and the world were fine, that it's all good. I could've said he can do anything he puts his mind to, that his dreams will all come true if he only believes, because that's how the world works and that's how God works. But instead I thought I'd be honest—because even adults need to be honest once in a while. So I decided to confirm his suspicion: God—functionally speaking—does not "work." At least not like clonazepam and denial work. Neither does God make for a very good Band-Aid, something you can slap onto your life and be on your merry way. Just ask anybody whose heartfelt prayers failed to yield the desired results. Pensions evaporate, levees break, parents bury children, children become orphans. All of this is "normal." All this is The Way Things Are, and Palo knew it. So I figured I'd go ahead and give it a name.

That day on the porch, I told Palo he might never make a lot of money or have a swanky car. I told him he might never have the kind of life that the Real World tells us we're supposed to have . . . or supposed to want. I told him he was right: that the world really is a mess, and that remarkable young men sometimes suffer terrible, terrible wounds, from which they never fully recover. But I also told him that none of those potential realities precluded the possibility of living a beautiful life, of knowing and being known, or loving and being loved. "The Lord is close to the brokenhearted,"[822] said the psalmist. And the New Testament gives the distinct impression that, in Jesus' kingdom, only broken cups runneth over.

Homesick

You know the weirdest thing about Palo? He got homesick. Sometimes I'd find him alone in his room, staring off into nowhere like my dad used to do in the ICU. "I wanna go home," he'd say. But I knew Palo's situation well enough to know that that wasn't the home he was longing for.

The other boys got homesick too, gripped by a longing to return to a familiar place they've never been. So did Bonhoeffer. He spoke of humanity as living under a dark spell: "The curse of homelessness which hangs heavy over the world."[823] And that's where God enters: in the weakness and wanting of our world—the Real World, where all is not well. It is *here* and *now* that we encounter the God given in Jesus, a man who lived and loved under the same curse of homelessness. In Jesus, we discover a way home: "If anyone loves me, he will keep my Word, and my Father will love him, and we will come to him and make our home with him."[824]

The Problem of Life isn't something you can solve by sheer force of will, no matter how pathologically peppy you may be. Even if, by some gravity-defying miracle, you're able to pull yourself up by your bootstraps, you can't pull the whole world up with you. Neither can you pull up the past, the history that precedes you. Optimism can help overcome some problems, but not *the* Problem.

Which is not to say all our efforts are fruitless. There's an abundance of research demonstrating how optimism can contribute to physical and mental health.[825] Positive thinking can boost your mood and get you out of a rut. It can help you see things from a new, more uplifting perspective. It can even help you construct your own version of reality. And if you're really, really good at it, you might even be able to impose said reality construct upon whatever little slivers of the Real World you choose to let in. But optimism can't remedy the world *as it really is*. It can't fix the concrete realities that exist outside your skull-locked self. Neither can it rewrite or redeem the tragedies of the past—not Palo's, not mine, not yours. So it would seem that the skeptics are right: the world is a mess, everything's broken, and we lack the power to fix it.

This is usually where the serial optimist summons his inner Tony Robbins and exclaims, "You're giving your circumstances too much power. Remember: mind over matter! Happiness is an inside job!" And again, there's some real truth to that. It *is*, in fact, possible to experience inner peace while enduring difficult circumstances. "Even though I walk through the valley of the shadow of death, I will fear no evil, for you are with me . . ."[826] God really is close to the brokenhearted. But inner peace and blissful ignorance are not the same thing. There's a big difference between experiencing spiritual consolation in the midst of death's dark valley and denying that the dark valley even exists. That's the problem with regurgitating clichés about "creating your own happiness": it can be a form of evasion, or even self-deception. And besides, it's easy to claim victory over your circumstances when you're facing First World problems; when the air you breathe is, quite literally, conditioned to your own liking. Not so easy when you're an Auschwitz survivor, or somebody's sex slave, or Palo.

The Courage of Despair

Karl Barth, the famous pastor-turned-theologian, praised atheism for its willingness to look the Real Word in the eye: "Only because they have nothing better, only because they lack the courage of despair, do the generality of men on this side [of the] resurrection avoid falling into blatant atheism."[827] The "they" to whom Barth refers are ordinary, decent people, like you and me. They—"the generality of men"—pay their taxes and toe the line. Good neighbors, responsible citizens. Many are chivalrous and kind, perhaps even charitable. They've got their fair share of admirable qualities, to be sure. But "the courage of despair" isn't one of them.

Speaking of despair, a journalist once asked Holocaust survivor, Primo Levi, if he was a man of faith. In typical, unblunted eloquence, Levi replied, "No, I never have been. I'd like to be, but I don't succeed . . . There is Auschwitz, and so there cannot be God. I don't find a solution to this dilemma. I keep looking, but I don't find it."[828] Behold: the courage of despair.

Herein lies the essential difference between pathological optimism and the informed skepticism of people like Barth, Buddha, Nietzsche, and Levi. Pessimists take honest stock of the world, compile the evidence, then endeavor to make sense of it all. Irrational optimists take no such inventory, opting instead to reimagine the world in their own image. Skeptics keep their eyes peeled and their ears to the ground. Irrational optimists listen only to the sound of their own positive self-talk. Informed pessimists—including some of history's most hardened atheists—do their homework and face the facts. Irrational optimists keep their heads in the clouds. Only after taking it all in and thinking things through, the informed atheist concludes, "This world, this life, *this* is all there is," while the optimist triumphantly declares, "*I* am all there is!" Call me gloomy, but I prefer the atheist.

16

The Departed

Death is the opposite of everything.

—Susan Sontag[829]

Love and Death

My wife's friend is a death coach. Or, more formally, an "end-of-life doula." She literally coaches people on dying. And judging by her success rate—she's currently batting a thousand—I'd say she's really good at it.

But that's the thing about death: we all do it eventually, with or without the benefit of coaching. Like taxes, it's unavoidable. The difference, of course, is that it's actually possible to cheat on your taxes.

I remember my first personal encounter with the Grim Reaper. I was maybe seven or eight. Our Boston Terrier died. That was the window through which I made a terrible, terrible discovery: *everyone* dies. Every pet, every president, every parent, every person, ever. Even people I hadn't met yet. Even me. An alarming realization for a wee young lad. More than alarming, it was annoying.

Not that I was peeved at the Grim Reaper, per se. It was the world's adults that I suddenly found agitating. How could everyone just keep on keepin' on, as if the void weren't rushing towards us in a pitiless sprint? The world's grownups were content to go on playing pretend, scampering around from place to place, desperate to make more and more money so they could buy more and more things—like shoes, Twinkies, milk frothers, and gluten-free dog treats—all things destined to disintegrate, just like them (except maybe the Twinkies).

Worse still were the various and insipid comments I started noticing, lame attempts to minimize the horror of mortality. "She's in a better place." Really? *Where*, exactly? Or this one: "She'll always be with us." How so? In our "memories," which are really just jumbles of neurons firing in our brains? In our "hearts," or our "spirits," like how Mufasa's spirit "lives on" in Simba? Seriously, is that the best we got? Personally, I've always resonated more with Woody Allen's take on mortality: "Rather than live on in the hearts and minds of my fellow man, I'd prefer to live on in my apartment."[830]

Death Anxiety

Like the gloomiest of existentialist philosophers, Christianity takes death seriously. But only because death takes you seriously. We are, as Cornel West is fond of saying, "featherless, two-legged, linguistically conscious creatures born between urine and feces . . . our bodies will be the delight of terrestrial worms."[831] The Grim Reaper may not be a part of your plans, but you're definitely part of his.

Modern physics has only confirmed what the prophets of old believed: from dust we came and to dust we shall return. "Stardust" perhaps, the re-configured remains of heavenly bodies that exploded billions of years ago, but dust nonetheless.[832] It's a troubling thought. Makes you wonder why the dust ever bothered to settle.

So maybe the trick is to get rid of death. Medical science has already made more breakthroughs than any medieval alchemist or bloodletting sha-man could've possibly imagined. Why not immortality? Wouldn't that fix the Problem? After all, don't most of our human troubles boil down to what they call "death anxiety"?[833] According to the apocryphal book of Sirach,

> Perplexities and fear of heart are theirs,
> and anxious thought of the day of their death.
> From the one who sits on a splendid throne
> to the one who grovels in dust and ashes. . .
> there is anger and envy and trouble and unrest,
> and fear of death, and fury and strife.[834]

Dying. *That's* what we're scared of. It's the "worm at the core" of our exis-tence, the Why behind our endless strivings. According to what psycholo-gists call "terror management theory," almost everything we do is motivated by a desperate desire to alleviate death anxiety. It's what drives the bulk of our behaviors and beliefs, if only subconsciously.[835] We want to live on and be remembered. We want to "make a name for ourselves" and play an important role in the story of human history. We want to cheat death. And we suck at it.

Freud believed death anxiety drove our prehistoric ancestors to invent the concept of the spirit world, especially the immortal soul.[836] The Bible actually calls us "slaves" to the fear of death[837]—meaning mortality is more than just a minor glitch. It is our master, the dark overlord under whose shadow we spend our lives in faithful, involuntary subjugation.

The whole death problem really bothered Jesus. Dealing with it was one of his main objectives.[838] It was central to his mission and purpose, near the top of his messianic to-do list. And he dealt with it in the most peculiar of ways. He dealt with death by dying.

Death on the Ropes

When God became human, dying was part of the deal, just as it is for the rest of us. Recall young Pi's ruminations: "If the Son is to die, it cannot be fake. If God on the Cross is God shamming a human tragedy, it turns the Passion of Christ into the Farce of Christ. The death of the Son must be real . . ." And so it was.

Remember: the God incarnate in Jesus is a God to whom "nothing human is alien." And you can't be fully human without knowing firsthand the fear of death. There's no SparkNotes version; no crash course in life as it is actually lived. You don't get to skip the hardest parts and still claim solidarity with the rest of us. Either you experience the full agony and ecstasy of The Way Things Are, or you don't.

Jesus knew he was going to die: "The Son of Man will be betrayed . . . They will condemn him to death and will turn him over to the Gentiles to be mocked and flogged and crucified."[839] More strikingly, Jesus willingly submitted to crucifixion—not out of some masochistic, ego-driven desire for martyrdom, but in order to defang the powers of darkness, to free the world from fear and death. That's why Jesus shared in our humanity, "so that by his death he might break the power of him who holds the power of death"—the overlord—"and free those who all their lives were held in slavery by their fear of death."[840]

It's a radical idea, this notion of being freed from fear and death. We see hints of it in the martyrdom of Moses the Black, in the munificent recklessness of St. Francis, and in MLK's "Mountaintop" speech: "I'm not fearing any man . . ." The ancient Christians believed such freedom was a supernatural gift from God, a.k.a. a *miracle*—something that exceeds the scope of human possibility. That's how Athanasius of Alexandria described it in the fourth century: "For men who, before they believe in Christ, think death horrible and are afraid of it, once they are converted despise it so completely that they go eagerly to meet it, and themselves become witnesses of the Savior's resurrection from it." Somehow, Jesus' death and resurrection emptied death of its power—it's "sting." And to Athanasius, this was compelling evidence of the reality of Christ's coming kingdom:

> Now that the Savior has raised His body, death is no longer terrible, but all those who believe in Christ tread it underfoot as nothing . . . knowing full well that when they die they do not perish, but live indeed, and become incorruptible through the resurrection.[841]

By rising from the grave, Jesus defeated death. More than that, Jesus said *we* would do the same. Death would no longer have the last word. Like Jesus, we would rise again. Through him, humanity would be saved.

Defeating death is serious business. Some say it was Jesus' *only* business, the sum total of his mission. But respectfully, I disagree. Solving the death problem couldn't have been Jesus' *only* objective, because immortality wouldn't fix all of our troubles. Without some sort of drastic treatment for the deeper Problem, what would "eternal life" mean but the endless reduplication of a hopelessly deficient now?

On Immortality

If heaven involves the sort of suffering we currently bear, who'd want to live forever? Not Job. After enduring the loss of his home and family, Job was ready to call it quits: "I despise my life; I would not live forever . . . my days have no meaning."[842] Immortality isn't necessarily "good news." The mere extension of life offers no real remedy for life's ills, no "salvation" (*salus*) or "healing."[843] And that's what Job was after: *salus*. Job wanted *healing*, from the inside out. That's what I learned to want by reading the Bible and the dead saints. And also, *Tuck Everlasting* . . . and most importantly, *X-Men*.

What is Wolverine's real struggle, the main source of his vulnerability? Simple: invulnerability. Logan wants nothing more than the freedom to die. And it's the one thing he's powerless to bring about. So he wanders the earth, doomed to live century after century as countless friends succumb to cruel inevitability. Regeneration is his affliction, immortality his curse. Things never get easier for Wolverine. Same old muttonchops, same character flaws and retractable claws, same Old Man Logan. If only he could break free from the endless *saṃsāra* of war-torn lifecycles and disappointing summer sequels (though *Logan* and *Days of Future Past* did kinda rule).

Freud dismissed the afterlife as a wish-fulfilling illusion. An effective source of comfort for some, but so are porn, cat posters, and Percocet. More than merely bogus, Freud thought heaven was pointless: "With the mere lengthening of the period of life nothing would be gained unless much in the conditions of life were radically changed as well . . ."[844] For heaven to be any good, it would require the wholesale renovation of reality. Renewal. *Salus*. And not just private, "spiritual," inner healing for isolated individuals. I'm talking about restored communities. I'm talking radically changed cultures, conditions, and ways of being. Existence redefined.

Jean Paul Sartre said hell is other people, and he had a point: If eternal life involves no fundamental transformation, no real healing of the human heart, what would heaven be but perpetual fellowship with the very people you're currently do your best to avoid, including that guy from work who always reheats fish in the office microwave, spits when he talks, and drops silent-but-deadlys in the elevator? "Heaven," thus conceived, would mean unredeemed madness. Even if science can render our mortal bodies incorruptible, it wouldn't do a thing to address our most essential problems.

But what is the essential Problem, if not mortality?

Beyond Good and Evil

Sometimes we need the court jester to point out the obvious. Enter Louis C. K. In one of his well-known comedy bits, C. K. talks about how he drives an Infiniti, knowing full well there are starving people out there who would benefit greatly from some of the money he'd spent on his gratuitously pimped-out ride. He knows he could easily sell his Infiniti and buy a slightly less luxurious car—say, a fully loaded Ford Focus, fresh off the lot—and still have thousands of dollars left over to help all those starving people. But every day, he doesn't do it—which is as normal and ubiquitous as it is evil. Every day, he fails to make one mildly self-sacrificial decision that would literally save lives. Every day, he makes people die with his car.[845]

Before his calamitous #MeToo moment, Louis C. K. was what most people would've called a "good guy": witty, insightful, self-deprecating; a reliable friend; a dialed-in dad. He also strikes me as the kind of guy who knows how utterly meaningless it is to be called a "good guy." That's what we used to call frat guys in college who were tolerable to be around: "Yeah, he's a solid dude. A good hang. I wouldn't want him dating my sister, but . . . you know . . . he's a good guy."

And this is essential to the Problem. In presuming every person in the world is generically good-*ish*, we gloss over the real horrors of the world at large. The word "good" becomes a sloppy synonym for "not that bad," and certainly "not as bad as *that* guy." Good rebranded as "Diet Good." Good-*Lite*. Tsunamis, school shooters, terrorists, even Louis C. K. after being outed—those are the *real* (and only?) evils, things we can point to and say, "*That's* the problem!" What feels better than that? Social psychologists call it the "myth of pure evil." It's the supreme self-serving bias, the ultimate scapegoat. Evil is something absolute and obvious, a monster we can identify and (hopefully) isolate, something "over there" we can blame for the world's woes.[846]

But the myth of pure evil is just that: a fantasy. A vain exercise in wish fulfillment. In reality, the fallenness of the world is only ever propagated by ordinary, "decent" people.[847] That was one of Primo Levi's insights when reflecting upon the Holocaust: "Monsters exist, but they are too few in number to be truly dangerous. More dangerous are the common men, the functionaries ready to believe and to act without asking questions."[848] Turns out, you don't need monsters to perpetuate the Problem. You need polite, compliant people. Contented citizens. You need decent people doing a decent job of living decent lives.

But could *I* really be part of the Problem? I never killed anybody or built any bombs in my basement. I don't even drive an Infiniti. And my little fuel-efficient, two-door Accord never hurt anybody.

I think I spent the first half of my life thinking this way. It's the fault of the few bad apples for screwing things up for the rest of us. And since the world was a mess long before I came along, I never really thought of myself as being part of the Problem.

I have Augustine and MLK to thank for bursting that little bubble. Both had a lot to say about the hidden intentions of the human heart. They described evil as being far more insidious than we are wont to imagine, let alone admit. According to King, it's not just a few scary White dudes in scary white sheets who are responsible for society's ills: "He who passively accepts evil is as much involved in it as he who helps to perpetrate it. He who accepts evil without protesting against it is really cooperating with it."[849] Which is a poetic way of saying that if you're not part of the solution, you're part of the problem. And that means *I* am part of the Problem, simply by virtue of that fact that I neglect to do the right thing at all times. "Sins of omission," some call it. I make my peace with the evils of the world, little truces of convenience, so I can get on with my day. And to MLK, this was a big deal. He thought of humanity as an "an inescapable network of mutuality," not a loose collection of self-contained individuals. Everything we do (or fail to do) affects everyone around us. Hence, "injustice anywhere is a threat to justice everywhere."[850] Similarly, Augustine described society as an organic whole, infected throughout by an almost imperceptible corruptive influence. Most of history's great Christian thinkers have spoken of evil this way—as something we breathe in and out, without even noticing.

I've never really enjoyed the notion that there's Something Wrong with the world. And "sin"? Suffice it to say, the S-word had not been a part of my native vocabulary . . . until MLK and Augustine brought it to the fore and put me on the hook. But along with their unflinching realism came an unexpected blessing.

It can take a long time to see the sunny side of Christian pessimism. It can bring an unexpected sense of relief—mostly because it confirms that you're not crazy. The world really is rife with problems, and you're not alone in seeing it. No more need to play pretend. As Chesterton put it, "The glad good news brought by the Gospel was the news of original sin."[851] Finally, somebody named it for me.

17

Dead Saints and Decent People

Original sin is the only empirically verifiable doctrine of the Christian faith.

—REINHOLD NIEBUHR[852]

Psychoanalysis is no more than confirming the habitual pronouncement
of the pious: we are all miserable sinners.

—SIGMUND FREUD[853]

Original Sin

WHEN KIDS PLAY PRETEND, they all want to be the hero. Like my niece and
her friends. They have these adorable little Disney parties, where everybody
dresses up like Cinderella, Jasmine, Elsa, or Pocahontas. I notice none of
them ever calls dibs on being the Wicked Witch. So it goes with the world's
adults: no one ever sets out to be the bad guy. Yet here we are.

A long time ago, on a continent far, far away, a young boy named Augustine stole some pears from the neighbor's tree. It's not like he didn't know
any better. Augustine's mother was an upright and devout woman. He grew
up going church. He knew the Ten Commandments by heart, including,
"Thou shalt not steal." But that didn't stop him Lil' Auggie.

Years later, when reflecting upon his prepubescent venture into thiev-
ery, what really bugged Augustine was the sheer irrationality of it all, the
utter lack of any intelligible motive. His parents had plenty of pear trees

in their own back yard—bigger trees with better pears than the one from which he stole. Besides, he didn't even like pears in the first place.

So why'd he do it? Why steal something you don't even want? After much soul-searching, Lil' Auggie realized he probably wouldn't have stolen the pears if he was alone. Something about being with his hoodlum friends made it all the more appetizing. Equally important, he knew he couldn't pin the blame on his buddies. His friends didn't make him become a thief. There was no egging on, no coercion. He did it because he wanted to do it. It seemed like a good idea at the time. But why? Why is stealing something you neither want, nor need, so much fun?[854]

I remember being on a college road trip with a few friends. I was sitting in the back seat of my buddy's Mustang GTO, careening down the interstate at about a million miles an hour. All of a sudden, we heard a deafening *weeeee-errrrrrr-weeeee-errrrrrr*, accompanied by the dreadful flashing of red-and-blue lights. We'd thought we were in the clear, what with my friend's radar detector on board. Apparently not.

Panic set in as the officer approached. Not only had we been caught going 30 mph over, but somehow the cop knew we had a radar detector—a misdemeanor in the state of Virginia. He leaned over the driver's side window, belly protruding, and commenced interrogation: "Y'all look to be in some kinda rush," he mumbled, a pinch of chaw in his right cheek. At some point during that clumsy confrontation, one of us gathered the courage to ask, "Sir, how did you know we had a radar detector?" He responded: "Cause I got me a radar detector detector."

The next thing that happened was a bit of a blur. I recall being seized by a nearly irresistible urge to speak. I could almost see each ill-fated word as it escaped my mouth: "Oh, yeah? Well, *we* have a radar detector *detector* detector." Silence. The air grew thick with a palpable tension. Somewhere, a lonely tumbleweed rustled across the road. Creeping death. Then, a series of strangled snickers from the back seat. The officer was not pleased. Neither was my buddy who was driving. But at least my friends got a really, really big laugh out of it. Except for the one who was driving, who got a really, really big ticket.

The Importance of Everything

It was Augustine who said friendship can be a dangerous enemy.[855] I think he was talking about something more than just "peer pressure." Back in middle school, when I worked in a deli, my boss—a convicted felon—ordered me to take a hundred dollars out of the register at the end of each shift. I was to then put the cash in an envelope and slide it under the prosciutto, on the bottom shelf of the walk-in. Later on, I discovered what I had been doing was called "skimming off the top," and it's highly illegal. Now here's a clear-cut case of being coerced into unlawful behavior by an external force—namely, my ex-con boss with two counts of voluntary manslaughter on his rap sheet. But I don't think this is the kind of fear-based motivation Augustine was talking about. I think he meant that friends can be like gasoline on a spark: they fuel the fire of our already-present inclinations. Imperceptibly, perhaps even unconsciously, they conspire to trigger the twisted choices we end up making. *Trigger*, not *cause*.

Maybe it's because we all long to belong. I wouldn't have made the "radar detector detector detector" comment if it was just me and the cop.[856] I don't even think it would've crossed my mind. Something about being in the company of others helped draw out my incipient obnoxiousness. I wanted to feel "part of."

Not that my comment was "evil" in some Hannibal Lecter sense. No real harm done, so why sweat it? This is a common criticism of Christianity, by the way—it makes too big a deal of the minutiae. What's a few missing pears and one whopping speeding ticket in the grand scheme of things? Is it really that important? Don't these things only seem significant when they directly involve *me*? *My* actions, my deep-seated Freudian guilt? With this criticism in mind, Christopher Hitchens called Augustine a "self-centered fantasist": "He was guiltily convinced that god cared about his trivial theft from some unimportant pear trees, and quite persuaded—by an analogous solipsism—that the sun revolved around the earth."[857]

It's easy to imagine existence as a one-man show with only God in the audience, as if the universe were merely a backdrop for my life-sized solo performance. Maybe that's what King David meant by the following confession, written after his infamous extramarital affair with Bathsheba, the local beauty: "Against you, and you alone, have I sinned."[858] You sure about that, David? You sure God is the only one you've wronged? How 'bout Bathsheba's husband? Maybe "her beauty and the moonlight overthrew ya," but now she's preggers, you're her baby daddy, and her husband's dead—conveniently dispatched to the front lines by none other than you, O great and righteous king.

If life is really all about *my* storied struggle to feel good about myself, then everything that happens outside me is secondary and incidental, an assembly of plot devices serving only to keep my internal narrative moving along. Thus understood, the world's people, places, and things have meaning only insofar as they relate to my inner "spiritual" reality. Even God becomes a prop.

But this scenario stands in stark contrast to the reality described by Jesus. He labored under the conviction that everything mattered: from our innermost intentions, to the well-being of our enemies. To condemn a fellow human being was, according to Jesus, to commit murder. What we call "character assassination," he called assassination. There was no distinguishing hidden thoughts from externalized actions, no dualism of body vs. mind/spirit, no division between the inner self and the outer, visible world. Because, to Jesus, there was only one world—the Real World, as it is—where everything matters, if anything does.

And isn't that the case? If even one thing in the universe has stable and substantial value, must not everything? Including the very things, and the very people, we are wont to overlook?

In a proclamation that probably shocked his first-century audience, Jesus directly associated himself with the poorest of the poor: "Whatever you did for one of the least of these brothers and sisters of mine, you did for me."[859] Worse still, the same Bible warns, "Whoever claims to love God yet hates a brother or sister is a liar."[860] It's easy to say you love God, and still easier to assume you do. Not so simple when speaking of your flatulent coworker. The implication is clear: when it comes to love, the words "self," "God," and "neighbor," are indissolubly enmeshed. To Jesus, a failure to love anyone constituted a failure to love God. It was that serious. It still is. And maybe that's what David meant: a sin against Bathsheba (and her unsuspecting husband) was a sin against God.

Infinite Obligation, Mutual Responsibility

"There are no ordinary people," wrote C. S. Lewis, "You have never talked to a mere mortal."[861] Unlike the price of gasoline or the trade value of Google stock, human dignity is not determined by fickle market trends. Which is not to suggest that we're all "equal" is some sloppy, sentimental sense. Americans don't much like having our egalitarian buttons pushed, but I can pretty much guarantee that you and I have some pronounced areas of inequality. I bet you're a better baseball player than I am. Probably taller, too. And if you're an even remotely competent financial planner, it's a safe bet you've got more cash stashed away than I ever will. But when it comes to a head-to-head guitar duel, I like my chances . . . none of which has even the slightest thing to do with what C. S. Lewis was talking about, which is that, at bottom, we're all equal—not in terms of aptitude, physical or mental attributes, personality type, or character traits, but *in the eyes of God*.

"In the image of God he created them; male and female he created them."[862] There it is, right at the beginning of the Bible. Roughly translated, it means that each of us is an extraordinary work of art. An unfinished work, no doubt, but extraordinary, nonetheless—which means we should all be treating each other in an altogether different way. To paraphrase the philosopher Emmanuel Levinas, and Kierkegaard before him, each of us is infinitely obligated to "the other."[863] This is the deadly seriousness of it all. This is the terrible worth of every human being. Implicit here is the answer to the most haunting rhetorical question of all time: "Am I my brother's keeper?" And it's a question that each one of us has to answer for ourselves.

Behold, the absolute, concrete claim of Christ over all creation. And by contemporary standards, this might be one of Christ's least likeable qualities: this inflexible, all-encompassing absoluteness. It's about everything and everyone. It both includes and incriminates us all, since we all exist under the shadow of God's universal call to love, to live in the present reality of God's kingdom. And we fail. On the daily.

Hereditary Evil?

Okay, failure is one thing. But *sin*? Sure, humanity has its problems. We've all got our little quirks and neuroses. But invoking the S-word is another thing altogether. *Sin*—is there even such a thing?

Most of us think of sin as a rhetorical relic, like so many leftovers on the bottom shelf of the refrigerator of history. Maybe the concept of sin used to make sense, back when witch trials and scarlet letters still blighted the cultural landscape, but surely not now. For my part, reading Augustine's rants about "original sin" felt like passing a peanut-sized kidney stone. He thought of sin as something passed down from parents to children, as if Adam's original transgression had resulted in a genetic defect, effectively re-wiring human nature. The result? We are all born sinners. It affects even our deepest desires and subconscious urges. All who are "born from Adam"[864] are tainted by this ancient, "hereditary evil." What's worse, we've actually inherited Adam's *guilt*—meaning each of us is personally responsible for the ruin of the universe.[865] It's a grim, discomfiting prognosis . . . and not one embraced by all Christians at all times.[866]

Theologian Herbert McCabe has a bit of a different take. To McCabe, the words "original sin" refer not to some prehistoric mishap, but to *your* origin, your personal history and original background story, your "coming into being." Remember: you don't enter this life as a fully formed, autonomous self, floating above all environmental influence. There is no "I" in Y-O-U. You only *become* yourself by being born into the Something Wrong: an already-wounded world that shapes and informs you at every turn. And it all happens without you even realizing it.

Nature vs. Nurture

I have this friend named Dabney, who, second to Bigoted Becky, might be the Whitest person I've ever met. Dabney talks about his dad in ways that are unfamiliar to me. Apparently, he was a big-time banker/venture capitalist who somehow never missed a single one of his son's Little League games. In his spare time, he taught Dabney how to do things like fix a carburetor, tie a square knot, and balance a checkbook. How the guy was able to accomplish all this while holding down a full-time job remains a mystery.

My dad didn't do any of that stuff. At least, not when I was a little kid. Not that he didn't want to. He just didn't know how, mostly because his parents didn't know how . . . and so on and so on, in an infinite regress of best efforts and good intentions. My father spent the better part of his early adulthood gigging up and down the East Coast, occasionally rubbing elbows with the likes of B. B. King and Screamin' Jay Hawkins. As a teenager, in 1962, he played the Apollo Theatre in Harlem with his first band, The Orients, just a few years after Buddy Holly's legendary "Who brought the White guy?" appearance. By the time I was born, he'd already come off the road and picked up more shifts at the bar. At any hour of the day, he was either cooking, gigging, bartending, drinking, or recovering.

The Orients, 1962 (hint: my dad's the White kid on the right)

My dad redoubled his efforts at being a good father once he got sober. It was a beautiful thing to witness. Every once in a while, he'd sit down with us on the couch and play us a song, usually "Mr. Bojangles." "I knew a man Bojangles and he'd dance for you in worn out shoes . . ." Years before I'd seen my first photo of Bojangles, I'd already imagined him in vivid detail—a black-and-white image of an old, leather-faced man, smiling and dancing, yet somehow sad. I pictured him watching younger, Whiter people mimicking his craft, studying his every step, then bringing his moves to the big screen, where they'd proceed to make millions and forget his name. It was the perfect song. It was as if my dad was saying, "This is it kid; this is all I got." A couple of chords. Some sad, shimmering moments. Longing.

This was, and is, my genesis—my beginning, my origin. And my father never beat me with a pipe wrench or burned me with me cigarettes. He didn't turn me over to the state, like Palo's parents did. He taught me many good and beautiful things. He showed me that helping those who are hurting is worth it, even when you get yourself hurt in the process. He showed me how to be vulnerable, to make amends, and begin anew. And in countless ways, my father loved me well. He remains one of the great heroes of my life, along with my mother. But like all people and all parents, he did only what he could—which was, in an ultimate sense, deficient. And in this world, in this life, even the slightest shortcomings can constitute a failure to meet another person's desperate need to be loved. Like Dabney's dad, who did his best, but died too young. So much the worse when you're Palo, and your origin, the very soil in which you're planted, is one of barren indifference.

Sick Home

"Home may be where the heart is, but it's no place to spend Wednesday afternoon," wrote Walker Percy.[867] "Sin," if I can dare use the word, is a *place*. More specifically, it's *this* place—which, for you and me, is the only place. It's civilization: the historical totality of every culture, society, and individual that has ever been. It's *home*. It might not the home we're longing for, but it's the only home we find when we enter this world. And here, in this place, there ain't no "right side of the tracks."

Sin isn't something we "do" in spurts. It's the air we breathe, the water we swim in. Even if, in the name of modern psychology, we bracket traditional categories of "right" vs. "wrong," it's hard to live a life of sober watchfulness while continuing to deny the Something Wrong.

The Hebrew word for "sin" (*chata'*) means, among other things, "to miss the target."[868] Sounds a bit more palatable to our modern ears than "moral licentiousness," or "hardened rebellion against God." Maybe you "miss the target" because you can't see it clearly. Maybe you've tried your best but keep coming up just shy. If you're anything like the rest of us, then one thing's for certain: missing the mark is now a regular occurrence. Call it the "habitual not-quite-ness of life," the phenomenon of perpetually deferred desire. Call it "without-ness," or the pervasive human experience of lack. Call it *chata'*, if you prefer. Call it whatever you want. It'll still be there, with or without being named.

Returning to original sin: my *chata'* is "original" to me in the sense that it is *my* origin. It's where I cut my teeth. It's home, the one and only training ground where I became myself. From day one, life was busy nurturing the warped wants I've grown to know and love . . . and hardly even recognize. Long before that cop ever clicked on his red-and-blue lights, my wanting mechanisms were already prone to generating all manner of misshapen desire. I am, like you, a socially constructed being—a "product of my environment"—at least, in part. There is no pristine version of me that predates my embodied existence. This me is the only me I've ever met . . . and he has problems.

Wrath & Will

I take no pleasure in bursting self-esteem bubbles, especially my own. "Me" is a likeable enough guy. Lovable, even. But at the very least, I am guilty of perpetuating the same patterns of fear and lack as the generations before me. Their symptoms are now mine.

Actually, that's not quite true. We don't merely suffer the superficial symptoms of our parents' (or even Adam and Eve's) problems. We *are* our symptoms. And the gripping "It's not your fault" scene from *Good Will Hunting* notwithstanding, the question of whether or not you're to blame for the present messiness of life is not really the issue. Regardless of who's responsible for the Problem, it's now *your* problem. You are in it, living and enacting the drama of your life, willing it into being. Because to *be* is to *will*.

Even if you reject folksy concepts of "free will"; even if you understand "will" as merely the result of basic biological processes occurring in your noggin;[869] even if, in a lackluster protest, you choose *not* to choose (like your stoner college roommate), you're still making a choice. You are not free to forswear your freedom. You've got no choice but to choose. "You are embarked," Pascal said.[870] The train has left the station. You're a pilgrim, like it or not. You can't *not* be on the journey, heading somewhere, towards something. Such is life. Such is the world. Such is our fallen, finite freedom.

Gods and Worms

"We are all worms," Churchill mused, "but I do believe that I am a glow-worm."[871] Well spoken, sir . . . though I might add that we're worms who'll one day be food for worms, regardless of how brightly we glow in the interim. While not everyone is endowed with a Churchill-sized ego, most of us have at least a mild case of "God-bug syndrome": the feeling of being both special and insignificant, wormlike yet godlike, larger than life yet unbearably small.[872] Our longings and aspirations soar higher than the heavens, but we're destined for the dirt—six feet under, to be precise. Such is the paradoxical nature of being a person. And when it comes to The Way Things Are, this dichotomy is even more apparent, since each of us plays the part of both perpetrator and prey, origin and victim.

And yes, you really are a victim. Really and truly. Don't let any crusty curmudgeons tell you otherwise. Somebody's hurt you along the way, and they had no excuse for doing so. You've stumbled upon unjust systems and situations that you had no part in creating, yet you were left to bear at least some of the brunt . . . and you've still got the scars to prove it. Biblically speaking, you're a "captive," a prisoner held in bondage by the three-headed hydra of darkness, evil, and death. So am I. We're all in the same boat—the *USS Victim*—and it's sinking.

Victimhood

As a work of ancient religious literature, the Bible is unique in that it speaks from the point of view of the victim. It looks at the world from the margins. Shockingly, and without apology, it tells the losers' story—the suckers, the scapegoats, the second-best.[873] The God of the Bible sides with Abel, not Cain; with Job, not his highfalutin friends; with Jesus, not the dark powers and principalities that put him to death. And Jesus was all about setting the oppressed free. For this very reason, the New Testament refers to Jesus as "ransom": a one-time payment, made by God, to redeem (or "buy back") humanity from captivity (a.k.a. the *Christus Victor* and/or "ransom theory" of atonement[874]). "The Son of Man did not come to be served, but to serve," Jesus said, "and to give his life as a ransom for many."[875]

And why does anybody ever pay a ransom? Why would any parent fork over a personal fortune to secure the return of their kidnapped child?

Simple: for the sake of the child, the object of the parent's undying affection and desire. It's got nothing to do with guilt or innocence. Maybe the child is exceptionally well-behaved, or maddeningly disobedient, or somewhere in between. Doesn't matter. The parent pays the ransom for one reason, and one reason only: for love of the child.

Glory and Refuse

But we are more than mere victims in the human story. We also play the part of the perpetrator. Right-wingers are right about this: we really are accountable for what we do, and for how we respond to life's ups and downs. That's part of what it means to be a person, a "moral agent," a responsible self. It means you're able to affect things around you, for good or for ill. It means there are people counting on you: friends, family, customers, clients, even complete strangers who trust you to stop at red so they can safely go on green. That's the deal. If Harry doesn't sacrifice himself to destroy the last horcrux, then the darkness will prevail. If Frodo doesn't drop the One Ring into the fires of Mount Doom, Middle earth is lost. That's how it works. As chaos theorists have explained, your actions ripple out into the world, the results of which are almost impossible to predict, let alone imagine (a.k.a. the "butterfly effect").[876] And only you can answer for your actions, since without you, they wouldn't've happened. That's what Augustine discovered: "I knew myself both to have a will and to be alive. Therefore, when I willed or did not will something, I was utterly certain that *none other than myself* was willing or not willing."[877] Same goes for you. Only you can will to do what you will to do. There's no one else to blame. Only you are responsible for enacting the decisions you've chosen to make. Your fingerprints are all over the crime scene, and you're accountable for them—which is not all bad news, since (as Sebastian Junger and Jordan Peterson have argued) one's sense of meaning and purpose is proportional to the amount of responsibility one willingly assumes.[878]

If, as previously suggested, "to *be* is to *will*," then it's equally true that to *will* is to *wound*—which is a big part of the Problem of Life. We humans have a knack for hurting one another, including the ones we love most (not to mention the ones we resent). In so doing, we fail to live up to our inner sense of "oughtness," thereby violating the timeless principle of moral, social, and cosmic order, which MLK and Aquinas called "natural law."[879] The ancient Egyptians called it *Ma'at*—the eternal embodiment of truth, justice, and harmony. To the Chinese, it's *Tao*. To America's indigenous people, it's *Wakan Tanka* ("Great Spirit" or "Great Mystery"[880]). Hindus call it *Rta*. The ancient Greeks and early Christians called it the *Logos*.[881] It's that nagging inner voice that tells you what kind of person you're supposed to be. You know . . . *that* voice. It whispers to you in those rare, silent moments, reminding you to seek justice, speak truth, defend the defenseless, and love your neighbor as yourself.[882] And you don't. Neither do I. We're on the same sinking ship . . . so don't go blaming me for your own inner voice. I didn't put it there. It's *yours*, just as your highest ideals are *yours*. Even now, you stand directly under their judgment, as I stand under mine.

And speaking of high ideals, there's none more lofty than our longing to love and be loved. It's the apex of our aspirations, the high point of all our hopes. There is no greater goal, nothing more "excellent" (1 Cor 12–13). But when it comes to loving others, we "miss the mark." Over and over and over again. This is our human plight. "What sort of freak then is man!" Pascal wondered, "How novel, how monstrous, how chaotic, how paradoxical . . . Judge of all things, feeble earthworm, repository of truth . . . the glory and refuse of the universe!"[883]

None of this seems particularly fair. We didn't ask to be born, yet here we are, with heavy loads of responsibility, privilege, and freedom all placed at our feet. And freedom is a funny thing: we've got more of it now than anybody ever has, yet we're more anxious and unhappy than ever. Our choices are limitless (almond milk, 2 percent, coconut, or soy?), our liberties beyond number. But the apostle Paul had a word for this sort of radical, unfettered freedom: "wrath." More precisely, *God's* wrath. Our hell is getting to do whatever the hell we want. The punishment is the reward; the penalty, pleasure. And our choices are avenged by their success. This is The Way Things Are. Behold, the terrible wrath of God.[884]

Doing Evil by Wanting Good

Whatever we mean by the word "sin," it can't be something "over there," a lone wolf we can isolate and contain. Remember: the "myth of pure evil" is just that—a self-serving bias. A convenient untruth. *Chata'* isn't confined to the actions of a few bad apples. It's much more mundane than that.

Evil is, as psychologists keep telling us, "banal." Ordinary. Commonplace. Dare I say, dull. No "monsters" necessary—which is precisely what was so disturbing about the Nazis. Wrote one SS officer in his diary, "On 17 July 1941 nothing much happened. I messed around with the Jews some more—and that's my work."[885] Nazis riffed about the weather, what they ate for dinner, how much they missed their children, and how many Jews they killed that day, all in the same breath. Most were average, compliant people. Family men. Faithful patriots who fulfilled their duty.[886]

Even the most egregious evils usually boil down to something that the guilty party perceives as "good," i.e., desirable, valuable, worthy of pursuit. Just ask Len Wein, the guy who created Wolverine: "Almost every villainous character worth his salt is somebody who believes they're doing the right thing."[887] That's why Wolverine is just a hair's breadth away from Magneto. And according to Jesus, so are we. We pursue things we want, things that seem right and good. In Magneto's case, it's exacting revenge against the mutant-hating scum who made his life a living hell. Why does Thanos want to kill half the universe? To save the other half. To restore the cosmic balance. He's the ultimate, intergalactic ecoterrorist.

In his book, *I Wear the Black Hat*, Klosterman asks, "Why would anyone *want* to be evil?"[888] It's an age-old question that plagued even Plato, who concluded that nobody really wants to be evil. It's like my niece and her friends: none of them ever chooses to be the villain. Following Plato, Christians from Athanasius to Dionysius to Aquinas all agreed: "No one acts intending evil."[889] We make choices based on what we want, and we want them because, to us, they're "good."

And that's just the thing: they *are* good. Or, at least, a type of good. "God created the heavens and the earth . . . and God saw that it was good." The world is full of good things, things worthy of being wanted, even loved. The problem, of course, is that we love things in the wrong way and in the wrong order. Augustine called it "disordered love," and we do it all the time.

We love eating ice cream more than we love being healthy. We love feeling "part of" more than standing up for what's right. I like columnist David Brooks's example: "If a friend tells you a secret and you blab it at a dinner party, you're putting your love of popularity above your love of friendship."[890] That's loving in the wrong order. And you know what? I *love* popularity. I like the way it makes me feel. That's partly why I played cover songs at college frat parties. I love to feel loved, to be seen and recognized. Apparently, so did Augustine. And that's precisely what gets us into trouble.

When you get right down to it, nobody does evil for the sake of being evil. Even serial killers do what they do because they enjoy it, plain and simple. They don't kill in order to advance the general cause of evil. They do it because, to them, it's "good"—a.k.a. desirable, natural, satisfying, worthwhile—like Thanos with his genocidal scheming, or Magneto with his humanity hating . . . or, on an admittedly smaller scale, like Augustine with his stolen pears. And me with my radar detector-detector-detector.

But enough about me. Let's talk about Satan.

Empathy for the Devil

The devil was once an angel of light who fell from grace. And what was his basic, unpardonable offense? He wanted to be great. He wanted to soar ever upward, higher than any other creature—higher even than God. He wanted to be the overlord of all things: "You said in your heart, 'I will ascend to the heavens; I will raise my throne above the stars of God . . . I will ascend above the tops of the clouds; I will make myself like the Most High'".[891] Satan fell prey to what some call "the pride of life," which is nothing other than an overdeveloped desire to imitate God.[892] It's wanting to be the greatest, to be loved, revered, and remembered, maybe even feared. You saw it played out in that spookiest of *Lord of the Rings* scenes, when Galadriel the Elf briefly considers taking the One Ring for herself and becoming the all-powerful empress of Middle Earth:

> In place of the Dark Lord you will set up a Queen. And I shall not be dark, but beautiful and terrible as the Morning and the Night! Fair as the Sea and the Sun and the Snow upon the Mountain! Dreadful as the Storm and the Lightning! Stronger than the foundations of the earth. All shall love me and despair![893]

Galadriel is one of the "good guys," by the way.

Are the temptations of demons and she-elves really so foreign? Who doesn't like a little glory now and then? Aren't we always telling our kids to write their own destinies, reach for the stars, etc.? Is self-directed ambition really such perilous business? Apparently, for alcoholics, it is: "Any life run on self-will can hardly be a success. On that basis we are almost always in collision with something or somebody, *even though our motives are good.*"[894] Regardless of our intentions, self-will has the inevitable effect of alienating us from our neighbors. Our wants and ambitions clash with theirs. The Bible has even stronger words on the subject: "God opposes the proud but gives grace to the humble"; "He has scattered those who are proud in their inmost thoughts."[895] Behold, the essence of what Christians call "sin." And it isn't a wicked witch in a dark and faraway tower, casting hexes on a hapless humanity. That's far too naive and self-serving of a picture.

Perhaps the ancients were right. Maybe nobody knowingly chooses evil. Maybe everybody, in their heart of hearts, "means well"—including Satan, the angel of hell. Well apparently, "meaning well" doesn't mean a whole hell of a lot.

Good Intentions

Take Cecil Rhodes, that infamous imperialist who "meant well" when he transformed southern Africa into his own personal diamond mine, mowing down any and all natives who got in his way: "The more of the world we [White Anglo-Saxons] inhabit the better it is for the human race."[896] Then there was the eugenics craze of the late eighteenth through early nineteenth century. Teddy Roosevelt, a contemporary of Rhodes, believed it was the "prime duty" of every good citizen to pass on their superior genetic material through selective breeding: "We have no business to permit the perpetuation of citizens of the wrong type."[897] Woodrow Wilson (nephew of theologian James Woodrow) even signed a bill to authorize the "sterilization of feeble-minded," including "idiots," epileptics, "imbeciles and morons," and other "defectives."[898] Clarence Darrow, the famous Scopes "Monkey" Trial litigator, and the mathematician Bertrand Russell, also sympathized with the eugenicists' cause (Russell supported the implementation of government-issued, color-coded "procreation tickets," which would determine which citizens were fit to bear children, and with whom).[899] These were men of great sincerity and ambition, and in the case of Woodrow and Roosevelt, great optimism. True "progressives," in the turn-of-the-twentieth-century sense of the word. They were genuinely interested in the betterment of human society. They "meant well." But as the old saying goes, "The road to hell is paved with good intentions."

I love teaching my students about Cecil Rhodes. He's an easy historical figure for them to latch on to, mostly because he's such a despicable scoundrel . . . and what could be more memorable than a despicable scoundrel? Nobody ever gets the Cecil Rhodes question wrong on the midterm. There's something so unforgettable, so strangely satisfying about notoriously evil people, especially if and when they get their just deserts. What isn't so satisfying is the prospect that you, me, and Rhodes aren't all that different.

I'm not suggesting that we're all genocidal maniacs in the making. Most of us are ordinary, decent people. We do our duty. We respond when needed and pay our taxes. We act out our assigned roles in a societal narrative that we didn't write. But one of the many disturbing lessons of WWII is that ordinary, decent people are quite capable of committing evil, especially when situated within organizational hierarchies where evil has become normalized. When everyone around us is doing something dastardly, we assume we're supposed to be doing it—or at the very least, we feel less personal responsibility for participating. That was Hitler's great secret: convince the everyday German that they're "just following orders," or better yet, that's it's for the sake of the "greater good" (i.e., the flourishing of the German state).

As psychologists and Holocaust scholars can attest, none of us is immune to the tugs of conformity and groupthink. Not even you (read Blumenthal's *The Banality of Good and Evil* or Zimbardo's *The Lucifer Effect* if you want more proof). I don't care how much of rugged individualist you are, how contrarian your personality, how militantly you march to the beat of your own libertarian drum. Statistically speaking, most of us will do the dirty work till the bitter end, even if it means leaving our morals by the wayside.[900]

Themification

Here's where Jesus becomes particularly unsettling. He insists that the Something Wrong isn't "out there." That means you can't delimit the Problem to the actions and intentions of an externalizable "them." No more getting yourself off the hook by blaming everybody else. This was Aleksandr Solzhenitsyn's realization after a decade of imprisonment under the brutal Stalinist regime. The tempting thing, the all too simple thing, is to divide humanity into two categories: the malevolent oppressors (e.g., the Stalinists, Nazis, etc.) and the harmless rest of us. Evil, thus construed, is something we can quarantine and extinguish with relative ease. But as Solzhenitsyn recognized, "the line dividing good and evil cuts through the heart of every human being." And who among us is willing to uncover, let alone extinguish, the evil hidden in his own heart?[901]

A century earlier, another Russian author was busy writing his magnum opus, *The Brothers Karamazov*. Dostoyevsky, like Solzhenitsyn, spent time in a Russian prison, experienced a dramatic conversion, and came to embrace the reality of the ubiquity of evil. In *Karamazov*, Dostoyevsky depicts Father Zosima as a mind-bogglingly compassionate man. Yet in spite of his holiness—or maybe because of it—Zosima sees himself as culpable for the sins of the whole world, "on behalf of all and for all, for all human sins, the world's and each person's."[902]

But hey, Zosima's a fictional character. It's easy for him to be self-effacing. Nobody's ever that humble in real life . . . right?

Christian

In 1996, a group of Algerian terrorists kidnapped and butchered seven Catholic monks. Long before being kidnapped, one of the monks, a man named Christian, sent a letter to his family, to be opened in the event of his death. The letter included the following prayer:

> My life has no more value than any other. Nor any less value . . .
> I have lived long enough to know that I share in the evil which
> seems, alas, to prevail in the world, even in that which would
> strike me blindly. I should like, when the time comes, to have a
> clear space which would allow me to beg forgiveness of God and
> of all my fellow human beings, and at the same time to forgive
> with all my heart the one who would strike me down.[903]

That was Christian's realization: he shared in the very same evil that would soon claim his life. Like Dostoyevsky before him, he saw himself as belonging to the same "inescapable network of mutuality" of which MLK spoke. And his dying wish? To be forgiven by God, and by the whole of humanity. But being forgiven means forgiving others, including the very jihadists who might someday slit your throat.

The apostle Paul called himself "chief among sinners."[904] That's what saints are like. No themification. No one-upmanship or putting on airs. Saints are utterly uninterested in playing the comparison game. They don't mind being called out, even laughed at. They know they're entangled by the same human web that ensnares us all. Saints expect no parades in their honor, mostly because they don't expect much of anything—and that, of course, is their great secret. To them, it's all a gift. Which is why they're grateful for everything.

Adam and Eve, on a Raft

In the end, getting rid of Adam and Eve doesn't get rid of the Problem of Life. Whether you think of "sin" as something socially habituated or genetically encoded, it's as self-evident as it is pervasive. And for all of modern science's accomplishments, it hasn't been able to solve this basic problem, the plight of being a person. Modern psychotherapy corroborates the great world religions on one crucial point: namely, that being human means navigating life with a broken rudder. It doesn't really matter whether you interpret the creation story literally or figuratively. We do what we don't want to do and fail to do the very things we believe we should—the beautiful, selfless things.

For anybody willing to take a good, hard look at the Real World, it can be tempting to join our Buddhist friends in denying its existence. It's all a grand illusion, a veil of appearances, "dust in the wind." Except that it's not . . . and you know it. Even now, you can feel it bearing down on you, the realness of it all, breathing on the back of your neck. It's as infuriating as it is lovely. Look away, if you must. Or take the red pill and get your irrational optimism on. Stay suspended in the clouds. Because looking the Real World in the eye can feel like plunging into an acid bath. Even the world's beauty, when seen aright, is haunting. "Beauty will be convulsive or will not be at all," wrote André Breton. And if we have eyes to see, all the terror and splendor of life will leave us uneasy—perhaps permanently so.[905] It can rend us to the hub of our hearts. It can push us to the end of our wits and out of our minds.

Heads or Tails?

The Gospel of John contains some of Scripture's most uplifting statements: "I have come that they may have life, and have it to the full"; "You will know the truth, and the truth will set you free"; etc. But against the knee-jerk optimism of our age, John portrays a world in dire straits, a world in need of much more than a pep talk. John isn't interested in making the world "a better place." He's about *judgment*—and the verdict is this: if our world is indeed worthy of repair, if it's even remotely salvageable, it needs to be gutted to the studs. Revolutionized. Rebuilt from the bottom up.

In one of my all-time favorite *Simpsons* episodes, Homer and Marge are listening to the Debbie Boon classic "You Light Up My Life" on the radio. As the song winds down, Homer says, "I bet the guy she was singing that about was real happy." Marge corrects him "Well, actually, she was singing about God." Disappointedly, Homer replies, "Oh, well, He's always happy . . . No, wait, He's always mad."[906]

So which one is it? Is God eternally angry? Or does God really love the world, and take delight in it? Heads or tails—which will it be?

18

Fourth and One

The shattered water made a misty din.
Great waves looked over others coming in,
And thought of doing something to the shore
That water never did to land before.
The clouds were low and hairy in the skies,
Like locks blown forward in the gleam of eyes.
You could not tell, and yet it looked as if
The shore was lucky in being backed by cliff,
The cliff in being backed by continent;
It looked as if a night of dark intent
Was coming, and not only a night, an age.
Someone had better be prepared for rage.
There would be more than ocean-water broken
Before God's last PUT OUT THE LIGHT was spoken.

—ROBERT FROST[907]

PUT OUT THE LIGHT!

THERE ONCE LIVED A crabby old philosopher named Diogenes. According
to legend, he spent most of his days meandering around ancient Greece,
lamp in hand, scouring the sunlit city streets in search of an honest man.

Apparently, he never found any. A homeless wanderer, he preferred the company of wild dogs to any human companion. Diogenes the Cynic, they called him. Word of his antics got around until even Alexander the Great became one of his admirers. When the star-struck conqueror finally met his ill-tempered idol, Diogenes was doing what he did best: loafing around under the Mediterranean sun. Gathering his courage, Alexander made a timid approach and asked, "Diogenes, is there anything I can do for you?" Diogenes answered, "Yes. You can get out of my sunlight."[908] The two crossed paths on another occasion, this time at a local cemetery, where Diogenes was busy examining some discarded skeletons. When Alexander asked Diogenes what he was up to, he replied, "I'm looking for the bones of your father, but I can't seem to tell them apart from the bones of my slave."[909]

Here's a man in whom there was no guile. 24/7/365, he kept it 100. Diogenes wasn't interested in broadening his platform or strengthening his brand. He was looking for truth, or nothing at all. And after making careful survey of the Real World, with its various cultural offerings and achievements, its popular explanations of morality, cosmology and purpose, Diogenes settled on cynicism as the best available option.

If Diogenes, John Calvin, N.W.A., and even a momentarily disheartened Oprah were correct, if the world is indeed a mess, then maybe it's time to punt? Instead of hoping for a better tomorrow, maybe we should all be praying for Robert Frost's ominous words to come to fruition? "PUT OUT THE LIGHT!" Or at the very least, reject the Real World in all its bloated absurdity.

We see flashes of such cynicism in Jesus himself. He dismissed long-cherished religious conventions by befriending sinners, prostitutes, political enemies, foreigners, and people of ill repute. Like Diogenes, Jesus spurned superficiality and materialistic ambition in favor of an ascetic lifestyle: "Foxes have dens and birds have nests, but the Son of Man has no place to lay his head" (Matt 8:20); and elsewhere, "Go, sell everything you have and give to the poor, and you will have treasure in heaven. Then come, follow me."[910] The controversial biblical scholar John Dominic Crossan paints Jesus as a "cynic philosopher" in the pattern of Diogenes. Other credible historians agree.[911] To Jesus, the world was something to be wrestled with and overcome: "Do not suppose that I have come to bring peace to the earth. I did not come to bring peace, but a sword."[912] In a similar vein, his apostles advised: "Do not love the world or anything in the world. If anyone loves the world, love for the Father is not in them."[913] There would be no "fitting in" for Jesus and his followers. Not an ounce of irrational optimism in their camp. The world was a Problem to be solved . . . or abandoned . . . or outright obliterated.

Furious, Vengeful Antipathy

If Christ was a committed pessimist, what, then, of the Christian? Must Christ-followers embrace Jesus' brand of countercultural cynicism, and do we? Nietzsche certainly thought so. Christians were, in his assessment, a miserable lot, perpetually crushed by the weight of God's "eternal No," obsessed with an ostensibly "better" world "beyond," consumed by a "furious, vengeful antipathy to life itself."[914] Maybe Nietzsche was a tad melodramatic. But maybe not. After all, it was Jesus who said, "If anyone comes to me and does not hate father and mother, wife and children, brothers and sisters—yes, even their own life—such a person cannot be my disciple."[915] Sure sounds like "furious, vengeful antipathy" to me.

Reminds me of Anne Rice's appraisal of Christianity. "Anti-life," she called it. And in one sense, why shouldn't it be? Why be "pro-life," if life is the one and only location in which all of our worst experiences take place? It was Darwin who said there was "too much misery in the world," and maybe he was right. Aren't there days when it seems we'd be better off if there was no world, no life, no humanity to contend with? "And the Lord was sorry that he had made man on the earth, and it grieved him to his heart."[916] Can we really blame him? Has not the world warranted disdain, even divine disdain? In Goethe's *Faust*, the devil laments:

> I am the spirit that negates.
> And rightly so, for all that comes to be
> Deserves to perish wretchedly;
> 'Twere better nothing would begin.[917]

Maybe the devil had a point. From Hamlet to Heidegger, Buddha to Socrates, Schopenhauer to Solomon—all have said similar things, aptly encapsulated by Tolstoy in the following pessimistic synthesis: "Happy is he who has not been born."[918] Bertrand Russell had a slightly wittier, yet somehow more depressing take on happiness: "The secret of happiness is to face the fact that the world is horrible, horrible, *horrible*."[919]

Ah, the joys of cynicism. Gloating over the world's shortcomings can be enormously satisfying. Addictive, even. That's how resentment works—like a spring-loaded, internally dispensed drug of limitless supply, ever ready to remind us, "It's all *their* fault!" And what better way to get your fix than by informing "them" of their impending doom? "The Lord is going to lay waste the earth and devastate it."[920] Take that, humanity. Didn't we all find ourselves tantalized by Heath Ledger's Joker, that insightful madman who scorched multi-million-dollar mounds of money just to watch it burn, just to have the satisfaction of snubbing that which this world treasures most?

Maybe it's time God shut this whole thing down and called it a day (though not necessarily twenty-four literal hours).

Of course, if the prospect of delighting in destruction doesn't sit well with you, there's always Option B: create an insular, self-segregated Christian ghetto, where the righteous and fragile can live in relative peace.

Pro-Life?

Apocalyptic anticipation is nothing new. Neither is it uniquely Christian. From the ancient Mayans to medieval Norsemen, prophets aplenty have been heralding the end of days since the beginning of days. But in the U.S., Christian apocalypticism picked up some serious steam during the eighteenth and nineteenth centuries.[921] That's when Christians began promulgating a somewhat novel theology known as "premillennial dispensationalism," including the belief that the faithful few would soon be extricated—or "raptured"—from the earth, leaving the rest of humanity behind to endure a period of untold misery and tribulation.[922]

It was premillennial dispensationalism that gave modern Christians permission to hate the world. And boy, did it catch on. Over the course of the twentieth century, growing numbers of Christian fundamentalists started speaking of the imminent rapture as if it were a matter of course.[923] And in their defense, it certainly looked that way. World Wars I and II, the Holocaust, the atom bomb, Vietnam . . . the world was going to hell in a hand basket. Who wouldn't want to escape, to oppose a secular, nihilistic culture that gave rise to such horrors? By the 1970s, books like Hal Lindsey's *The Late, Great Planet Earth* started counting down the days . . .[924]

But Christianity didn't used to be known for its escapism. In the late nineteenth century, the influential German pastor Christoph Blumhardt labelled such escapist theology a "completely new and unbiblical" form of Christianity.[925] Maybe he was right, but it sure has become a popular one, especially in America. You've probably noticed (*Left Behind*, anyone?). These days, Christians often seem more interested in ushering in Armageddon than in loving our neighbors—let alone forgiving our enemies.

In his "Letter from a Birmingham Jail," MLK echoed Blumhardt's basic concern: "I have watched many churches commit themselves to a completely otherworldly religion which made a strange distinction between body and soul, the sacred and the secular."[926] King was lamenting the apathy of his churchgoing contemporaries, who were eager to save souls but uninterested in embodying God's kingdom, "on earth as it is in heaven." The logic is transparent: Why endeavor to emulate Jesus in this life, if he only functions as an escape hatch to the next? Why love your neighbor if they're basically kindling? And for God's sake, why work towards justice, cultural flourishing, and the common good if the "secular world" is predestined for destruction?[927] Let's get this rapture party started. To hell with it. Let it burn. "I have come to bring fire on the earth," Jesus vented, "and how I wish it were already kindled!"[928] So long, cruel world. It's been real.

There's no denying the appeal of this kind of visceral, apocalyptic language. It's shot through much of today's pop Christianity, especially premillennialism, with its army of adherents in America—and they're not all driven by bitterness. On a bad day, I think a lot of us can sympathize with escapist theology, particularly the impulse to hit the cosmic reset button on life. We hear some of it in the old slave songs, with their repetitive refrains, like apocalyptic mantras set to music:

> Soon-a will be done a-with the troubles of the world,
> the troubles of the world, the troubles of the world,
> Soon-a will be done a-with the troubles of the world,
> I'm goin' home to live with God . . .

Born out of the hell of the American slave experience, the old gospel hymns give voice to a desperate, deeply human desire for liberation, both physical and spiritual: "Now the Gospel train's at hand, be in time. Crowds at the station stand, with passport in their hand, to start for Zion's land, be in time, be in time. . . " With hands open and raised, they sing of release and escape, as if beckoning the end of the world. I think a lot of today's premillennialists are driven by a similar impulse, if only subconsciously. Which is not to say we can (or should) compare our First World problems with the sufferings of antebellum slaves. But even for the most privileged Americans, the here-and-now can be heartbreakingly difficult. There's mental illness, disillusionment with the American dream, the opioid epidemic, White middle-class male malaise, the list goes on (note: White males make up 30 percent of the U.S. population and account for 70 percent of suicides[929]). Remember the Buddha's revelation: "Life is suffering"—and we modern Westerners are no exception.

One of the primary appeals of premillennialism is that it promises a swift end to the horrible, a final emancipation from the anguish and anxieties of everyday life.[930] It's more about escape than "vengeful antipathy." Moreover, plenty of premillennialists are driven by a genuine, altruistic desire to see as many souls saved as possible before the coming apocalypse. They're zealous in their efforts to evangelize, precisely because they *do* care about life—specifically, the lives of others. They want their loved ones to be spared when Armageddon hits and all hell breaks loose. Nevertheless, they remain ready—even eager—for the end.

"Bring Again"

In spite of everything, most of us are still nagged by an undeniable urge to go on living; to embrace life, to love the world as it is. In a famous letter written from a Nazi prison, Dietrich Bonhoeffer cited one of his favorite hymns: "Let pass, dear brothers, every pain; What you have missed I'll bring again." Bonhoeffer wondered:

> What does 'I'll bring again' mean? It means that nothing is lost, that everything is taken up in Christ, although it is transformed, made transparent, clear and free from all selfish desire. Christ restores all this as God originally intended it to be, without the distortion resulting from our sins . . . Doesn't this passage, in its ecstatic longing combined with pure devotion, suggest the 'bringing again' of all earthly desire? . . . 'I will bring again'—that is, we cannot and should not take it back ourselves, but allow Christ to give it back to us.[931]

Bonhoeffer knew the world was a mess, but he loved it anyway. He longed for it to be healed, transformed, and turned upside down, precisely because he loved it. For this very reason, and in the best possible sense, Bonhoeffer refused to make peace with The Way Things Are.

The late liberation theologian James Cone once wrote, "The cross, as a locus of divine revelation, is not good news for the powerful, for those who are comfortable with the way things are."[932] There's nothing alluring about the cross if you're a committed pain avoider or pathological optimist. The gospel offers nothing to those interested in maintaining the status quo. There is no "reaching" people who will not look upon the Something Wrong, who can't imagine why God would ever rock humanity's boat, let alone turn the whole thing upside down. But Bonhoeffer and Cone wouldn't play nice with the world order.

We see this same sort of prophetic defiance in the great sages of Scripture: Jeremiah, Isaiah, John the Baptist. It's the false prophets who prescribe Band-Aids for bullet wounds, saying, "'Peace, peace,' where there is no peace."[933] But Bonhoeffer wouldn't have it. He knew full well the hells of war. And because of that, he knew the merits of measured pessimism. But Bonhoeffer was no cynic. Any antipathy he felt towards the world was fueled by an insatiable desire to see it reborn, given back, and brought again.

Bonhoeffer's prison prayer notwithstanding, cynicism is perfectly natural. Rational, even. It's what we do. We negate life. We assassinate character. We blame, complain, and condemn. With furious antipathy, we reject the world.

But thankfully, for Jesus, "No!" is not the final word.

Worthy and Real

When I think about the possibility of truly cherishing the world, I remember Rilke's love poems to the Lord:

> Dear darkening ground,
> you've endured so patiently the walls we've built,
> perhaps you'll give the cities one more hour
>
> and grant the churches and cloisters two.
> And those that labor—let their work
> grip them another five hours, or seven,
>
> before you become forest again, and water, and widening wilderness
> in that hour of inconceivable terror
> when you take back your name
> from all things.
>
> Just give me a little more time!
> I want to love the things
> as no one has thought to love them,
> until they're worthy of you and real.[934]

Does God love the world like *that*?

It's a yes-or-no question, and one from which we must not shirk. Does *this* place, the Real World, really matter? Is the struggle worth it? To be, or not to be, to love or not to love? These are the questions, and the great world religions are right to take them seriously. It's what drove the Buddha to re-examine—and ultimately renounce—life itself (*nekkhamma*).

Both Buddhism and Christianity agree that self-centeredness is a problem of epidemic proportions. Both admonish us to wage war against the ego and, if at all possible, to put it to death (though followers of the Way believe God does all the heavy lifting). Both try their best to see the Real World as it is: fraught with suffering and ambiguity. But unlike Buddhism, Christianity is not a decree to detach from the world or abandon all desire. Quite the opposite. While confirming that the world is in desperate need of repair, the good news of Jesus is that God has declared this world to be worthy of love—of *God's* love, as well as our own.[935] That's what Jesus' life, death, and resurrection are all about.

In life, Jesus embodied and fulfilled the law of God, obeying every imperative to love God and neighbor. In dying and rising again, Jesus reconciled heaven and earth: "For God was pleased to have all his fullness dwell in him, and through him to reconcile to himself all things . . ."[936] In inaugurating God's kingdom, Jesus initiated the "renewal of all things," the final healing of the cosmos (*apocastasis*). And why did the incarnate God go to all this trouble? Simple: for love of the world.

"I did not come to judge the world," Jesus said, "but to *save* it." That's the good news. He didn't come to crush life under God's gavel, but to bring life "to the full." And he isn't talking about some hypothetical dream world, but the Real World—*this* world—the only world there is.[937]

A Good Dose of Atheism

If you've spent a lifetime being suckled on the teat of indiscriminate affirmation, maybe the love of God seems self-evident or casual, i.e., something to which you are entitled. But historically speaking, God's love for humanity is a radical concept whose introduction we can blame on that quirky carpenter from Nazareth. It was Jesus, after all, who first presented God to the world as "Father"—not a tribal, desert deity, but the Creator and Redeemer of the cosmos. Likewise, it was Jesus who taught us to cry, "Abba," meaning God is not merely a master of servants, but a loving parent. Only Jesus taught his followers to see themselves always as children, the beloved sons and daughters of God: "Unless you turn and become like children . . ."

It was also Jesus who called his disciples "friends," equating his affection for them with God's affection for him: "As the Father has loved me, so I have loved you."[938] There's nothing obvious about this manner of love (*agape*). You don't stumble upon it, dream it up, or derive it from observation or experience—and this is precisely where we could use a good dose of atheism. What could be *less* credible, *less* believable than the unfailing love of an invisible God?

A Many-Splendored Thing

Sometimes I think the word "love" has lost all meaning. What are we even saying when we say it? Do we mean something abstract, impersonal, or obligatory? Something God is theologically required to feel? Or does God love *for real*—like a mother who embraces her dying child, pulls her up towards her lips, and kisses her slowly balding head with a devouring kiss, as if she wants only to consume every ounce of her child's beauty and agony, every millimeter of her cancerous, dying, irreplaceable self? With absolute abandon, she *wants*. Come what may, she is unwilling to lose the object of her love. Nothing "spiritual" about it. Does God love the world in the sense that God *wants it to be*?

Channeling his inner Nietzsche, Karl Barth proclaimed, "Better to hear everywhere *only* the No than to hear an unreal, unconfirmed, merely religious Yes."[939] Barth appreciated atheism, mainly because it reminds us that God's existence isn't obvious, let alone a personal God who is in love with the world and hell-bent on its rescue. And that's what (and who) we're talking about: *Yahweh*—or, more accurately, *YHWH*; the uncreated Creator whose proper name is, strictly speaking, unpronounceable; a vowelless refusal of being named. This God is Someone Else, a divine Stranger. And it is this particular God whom Jesus "fleshes out." It is this particular kingdom that Jesus proclaims and fulfills.

So we postmodern pilgrims are in a bit of a pickle. On the one hand, sky-high self-esteem makes the love of God seem self-evident. On the other, modern skepticism makes the love of God seem unimaginable. In a contemporary culture caught between pathological optimism and enlightened skepticism, it's harder than ever to give the good news a good hearing. And premillennial theology has only made things harder. This brand of (almost exclusively American) fundamentalism has overshadowed a deeper, more ancient strand of sacred truth—namely, that Rilke was right: God is in love with the world, after all.

"For God so loved *the world* . . ."[940] Such is the global, enveloping scope of God's kingdom, which reverberates through Paul's second letter to the Corinthians: "God was reconciling the *world* to himself in Christ, not counting people's sins against them."[941] Such is the love of Jesus, "the lamb of God who takes away the sin of the *world*."[942] Such is the compassion of God, "who desires everyone to be saved and to come to the knowledge of the truth."[943] And such is the proper disposition of the Christian heart, yearning as it does for *apocastasis,* "the renewal of all things," or what Barth called the "absolutely otherworldly reconstruction of *all* that is creaturely"[944]—every person, every neighbor, every enemy (whether fancied or real), every culture and community, every atom of creation.[945] Far from "spiritual," God's love is gritty and real, with dirt under its fingers. It's hungry and jealous, though never stingy. And God will not be robbed of his creation.

But make no mistake: "*re*construction" also implies *de*struction, as John's Gospel points out. Jesus came to "bring fire on the earth," to overcome the great halls of power and monuments of worldly wisdom, to tear down the Jerusalem temple—and indeed, *all* temples.[946] "A time is coming when you will worship the Father neither on this mountain nor in Jerusalem . . . the true worshipers will worship the Father in the Spirit and in truth, for they are the kind of worshipers the Father seeks."[947] The world will not be whitewashed, but resurrected.

"To clasp the hands in prayer," said Barth, "is the beginning of an uprising against the disorder of the world."[948] By definition, Christianity implies rebellion—but a rebellion of a strange sort. It means insurrection against the self-ruin of the world; rebellion against rebellion; a rousing against denial, lethargy, and resentment; against fear, fallenness, and the frightening finality of death. This is what punk and hip-hop always got right. This is what corny Christian pop always gets wrong. This is why Rage, N.W.A., Steinbeck, and Dostoyevsky always have and always will be closer to the truth than the blithe optimism of syrupy spirituality.

God So Loved the World

When faced with the death of his friend Lazarus, Jesus was overcome with anguish—"deeply moved," the Bible says, from the Greek *embrimaomai*, meaning Jesus was not only saddened, but enraged. *Embrimaomai* means to snort with fury, like a bridled horse trudging its way uphill under the cruel crack of the whip. And this is the sort of irreverent discontent Jesus displayed at Lazarus' grave, abandoning all propriety. Nothing detached or "spiritual" about it. Jesus made his stand against The Way Things Are, where people like Lazarus live under the long shadow of evil, suffering, and death, because he is in love with the world and longs for its redemption. Isaac the Syrian felt the same longing, which he expressed in an almost unpardonably pagan prayer:

> What is a compassionate heart? . . . It is a heart on fire for the whole of creation, for humanity, for the animals, for the demons, for all that exists. At the recollection and at the sight of them such a person's eyes overflow with tears owing to the vehemence of the compassion which grips his heart; because of his deep mercy he cannot bear to hear or to look upon any injury or the slightest suffering of anything in creation.[949]

That includes the suffering of cop killers, terrorists, and school shooters. Against all defensible cries for vengeance, the kingdom of God is a kingdom of forgiveness, if it is anything at all.

Turns out the ancient pagans were half-right, enamored as they were by the beauty of nature. Star-crossed lovers and dirt-worshipping hippies are not complete idiots. There's something profoundly Christian about loving the sensual, temporal world. There's something really right about loving creation so fiercely that we're unwilling to let it die. Like Maurice Sendak,

Isaac the Syrian, Bonhoeffer, and even my dad, Jesus refused to let his be-loved creation "go gently into that good night." And so, in utter defiance of The Way Things Are, Christ cracked open the world, unleashing his king-dom from within the confines of creation.

But we only taste and see God's kingdom when we relinquish our own. We only gain the world by first letting it go. "Whoever wants to save their life will lose it," Jesus said, "but whoever loses their life for me will find it."[950] And elsewhere: "Do not love the world or anything in it"—and he meant *our* version of the world, the version we've made in our image, or as N. T. Wright puts it, "The world as it places itself over against God."[951]

So it's not that loving the world is inherently wrong, or even inherently problematic. It's that the kingdoms of this world are all hopelessly deficient. At best, humanly contrived kingdoms serve to protect our individual rights by enforcing well-conceived laws. At worst, worldly governments violate human dignity through violence, coercion, and exploitation. Neither ex-treme is capable of generating the kind of curative love for which we all long. Neither liberates us from the grip of our own rapacious egos. Nor can any earthly kingdom bring salvation (*salus*) and healing to the human heart, from the inside out.[952]

"To believe in God is easy," Blumhardt wrote, "but to believe that the world will become different—to do that, one must be faithful unto death."[953] Some call it "Easter faith," and it means trusting that God is actually capable of building the kingdom Jesus proclaimed—not in spite of this world, but for its sake. Equally important, it means the same God who raised Jesus from the dead can raise us, too. Starting now.

19

What Does Jesus Do?

All shall be well, and all shall be well, and all manner of thing shall be well.

—JULIAN OF NORWICH[954]

How to Spend a Life

ONCE UPON A LEISURELY afternoon, when the Buddha was strolling through the forest, he happened upon a hungry tigress and her litter of cubs. The tigress was too feeble and famished to move, let alone suckle her young with mother's milk. Soon, she would either starve to death, or worse, succumb to brute instinct and consume her own offspring. So the Buddha thought it over: "This body being foul and a source of suffering, he is not wise who would not rejoice at its being spent for the benefit of another."[955] Moved by compassion, he decided to sacrifice himself, that the tigress and her cubs might live. Calmly, quietly, and without any fuss, he lied himself down near the tigress' mouth, slit his own throat, and let himself be devoured.

History is bespeckled by stories of such heroes. Every now and then, some rare soul comes along and chooses to make the ultimate sacrifice "for the benefit of another"—a helpless child, an innocent victim in distress, a litter of hungry cubs. "Very rarely will anyone die for a righteous person," wrote the apostle Paul, "though for a good person someone might possibly dare to die."[956] The key words are *"might possibly"*—as in, hardly ever. So rare, in fact, are such heroes that we erect monuments in their honor. We adorn them with medals, immortalize them in song, and remember their names. We celebrate the fact that, against all odds, heroes happen.

Now here's a hard question for your average pop-culture Christian to ponder: Was Jesus a *hero*? It's a serious question. Was Christ as brave as the Buddha? Brave enough to stand strong in the face of death, and without backing down? Did he possess the same sort of steely resolve as the Gandhis, MLKs, and Harriet Tubmans of history?

Well, no.

At least, not according to the New Testament.

The Gospels tell the story of a trembling and terrified Christ, a man overcome by fear of death—much more so than his own disciple, Paul, who testified, "My desire is to depart [this life] and be with Christ."[957] Jesus shared no such desire. For whatever reasons, Paul welcomed death's sweet embrace. He knew where he was going, and was ready to get there. But not Jesus. He wanted to live.

In another episode unbecoming of a hero, "Jesus wept."[958] We get no such tears from Socrates. Neither has any enlightened Easterner ever aspired to emulate Christ's grief. As the Buddha instructed,

> Longing gives rise to grief;
>   Longing gives rise to fear
> For someone released from longing
>   There is neither grief nor fear
> Affection gives rise to grief;
>   Affection gives rise to fear
> For someone released from affection
>   There is no grief;
> And from where would come fear?[959]

But Jesus was the "man of sorrows and acquainted with grief."[960] He knew full well the burden of anguish. The night before he was crucified, Christ nearly collapsed under the weight of his own fear: "He prayed more earnestly, and his sweat was like drops of blood falling to the ground."[961] So consuming was his fear of death that he begged God for a way out: "My Father, if it be possible, let this cup pass from me . . ."[962] Finally, at the end of his passion, Jesus cried out from the cross, *"Eloi, Eloi, lema sabachthani?,"* which means, "My God, my God, why have you forsaken me?"

An Unexpected Cameo

It was that last question that really bothered Augustine. If the great heroes of history were strong enough to stare down death, why wasn't Jesus? Wasn't he supposed to be the "King of kings," a God-man among men? Why, then, the last-minute plea for a way out? Socrates made no such appeal. Neither did Paul, nor Buddha, nor scores of early Christian martyrs. Why were other men so much braver than Jesus? After giving it some thought, Augustine concluded that Jesus must've been speaking in someone else's voice when he uttered those four famous words, "*Eloi, Eloi, lema sabachthani?*" He couldn't have spoken those words in his own name, or for his own sake. Surely not. Surely Jesus of Nazareth, the human son of Mary, a man who never once succumbed to the temptation to sin, could've mustered the strength to bite his tongue and look death in the eye, just as heroes had being doing since time immemorial.

Augustine continued to ponder, as was his wont: If Jesus wasn't speaking from a distinctly human perspective, i.e., as the biological son of Mary, then who? Perhaps he was speaking as the eternal Son of God. Remember: Jesus is fully God *and* fully man, two natures in one. Maybe when Jesus cries, "*Eloi, Eloi, lema sabachthani?*," it's the divine voice we're hearing—the *Logos*, the first and final Word, the eternal Son of God.

An interesting hypothesis, but it leads to some pretty obvious problems. For starters, why would God be afraid of death? Don't the words "*Logos*," "God," "eternal," and "divine" imply *immortality*—as in, the inability to die? Why would the uncreated Creator ever have cause to speak those four fateful words? And even if he did, who would he be talking to?

So the question remained: When Jesus cries out, "My God, my God, why have you forsaken me?," whose voice is it we're hearing? If not the human son of Mary, nor the divine Son of God, then who?

At long last, Augustine settled on an answer that's as surprising as it is profound: that fearful cry we hear from the cross—the voice of one who's overwhelmed by anxiety, doubt, and dread—is yours.[963]

You are the one speaking when Jesus utters those four words. *You* are the one who asks God why he's forsaken you. It is your voice we hear, just as it's mine. It's all of our voices: everyone who's ever fallen short of true heroism and valor, everyone who's scared to death of death. All who doubt, and are given to tremble.[964] All who want to believe enough, but don't. All who half-heartedly wish they could forget about Jesus and strike his all-seeing, all-loving, soul-piercing gaze from memory, but can't. It's all of us—the ordinary, decent, fearful people of the world—who speak out our fears through the voice of the crucified Christ. Who knew you'd make a cameo in the New Testament? And a speaking part, no less?

Body and Head

In his letter to the Christians in Rome, Paul refers to the community of faith as the "body of Christ," and Jesus, the "head."[965] It's an oddly organic picture of God's relationship with his people. Somehow, through the life, death, and resurrection of Jesus, we are joined to God in what Calvin called a "mystical union."[966] And while Christian theologians differ on some of the finer details of this union, the general consensus is that Jesus is the cause, the unique bonding agent between divinity and humanity, the bridge by which we are reconciled to God. Thus sayeth Calvin: "When the apostle [Paul] defines the Gospel, and the use of it, he says that we are called to be partakers of our Lord Jesus Christ, and to be made one with Him, and to dwell in Him, and He in us; and that we be joined together in an inseparable bond."[967] That's what Jesus does. He forges a redemptive link between God and the world, weaving us into the very cloth of God's life.

In the Eastern church, when fledgling followers of the Way undergo the public ritual of baptism, they're asked to respond to the question, "Do you unite yourself to Christ?"[968] Three times they're asked. It's that crucial of a concept, that integral to a historically orthodox understanding of salvation. From Calvin, to the church fathers, to the first-century apostles and medieval mystics, Christians have always used words like "united," "joined," "bond," "partake," "adoption," "participation," "indwelling," and "body and head" to describe God's relationship with redeemed humanity.[969] Augustine extended it even further: "If He [Jesus] is the head, we are the members: the *whole man* is He *and* we . . . The fullness of Christ, then, is head and members."[970] Don't miss the radicality of this claim. Augustine is saying that those who trust in Jesus become his "body"—and not in some hazy, impressionistic sense, but *actually*—for real, or not at all. Together, both "body" and "head" constitute the complete Christ. And as anyone who knows anything about anatomy can tell you, separating "body" from "head" means decapitating the "whole man." It's a package deal. You can't have one without the other. That's how strong of a bond it is, how serious and substantial a union—so substantial, in fact, that the crucified Christ is able to speak for us, and we through him, since we're a part of the same organic whole. And that's good news for the world, since it is *God* who establishes this redemptive union, not us. We are the recipients of divine grace, not the initiators. That's why they call it a "gift."[971]

It was also Augustine who urged, "Cast yourself upon him, do not be afraid . . . Make the leap without anxiety. He will catch you and heal you."[972] But for Jesus, the "leap of faith" was a fearful one. In the face of imminent crucifixion, in the pit of his own hell, Jesus made the same sort of leap we make, if we elect to do so. He chose to surrender, even though it felt as though he'd been abandoned. And in that desperate state, he cried with and for us, "My God, why have you forsaken me?" But he also said, "Nevertheless, not as I will, but as you will."[973] This is the "Thy will be done" of Jesus, spoken on our behalf; the divine "nevertheless" that changed the world.

Point of Contact

The incarnation marks the moment when God became human—"*fully* human in every way."[974] That's our point of contact with God: his humanity. His vulnerability. Nothing about our humanness is alien to Jesus, who was tempted "in *every way*, just as we are."[975] Just as Jesus ate, slept, and wept, he really did experience what we experience, including our feelings of fear, loneliness, anger, even panic. And he experienced those things in your name, and in mine. That's how Jesus redeems: by taking our fears and failures into himself. God's way down is our way up.

All of this means you're allowed to be scared. You don't have to hide your anxieties and misgivings. It's official: you have God's expressed permission to be afraid, just as the crucified Christ was afraid. Which is not to say you should wallow in worry, or camp out in your old problems. God wants you to live "more abundantly," not stay stuck. But getting unstuck usually means getting honest—and that's exactly what Jesus wants from you: honesty. Vulnerability. Christ came to carry your burdens, not to have you bury them.

Confidence and Unbelief

There's this Bible story about an unnamed man who asked Jesus to heal his ailing son. "If you can do anything," the man pleaded, "have compassion on us and help us." Jesus answered, "Everything is possible for one who believes." Then, in a moment of desperate, almost embarrassing honesty, the man cried out, "I believe; help my unbelief!" *That* was a faith that triumphed over Satan, a miniscule faith, "like a grain of mustard seed." But it was enough.[976]

The same Bible urges, "Let us then approach God's throne of grace with confidence, so that we may receive mercy and find grace to help us in our time of need."[977] Translation: you don't need to make yourself perfect before beginning your spiritual pilgrimage. And that should be a source of great relief, since you *can't* make yourself perfect—hence, the need for God's help. If you were capable of cleaning yourself up before approaching the throne of grace, you wouldn't need to approach the throne of grace. But you do. We all do.

As an old friend of mine, a licensed psychotherapist, always says, "Everybody's crazy." Maybe not *Silence of the Lambs*, finger-painting-with-your-own-poo crazy, but crazy enough to need help. Serious, divine help. And we can ask for it "with confidence," because the God revealed in Jesus is a God who empathizes with us; who knows what hurts us and wants to help, whatever the circumstances.[978] God knows how hard it can be, because he's been there. That's why you can be honest with him. As in, "I'm afraid I wanna have sex with the devil" honest. The more honest, the better. (It's no coincidence that people who experience profound spiritual healing tend to be profoundly honest people . . . or, at the very least, they're willing to become honest people.)

That's yet another benefit of the good news: you get to retire from the performance business. No more "brand management" or keeping up appearances. You get to bring it all to light—all your deepest, darkest, dirtiest secrets; those things you always thought you'd carry with you to the grave, and would rather die than talk about. God wants to carry those things too . . . especially those things, since, as you know already, they're the heaviest and hardest to bear.

The Great Exchange

The Bible has a lot to say about bearing each other's burdens. "Give to those who ask," Jesus said. "Wash one another's feet." Go the extra mile.[979] "Carry each other's burdens," Paul reiterated, "and in this way you will fulfill the law of Christ."[980] There's a profound spiritual principle at work here—namely, the principle of *exchange*, of sharing and participating in the lives of others. It's all over the New Testament, culminating in the crucifixion, where it's most clearly visible: "He [Jesus] himself bore our sins in his body on the tree, so that we might die to sins and live for righteousness; by his wounds you have been healed."[981] That's the crux of the gospel, and I confess, it's a transaction that I still find mysterious. Somehow, by living a sinless life of spiritual dependence and dying a criminal's death, Jesus exchanged his life for ours, taking all our wounds and wrongdoings upon himself.[982] And he was able to do so because he plumbed the full gamut of human frailty and fear, sharing in our selfsame hardships, "yet he did not sin."[983] Even though we're the ones responsible for causing and perpetuating The Way Things Are, Jesus, "who knew no sin," bore the full burden of it, as if the ruin of the world were entirely his fault.[984] Behold, the Great Exchange.

To be clear, we're talking about *God* here, not just a pious Jew from first-century Palestine.[985] Nothing against pious Palestinian Jews, but Jesus' humanness is only half the picture. Remember: Jesus is fully God *and* fully man, which means it really is God up on that cross—and when you think about it, that has some pretty hefty theological implications.

For one thing, it means God isn't a celestial rageaholic who beat the hell out of his own human son in order to satiate his pent-up anger. The crucifixion isn't about appeasing some cranky old man in the sky; a distant, divine drill sergeant. And it's definitely not about God the Father fulfilling some obligation to a "higher" law or principle, i.e., "justice"—as if justice were something above or outside of God. To paraphrase Aquinas, "God *is* what God *has*," meaning God and his attributes are one in the same.[986] God doesn't have to answer to any "higher" authority, be it justice, or truth, or the "rule of law" (e.g., "an eye for an eye"), or even capital-L Love. Because God *is* truth, and God *is* love—and, most crucially, God is like Jesus, "who takes away the sin of the world."[987]

So let's avoid any unnecessary confusion on this: it is *God* who substituted himself for humanity on the cross, suffering in our stead. It is *God* who absorbed the cost of our clemency.[988] And it is *God* who exchanged innocence for guilt, faithfulness for inconstancy, *agape* for apathy, and righteousness for *chata'*.[989] Rather than let us be crushed and condemned by the weight of our own wrongs, the incarnate God surrendered himself to The Way Things Are, to the ruling powers and warped priorities of this "dark world."[990] In so doing, the incarnate God turned the principle of "what goes around, comes around" on its head. No more "you'll get what's coming to you." No more "an eye for an eye." Jesus forever broke the chain of cause and effect. Where there was once judgement, now there is grace, freedom, and forgiveness. That's the Great Exchange.

And don't get bent out of shape over all this "substitution" and "exchange" business. As much as it grates against our individualistic impulses, we really do live in an "inescapable network of mutuality." MLK was right about that. Our lives overlap in ways we are wont to minimize or overlook. The poet and playwright Charles Williams observed, "It is regarded as Christian to live '*for*' others; it is not so often regarded as Christian doctrine that we live '*from*' others."[991] And we do. We live *from* others, at least as much as *for* others, even when we don't realize it. Williams called it "coinherence." It's Frederick Douglass's friends suffering alongside him, sharing in his personal hardships, even though they didn't have to. It's MLK forgiving the thugs who bombed his home, absorbing the cost of their transgressions, choosing not to repay evil for evil. It's my professor, Mr. Mead, having me over for tea, playing the piano for me, giving me more of his time than

I could ever return, drawing me out of myself, listening me into speech. That's *coinherence* at work—a gloriously imprecise calculus of giving and receiving, of sharing in each other's lives, such that we become integral parts of one another.

As Cornel West says, "I am who I am because somebody loved me."[992] We are all, each of us, indebted to one another. We help make each other who we are. Without my parents, I never would've been. Without me, this sentence would never have been, nor would the thoughts you're having as a result of reading it. Without my wife, my son would never have been, as I am incapable of producing a child by myself. We both do our part, but she (literally) carried our child in her womb, substituting her body for his, until he was ready to be born. That's how it works. We live *from* others, accruing untold benefits from their participation in our lives, receiving far more than we could ever have earned by and for ourselves. And this is what Jesus does—though on a much more cosmic and mysterious scale.[993]

Participation Trophies

In addition to "the body of Christ," Paul called Jesus' followers "coheirs with Christ"—an equally startling, and significant, designation. It means that those who trust in Jesus are "adopted" as God's children—as the siblings of Christ—and are thereby enabled to "participate in the divine nature," just like Jesus. That's the language Paul and the apostles used, the language of adoption and participation. By grace, through faith, we're given a share in Jesus' "inheritance," in the same spiritual "riches" and resources he enjoyed, including peace, joy, *agape*, and intimate communion with God and neighbor.[994]

Remember Jesus' words: "As the Father has loved me, so have I loved you."[995] Think about that for a minute. The Son loves you as much as the Father loves the Son. The Father loves you so much that he gave his only Son. When you love your neighbor, you are loving Jesus, the Son: "Whatever you did for one of the least of these . . . you did for me." In loving Jesus, you are loving the Father, who is "one in being" with the Son.[996] That's the kingdom of God in action: *agape* love, running over and pouring out in all directions. And that's what the journey of faith is about—learning to enjoy and embody the love of God, "on earth as it is in heaven."

Crucified with Christ

In another letter, Paul writes, "I have been crucified with Christ and I no longer live, but Christ lives in me. The life I now live in the body, I live by faith in the Son of God, who loved me and gave himself for me."[997] As far as metaphysical statements go, it doesn't get much weirder than that. For starters, it's kinda hard to write a letter when you're already dead. So what's all this about being "crucified with Christ"? As in, deceased? Clearly, Paul couldn't've been talking about his own physical death. So what's he saying?

Like much of the New Testament, the phrase "I have been crucified with Christ" only makes sense when read through the lens of coinherence. Paul is talking about participation in the divine life, through participation in Jesus' death—which sounds patently absurd, unless you're open to the genuine possibility of sharing in something (or someone) outside yourself. In a similarly bizarre turn of phrase, Paul speaks of being "in Christ" (or "in the Lord") over one hundred times in his letters.[998] Yet again, this makes no earthly sense, since nobody is "in" Jesus Christ—at least, not in any literal, spatial sense (yet another reason to be wary of biblicist literalism). The whole thing hinges on coinherence. That's the spiritual principle Paul is working with. So is Jesus, when he says things like, "Whoever wants to be my disciple must deny themselves and take up their cross daily and follow me."[999] You'll notice how none of his followers took him up on it. At least, not literally. We have no record of any ancient disciples lugging wooden crosses around while retracing Jesus' literal footsteps from place to place. They knew better. They realized Jesus was talking about something much, much deeper than that.

To be "crucified with Christ" is to let your "old self" die—the "imposter" self; the wounded, fearful, self-centered, performer self; the "false self."[1000] It's a spiritual death, a saying goodbye to the polished and presentable "you" that you've been showing to the world since before you can remember, so you can become someone new: the reborn self. And all of this happens through "mystical union" with Christ. As Paul puts it, "We have been buried with him [Jesus] by baptism into death, so that, just as Christ was raised from the dead by the glory of the Father, so we too might walk in newness of life."[1001] Which means Jesus' resurrection can also be your resurrection.

New Self, New Life

Ever notice how evangelicals make such a big deal out of being "born again"? This is what they're talking about: spiritual rebirth. Resurrection with Christ, into "newness of life." Coinherence on steroids. But there's no resurrection without crucifixion. You can't rise from the grave without dying first. And that's precisely what Paul is getting at. He's talking about being "buried with" Christ, coinhering in Jesus' death, so you can be raised with him, too.

Spiritual rebirth means letting go of the "old self"—all the coping and defense mechanisms we've been relying on since forever; all those unhealthy habits and destructive desires; the secrets, the scheming, the compulsions; the mad scramble to "control the narrative"; the shame, blame, and bitterness; the fear of being "found out"—all of it. We bury it in the dirt. We let it die, that we might "put on" the "new self"—the resurrected self.[1002]

And I've seen it happen. More times than I can count, and to more kinds of people. Maybe words like "rebirth" and "coinherence" sound like pseudo-spiritual woo-woo to you, but rest assured, the whole thing is as earthy and real as the ground beneath your feet. And it can happen for anyone. Remember Kierkegaard's insight: "Faith is a marvel, and yet no human being is excluded from it." By "marvel," he meant a *miracle*—i.e., an absolute human impossibility. And for this very reason, faith is open to all, since none of us can "do" it in our own strength.

You can be an abusive bigot and be reborn. You can be a cheat, a philanderer, or a murderer and be reborn. You can even be reborn and be reborn ("born again" Christians need Jesus too). It's a lifelong pilgrimage, this journey of faith, full of fits and starts and start agains. There are dry seasons and dreary patches, and dark nights of the soul. The "old self" has a way of cropping up—hence, the need for sharing your burdens with other travelers along the Way, fellow members of the "body of Christ," who are all just as scared, wounded, and worthwhile as you are.

Finding Yourself

One of the great paradoxes of the Christian faith is that you find yourself by losing yourself. To save your life, you've got to lose it. By taking up your cross and denying yourself, you become someone new—and you lighten your load in the process. That's what Jesus promised: "My yoke [harness] is easy and my burden is light."[1003] Sounds strange, but it's actually easier to die to self than it is to live for self. Granted, the leap of faith is a frightening one, and dying to the old self can be a painful process, but it's a lot more doable than trying to run your own show. After all, the false self is a far heavier load than the cross Jesus wants you to carry.

"Newness of life." Freedom from captivity. An easy yoke. That's the promise. And fear not, fellow sojourner! The promise is not made in vain.

God's kingdom is not one possible outcome among many. "It is finished,"[1004] Jesus said. And it's worth it. The whole journey is worth it. The leap, the risk, the opening up, the dying to self—all of it.

And you're right to want it, by the way. Heaven, I mean. The kingdom of God. The "all shall be well." You're right to pine after Eden, and you're right to be restless and dissatisfied by The Way Things Are. You always have been.

You remember, don't you? All those longings? Those pangs of "oughtness"? Your highest hopes and ideals, before it all went dark? You were right about those. You always have been. Don't let anybody tell you otherwise. And for Christ's sake, don't let *me* tell you otherwise. If it helps, I'm sorry that the world let you down, and that I've played a part in that. Forgive me.

Adieu

One final thing, fellow sojourner. If, upon serious reflection, you've concluded that the kingdom of God is not for you; if you remain unstirred by the life of Jesus and uninterested in the life of faith; if you're perfectly contented with The Way Things Are, thank you very much, and you see no need for shedding the "old self" in favor of the new; if you feel no sense of solidarity, no inner resonance with the "My God, my God, why have you forsaken me?" of the crucified Christ; if you're convinced of the folly of faith, and are certain that God is a superstition; and if, perchance, you take pity on poor, idiotic souls like mine—who would have God's kingdom or die thirsting after it—then please, if you have the time and sympathy to spare, please pray for us.

Endnotes

1. Meier, *Marginal Jew*, 1.

2. Mayer, "Stop this Train."

3. For more on the term "evangelicalism," see Worthen, *Apostles of Reason*, 3–7.

4. According to the *Oxford English Dictionary*, the adjective "secular" denotes "attitudes, activities, or other things that have no religious or spiritual basis." "Secular," *Lexico*, http://oxforddictionaries.com/us/definition/american_english/secular.

5. Habermas, "Awareness of What Is Missing," 16.

6. For example, see Berger, *Desecularization of the World*, 2. By "West," I mean those European and North American nations that pioneered the industrial revolution and have dominated the global economic stage for the last few centuries. See also Smith et al., "Twenty-Three Theses," 921.

7. The term "secular" was first coined by nineteenth-century "freethinkers" and Deists who did not want to be associated with atheism. Asad, *Formations of the Secular*, 23.

8. As explained by the philosopher Charles Taylor, ours is a "fractured culture" characterized by "an ever-widening variety of moral/spiritual options" and proposed "third ways" as alternatives to traditional orthodoxy and radical atheism. Taylor, *Secular Age*, 300–302.

9. In 1973, organized religion was the highest-rated institution in Gallup's "confidence in institutions measure." Gallup, "Confidence in Organized Religion."

10. The percentage of religiously unaffiliated Americans is up from about 15 percent in 2007 to almost 20 percent of all U.S. adults in 2012. Pew Research Center, "'Nones' on the Rise." Moreover, the percentage of Americans in their twenties who say they've never doubted the existence of God is at an all-time low. Pew Research Center, "Section 6: Religion and Social Values."

11. Pew Research Center, "America's Changing Religious Landscape." According to the same study, fewer than six in ten millennials now identify with any particular branch of Christianity.

12. Pew Research Center, "'Nones' on the Rise."

13. Schultz, "Rise of the 'Dones.'"

14. Between 2008 and 2012 alone, fourteen million American adults said they no longer identified themselves as Christian. Kinnaman, "Lost and Found."

15. Jane Little credits digital media as contributing to the move away from traditional religious communities and towards new, often virtual communities and subject religious experiences. Little, "Media Coverage of Religion."

16. In *The Sociology of Colonies*, Rene Maunier observed, "It was the desire to convert the heathen which lured colonizers of modern times to seek to conquer the universal empire." In some cases, this was the colonizer's "chief motive." Quoted in Dube, *Postcolonial Feminist Interpretations*, 129.

17. Raboteau, "African Americans, Exodus," 81–83.

18. Hochschild, *King Leopold's Ghost*, 106.

19. Irons, *Origins of Proslavery Christianity*, 13–14. See also Cone, *Black Theology of Liberation*, 65.

20. Compare Col 3:22 with Luke 4:18.

21. Raboteau, *Slave Religion*, 151–73. See also Sugirtharajah, "Postcolonial Notes," 146–63.

22. Westerkamp, *Women and Religion*, 54. See also Linda Kay Klein's autobiographical account of being "raised hearing horror stories about harlots (a nice, Christian term for a manipulative whore) who destroy good, God-fearing men." Klein, *Pure*, 4.

23. See Col 3:18; 1 Pet 3:1; Eph 5:22. According to Dr. Lynne Baker, a professional counselor and educator who works with Christian women suffering under domestic violence, "Scriptures may be used by the perpetrator as a point of authority to condone his actions, or perhaps to 'prove' to the victim that she is not fulfilling her marital obligations." Research supports Baker's observation that women are often told by church leaders to tolerate domestic violence and abuse. See Baird and Gleeson, "Submit to Your Husbands."

24. In general, White evangelical Christians are more explicitly patriotic than the average American. Cox, et al., "Proud to be American."

25. Ryken, "New Jerusalem," 297.

26. See Jas 1:27; Ps 82:3; 146:9; Isa 58:7. The second-century philosopher Celsus disparaged Christianity precisely because it welcomed and appealed to the uneducated lower classes, including "women and children . . . workers in wool and leather," whom Christians deemed "worthy of their God." See Origen, *Contra Celsum*, III.44, 55. Scholar Warren Carter described the early church as an alternative community that was markedly "inclusive, merciful, non-violent, protective of the weak, genuinely structured for the good of all, committed to wholeness, oriented to the loving pursuit of the good of the other (service) in reciprocal practices, providing all with just access to resources necessary to sustain good life." Carter, "Gospel of Matthew," 100. Similarly, sociologist Rodney Stark argues that Christianity flourished in the ancient world at least in part because it successfully provided consolation and a vision of reality that was far more satisfying to the layperson than the Hellenistic philosophies of the day. In particular, the Christian emphasis on compassion, coupled with the promise of eternal life, were welcome and comforting novelties in the ancient world. "The *contents* of Christian and pagan beliefs were different in ways that greatly determined not only their explanatory capacities, but also their relative capacities to mobilize human resources . . . At a time when all other faiths were called to question, Christianity offered explanation and comfort. Even more important, Christian doctrine provided a prescription for action. That is, the Christian way appeared to work." Stark, "Epidemics, Network," 164–65. When an epidemic swept through the Roman Empire in 165 CE, killing somewhere between a quarter to a third of the population, Christians mobilized to offer aid: "Christian values of love and charity were translated into practices of social service in the times of crisis, thereby creating a network of medical care. . .Christian values of love and charity had, from the beginning, been translated into norms of social service and community solidarity." Stark, "Epidemics, Network," 159–60.

27. Stark, "Epidemics, Network," 167, 169, 177.

28. See Acts 9:2; 19:9, 23; 22:4; 24:14, 22. Many of the earliest Christians used similar language. See *First Clement* 35 and *Didache* 1–6.

29. See Stevenson's *Brand Jesus*.

30. Kinnaman and Lyons, *UnChristian*, 27. See also Anne Rice's statement on why she abandoned institutional Christianity. Shuler, "Anne Rice Quits Christianity."

31. Boyle, "'Pit of Hell.'" Ben Carson, former Director of Pediatric Neurosurgery at Johns Hopkins and current Secretary of Housing and Urban Development, has said similar things. Krauss, "Ben Carson's Scientific Ignorance."

32. Galileo, "Galileo to Castelli," 53; Galileo, "Galileo's Considerations," 70–86.

33. Ps 113:3 (CEB). See also Eccl 1:5.

34. Late medieval scholars also referred to the Psalms as proof of a geocentric universe,

e.g., "He set the earth on its foundations; it can never be moved (Ps 104:5)." For an example of the biblical rationale for the Aristotelian-Ptolemaic picture of a geocentric universe, see Bellarmine, "Letter to Foscarini."

35. This would include the Investiture Controversy of eleventh and twelfth centuries and ensuing conflicts between state and ecclesial authorities, as well as the Antipope Controversy of the fourteenth century.

36. Nichols, *Corporate Worship*, 15; Williams, *Retrieving the Tradition*, 19. Priests like the infamous Johann Tetzel sold indulgences to whoever was willing to cough up the dough, regardless of their spiritual sincerity or commitment.

37. Galileo, "Galileo to Castelli," 51. See also Galileo's "Letter to the Grand Duchess," in which he describes the written contents of Scripture as "propositions uttered by the Holy Ghost," which were "set down in that manner by the sacred scribes in order to accommodate them to the capacities of the common people who are rude and unlearned" (44).

38. Galileo, "Galileo to Castelli," 49. Charles Hodge, an early apologist for biblical inerrancy and outspoken critic of Darwinian evolution, admitted that the infallibility of the Bible does not guarantee the accuracy of any given interpretation. Dorrien, *Remaking of Evangelical Theology*, 18.

39. See Marx, *Hegel's 'Philosophy of Right'*, 127. In the eighteenth century, opium was often used for its powerful medicinal effects in the treatment of disease and chronic pain.

40. Freud, *Future of An Illusion*, 38.

41. Bowler, *Evolution*, 86–92. Charles Lyell's research suggested the earth was actually millions of years old. Gould, *Time's Arrow*, 99–146. Incidentally, "survival of the fittest" was Herbert Spencer's term, not Darwin's.

42. Nietzsche, *Gay Science*, 181–82.

43. Nietzsche, *Genealogy of Morals*, 44–45.

44. Chambers, "Baffling Call of God."

45. Patterson, *God of Jesus*, 68.

46. Compare Col 3:22 with Luke 4:18.

47. Col 1:15–19; Heb 1:3.

48. 1 Cor 1:18–25.

49. Buechner, *Magnificent Defeat*, 30.

50. Zacharias, *Jesus Among Other Gods*, 149–50.

51. Blue Letter Bible, s.v. *kenoō*.

52. Rohr and Feister, *Jesus' Plan for a New World*, 3.

53. In *The Crucifixion*, Fleming Rutledge remarks, "The preaching of the cross is an announcement of a *living reality* that continues to transform human existence and human destiny more than two thousand years after it originally occurred" (xvii).

54. Cassin et al., *Dictionary of Untranslatables*, 187.

55. "Progressive," *Merriam-Webster Dictionary*, https://www.merriam-webster.com/dictionary/progressive.

56. Rohane, "Discarding the 'Evangelical' Label?"

57. Foxworthy, interview.

58. MacArthur, *Battle for the Beginning*, 17–18. MacArthur reiterated these sentiments in a 2005 interview with Larry King. MacArthur, interview.

59. Inskeep, "James Dobson Signs Off."

60. Bailey, "Lasting Damage to American Christianity." See also Evans, "Why Millennials Are Leaving."

61. Hitchens, *God Is Not Great*, 64.

62. As stated by evolutionary psychologist Steven Pinker, "The more we learn about the world in which we live, the less reason there is to believe in God." Padilla, "Faith-vs.-Science Debate."

63. When it comes to spiritual practices and beliefs, sociologists and religious scholars have found it nearly impossible to fit Americans into one neat and tidy category. For

example, according to a recent Pew study, there has been almost no change in the percentage of Americans who claim prayer plays an important role in their daily life (76 percent in 2012, the same percentage in 1987). See Pew Research Center, "'Nones' on the Rise."

64. Carlson and Fogleman, "Losing My Religion?"

65. Augustine, *Confessions*, II.ii.2.

66. Oberst, "Let's Not."

67. Simon, "Slip Slidin' Away."

68. There were several distinct Jewish sects that existed simultaneously in the first century, including the Pharisees, Sadducees, and Essenes. The earliest Christians were mostly Jews who probably participated in diverse forms of Jewish worship. According to historian Robert Goldenberg, "At the end of the 1st century CE there were not yet two separate religions called 'Judaism' and 'Christianity.'" Goldenberg, "Review," 586–88). Over time, more Gentiles (non-Jews) started converting to Christianity, especially in response to the preaching of evangelists like the apostle Paul (see Acts 17).

69. Kinnaman and Lyons, *UnChristian*, 26.

70. Compare with 1 Thess 5:15: "Make sure that nobody pays back wrong for wrong"; "Do not repay evil with evil" (1 Pet 3:9); "Do not take revenge (Rom 12:19)."

71. Corn, "Obsessed with Revenge"; *Fresh Air*, "Trump Off Camera"; Fox News, "Trump Warns GOPers." Melania Trump uses similar language when describing her husband's "get even" policy. Vitali, "Melania Stumps for Trump."

72. Smith and Martínez, "How the Faithful Voted."

73. Continued Holder, "That's what this new Democratic Party is about." Blake, "Eric Holder."

74. Pew Research Center, "'Nones' on the Rise."

75. 1 Cor 1:18–31.

76. Kinnaman and Lyons, *UnChristian*, 28–29.

77. John 16:33; Luke 10:3.

78. Corcoran, "Katy Perry Kisses and Tells," 37.

79. In 2013, Perry stated, "I'm not Buddhist, I'm not Hindu, I'm not Christian, but I still feel like I have a deep connection with God." Hallowell, "I'm Not a Christian."

80. Kinnaman, *You Lost Me*, 66.

81. Golem, "Hardcore Christian."

82. Hobbs, "No Longer a Christian."

83. Ehrman, "Problem of Pain."

84. McEvoy, "Interview: John Green."

85. Huckabee, "Evolving Faith."

86. This is not to say that American ghettos are in any way benign. It can be argued that American ghettos are the result of racist economic and political practices (e.g., federal and local housing regulations of the 1920s and 1930s, the creation of interstates, redlining, "White flight," etc.) and that, for a number of historical reasons, residents now find it nearly impossible to escape. See Rothstein, *Color of Law*, 17–114.

87. Acts 2:42–47; 4:32–37.

88. In *Evangelii Gaudium*, the pope warned his global audience of a culture-wide "idolatry of money," going as far as to say, "The rich *must* help, respect and promote the poor." Pope Francis, *Evangelii Gaudium*, II.i.53, 55, 58.

89. Zenit, "Pope's Address to 'Popular Movements.'" No doubt about it, the pope has issued a public call to curtail capitalism and, if need be, tweak governmental policies and socioeconomic structures for the benefit of the poor. But this doesn't make him a Marxist. Anyone who knows anything about Marx knows "pure" Marxists are atheists by definition. Clearly this is not what the pope is saying . . . unless he's trying to talk himself out of a job.

90. From Chrysostom's *De Lazaro Concio*, cited in Benestad, *Church and Politics*, 200.

91. In a rare moment of bipartisan consensus on Anderson Cooper's *AC360*, politically conservative pundit Ross Douthat concurred with left-leaning Christiane Amanpour on

one basic point: the pope's encyclical says nothing "shocking, dramatic and new," since concern for the poor has been a historically Catholic, biblical, and essentially Christian concern for two millennia. Warren, "Interview." Douthat, a card-carrying Republican and practicing Catholic, called the pope's statement "completely consistent with the language that previous popes have used" (Douthat, interview), including official pronouncements made by the recently retired (and infamously conservative) Pope Benedict—who, by Limbaugh's standards, would also qualify as Marxist. In his 2009 encyclical *Caritas in Veritate* ("Charity in Truth"), Pope Benedict said the following: "I would like to remind everyone, especially governments engaged in boosting the world's economic and social assets, that the primary capital to be safeguarded and valued is man, the human person in his or her integrity." Urging political and business leaders to base their decisions on more than just the profit motive, Benedict quoted a statement by the Second Vatican Ecumenical Council: "Man is the source, the focus and the aim of all economic and social life." Benedict went on to insist that private business embrace their collective "moral" and "social responsibility," including care for workers worldwide. For Benedict, the "human family" necessarily involved personal interpenetration and cooperation grounded "in the light of the revealed mystery of the Trinity." Pope Benedict, *Caritas in Veritate*. And Benedict was certainly no Marxist; see Susan Berry's article on Breitbart.com, "Marxism Doesn't Work." Of course, an international Christian vision of justice is not a distinctly Catholic concept. After winning the Nobel Peace Prize in 1964, Martin Luther King Jr. began extending his efforts and rhetoric beyond civil rights in the U.S. to include the entirety of the "world house." In his book *The Trumpet of Conscience*, King identified himself as a "citizen of the world," and his increasing willingness to openly oppose the war in Vietnam testifies to his trans-local commitment (31).

 92. Kelly-Gangi, *Mother Theresa*, 100.

 93. Chesterton, *Miscellany of Men*, 98. Ten years later, Chesterton converted to Roman Catholicism.

 94. Today there are slightly more evangelical Christians in the U.S. than Catholics. Pew Research Center, "Changing Religious Composition."

 95. Olson, *Calvin and Social Welfare*, 11–12.

 96. See Exod 22:21; 23:9; Lev 19:10; Deut 10:18–19; 24:14–18; Job 31:32; Ps 146:9; Matt 25:35–43; 3 John 1:5.

 97. Calvin, *Institutes*, II.viii.51.

 98. Idleman, *Not a Fan*, 82; Chan, *Crazy Love*, 72–84; Platt, *Radical*, 11–21.

 99. Warren, interview, *Piers Morgan Live*.

 100. Luke 4:18.

 101. Matt 19:21.

 102. John the Baptist spent most of his time preaching repentance and warning listeners of God's impending judgment. Oddly enough, the author of Luke interpreted John's prophetic message as "good news"—which should tell us something. John also exhorted listeners to serve the poor: "Anyone who has two shirts should share with the one who has none, and anyone who has food should do the same." Luke 3:11. He saw an intimate connection between the practice of generosity and being a person for whom God's impending apocalypse is "good news."

 103. Wallis, *God's Politics*, 18, 58, 262.

 104. See John 18:36. Compare the NRSV, ESV, NLT, ISV, and NIV translations of Luke 17:21. Emphasis mine.

 105. See 2 Cor 13; Jas 1:19–20; 1 John 2:6–11.

 106. Shuler, "Anne Rice Quits Christianity."

 107. Weil's statement is preceded by the following remarks, written in 1942: "The Church has borne too many evil fruits for there not to have been some mistake at the beginning . . . Missionary zeal has not Christianized Africa, Asia and Oceania, but has brought these territories under the cold, cruel and destructive domination of the White

race, which has trodden down everything." Weil, *Letter to a Priest*, 32. Two years later, Lewis delineated between those who have "never heard of Christ" and those "who have misunderstood and refused to accept him." Lewis, "On the Reading of Old Books," 8. Weil and Lewis shared an affinity for Platonism and were well acquainted with the Hellenistic understanding of vice—namely, that we sin out of ignorance, or an inability to see and discern the good.

108. Perrin and Thibon, *Weil as We Knew Her*, xiii.

109. Miles, *Weil: An Anthology*, 26. Biblical quote is from Mark 2:17.

110. Williams, *Dostoevsky: Language, Faith*, 27–28.

111. John 10:10.

112. While Puritan preachers taught early versions of rapture theology in the eighteenth century, C. I. Scofield is usually credited with popularizing dispensationalist theology more broadly. See Magnum and Sweetnam, *Scofield Bible*, 71–89, 188–95.

113. Nietzsche, *Birth of Tragedy*, 23.

114. Historians like Nathan Hatch argue that the religious revivals of the First Great Awakening set the stage for the American Revolution by encouraging the average American to think independently, reject tradition, and question authority. Others disagree; see Kidd, *Great Awakening*, xvii–xix, 288–307; Butler, "Enthusiasm Described and Decried," 305–25.

115. Hatch, *Democratization of American Christianity*, 163. Still smarting from centuries of European oppression whereby the king's religion determined the religion of the kingdom, early Americans distrusted any and all forms of hierarchy. Williams, *Retrieving the Tradition*, 3.

116. Kinnaman and Lyons, *Unchristian*, 23. See also Gallup, "Confidence in Organized Religion." Swift, "Americans' Trust in Mass Media."

117. Hawking, *Brief Answers*, 202.

118. Dawkins, *God Delusion*, 299. See fellow atheist Theodore Dalrymple's critique of Dawkins' all-encompassing, self-defeating skepticism: Dalrymple, "New Atheists Don't See."

119. According to one person interviewed by sociologist Robert Wuthnow, "Spirituality no longer is true or good because it meets absolute standards of truth or goodness, but because it helps me get along. I am the judge of its worth . . ." Wuthnow, "Small Groups," 1239–40. In America, "Everybody has the authority to make up their own minds." Wuthnow, *After the Baby Boomers*, 93.

120. Contemporary theologian Ellen Armour made the following observation of her students: "'Spirituality' is their term for one's private religious life. It includes beliefs, also one's devotional practices (mostly but not exclusively private)." Armour, "Toward an Elemental Theology," 46.

121. According to LifeWay Christian Resources' 2010 survey of 1,200 millennials, 72 percent describe themselves as "more spiritual than religious." Grossman, "More Spiritual than Religious."

122. Little, "Media Coverage of Religion."

123. Alexander Campbell, one of the founding fathers of the Church of Christ denomination, insisted on a "Bible-only-ism" approach to reading Scripture. According to Campbell, the Christian individual needs "no creed but Christ." Neither do believers require a pastor's expertise or guidance. Williams, *Retrieving the Tradition*, 20. See also Wuthnow, *After the Baby Boomers*, 105.

124. In *Did Jesus Exist?*, scholar and religious skeptic Bart Ehrman ruffled some agnostic feathers by affirming the historical reality of Jesus of Nazareth. Like many historians and biblical scholars before him, Ehrman cites several sources outside the Bible that refer to Jesus, including Josephus, Pliny the Younger, and Tacitus (44–51).

125. Aslan, *Zealot*, xix. For not altogether different reasons, N. T. Wright offers a similar analysis of the detached Christ common to contemporary evangelical understanding:

"To speak of Jesus's divinity without speaking of his kingdom coming on earth as in heaven is to take a large step toward the detached spirituality . . . that the first two centuries of the church firmly rejected." Wright, *How God Became King*, 56, emphasis mine.

126. Aslan, *Zealot*, xix, emphasis mine. No doubt fueled by a similar frustration with Christianity in its current, popular form(s), feminist author and an unapologetically old-school lefty Barbara Ehrenreich made a similar observation at an outdoor Christian gathering in rural Maine: "Jesus makes his appearance here only as a corpse; the *living man*, the wine-guzzling vagrant and precocious socialist, is never once mentioned, nor anything he ever had to say. Christ crucified rules, and it may be that the true business of modern Christianity is to crucify him again and again so that he can never get a word out of his mouth." Obviously, Ehrenreich has her own set of deeply entrenched ideological presuppositions (Jesus the "wine-guzzling," nomadic socialist is a bit of a caricature). But her question as to the relation between Jesus the "living man" and the Christ of contemporary Christianity is both insightful and important. Ehrenreich, *Nickel and Dimed*, 68–69, emphasis mine.

127. The Dark Ages were not entirely devoid of intellectual and cultural vibrance. For this reason, many historians dispute the pejorative periodization of the early medieval period as "dark." There were advances made in the fields of philosophy and theology (e.g., Boethius), and under the reign Charlemagne in the late eigth and early ninth centuries, monasteries became centers of education, with monks often serving as scribes, schoolmasters, and translators.

128. The Council of Trent reaffirmed the exclusive teaching authority of the Church Magisterium: "No one relying in his judgment shall, in matters of faith and morals pertaining to the edification of Christian doctrine. . .presume to interpret contrary to that sense which holy mother Church, to whom it belongs to judge their true sense and interpretation." Fourth Session, 1546. https://history.hanover.edu/courses/excerpts/111ct.html.

129. Example: Pope Boniface VIII developed the "theory of the two swords" by loosely interpreting Luke 22:38 and Rom 13:4 as symbolizing the relationship between "spiritual" and "terrestrial" (secular, temporal, governmental or "state") power, with the spiritual sword of the papacy having authority over all. See *Catholic Encyclopedia*, 126. Theologian Daniel Williams frames the birth of Protestant Christianity in precisely these terms: "Protestantism was born in reaction to the tyranny of ecclesiastical authority." Williams, *Retrieving the Tradition*, 19)

130. That is, sins committed after being baptized. See Pope Clement VI's pronouncement *Unigenitus* (56–57), and Albert of Mainz's *Instructio summaria* (57–58) in *Reformation Reader*.

131. I'm thinking not only of the Renaissance popes, but other papal excesses like Boniface VIII's notorious *Unam Sanctam*: "If the terrestrial power err, it will be judged by the spiritual power; but if a minor spiritual power err, it will be judged by a superior spiritual power; but if the highest power of all err, it can be judged only by God, and not by man, according to the testimony of the Apostle: 'The spiritual man judgeth of all things and he himself is judged by no man' [1 Cor 2:15]. This authority, however, (though it has been given to man and is exercised by man), is not human but rather divine, granted to Peter by a divine word and reaffirmed to him (Peter) and his successors by the One Whom Peter confessed. . .Furthermore, we declare, we proclaim, we define that it is absolutely necessary for salvation that every human creature be subject to the Roman Pontiff." Boniface VIII, *Unam Sanctam*. Then there's Pope Julius II—a.k.a. the "Warrior Pope"—who peddled indulgences to peasants and created church offices only to sell them off to the highest bidder. Julius even contracted syphilis from one of his several mistresses. King, *Pope's Ceiling*, 29, 189.

132. The contributing historical causes of what eventually became known as the "Reformation" are legion, including (but not limited to) the enduring influence of humanism, an increased interest in the writings of the church fathers during the High Middle Ages,

ongoing feudal tensions between the Vatican and the local nobility, complex social dynamics, etc. Lindberg, *European Reformation*, 13, 19–20. Catholic scholar Bruce Morrill identifies the Fourth Lateran Council as having deleterious effects on medieval liturgical life and pastoral care. Lay people began receiving Communion less frequently as the ritual itself became focused on the role of the priestly celebrant, who mumbled unintelligible prayers in Latin, often in a low voice with his back towards the congregation, such that few congregants could hear or understand the meaning of the sacrament. The central moment in the ritual became not the reception but the viewing of the bread and cup from a distance—a.k.a. the "gaze that saves"—watching from afar the finished drama of Christ's life and receiving the cosmic efficacy of the sacrament. Morrill, "Christ's Sacramental Presence," 3–25.

133. Citing Gregory the Great as his inspiration, John Paul II understood his special position as *servus servorum Dei*, "servant of the servants of God." As pope, he felt obliged to labor on behalf of the laity, thereby keeping with the pattern established by Jesus, who said, "I am among you as one who serves." John Paul II, *Ut Unum Sint* (1995), 88.

134. Long before Luther, Christians like John Wycliffe and Jan Hus were already getting antsy about the medieval church's shady practices and sketchier teachings. Desiderius Erasmus called for drastic reforms within the medieval church, including a return to the "philosophy of Christ" and a more meticulous, dedicated approach to studying Scripture. Of medieval pontiffs, Erasmus confessed, "It is always a source of amazement to me that popes and bishops so indiscreetly wish to be called lords or masters when Christ forbade his disciples to be called either." Erasmus, "Handbook of the Militant Christian," 74. And in "Paraclesis" Erasmus wrote, "I absolutely dissent from those people who don't want the holy Scriptures to be read in translation by the unlearned—as if, forsooth, Christ taught such a complex doctrine that hardly anyone outside a handful of theologians could understand it, or as if the chief strength of the Christian religion lay in people's ignorance of it." Parish, *Short History of the Reformation*, 86. Of Erasmus, historian Johan Huizinga writes, "He does not reject [religious practices and ceremonies] them offhand and altogether: what revolts him is that they are so often performed without understanding and right feeling." Huizinga, *Erasmus and the Age*, 100–101.

135. Luther probably would've been somewhat puzzled by today's highly individualistic Christian spirituality. He remained a "high church," pro-hierarchy, liturgical Christian till his dying day, as did most of his followers. In the wake of the Protestant Reformation, newly Lutheranized congregations continued to rely on bishops to preach, teach, and expound upon Scripture. Askew and Pierard, *American Church Experience*, 21. By contemporary standards, men like Luther and Calvin were disappointingly pro-aristocracy, liturgical, establishment Christians. It was Luther called upon the German princes to reform the Christian church by force. Luther, "To the Christian Nobility," 7–112. See also Marty, *Martin Luther*, 39–68; and Dillenberger, "Introduction," xxiii.

136. See Mark C. Taylor's incisive analysis of Luther's revolutionary "turn to the subject": "By privatizing, deregulating, and decentering the relation between the believer and God, Luther initiated a revolution that was not confined to religion but extended to politics and economics . . ." Taylor, *After God*, xvi.

137. In most evangelical circles today, the twin teachings of penal substitutionary atonement and eternal torment are now presumed to be central and incontestable, to the exclusion all other competing theories of atonement salvation. But it weren't always so. For one thing, many early Christians didn't even believe in the innate immortality of the human soul. To them, eternal life was a gift given and revealed by Christ, part and parcel to the "good news." See first-century bishop Ignatius of Antioch's letter to the Ephesians: "For this end did the Lord allow the ointment to be poured upon His head, that He might breathe immortality into His Church (17:1)." And a few paragraphs later, Iggy refers to Communion bread (a.k.a. the "Body of Christ," Eucharist, or Lord's Supper) as "the medicine of immortality . . . the antidote which prevents us from dying, [which causes] that we

should live forever in Jesus Christ." In other words: no Communion bread, no life after death. Ignatius of Antioch, Letter to the Ephesians.

138. Shelley, *Plain Language*, 384.

139. Finney's 1835 *Lectures on Revivals of Religion* functioned as a veritable how-to manual for preachers desiring to learn and implement effective, utilitarian worship techniques. See Smith, *New Measures*, 52–66.

140. Senn, *Christian Liturgy*, 563–64. In truth, Christians long before Finney emphasized what A. W. Tozer called "personal heart religion." Tozer, *Pursuit of God*, 13. Famously, in the eighteenth century, John Wesley described his conversion as follows: "In the evening I went very unwillingly to a society in Aldersgate Street, where one was reading Luther's preface to the Epistle to the Romans. About a quarter before nine, while one was describing the change which God works in the heart through faith in Christ, I felt my heart strangely warmed. I felt I did trust in Christ, Christ alone, for salvation; and an assurance was given me that He had taken away my sins, even mine, and saved me from the law of sin and death." *Wesley*, "Strangely Warmed." Though Wesley and the revivalists who followed in his footsteps brought new emphasis to the heart, it was not a modern innovation. In the late fourth century, Augustine began his *Confessions* by stating, "our hearts are restless until they find their rest in Thee" (I.i.1). One of the main themes of *Confessions* is the necessity of a renewal of the heart by Christ. The seventh-century ascetic Isaac the Syrian wrote, "God is reality. The person whose mind has become aware of God does not even possess a tongue with which to speak, but God resides in his heart in great serenity." Isaac the Syrian, *Daily Readings*, 61. The sixteenth-century Catholic reformer Erasmus urged fellow Christians to make God "real in our *hearts*," not merely superficial obedience in ritual and external behavior Erasmus, "Correspondence of Erasmus," 239. Foreshadowing Calvin, Erasmus also believed it was the Holy Spirit who enabled Christians to discern the spiritual meaning of Scripture through the "illumined eyes of the *heart*." Schreiner, *Are You Alone Wise?*, 215. See also Tracy, *Erasmus of the Low Countries*, 105.

141. Kilde, *When Church Became Theatre*, 215.

142. See Idleman's confession, *Not a Fan*, 13.

143. "Barna Examines Trends."

144. See http://www.wikihow.com/Accept-Jesus-Into-Your-Life. See also the "four spiritual laws" of Cru—formerly Campus Crusade for Christ—for similar instructions on how to invite Jesus into your heart: Crustore.org, "Four Spiritual Laws English."

145. Fonda, "Christianity Is My Spiritual Home." See also Patricia Seller's article "Ted Turner at 75."

146. Misener, "Why I Miss."

147. See Shermer, *Believing Brain*, 37–39.

148. Sullivan, "Upon This Rock," 28.

149. In the midst of World War I, a conflict pitting the most powerful "Christian" nations of Europe against one another, theologian Karl Barth asked, "Can one read or hear read even as much as two chapters from the Bible and still with good conscience say, 'God's word went forth to humanity . . . all in order that here and there specimens of men like you and me might be "converted," find some inner "peace," and by a redeeming death go some day to "heaven."' Is *that* all?" Barth, "Strange New World," 46–47.

150. In Tozer's assessment, "The whole transaction of religious conversion has been made mechanical and spiritless. . .Christ may be 'received' without creating any special love for Him in the soul of the receiver. The man is 'saved,' but he is not hungry nor thirsty after God." Tozer, *Pursuit of God*, 22–26. Reinhold Niebuhr shared similar concerns: "We are all concerned not only with a breathless Billy Sunday or Billy Graham artificial minute for our soul's salvation, but with the whole of an abundant life, where nothing human is foreign to us . . . Consciously or unconsciously the Billy Sunday type of evangelist short-circuits eternity and this eternal gospel by an overemphasis upon two moments. One, the moment of conversion like the Philippian jailor when he is saved forever; the other the moment of

death when he is supposed by many to be clapped into a mold and perfected—all made alike in doctrine and character to enter the monotony of flat, stagnant, eternal heaven of bliss and harp-playing on golden streets." http://www.onbeing.org/program/moral-man-and-immoral-society-rediscovering-reinhold-niebuhr/extra/reinhold-niebuhr-timel-38. Contemporary evangelical pastor David Platt has made similar observations: http://www.christianitytoday.com/ct/2013/february-web-only/david-platt-wants-you-to-get-serious-about-following-christ.html?paging=off.

151. http://www.onbeing.org/program/moral-man-and-immoral-society-rediscovering-reinhold-niebuhr/extra/reinhold-niebuhr-timel-38.

152. Aikin, ""So What If Horses?"

153. See Voltaire's famous statement in *OEuvres Complètes De Voltaire*, 562. Other Enlightenment thinkers echoed Xenophanes' earlier insight, e.g., David Hume: "There is a universal tendency among mankind to conceive all beings like themselves, and to transfer to every object those qualities with which they are familiarly acquainted, and of which they are intimately conscious." Hume, *Natural History of Religion*, 9.

154. Nietzsche, *Genealogy of Morals*, 44–45.

155. Cohen, *Beautiful Losers*, 164.

156. McCormick, "Tom Petty," *The Telegraph*, June 16, 2012.

157. Monro, *Modes of Ancient Greek Music*, 1; Blackwell, *Sacred in Music*, 169–70.

158. Cornford, "Preface" to the *Geneva Psalter*, 3.399c, 87.

159. Rowling, *Sorcerer's Stone*, 128.

160. Weber, "Science as a Vocation," 155.

161. Olenick and Goodstein, *Mechanical Universe*, 111–16, 359–61.

162. Gribbin, *Science: A History*, 237–42.

163. Although Newton discovered the principles of gravitation and motion, Edward Davis argues that Newton is wrongly depicted as having therefore made God obsolete: "The typical picture of Isaac Newton as the paragon of Enlightenment deism—responsible for recasting god as a divine clockmaker with nothing more to do once he had completed his creation—is more than just badly mistaken: it is precisely the opposite of the truth." Davis makes the point that Newton flatly rejected the clockwork metaphor, as well as the mechanistic conceptions of the universe upon which it is grounded. Newton's thought, according to Davis, always included a "deep commitment to the constant activity of the divine will." Davis, "Isaac Newton's Mechanistic Cosmology," 116. According to Davis's reading of Newton's *Opticks*, written after Newton's more widely known *Principia*, the omnipresent God is the "direct, immediate cause of gravitation" (120).

164. So argued seventeenth-century theologian and pastor Thomas Burnet. See Gould, *Rocks of Ages*, 23–24. With this in mind, the famous philosopher Gottfried Leibniz critiqued Newton for insisting that God's constant and direct power was necessary in order to keep the universe going: "Sir Isaac Newton, and his followers, have also a very odd opinion concerning the work of God. According to their doctrine, God Almighty wants to wind up his watch from time to time: otherwise it would cease to move. He had not, it seems, sufficient foresight to make it a perpetual motion. Nay, the machine of God's making, is so imperfect, according to these gentlemen, that he is obliged to clean it now and then by an extraordinary concourse, and even to mend it, as a clockmaker mends his work; who must consequently be so much the more unskillful a workman, as he is often obliged to mend his work and to set it right." Wainwright, *Oxford Handbook*, 285.

165. Force, "Newtonians and Deism," 53. See also Westfall, *Never at Rest*, 23.

166. Though he considered himself a Christian, Franklin identified himself as a deist. He believed in an eternal, divine Source of human morality—not because the Bible told him so, but because he thought it was logically necessary for any functional, civilized society. Franklin, *Autobiography and Other Writings*, 52. Franklin's Christian deism included neither a doctrine of salvation nor belief in the divinity of Jesus. Franklin, "Belief and Acts of Religion." For Franklin, God was providentially responsible for the success of the

American campaign for independence. Isaacson, *Benjamin Franklin*, 486.

167. Franklin, "Belief and Acts of Religion." During the French Revolution, as France began its deliberate process of "deChristianisation" and removed the remaining vestiges of medieval Catholicism, Maximilien Robespierre thought the unenlightened commoners still needed a Supreme Being to believe in. So he reimagined divinity as the Goddess of Reason, even constructing monuments in her honor. Jordan, *Revolutionary Career of Maximilien Robespierre*, 192–200, 286. Robespierre thus fulfilled the satirical prophecy of Horace: "Once I was a little fig tree trunk, a useless bit of wood, when the workman, in doubt whether he should make a stool, preferred that I be a god." Quoted in Calvin, *Institutes*, I.xi.4.

168. British deist Thomas Morgan believed God stuck to the rational laws of nature that he himself created. Wrote Morgan: "God governs the World, and directs all Affairs, not by particular and occasional, but by general, uniform and established Laws; and the Reason why he does not miraculously interpose, as they would have him, by suspending or setting aside the general, established Laws of Nature and Providence, is, because this would subvert the whole Order of the Universe, and destroy all the Wisdom and Contrivance of the first Plan." Waligore, "Piety of the English Deists," 181–97.

169. Prothero, *American Jesus*, 12–13. See also Olson, *Mosaic of Christian Belief*, 95. Jefferson became a Unitarian and rejected Christian teachings on the Trinity and virgin birth. Said Jefferson, "The day will come when the mystical conception of Jesus by the Supreme Being as his Father in the womb of a virgin will be classed with the fable of the conception of Minerva in the brain of Jupiter." Graham, *Myths of the Bible*, 304.

170. Dawkins, *Greatest Show on Earth*, 147.

171. von Sydow, "Darwin: A Christian," 141–56.

172. Taylor, *After God*, 131–32.

173. Yeats, "Second Coming," 198–99.

174. Percy, *Strange Land*, 302.

175. Habermas, "Awareness of What Is Missing," 16.

176. Tyson, "Perimeter of Ignorance."

177. Wuthnow, *After the Baby Boomers*, 89.

178. Bonhoeffer, *Letters and Papers*, 369–70.

179. Bonhoeffer, *Letters and Papers*, 324–29.

180. See Eagleton's *Reason, Faith, and Revolution*, 7.

181. Smith et al., "Twenty-Three Theses," 906. See also Taylor, *After God*, xiii.

182. Cited in Muñoz, *God and the Founders*, 104.

183. Stanley, *Global Diffusion of Evangelicalism*, 38.

184. Taylor, *After God*, 130.

185. Amanpour, *Larry King Live*, "God's Warriors."

186. Habermas, "Awareness of What Is Missing," 19. Habermas now urges fellow secularists to embrace cooperation with religious communities. See also Habermas, *Religion and Rationality*, 77, 162.

187. Little, "Media Coverage of Religion."

188. Armstrong, "Let's Revive the Golden Rule."

189. Murray, "My Fellow Atheists," http://www.spectator.co.uk/features/8839081/call-off-the-faith-wars/.

190. "Maurice Sendak's Latest," http://www.npr.org/2011/09/20/140435330/this-pig-wants-to-party-maurice-sendaks-latest. Emphasis mine.

191. Cavanaugh, *Torture and Eucharist*, 192.

192. See Isaiah Berlin's famous distinction between "negative" and "positive" accounts of freedom in "Two Concepts of Liberty," 166–217.

193. According to Talal Asad, "Religion is by no means disappearing in the modern world." Asad, *Formations of the Secular*, 2.

194. Landy and Saler, "Varieties of Modern Enchantment," 1–14.

195. Habermas, "Secularism's Crisis of Faith," 17–29.

196. Smith et al., "Twenty-Three Theses," 913.

197. See Plato's *Republic*, book VII: "Until the person is able to abstract and define rationally the idea of good, and unless he can run the gauntlet of all objections, and is ready to disprove them, not by appeals to opinion, but to absolute truth, never faltering at any step of the argument—unless he can do all this, you would say that he knows neither the idea of good nor any other good; he apprehends only a shadow, if anything at all, which is given by opinion and not by science."

198. Klosterman, *Sex, Drugs & Cocoa Puffs*, 228, emphasis mine.

199. Biblical scholar Mark Coleridge describes the postmodern mindset as colored by the death of the metanarrative and therefore averse to anything all-encompassing. Coleridge, "Life in the Crypt," 14–17.

200. Paul Feyerabend offered a penetrating definition of fundamentalism as a phenomenon that is in no way limited to the realm of religion: "The desire of philosophers like Russell and Moore, at the dawn of modern analytical philosophy in Cambridge, to get down to the primitive sense-data in order to find a level of experience that would supposedly be free of all interpretation, subjective distortion etc, is fundamentalism transposed into an adjacent discourse." Quoted in Fergus Kerr's *Theology after Wittgenstein*, 24. Feyerabend, like Karl Popper, was quite critical of the tendency among modern scientists to presume impartiality when designing, conducting, and (especially) interpreting the results of experiments. See Linda Mercadante's "Good News about the 'Spiritual but Not Religious,'" http://religion.blogs.cnn.com/2014/02/22/good-news-about-the-spiritual-but-not-religious/?hpt=hp_c3.

201. See former SPIN columnist Andrew Beaujon's admission that atheism requires "too much of a commitment." Beaujon, *Body Piercing*, 2. In step with Beaujon, only about one quarter of Americans with nor clear religious affiliation are comfortable describing themselves as atheists. Pew Research Center, "Changing Religious Composition," https://www.pewforum.org/2015/05/12/chapter-1-the-changing-religious-composition-of-the-u-s/.

202. LaMott, *Traveling Mercies*, 264.

203. Bonhoeffer lived in Harlem in the 1930s and worshipped at a predominantly African-American church. McBride, *Church for the World*, 38.

204. For a brief, helpful description of Augustine's Hellenistic conception of a compound universe in which everything has its definite and intended place, see Ehrenberg, *Civil Society*, 40–41.

205. Ricoeur, "Idea of Revelation," 73–118. See also Williams, *On Christian Theology*, 132–33.

206. Cytowic, *Man Who Tasted Shapes*, 56.

207. Augustine, *Confessions*, V.xiv.24.

208. Augustine, *Confessions*, V.xiii.23.

209. Augustine, *Confessions*, VI.iv.6.

210. Clifford et al., eds., *Ethics of Belief*, 18. As Methodist theologian Christopher Morse explains, "To believe or give assent without sufficient evidence is," for the modern individual, "*immoral* as well as irrational." Morse , *Not Every Spirit*, 6, emphasis mine.

211. Among some Enlightenment thinkers, the methodological incredulity of the more skeptical Greeks of old came back into fashion. Phillipson, *Adam Smith*, 19.

212. As Christopher Morse observed, "Descartes, Locke, Hume, and Kant permanently affected the future accounting Christian faith claims by their critical analyses of the justification of belief." Morse , *Not Every Spirit*, 6.

213. John 7:17, emphasis mine.

214. Armstrong, *Case for God*, 87, 132, 145. It is certainly true that Aquinas, building on Augustine, defined faith as thinking something through "with assent" well before the advent of the modern Enlightenment period. However, Aquinas was careful to distinguish between various types of deliberation, making clear that faith is a kind of thinking that has

not been brought to "perfection" (or completion), since the object under consideration/
investigation is God, who cannot be seen or known with "perfection of clear sight" by the
unaided human powers of reason (Summa, II/IIiiq2).

215. Lewis, *Surprised by Joy*, 206–16. Lewis was significantly influenced here by fellow
Oxford Inkling, Owen Barfield.

216. John 1:46.

217. Said Bultmann, "It is impossible to repristinate a past world picture by sheer
resolve, especially a mythical world picture, now that all of our thinking is irrevocably
formed by science." Bultmann, *New Testament & Mythology*, 3.

218. From Hegel's "Lectures on the Philosophy of Religion," as quoted in Shestov's
Athens and Jerusalem, 108. Another translation renders the same passage thus: "If this
distinction is not made, then people are expected to believe things which those who stand
at a certain level of culture no longer *can* believe. For example, they are supposed to believe
in miracles . . ." Hegel, *Lectures on the Philosophy of Religion*, 338. Hegel defined miracles
as follows: "A miracle is nothing but a violation of natural relationships and, by the same
token, nothing but a violation of the Spirit." Quoted in Shestov's *Athens and Jerusalem*,
109. Hegel's definition was anticipated by David Hume in the mid-1700s: "A miracle is a
violation of the laws of nature." *Enquiry Concerning Human Understanding*, 52.

219. Bultmann, *New Testament & Mythology*, 4.

220. Augustine, *Confessions*, XII. For a careful examination of the psychological complexities of myth, belief, and truth in the ancient world, see Veyne's *Did the Greeks Believe?*
Veyne observes, "A Greek put the gods 'in heaven,' but he would have been astounded to
see them in the sky" (18).

221. Bultmann, *New Testament & Mythology*, 3–18.

222. MacCulloch, *First Three Thousand Years*, 2.

223. Bremmer, "Atheism in Antiquity," 11–26.

224. Pelikan, *Christian Tradition*, 194–96, 230–31, 256. See also Kelly, *Early Christian
Doctrines*, 154, 283.

225. Evans, "Introduction: Understanding Jesus," 11.

226. Coakley, "Rest on a Mistake?," 257.

227. Coakley, *Powers and Submissions*, 10.

228. Referring to the cumulative scholarship of A. Harnack, B. H. Streeter, and J. A. T.
Robinson, F. F. Bruce dates the completion of the New Testament between 64 and 100 CE.
Bruce, *New Testament Writings*, 7.

229. Matt 16:17.

230. Kierkegaard tackles the intersection of time and eternity and the similarity between "the contemporary disciple" (to Christ) and "discipline at the second hand" (e.g.,
modern Christians) in *Philosophical Fragments*, 8–13, 44–47. See especially Kierkegaard's
discussion of what it means for a learner to receive knowledge from a source extrinsic to
herself (contra Socrates' theory of learning and the role of the teacher).

231. Augustine, *Confessions*, VIII.xi.27.

232. Nineham, "Epilogue," *Myth of God Incarnate*, 195.

233. Foucault, *Use of Pleasure*, 8.

234. Kierkegaard, *Works of Love*, 46.

235. Also "excessive," "long-suffering" and "aggressive." See Ansbro, *Martin Luther
King, Jr.*, 1–3, 17. See also King's "An Experiment in Love," 19.

236. Ansbro, *Nonviolent Strategies*, 33.

237. King, "Walk for Freedom," 83.

238. Updike, *Rabbit Redux*, 294.

239. The Protestant Reformers made careful and repeated distinctions between justification (a.k.a. "pardoning grace") and sanctification (a.k.a. "empowering grace"), neither of
which is merited by human effort, behavior modification or adherence to moral or ritual
laws. Piper, *Future Grace*, 21. For instance, the Augsburg Confession: "By faith alone is

apprehended remission of sins and grace. And because the Holy Spirit is received by faith, our hearts are now *renewed*, and so put on *new affections* [or desires], so that they are *able* to bring forth good works. For thus saith Ambrose: 'Faith is the begetter of a good will and of good actions.'" XX.26, http://www.ccel.org/ccel/schaff/creeds3.iii.ii.html, emphasis mine. See also from the Second Helvetic Confession: "We do not divide justification by ascribing it partly to the grace of God or to Christ, and partly to our works or merits, but solely and exclusively to the grace of God in Christ through faith. We must first be justified before we can do good works. Love is derived from faith." XV, http://www.ccel.org/ccel/schaff/creeds1.ix.ii.v.html. And in even more clear language, the First Helvetic Confession, which defines saving faith as the "pure gift and favor of God," not the result of good works. Article XIV further clarifies, "This same faith is a certain, firm, yes, undoubting ground, and a grasping of all things that one hopes from God. *From it love grows as a fruit*, and, by this love, come all kinds of virtues and good works." Piper, *Future Grace*, 25, emphasis mine.

240. "Super," *Latdict*, http://www.latin-dictionary.net/search/latin/super.

241. I borrowed the rabbit example from Nicholas Lash's essay "Creation, Courtesy," 168.

242. As A.A. cofounder Bill Wilson explained, "It relieved me somewhat to learn that in alcoholics the will is amazingly weakened when it comes to combating liquor, though it often remains strong in other respects . . . understanding myself now, I fared forth in high hope . . . Surely this was the answer—self-knowledge. But it was not, for the frightful day came when I drank once more . . . I had been overwhelmed. Alcohol was my master." *Alcoholics Anonymous: The Big Book*, 8–9, 26, 39. Elsewhere in the *Big Book*, one highly educated, scientifically schooled woman recounts, "I read everything I could about this disease I have . . . I had access to a good medical library, but after a while, I realized the genetics and chemistry of the disease were of no use to me as an alcoholic. "Because I'm an Alcoholic," in *Alcoholics Anonymous: The Big Book*, 344. See also in the *Big Book*, "We Agnostics": "If a mere code of morals or a better philosophy of life were sufficient to overcome alcoholism, many of us would have recovered long ago . . . but the needed *power* wasn't there . . . *Lack of power*, that was out dilemma" (45, emphasis mine). See also Jean Pierre de Caussade's description of "head-knowledge," i.e., intellectual understanding of *how* God redeems and sanctifies human beings, vs. firsthand experience of God's healing work. Sick physicians might know all the "hows" without ever experiencing the joys of a liberated simpleton. Caussade, *Joy of Full Surrender*, 16–17.

243. So says Alcoholics Anonymous: "When a man or a woman has a spiritual awakening, the most important meaning of it is that he has now become able to do, feel, and believe that which he could not do before on his unaided strength and resources alone. . .He finds himself in possession of a degree of honesty, tolerance, unselfishness, peace of mind, and love of which he had thought himself quite incapable." *Twelve Steps and Twelve Traditions*, 106–7.

244. See King's sermon "Faith in Man," https://kinginstitute.stanford.edu/king-papers/documents/faith-man.

245. Bruce, "Bible," 5.

246. Luke 10:14.

247. Following the instructions of the Sermon on the Mount in Matthew 6, Evagrius Ponticus urged disciples to exercise "exacting attention" when praying, giving alms and fasting, lest they suffer a "second shipwreck more dangerous than the first," viz. vainglory. Casiday, *Evagrius Ponticus*, 92.

248. Ps 42:1, 7, NRSV.

249. Matt 1:3–4, KJV.

250. Deut 23:1, NLT.

251. Williams, *On Christian Theology*, 195.

252. Taylor, *After God*, 35; see also Tillich, "Two Types of Philosophy," 10.

253. Feuerbach, *Essence of Christianity*, 125, 270.

254. Augustine, *Confessions*, VII.10.xvi. See also Pascal's account of God in *Pensées*: "If there is a God, He is infinitely incomprehensible, since, having neither parts nor limits, He has no affinity to us." http://www.stat.ucla.edu/history/pascal_wager.pdf. For a more thorough philosophical treatment of divine otherness, see Rudolf Otto's landmark study, *Idea of the Holy*, 26.

255. Dillard, *Teaching a Stone to Talk*, 40–41.

256. Job 42:4–6. See also the prophet Isaiah's cathartic cry: "I saw the Lord, high and exalted, seated on a throne . . . 'Woe to me!' I cried. 'I am ruined! For I am a man of unclean lips, and I live among a people of unclean lips, and my eyes have seen the King, the Lord Almighty.'" Isaiah 6:5.

257. Luke 5:8.

258. Augustine, *Confessions*, I.xv.24.

259. Caussade, *Abandonment to Divine Providence*, 70.

260. Augustine, *Confessions*, V.xiii.23

261. Isaac the Syrian, *Daily Readings*, 24.

262. Same goes for the late evangelical author A. W. Tozer, who described conversion not as an end but a beginning: "For now begins the glorious pursuit, the heart's happy exploration of the infinite riches of the Godhead. Tozer, *Pursuit of God*, 24.

263. Hitchens, *Portable Atheist*, xxii.

264. See Phil 4:6–7: "Do not be anxious about anything, but in every situation, by prayer and petition, with thanksgiving, present your requests to God. And the peace of God, which transcends all understanding, will guard your hearts and your minds in Christ Jesus."

265. Rom 15:13.

266. Augustine *Confessions*, VII.vii.2.

267. Greg Brown, "Lord, I Have Made You a Place in My Heart," in *Poet Game*.

268. Chua and Lubenfeld, *Triple Package*, 8–11.

269. Contemporary Christian writers like Thomas Merton, Brennan Manning, and Richard Rohr have often spoken of the dichotomy between the "true," "real," or "authentic" self, vs. the "false" or "imposter" self. These distinctions are often extremely helpful, especially pastorally, so long as the "true self" is understood as being formed gradually over the course of a lifetime. See Merton's *New Seeds of Contemplation*, 34–35. See also Rohr's *Immortal Diamond*, 3, 21–29; and Manning's *Abba's Child*, 9–28.

270. Augustine, *Confessions*, X.iii.3.

271. Calvin, *Institutes*, I.i.2.

272. James K. A. Smith defines *kardia* as "the fulcrum of your most fundamental longings-a visceral, subconscious *orientation* to the world." Smith, *You Are What You Love*, 8, 12. In the Bible, "heart" and "soul" usually refer to individual human consciousness, will, desire and understanding. In the Old Testament, "heart" is translated from the Hebrew word *lebab*. http://www.blueletterbible.org/lang/lexicon/lexicon.cfm?Strongs=H3824&t=NIV. See Pss 37:4, "Take delight in the Lord, and he will give you the desires of your heart"; 73:26, "My flesh and my heart may fail, but God is the strength of my heart and my portion forever"; 139:23, "Search me, God, and know my heart; test me and know my anxious thoughts"; 51:10, "Create in me a pure heart, O God . . ." Also Prov 4:23: "Above all else, guard your heart, for everything you do flows from it." In the New Testament, καρδία (*kardia*), translated as "soul," "will," "mind" or "understanding," means "the source and seat of thoughts, desires, urges, appetites, affections and purposes." Blue Letter Bible, s.v. *kardia*. For the contemporary reductive physicalist/materialist, "heart" would be a complex emergent property arising out of innumerably intricate neurological processes in the brain—including the subjective phenomena of consciousness and free will. See Nancey Murphy's definition of the "soul" as the "functional capacity of a complex physical organism, rather than a separate spiritual essence that somehow inhabits a body." Murphy,

"Human Nature," xiii.

273. Matt 5:21–22.

274. Pelikan, *Jesus Through the Centuries*, 15.

275. See Gal 4:9: "Now that you know God—or rather are known by God—how is it that you are turning back to those weak and miserable forces? Do you wish to be enslaved by them all over again?" See also 1 Cor 8:3, 13:12.

276. Augustine, *Confessions*, X.iv.6; v.7; ii.2.

277. Ps 139:7.

278. In the first entry of his famous daily devotional, *My Utmost for His Highest*, Chambers exhorts Christians toward an "absolute and irrevocable surrender of the will" to God. Chambers, "Let Us Keep to the Point."

279. For instance, see Eliot's *Murder in the Cathedral*, 49. In his *Pursuit of God*, Tozer writes, "The only thinkable relation between us is one of full lordship on His part and complete submission on ours" (89; cf. 31). Compare with Charles de Foucauld, *Modern Spiritual Masters*, 104. See Stanley's references to "raising the white flag" in *The Spirit-Filled Life*, 8, 75, 266; as well as Andrew Murray's *Absolute Surrender*, 7–26.

280. *Alcoholics Anonymous: The Big Book*, 420.

281. MacDonald, *Donal Grant*, 8.

282. 2 Cor 12:9.

283. Coakley, *Powers and Submissions*, 3–39.

284. Lewis, *Mere Christianity*, 78. See also Henri Nouwen's candid confession: "Dear God, I am so afraid to open my clenched fists! Who will I be when I have nothing left to hold on to? Who will I be when I stand before you with empty hands?" Nouwen, *With Open Hands*, 21).

285. Augustine, *Confessions*, VIII.xi.27. The word "salvation" is derived from the Latin, *salus*, for healing. Augustine frequently uses variations of this Latin term in his *Confessions* when speaking of salvation. http://www.eudict.com/?lang=lateng&word=in cruce salus.

286. Augustine, *Confessions*, V.xiv.23

287. Casiday, *Evagrius Ponticus*, 93. Two centuries earlier, Origen described God's final judgment and chastisement as "medicinal." See Kelly's explication of Origen's eschatology in *Early Christian Doctrines*, 474. If you're really into the Enneagram, Evagrius is counted as one of its early Christian precursors. Also, if you're really into the Enneagram, please stop talking about it all the time.

288. Ps 139:13–16.

289. Ps 139:9.

290. http://www.sbc.net/resolutions/13. See also Balmer, *Making of Evangelicalism*, 61.

291. . . . including W.A. Criswell, former president of the Southern Baptist Convention. See Balmer, *Making of Evangelicalism*, 59–72. And Jimmy Carter, an outspoken, born-again Southern Baptist. While Carter was "personally opposed" to abortion and believed it to be "morally wrong," he refused to support an anti-abortion amendment to the constitution. Balmer, *Life of Jimmy Carter*, 67–69.

292. Fourth-century bishop Athanasius of Alexandria asserts, "The sacred and in-spired Scriptures are sufficient to declare the truth" Athanasius, *Against the Heathen*, I.1. Likewise, the Roman Catholic Council of Trent affirms Scripture as "divinely inspired." *Catechism of the Council of Trent*, qXII, 9. Trent cites 2 Tim 3:17: "All Scripture is God-breathed and is useful for teaching, rebuking, correcting and training in righteousness, so that the servant of God may be thoroughly equipped for every good work." Compare with evangelical scholar Carl Henry's account of biblical inspiration as an historical Christian doctrine in "Authority of the Bible," 20. See also Packer, "Inspiration of the Bible," 30–31.

293. According to authors Tim Chaffey, Ken Ham, and Bodie Hodge, "The Bible is cannot and does not contain any legitimate contradictions or inconsistencies." Chaffey, *Demolishing Supposed Bible Contradictions*, 15. Similarly, in *Bible Contradictions?*, John Taylor directly equates belief in the Bible's internal consistency with a "Christian

perspective" (4).

294. In his second-century treatise *Against Praxeas*, the North African bishop Tertullian stated, "We believe Him to have suffered, died, and been buried, according to the Scriptures." The same basic formula is present in both the Apostles and Nicene Creeds and in the Bible itself. See 1 Cor 15:3; Rom 1:3–4; 8:34; 1 Thess 4:14; 2 Tim 2:8.

295. The New Testament was deemed "useful or "profitable" (*ōphelimos*) for spiritual instruction, just like the Old (see 2 Tim 3:16, as well as *Apostolic Tradition*, 36:1). The apostle Peter referred to Paul's writings as Scripture: "Bear in mind that our Lord's patience means salvation, just as our dear brother Paul also wrote you with the wisdom that God gave him . . . His letters contain some things that are hard to understand, which ignorant and unstable people distort, as they do the other Scriptures, to their own destruction" (2 Pet 3:15–16). See Bruce, "Bible," 3–4. See also Noll, *Turning Points*, 35. In the second century, the Hellenistic philosopher and Gentile Christian apologist Justin Martyr mentioned the "memoirs of the apostles" or "Gospels" as being on the same level as the Old Testament. Justin Martyr, "Dialogue with Trypho," 185, 186, 249. Around the same time, Bishop Irenaeus of Lyon noted four Gospels to be included in the canon of Holy Scripture (ibid., 428). Two centuries later, church historian Eusebius mentions four Gospels, and the Muratorian fragment shows there was a set of Christian writings somewhat similar to the current New Testament, including the four Gospels—though the first two are unnamed. Porter, *Reading the Gospels Today*, 175–76.

296. Kelly, *Early Christian Doctrines*, 42, 46. For example, second-century theologian Clement of Alexandria urged Christians to rely on Scripture as the core criterion for determining the orthodoxy of any proposed teaching. Said Clement, "But those who are ready to toil in the most excellent pursuits, will not desist from the search after truth, till they get the demonstration from the Scriptures themselves." Clement, *Stromata*, VII.16. Around the same time, Irenaeus accused heterodox theologians of relying on spurious sources outside the biblical canon as the basis for their ideas. Irenaeus, *Against Heresies*, I.viii.1, http://www.newadvent.org/fathers/02107.htm. The fourth-century bishop Athanasius appealed to the "divine Scriptures" when arguing against the dualists of his day. Athanasius, *Against the Heathen*, I.6. And a few decades later, Jerome relied upon Scripture when arguing for the virtues of virginity: "But as we do not deny what is written, so we do reject what is not written. We believe that God was born of the Virgin, because we read it." Jerome, *Perpetual Virginity of Blessed Mary, Against Helvidius*, 21, http://www.newadvent.org/fathers/3007.htm. See also Cyril of Jerusalem: "For concerning the divine and holy mysteries of the Faith, not even a casual statement must be delivered without the Holy Scriptures; nor must we be drawn aside by mere plausibility and artifices of speech. Even to me, who tell you these things, give not absolute credence, unless thou receive the proof of the things which I announce from the Divine Scriptures. For this salvation which we believe depends not on ingenious reasoning , but on demonstration of the Holy Scriptures." Cyril, *Catechetical Lectures*, 4.17, translated by Edwin Hamilton Gifford, http://www.newadvent.org/fathers/310104.htm.

297. See Francis Turretin's landmark work *Doctrine of Scripture*, 209–26. Turretin's work was published in the 1880s and served as a template and guideline for generations of Protestants thereafter.

298. Pelikan, *Christian Tradition*, 154. See also Justin Martyr's defense of Jesus' divinity in "Dialogue with Trypho," 249. Ignatius of Antioch was another early opponent of Docetism. Ignatius adamantly defended the reality of Jesus' fleshly, material embodiment. Ignatius, *Ignatius to the Smyrnaeans*, 1–6. See also McGuckin, *Westminster Handbook*, 15, 178.

299. *Apostolic Tradition*, 36:1.

300. See David Bebbington's landmark study *Evangelicalism in Modern Britain*, 12–14, 86–91, 188.

301. Smith, *Bible Made Impossible*, viii.

302. Smith, *Bible Made Impossible*, 5.

303. Cited in Noll, "Common Sense Traditions," 225.

304. Chafer, *Systematic Theology*, vol. 8, 5–6.

305. "It being true that two truths cannot contradict one another," Galileo argued, "it is the function of wise expositors to seek out the true senses of scriptural texts." Swindal and Gensler, eds., *Sheed and Ward Anthology*, 244.

306. Smith, *Bible Made Impossible*, 13, 112. See also Noll, "Common Sense Traditions," 223–29.

307. Hodge, *Systematic Theology*, vol. 1, ch. 1, sec. 5.

308. Warfield, *Inspiration and Authority*, 113–14, emphasis mine. Warfield's language anticipates the 1978 Chicago Statement on Biblical Inerrancy: "Holy Scripture, being God's own Word, written by men prepared and superintended by His Spirit, is of infallible divine authority in all matters upon which it touches: it is to be believed, as God's instruction, in all that it affirms." http://www.churchcouncil.org/ICCP_org/Documents_ICCP/English/01_Biblical_Inerrancy_A&D.pdf.

309. According to Warfield, "every one of its [the Bible's] affirmations *of whatever kind* is to be esteemed as the utterance of God, of infallible truth and authority" (emphasis mine). Warfield, *Inspiration and Authority*, 112. See also Bebbington, *Evangelicalism in Modern Britain*, 13, 86, 91.

310. Worthen, *Apostles of Reason*, 16.

311. Smith, *Bible Made Impossible*, 112.

312. Quoted in Smith, *Bible Made Impossible*, 6.

313. Ehrman, *Misquoting Jesus*, 13.

314. Influential spokesmen for the biblicist view of Scripture include R. C. Sproul (see *Can I Trust the Bible?*), John MacArthur (*Think Biblically!: Recovering a Christian Worldview*), Lee Strobel (*The Case for Christianity Answer Book*, 41–92), Norman Geisler (*The Big Book of Bible Difficulties*), and Josh MacDowell (*More Than a Carpenter*, 37–55, 119–20).

315. For an articulate exposition of the Biblicist position, see Mohler, "When the Bible Speaks," especially 51–54.

316. Wuthnow, *After the Baby Boomers*, 103. The philosopher Slavoj Žižek follows Hegel in defining one of the main historical manifestations of religion as *Volksreligion*, "the people's religion," meaning religion that is indoctrinated through customs and social norms. "It required no special reflexive act of faith." Žižek, *Puppet and the Dwarf*, 4. I'd imagine a lot of Christians who grow up in evangelical and fundamentalist churches accept the Bible's unique status because it's what they grow up hearing and believing.

317. Wuthnow, *After the Baby Boomers*, 104.

318. For Gandhi, Jesus' teachings in the Sermon on Mount summarized the universal law of love and were fundamental to his practice as a religious and political leader. As a source of guidance and inspiration, Gandhi wrote, "The New Testament gave me comfort and boundless joy." Gandhi, *Gita the Mother*, 51.

319. Wuthnow, *After the Baby Boomers*, 103.

320. As prominent evangelical scholar J. I. Packer acknowledged, "The doctrine [of inerrancy] has sometimes been unnecessarily clouded by extreme conservative apologists who have overstated what biblical authority presupposes and implies." Packer saw this as a problem, warning against the tendency to distinguish "real" or "true" believers from "false Christians" purely on the basis of their view of Scripture. It's a problem precisely because it imposes a new set of laws and requirements in addition to the gospel. See Packer, "Inspiration of the Bible," 20. In a similar vein, the famous fundamentalist J. Gresham Machen believed it was possible to be a genuine follower of Jesus while denying the doctrine of biblical inerrancy. Such people should be considered true Christians, Machen argued, because they've embraced and believed in the good news, accepting the gospel message of as true. Yet they believe the message "has come to us merely on the authority of trustworthy

witnesses unaided in their literary work by supernatural guidance of the Spirit of God." Such people might even believe the Bible contains errors or related to secondary, but is nevertheless reliable and accurate in its communication of the gospel message. Machen, *Christianity and Liberalism*, 64.

321. Williams, *Evangelicals and Tradition*, 31. See also Gamble, *Books and Readers*, 2–6.

322. *Apostolic Tradition*, 36:1; Acts 2:42.

323. I'm referring to the Councils of Hippo (393 CE) and Carthage (397 and 419 CE). See Bruce, *Are They Reliable?*, 7.

324. Same goes for medieval Christians. Even if you could afford a hand-written copy of the Good Book, you'd need to be fluent in Latin to read it—which was a problem for the average, barely literate peasant, since local vernacular languages were becoming more and more popular and Latin had been on the decline for centuries.

325. Lash, "Ideology, Metaphor, and Analogy," 105–12; and "Reflections on a Metaphor," 158–66.

326. Matt 7:5.

327. L'Engle, *Rock That Is Higher*, 93.

328. Amos 7:14.

329. See Ps 91:4: "He will cover you with his feathers, and under his wings you will find refuge." Compare with anthropomorphic portrayals of God in Ps 139:9 ("even there your hand will guide me") and Ps 136:12 ("a mighty hand and outstretched arm"). And in the Exodus story, Moses and other Hebrew leaders catch a glimpse of God on Mount Sinai, "and under His feet there appeared to be a pavement of sapphire" (Exod 24:10, NASB). See John 4:24.

330. Ezek 7:2; Isa 11:12.

331. Isa 40:22: "He sits enthroned above the circle of the earth . . ."

332. A quick shout-out to Copernicus (1473–1543), the first Renaissance astronomer to provide a mathematical model of a heliocentric universe. A few decades after Copernicus's death, Galileo picked up heliocentrism and ran with it.

333. Galileo, "Letter to the Grand Duchess," 46.

334. See physicist Karl Giberson's article, "The Bible Is a Library, Not a Book," http://www.huffingtonpost.com/karl-giberson-phd/the-bible-is-a-library-no_b_923690.html. See also Giberson and Collins, *Language of Science and Faith*, 94.

335. From the fourth book of Origen's *On First Principles*, quoted in Bovell, *Interdisciplinary Perspectives*, 276. See also Stephen Jay Gould's discussion of Burnet's allegorical interpretation of Genesis 1: Gould, *Rocks of Ages*, 87.

336. Augustine, *Literal Meaning of Genesis*, 42–43. See also Steinmetz, "Superiority of Pre-Critical Exegesis," 26–38.

337. Quoted in Mitchell, *Paul, the Corinthians*, 3.

338. Steinmetz, "Superiority of Pre-Critical Exegesis," 28–29. See also See theologian Hans Frei's commentary on the "literal sense" of Scripture, which has priority over other "legitimate" interpretations, "although the allegorical or spiritual sense is permissible where the literal leaves you in the dark, or where the text says something that, when taken literally, is unworthy of God." Frei, *Types of Christian Theology*, 5, 14.

339. Steinmetz, "Superiority of Pre-Critical Exegesis," 28.

340. Galileo, "Letter to the Grand Duchess," 44.

341. 2 Chr 16:9 reads, "For the eyes of the Lord run to and fro throughout the whole earth." See also Exod 24:10.

342. Augustine, *Confessions*, V.xiv.24, VI.iii.6.

343. Huckabee, "Evolving Faith."

344. Augustine, *Confessions*, V.xiv.24, VI.iii.6.

345. In his preface to the New Testament, Luther claimed the book of James opposes Paul's theology by teaching justification by works, not the doctrine of *sola fide*. In the

earliest editions of his German Bible, Luther wrote, "St. James Epistle is really an epistle of straw compared to [St. Paul's letters], for it lacks this evangelical character." Cited in Jenkins, *New Faces of Christianity*, 60–61.

346. Evangelical pastor Greg Boyd knows the drill: "As most freshmen taking a course in 'The Bible as Literature' at a secular University learn, the historical accuracy of some biblical stories are questioned by many scholars, and it's hard to deny that the Bible contains some apparent contradictions and some material that seems to fly in the face of modern science." Boyd, interview.

347. Bebbington, *Evangelicalism in Modern Britain*, 14. See also Scholz, "Preface," xiii–xvii.

348. See Hobbe's *Leviathan*: "It is therefore sufficiently evident that the five Books of Moses were written after his time" (III:33; p. 261).

349. See Deut 34:5–8.

350. It's worth noting that plenty of scholars, most notably Umberto Cassuto, have ripped Wellhausen's Documentary Hypothesis to shreds. Cassuto wasn't trying to make a case for evangelical doctrines of divine inspiration and plenary inerrancy, nor was he a biblical literalist. He simply concluded that the Pentateuch was a unified composition derived from oral and written traditions. Cassuto, *Documentary Hypothesis*, 124. See also Campbell and O'Brien, *Sources of the Pentateuch*, 240.

351. Levine, "Introduction," 4. See Matt 26:17–19; Mark 14:12–16; Luke 22:7–13; John 13:1; 18:28; 19:31.

352. Bandstra, *Reading the Old Testament*, 19–37.

353. Among other things, Strauss drew attention to the substantial similarities between the Synoptic Gospels—Matthew, Mark and Luke—and questioned the veracity of miracles. Coogan, "Gulf Between Scholars," 6–8.

354. Evangelical and fundamentalist authors like Norman Geisler, Hank Hanegraaff, Ray Comfort, John MacArthur, and Ken Ham go to great lengths in arguing the case for biblicism by attempting to harmonize any apparent inconsistencies in the Bible. In the impressive and intelligently written *The Big Book of Bible Difficulties*, Norman Geisler and Thomas Howe address some of the most frequently cited examples of biblical contradictions (15, 20, 33, 38, 51, 53–54, 60, 73–74, 89, 104, 120, 123–24, 129, 141, 147, 159, 164, 183, 210, 235, 243, 246, 280, etc.). See also Comfort, "Supposed Bible Contradictions."

355. Historian Mark Noll taught at the historically evangelical Christian Wheaton College for over twenty-seven years. He's one of the world's authorities on American Christian history and a practicing evangelical himself. Nevertheless, Noll warns against Biblicist naiveté: "As comfortable as it would make Protestants to think that the New Testament always existed with firm, crisp boundaries marking it off from all other kinds of literature, the existing historical evidence shows that . . . it took more than two centuries to define the precise shape of the New Testament." Noll, *Turning Points*, 35.

356. For example, the apostle Paul quoted pagan philosophers while addressing a Hellenistic audience in Acts 17:28. And in Jude 1:14–15, the author quotes from the apocryphal book of Enoch, which Tertullian considered canonical. Tertullian, *De cultu foeminarum*, I.3. See also Coon, *Sacred Fictions*, 37. Likewise, Irenaeus considered Enoch part of Scripture (*Against Heresies*, IV.16.2), though it was eventually excluded from the canon. Boccaccini, *Beyond the Essene Hypothesis*, 168. It is also possible Jesus quoted from the apocryphal book Sirach—a.k.a. Ecclesiasticus—either directly or indirectly. Compare Matt 7:16–20 with Sir 27:6; Matt 6:12 with Sir 28:2; Mark 4:5, 16–17 with Sir 40:15; and Matt 11:28 with Sir 51:27. For Sirach online, see https://www.biblegateway.com/passage/?search=Sirach+1&version=GNT.

357. Biblical evidence suggests that Third and Fourth Corinthians were also read by early churches, though there are no extant copies. The Epistle to Laodicea, which is mentioned in Colossians, was also lost: "And when this letter has been read among you, have it also read in the church of the Laodiceans; and see that you also read the letter from

Laodicea" (Col 4:16).

358. Wright, "Passing of Evolution," 60–72. See also Numbers and Stenhouse, *Disseminating Darwinism*, 27–29.

359. See Peter Enns's *Inspiration and Incarnation*, 18.

360. Mohler, "When the Bible Speaks," 54.

361. Aslan, *Zealot*, xix, emphasis mine.

362. Ehrman, *Misquoting Jesus*, 9–10.

363. Ehrman, *Misquoting Jesus*, 9, 11.

364. Ehrman, *Misquoting Jesus*, 13, 11.

365. Sullivan, "Upon This Rock," 32.

366. Misener, "Why I Miss," http://www.buzzfeed.com/jessicamisener/why-i-miss-being-a-born-again-christian, emphasis mine.

367. Misener, "Why I Miss."

368. McClymond, *Familiar Stranger*, 82.

369. "No single picture of Jesus has convinced all, or even most scholars." Levine, "Introduction," 1.

370. Tyrell, *Christianity at the Cross-Roads*, 44. Said Schweitzer, "Each individual created him in the image of his own personality." Cited in Kasper, *Jesus the Christ*, 19.

371. Cone, *Black Theology of Liberation*, 111–19.

372. Auden, *Prose*, 197.

373. Warren, "Michael Ramsey," http://anglicanpastor.com/the-theology-of-michael-ramsey-for-today/.

374. See Chesterton, *Orthodoxy*, 44–45. The full quote reads: "I have never been able to understand where people got the idea that democracy was in some way opposed to tradition. It is obvious that tradition is only democracy extended through time. It is trusting to a consensus of common human voices rather than to some isolated or arbitrary record . . . Tradition means giving votes to the most obscure of all classes, our ancestors. It is the democracy of the dead. Tradition refuses to submit to the small and arrogant oligarchy of those who merely happen to be walking about. All democrats object to men being disqualified by the accident of birth; tradition objects to their being disqualified by the accident of death. Democracy tells us not to neglect a good man's opinion, even if he is our groom; tradition asks us not to neglect a good man's opinion, even if he is our father. I, at any rate, cannot separate the two ideas of democracy and tradition; it seems evident to me that they are the same idea. We will have the dead at our councils. The ancient Greeks voted by stones; these shall vote by tombstones."

375. 1 Cor 12:27.

376. Stott, *Cross of Christ*, 12.

377. Calvin affirmed "the authority of the fathers" in his *Institutes* (II.ii.7-8; "Prefatory Address," 4). See Steinmetz, "Reformers Read the Fathers." See also Williams, *Retrieving the Tradition*, 25.

378. Duke professor David Steinmetz calls this modern bias the "single meaning" theory of interpretation. Steinmetz, "Superiority of Pre-Critical Exegesis," 26–28.

379. Frank Viola argues that modern Christians are too preoccupied with uncovering the original intent of the author, ignoring figurative and Christological interpretations along the way. See Viola, *Beyond Bible Study*.

380. See MacArthur's *Grace to You* online article "Study Your Bible."

381. For instance, Clement of Alexandria, Origen, Augustine, Gregory of Nyssa, John Cassianus, and Thomas Aquinas. Origen believed the Bible could be read and understood on three different levels: the literal, the moral and the allegorical. See Irvin and Sunquist, *World Christian Movement*, 124–25. See also Pelikan, *Christian Tradition*, 61. Though Aquinas was a strong advocate of the literal approach, he nevertheless affirmed and defended the multiple senses of Scripture. Aquinas, *Summa*, Iq1a10). More recently, the modern semiotician A. J. Greimas argued that reading and interpreting a text involves

making the text: by focusing on a single component and following a particular trajectory that becomes, for the reader, what is "truly" significant in the text. This is what medieval biblical interpreters knew well: there are several dimension or levels of Scripture and multiple ways of interpreting it from within a distinctly Christian framework. Patte, *Religious Dimensions*, 1–3. It wasn't till the arrival of Protestant Scholastics like Francis Turretin that the medieval "fourfold meaning [or 'sense'] of Scripture" came under serious, sustained attack and, subsequently, fell into disuse. Turretin, *Doctrine of Scripture*, 199–208. Nevertheless, modern Protestant evangelicals are at least aware of the multiple senses of Scripture, if only in lay practice. For instance, evangelicals freely eat shellfish, though doing so is explicitly forbidden by Leviticus (11:9–12). Thankfully, evangelicals are equally lax in their interpretation of Psalm 137. Former Promise Keeper and current evangelical/Pentecostal Jack Hayford refers to several "types of teachings" in the Old Testament, including: historical facts (literal sense), moral instruction (tropological sense), spiritual lessons, and "pictures of New Testament truth" (a.k.a. christological prophecies, shadows, and types). Hayford, *Rebuilding the Real You*, 4–5.

382. See Steinmetz's treatment of the fourfold sense of Scripture in "Superiority of Pre-Critical Exegesis," 26–38.

383. Augustine, *Confessions*, XI. See also Hawking, *Brief History of Time*, 8–9; and Hawking's online post "The Beginning of Time."

384. Augustine, *Literal Meaning of Genesis*, 43–44. See also Augustine, *City of God*, XI:6: "What kind of days these were it is extremely difficult, or perhaps impossible for us to conceive."

385. Augustine, *Confessions*, XII.xviii.27, emphasis mine. See XII.xvi.22–33 for Augustine's extended discussion of numerous orthodox interpretations of Genesis.

386. Saad, "Bible as Word of God," http://www.gallup.com/poll/170834/three-four-bible-word-god.aspx.

387. Bebbington argues that biblical inerrancy as we know it today was an innovation of the nineteenth century and took time to gain adherents among evangelicals. Bebbington, *Evangelicalism in Modern Britain*, 91. In the fourth century, Gregory of Nyssa already felt it necessary to address the issue of biblical literalism in the preface to his *Commentary on the Song of Songs*: "Since some ecclesiastics deem it right to stand always by the literal meaning of the holy scripture and do not agree that anything in it was said through enigmas and allegories for our benefit, I consider it necessary first to speak in defense of these things to those who bring such accusation against us, because in our view there is nothing unreasonable in our seriously studying all possible means of tracking down the benefit to be had from the divinely inspired scripture." Quoted in Mitchell, *Paul, the Corinthians*, 1.

388. See Bebbington, *Evangelicalism in Modern Britain*, 14, 86, 91, 188.

389. For further reference, see Langer, *Philosophy in a New Key*, 13–25, 266–76.

390. Postcolonial biblical scholar Fernando Segovia challenges the Enlightenment presupposition that modern, scientific methodologies are "applicable to all areas of inquiry," including biblical studies and interpretation, and can always be counted on to produce "objective" results. Segovia, *Decolonizing Biblical Studies*, 45. See also Segovia, "Postcolonial Criticism," 196.

391. Fleming Rutledge puts it elegantly: "Like virtually all the important Christian thinkers prior to the post-Enlightenment and modernist milieu that dominated biblical studies until the second half of the twentieth century, Irenaeus moved among various images of what Christ accomplished." Rutledge, *Crucifixion*, 540.

392. See Rev 21.

393. See Paul's figurative interpretations of Sarah, Hagar, Sinai, and Jerusalem in Gal 4:21–31.

394. John 5:46, emphasis mine.

395. John 14:6; 8:58.

396. Viola, *Beyond Bible Study*, 9. See also *Pursuit of God*, where Tozer interprets the

burning incense of the tabernacle as a "figure of unceasing prayer" (41).

397. In the New Testament, the book of Hebrews (10:1) says the Old Testament laws were a "shadow of the good things that are coming—not the realities themselves" Calvin, *Institutes*, II.vi.1.

398. In *Confessions*, XI.ii.4, Augustine interprets the Psalms and other Old Testament books as speaking of Jesus, e.g., "Moses wrote of him." See also *Confessions*, XII.xvi.22–33.

399. Calvin, *Institutes*, III.iv.4–6.

400. Calvin, *Commentary on John* 5:39. For specific examples of Calvin's christological hermeneutic in the *Institutes*, see his interpretations of David (II.vi.2); Old Testament prophecy (II.xi.6) and theophanies (I.i.3); the Egyptian bondage of Israel (II.viii.15); Moses, the Red Sea, and the manna from heaven (II.x.5); and the Law (II.vii.1; II.ix.3-4) as types, prefigurings, and foreshadowings of Christ.

401. Gen 6–7. See Augustine, *City of God*, XV.26–27; and *Contra Faustum*, XII.14–23, 39. See also Aquinas' *Summa*, IIIq73a3; and Milburn, *Early Christian Art*, 134.

402. Jesus' forty-day fast in the desert parallels the story of the Moses and the Hebrews wandering in the wilderness for forty years. See Exod 16:35, Josh 5:6, Matt 4:1–11, Mark 1:12–13, and Luke 4:1–13. Heb 3–4 interprets Jesus as the ultimate fulfillment of the Sabbath, as well as the prophecies of Moses and Joshua. Heb 8–10 interprets the tabernacle and sacrifices of the Hebrew Bible as pictures, figures, shadows, and "types" of Jesus and His eventual redemptive work.

403. Lewis, *Letters*, 273.

404. See Augustine, *Confessions*, XII.xxiv.33, wherein Augustine explains how a "true" and faithful reading of a passage of Scripture can be different than what the original author (i.e., Moses) had in mind.

405. Famously, Thomas Torrance, one of Barth's prized pupils, said the following: "There is no God behind the back of Jesus." Torrance, *Incarnation*, xxxi.

406. Naim Ateek, a contemporary christocentric theologian and Palestinian native of Israel, explains the christological hermeneutic as follows: "The *Word* of God incarnate in Jesus the Christ interprets for us the *word* of God in the Bible." Ateek calls Christ the "true hermeneutic"—i.e., the supreme interpretive key for reading and understanding the Bible, our most reliable and informative source of the knowledge of God. Ateek, "Palestinian Perspective," 398–99.

407. In his fourth-century commentary on the Song of Songs, Gregory of Nyssa encouraged the faithful to consider multiple senses of the biblical text: "When it comes to the insightful reading of such passages that comes via the elevated sense, we shall not beg to differ at all about its name—whether one wishes to call it *tropologia*, *allegoria*, or anything else—but only about whether it contains meanings that are beneficial." Quoted in Mitchell, *Paul, the Corinthians*, 1.

408. See Alexander Golitzin's commentary on Dionysius and the process of growing in likeness to God. Golitzin, *Mystagogy*, 117–21.

409. Bonhoeffer, *Letters and Papers*, 270.

410. Of the "cursing psalms," C. S. Lewis wrote, "We should be wicked if we in any way condoned or approved it, or (worse still) used it to justify similar passions in ourselves." Lewis, *Reflections on the Psalms*, 22. With these kinds of biblical passages in mind, Gregory of Nyssa references Paul's words in 2 Cor 3:6 as a check against indiscriminate literalism: "It is not necessary always to remain in the letter, on the grounds that the immediately apparent meaning of the things said in many instances causes us harm in the pursuit of the life of virtue . . . 'The letter kills, but the spirit gives life,' since oftentimes with biblical narrative, it will not provide us with examples of a good life if we stop short at the simple events." Mitchell, *Paul, the Corinthians*, 3.

411. Thejanlynn, "Notes from Q."

412. Warren, "Cost of Freedom."

413. Compare Phil 4:13 (NKJV) with 1 Thess 4:11 (NIV).

414. See the definition of "pride" in *Dictionary of the Christian Church*. See also Aquinas' treatment of Augustine's analysis of pride in *Summa*, IIq162.

415. Adapted, paraphrased, and possibly butchered, from Ward, *Desert Fathers*, 148, 165.

416. 1 Pet 5:5, ESV.

417. Matt 5:5, CSB.

418. John of the Cross, *John of the Cross*, 164–65.

419. Nietzsche, *Gay Science*, 87.

420. Barth, "Biblical Questions, Insights," 83.

421. Augustine, *Confessions*, XII.xxv.34. See also H. Richard Niebuhr's warning: "The God of a revelation that can be possessed must be God of the past, a God of the dead who communicated his truths to men in another time but who to all effects and purposes has now retired from the world." Niebuhr, *Meaning of Revelation*, 21.

422. Augustine, *Confessions*, X.xxxvii.60, emphasis mine. Augustine anticipated the eventual denial of a unified, homogenous "self" as popularized by psychotherapists and continental philosophers from Marx to Freud to Lacan to Zizek. Zizek and Milbank, *Monstrosity of Christ*, 11.

423. Wittgenstein, *Tractatus*, 5.633: "Where in the world is a metaphysical subject to be found? You will say that this is exactly like the case of the eye and the visual field. But really you do not see the eye. And nothing in the visual field allows you to infer that it is seen by an eye."

424. Chesterton, *Orthodoxy*, 51.

425. The philosopher Louis Althusser argued that the coherent, self-aware, and enduringly stable "ego" is a socioculturally constructed illusion. The list of Althusser's eminent students includes Michel Foucault, Jacques Derrida, and Alain Badiou who, along with Althusser himself and Ferdinand de Saussure, "question the humanistic assumption that individuals are the sole source of meaning or action." Loomba, *Colonialism/Postcolonialism*, 36. Likewise Jacques Lacan argued that one's "ego" or "self" is never present to oneself, just as there is no stable human subjectivity, no consciousness from which an ostensibly autonomous individual agency arises. Cautiously, one can see an analogy in Augustine, who likewise questioned the individual's capacity for self-assessment, especially when it comes to assessing one's spiritual progress. Said the Jesuit priest Jean-Pierre de Caussade, "Perfection is neither more not less than the soul's faithful cooperation with God. This co-operation begins, grows and comes to fruition in our souls so secretly that we are not aware of it . . . If a faithful soul accepts God's will and purpose in all simplicity, he will reach perfection without ever realizing it." Caussade, *Abandonment to Divine Providence*, 26. Similarly, Oswald Chambers, a Baptist minister of keen psychological insight, believed spiritual transformation (a.k.a. sanctification or *theosis*) occurs on both conscious and unconscious levels, whether or not the putatively objective "self" detects the Spirit's transformative work within: "The entrance into the kingdom of God is through the sharp, sudden pains of repentance colliding with man's respectable 'goodness.' Then the Holy Spirit, who produces these struggles, begins the formation of the Son of God in the person's life (see Gal 4:19). This new life will reveal itself in conscious repentance followed by unconscious holiness, never the other way around." Chambers, "Repentance."

426. See Mark C. Taylor's analysis of Luther's revolutionary "turn to the subject" and its global, cultural, and ideological aftereffects. Taylor, *After God*, xvi, 55, 62, 64, 68. In a similar vein, Patrick Collinson summarizes Thomas Carlyle's depiction of Luther as a heroic individual: "If Luther had not stuck to his guns at the Diet of Worms, where he stood before the Holy Roman emperor and refused to recant ('Here I stand'), there would have been no French Revolution and no America . . ." Collinson, *Reformation: A History*, 6.

427. Most committed Catholic scholars today acknowledge the unfortunate liturgical lapses and clerical abuses that prevailed in the medieval Roman Church. For instance, Father Bruce Morrill's critique of the dominant medieval understanding of the Eucharist

in "Christ's Sacramental Presence."

428. See Heiko A. Oberman's rendering of Luther's statement at the Diet of Worms (1521) in Oberman, *Luther: Man Between*, 39. See also Bainton, *Here I Stand*, 130.

429. A large contingent of scholars argue that the driving concern of the Reformation debates was the question of what constitutes reliable religious authority. Fulton and Webster, "Introduction," 1–10.

430. Nichols, *Corporate Worship*, 11.

431. Wright, "Some of His Critics," 352.

432. Hatch, *Democratization of American Christianity*, 214–16.

433. Lincoln, "Second Inaugural Address."

434. Hatch, *Democratization of American Christianity*, 163.

435. See Mark Noll's definition of "common sense realism" and its epistemology: "Our perceptions pretty much reveal the world as it is." Noll, "Common Sense Traditions," 223–29. Common sense realism was a Scottish Enlightenment philosophy of the 1700s. It was hugely influential for Thomas Jefferson, Thomas Paine, and others, including many early American seminaries—especially Yale and Princeton, where half of undergraduate students in the early nineteenth century went into full-time vocational ministry upon graduating. Jefferson, who opposed counterintuitive doctrines like the Trinity, idealized the self-sufficient "Yeoman farmer," endowed with sufficient common sense to navigate all moral, political, and theological decisions without the guidance of educated elites or entitled nobility. Noll, *Scandal of the Evangelical Mind*, 84–93.

436. Under the influence of John Cotton, individual citizens of the Massachusetts Bay Colony were urged to have personal and intimate knowledge of Scripture. Eberling, "Massachusetts Education Laws," 225–26. The Puritans believed all individuals should be able to read and interpret Scripture for themselves. Hence, literacy was of prime importance. In 1647, Massachusetts Puritans passed the "Old Deluder Satan Law," mandating that every town of ffity households or more hire a teacher for the purpose of instructing the populace in biblical literacy. Milson, "John Cotton," 1. A century after Cotton, primitivist leaders like Barton Stone and Alexander Campbell turned to "Bible-only-ism" in hopes of restoring the "biblical church" and ridding Christianity of any unwanted innovation and humanly contrived tradition. Academic theology would thus be replaced by commonsense "Bible-only-ism." Gaustad and Schmidt, *Religious History of America*, 155. See also Noll, *Old Religion*, 66.

437. Evangelicals like Charles Colson and J. I. Packer admitted as much in "Your Word Is Truth," a statement by Evangelicals and Catholics together in 2002. They warned, "The isolation of Scripture study from the believing community of faith (*nuda scriptura*) disregards the Holy Spirit's work in guiding the witness of the people of God to scriptural truths, and leaves the interpretation of that truth vulnerable to unfettered subjectivism." "Your Word Is Truth."

438. John Calvin understood the corporate gathering of believers in ritual and fellowship as crucial to Christian living. Wary of sectarianism, Calvin criticized Protestants who voluntarily deserted the "outward communion of the church." Calvin, *Institutes*, IV.i.19. He believed it was "not lawful for a private individual to separate from" even the most Libertine church bodies. Cited in Mannion and Eduardus, eds., *John Calvin's Ecclesiology*, 66.

439. In 1520, Luther called upon the German nobility to forcibly reform the church. Luther, "To the Christian Nobility," 7–112. Princes and nobles were valuable political allies for Luther. Frederick the Wise, elector of Saxony, protected Luther from the papacy and probably conspired to secure Luther's abduction to Wartburg Castle. Marty, *Martin Luther*, 39–68. See also Dillenberger, "Introduction," xxiii. During the German Peasants' War, Luther condemned the revolutionaries for breaking their vow "to be true and faithful, submissive and obedient, to their rulers." In all likelihood, the peasants were influenced and inspired by Luther's theological ideas concerning individual Christian freedom and the priesthood of all believers. Luther, *Freedom of a Christian*, 100. For example, in his

famous letter to the German nobles, Luther attacks the "Romanists" for religious and socioeconomic elitism: "It is intolerable that in canon law so much importance is attached to the freedom, life, and property of the clergy, as though the laity were not also as spiritual; and as good Christians as they, or did not also belong to the church. Why are your life and limb, your property and honor, so cheap and mine not, inasmuch as we are all Christians and have the same baptism, the same faith, the same Spirit, and all the rest? If a priest is murdered, the whole country is placed under interdict. Why not when a peasant is murdered?" Luther, "To the Christian Nobility," 17.

440. Francis of Assisi was tonsured by the church and received approval from Pope Innocent III. See Sabatier, *Life of St. Francis*, 57–72. See also Thompson, *Francis of Assisi*, 30–31, 92.

441. After the Protestant Reformation, newly Lutheranized congregations continued to rely on bishops to preach, teach, and expound upon the Bible. Askew and Pierard, *American Church Experience*, 21)

442. Calvin criticized Christians who dared "despise public assemblies and deem preaching superfluous," and who claimed to "profit enough from private reading" [of Scripture]. To Calvin, spiritual individualism led to spiritual delusion and idolatry. Calvin, *Institutes*, IV.1.5.

443. John 16:13.

444. See the definition of the Greek word *pas* in Blue Letter Bible.

445. 1 Peter 1:11; Romans 8:9. See also Westminster Confession, XIII.ii.7–13.

446. This is the title of his book.

447. Lewis, *Reflections on the Psalms*, 111.

448. Lewis, *Reflections on the Psalms*, 11, 53, 111.

449. Coleridge, *Confessions of an Inquiring Spirit*, 13. Coleridge actually says "supernatural dictation," but divine dictation is pithier. And yes, I just attempted to improve upon Coleridge.

450. "Evangelicals in America," Greenberg Quinlan Rosner Research, 4.

451. 1 Cor 1:16.

452. There's also the problem of misquotations in the Bible—or, more accurately, misquotations *of* the Bible *by* the Bible. New Testament authors were sometimes inaccurate when citing passages from the Old, as when Paul fudged a few details of Ps 51:4 in his letter to the Romans (3:4). Even curmudgeonly Calvin conceded, "We know that in repeating the words of Scripture [the Old Testament] the apostles were often pretty free." Calvin, *Institutes*, CR XLIX 49. *"Pretty free?"* This is *Calvin* we're talking about: pioneer of Puritanism, present-day hero to countless conservative evangelicals. Yet even Calvin fell afoul of popular biblicist standards. Case in point: noted evangelical scholar Peter Davids explains how the apostle Paul must have suffered a "slip of the mind" when quoting Num 25:9 in 1 Cor 10:8. Kaiser et al., *Hard Sayings*, 598–99. Davids attributes Paul's error to a momentary lapse in memory, which Eric Lyons of *Apologetics Press* finds unacceptable. In an online post entitled "The Myth of 'Factual' Bible Contradictions," Lyons criticizes Davids for considering the possibility that Paul fudged a minor detail.

453. Enns, *Inspiration and Incarnation*, 18.

454. Distinguished historian and self-identifying evangelical Mark Noll elaborates: "As comfortable as it would make Protestants to think that the New Testament always existed with firm, crisp boundaries marking it off from all other kinds of literature, the existing historical evidence shows that . . . it took more than two centuries to define the precise shape of the New Testament." Noll, *Turning Points*, 35.

455. See Warfield, *Revelation and Inspiration*, 429. See also Hodge and Warfield, "Inspiration," 245. In the 1970s, America's leading evangelicals agreed with Warfield. See Brown, "Inerrancy and Infallibility," 39.

456. See the Chicago Statement on Biblical Inerrancy, ratified by Francis Schaeffer, J. I. Packer, and R. C. Sproul, among others: "We affirm that God in His Work of inspiration

utilized the *distinctive personalities and literary styles of the writers* whom He had chosen and prepared." Signatories of the statement also denied that God in any way "overrode" the personalities of the biblical authors (vii–viii, emphasis mine).

457. At least, that *was* the explanation, till Luke Skywalker said otherwise in *The Last Jedi*. Don't test my *Star Wars* skills.

458. Docetism was an early heresy that denied Jesus' humanity and assumed Christ could not have a physical body.

459. I'm referring to Buddha's interaction with Saccaka. Thanissaro, "Shorter Discourse to Saccaka."

460. Genesis 1:31.

461. Aquinas, *Summa*, Iq103a6.

462. 1 Cor 1:4; Acts 18:1–17.

463. Aquinas did not see human will as necessarily engaged in constant competition with God's will. Aquinas, *Summa*, 1q103a8. Three centuries later, John Calvin said, "Man's [*sic*] action is not taken away by the movement of the Holy Spirit" (*Institutes*, II.v.14); and "man [*sic*], while he is acted upon by God, yet at the same time himself acts" (I.xviii.1.232)."

464. See Rowan William's discussion of the problem of dichotomizing spiritual and material realities: "It is perhaps because we are so generally inept at recognizing that the meaning of our acts and relations rests, moment by moment, on God's creative grace that we so readily end up in bad-tempered confrontations of a singularly unproductive sort over 'what we do' and 'what he does' in the sacraments—as if (thinking back to St. Thomas [Aquinas] once again) the purely spiritual and divine could be thought of as something side by side with the material and human." Williams, *On Christian Theology*, 205).

465. The fourth-century theologian Athanasius explained, "He became Himself an object of the senses, so that those who were seeking God in sensible things might apprehend the Father through the works which He, the Word of God, did in the body." Athanasius, *On the Incarnation*, 43.

466. John 1:14.

467. Col 1:15. Verse 19 describes Jesus as the embodied dwelling place of God's "fullness."

468. Heb 1:3

469. John 14:7, 9.

470. The Chalcedonian Creed of 451 describes Jesus as "truly God and truly man," foreshadowing the words of the Athanasian Creed: "fully God, fully man." http://www.reformed.org/documents/.

471. See John 1:1, 14; 8:58; Matt 1:23; Col 1:15; 2:9–10; 1 Tim 3:16; 2 John 1:7.

472. See 1 Cor 15:3; Rom 1:3–4; 8:34; 1 Thess 4:14; 2 Tim 2:8. See also Tertullian's *Against Praxeas* 2; as well as Ignatius of Antioch's assertions of Jesus' humanity in *The Epistle of Ignatius to the Smyrnaeans*, 1–6. http://www.newadvent.org/fathers/0109.htm.

473. See Augustine, *Confessions*, X.xlii.67. In his masterful essay "Fate and Idea in Theology," Karl Barth makes it clear that immateriality is not a privileged position or inherently superior state of being: "The spiritual realm, no less than the natural, has creaturely status, and that as such it therefore gives us no access to God." (Barth, "Fate and Idea," 48.

474. As the twentieth-century evangelical A. W. Tozer explained, the incarnation "sweeps away forever the evil notion that there is about the human body something innately offensive to the Deity of God." Tozer, *Pursuit of God*, 110.

475. Russell, *Mysticism and Logic*, 30.

476. Keeble, *Every Man an Artist*, 8. See also *Damascene On Holy Images*, 18.

477. Moltmann, "Eberhard Jüngel," 9–10.

478. Bonhoeffer, *Ethics*, 242, emphasis mine.

479. Weil, *Waiting on God*, 103, 108.

480. Percy, *Love in the Ruins*, 37.

481. Cohen, *Beautiful Losers*, 99. Similarly, Walker Percy contrasted incarnate religion

with the contemporary spirituality: "What she didn't understand, she being spiritual and seeing religion as spirit, was that it took religion to save me from the spirit world, from orbiting the earth like Lucifer and the angels, that it took nothing less than touching the thread off the misty interstates and eating Christ himself to make me mortal man again and let me inhabit my own flesh and love her in the morning." Percy, *Love in the Ruins*, 254.

482. Chesterton, *St. Thomas Aquinas*, 11.

483. Howell, *Ignatius of Antioch*, L29.

484. Mark 10:35–45; Matt 20:20–28.

485. John 21:25.

486. See Philip Ball's intriguing article "The Trouble with Scientists." Ball concedes that some researchers are "consciously cherry-picking" data in order to secure publication for their work and/or advance a particular position. "But the problems of false findings often begin with researchers unwittingly fooling themselves: they fall prey to cognitive biases, common modes of thinking that lure us toward wrong but convenient or attractive conclusions." Psychologist Brian Nosek of the University of Virginia calls it "motivated reasoning," meaning that we look for evidence to support conclusions we have already drawn, especially if doing so has the potential to lead to career advancement, tenure, securing grants, and the like.

487. As Hans Frei wrote, "We do not try to imagine the *inside* of it [a sculpture], but let our eyes wander over its surface and its mass, so that we may grasp its form, its proportions, and its balances." That's how you grasp the "meaning" of a piece of art. Frei, *Identity of Jesus Christ*, 133.

488. Evans, "Mirror of the Word."

489. Olson, *World on Paper*, 4. See also Bloomfield, *Language*, 219.

490. For instance, defining Jesus as the "image of God" is a formula repeated in Col 1:15 and 2 Cor 4:4. Dunn, *Epistles to the Colossians*, 87.

491. Williams, *Retrieving the Tradition*, 55.

492. Tertullian, *Against Praxeas 2*.

493. See 1 Cor 15:3; Rom 1:3–4; 8:34; 1 Thess 4:14; 2 Tim 2:8. Likewise, the Apostles', Nicene, and Chalcedonian Creeds all emphasize Jesus' crucifixion and burial.

494. See Phil 2:5–11, NRSV; Allen, "Between Text & Sermon," 72–74; Murphy-O'Connor, *Paul: A Critical Life*, 216; Coakley, "Rest on a Mistake?," 247. While Coakley argues that the church fathers were "bewilderingly creative" in their divergent readings of the "kenotic hymn," violating God's unchanging nature divine was not seriously considered by any of them. See also Pelikan, *Christian Tradition*, 229.

495. Williams, *Retrieving the Tradition*, 42. See also Heb 2:3.

496. Jenkins, *Lost History of Christianity*, 65.

497. Moffett, *Christianity in Asia*, 292.

498. Like the Mediterranean culture of the Roman Empire, Chinese civilization had developed writing and a substantial literary tradition. Irvin and Sunquist, *World Christian Movement*, 8.

499. Rom 6:17. See also 1 Tim 4:13: ". . . devote yourself to the public reading of Scripture, to preaching and to teaching."

500. 1 Thess 2:13.

501. "1 Thessalonians . . . is regarded by most scholars as the earliest document included in the New Testament. It is usually dated to late 50 or early 51 CE." McGaughy, *Authentic Letters of Paul*.

502. 2 Thess 2:15.

503. Gamble, "New Testament Canon," 282.

504. Irenaeus, *Against Heresies*, III.1.1, emphasis mine.

505. Even after the New Testament was completed, reading silently to yourself was kind of an oddity back in the day, even among the minority literate elites. Most reading was public and communal, including readings from the Bible. See Henry Chadwick's

footnote, "In antiquity silent reading was uncommon, not unknown." Augustine, *Confessions*, VI.iii.3.

506. See Tertullian, *On Prescription Against Heretics*, 12. See also Tertullian, *Against Praxeas*, 2, http://www.newadvent.org/fathers/0317.htm; and Irenaeus' *Against Heresies*, such as book 1.1.1, or book 3.2.2. The "tradition" was, contrary to the Gnostic view, public, never "secret."

507. Williams, *Retrieving the Tradition*, 35–45.

508. See John 1:1, 14.

509. Pelikan, *Christian Tradition*, 199.

510. As seen in Jerome's *Epistle 129*, written to Claudianus Postumus Dardanus, the basis for including the book of Hebrews in the New Testament canon was widespread acceptance and usage among a diversity of churches. Gregory, *Canon and Text*, 284. See also Williams, *Retrieving the Tradition*, 45. In his book *Lost Christianities*, Bart Ehrman enumerates four main criteria for inclusion in the New Testament canon. Any book under consideration for canonization had to be written by an apostle or an apostle's companion, at or near the time of Jesus, widely circulated and used among the established, ancient churches, and orthodox in its theology. Ehrman, *Lost Christianities*, 242–43. For an example of theological heterodoxy, the non-canonical Gospel of Judas, depicts Jesus as a disembodied spirit who neither suffers nor achieves genuine identification with humanity. Gathercole, *Gospel of Judas*, 162–71.

511. Kelly, *Early Christian Doctrines*, 40.

512. In *Against Heresies*, Irenaeus asked, "Even if the apostles had not left their writings to us, ought we not to follow the rule of the tradition which they handed down to those to whom they committed the churches?" (III.4.1).

513. Athanasius, *Serapion of Thmuis*, 1:28 (40).

514. According to the late Jesuit scholar Walter Ong, "Hard-core textualism [privileging the written word to the exclusion of oral transmission] is snobbery, often hardly disguised." Downing et al., eds., *Linguistics of Literacy*, 296.

515. Foley, *Homer's Traditional Art*, 13–17.

516. DeHart, *Trial of the Witnesses*, 18.

517. Jenson, *Canon and Creed*, 43.

518. Kelly, *Early Christian Creeds*, 102.

519. Charles Hodge was one of the forefathers of American fundamentalism, a hugely influential biblicist, and harsh critic of Roman Catholicism. But even Hodge readily acknowledged the essential doctrinal orthodoxy of Catholicism: "Indeed it is a matter of devout thankfulness to God that underneath the numerous grievous and destructive errors of the Romish Church, the great truths of the Gospel are preserved. The Trinity, the true divinity of Christ, the true doctrine concerning his person as God and man in two distinct natures and one person forever; salvation through his blood, regeneration and sanctification through the almighty power of the Spirit, the resurrection of the body, and eternal life, are doctrines on which the people of God in that communion live, and which have produced such saintly men as St. Bernard, Fenelon, and doubtless thousands of others who are of the number of God's elect. Every true worshipper of Christ must in his heart recognize as a Christian brother, wherever he may be found, any one who loves, worships, and trusts the Lord Jesus Christ as God manifest in the flesh and the only Saviour of men." Hodge, *Systematic Theology*, vol. 3, ch. 17, sec. 3, 135–36.

520. Clement of Alexandria, *Stromata*, VII.16.

521. Wright, *Simply Christian*, x.

522. White, *Guide to the Kingdom*, 23–24.

523. Quoted in Stark, "Epidemics, Network," 166.

524. Writes Stark, "Pagan and Christian writers are unanimous that not only did Christian scripture stress love and charity as the central duties of faith, but that these were sustained in everyday behavior." Stark, "Epidemics, Network," 166.

525. Carter, *Matthew and Empire*, 47–51.

526. Carter, *Matthew and Empire*, 47–51. A full 97 percent of the empire's population were excluded from the ruling elite. Carter, "Gospel of Matthew," 50.

527. See Acts 2:42–47; 4:32–37; *Didache* 4:5. See also Milavec, *Didache*, 201–13. When the apostle Paul went to Jerusalem to receive the approval of the other apostles, they affirmed his teaching and asked him only one thing: ". . . remember the poor, which was actually what I was eager to do" (Gal 2:10). Paul regularly took up collections for the Jerusalem church (1 Cor 16:1–4; 2 Cor 8:1—9:15; Rom 15:14–32), possibly to alleviate food shortages due to famine. See Winter, "Acts and Food Shortages," 59–78.

528. See Matt 5:3–6; 25:35–40; 5:7–9; 19:21.

529. Pelikan, *Christian Tradition*, 247.

530. See Jesus' instructions to the disciples in Matt 28:19: "Therefore go and make disciples of all nations, baptizing them in the name of the Father and of the Son and of the Holy Spirit." Compare with *Didache* 7 (http://www.newadvent.org/fathers/0714.htm). See also Tertullian, *Against Praxeas* 2 (http://www.newadvent.org/fathers/0317.htm); and Justin Martyr's *First Apology* 13 (http://www.newadvent.org/fathers/0126.htm).

531. Williams, *Retrieving the Tradition*, 28.

532. Meeks, "Nazi New Testament Professor," 527.

533. Blumenthal, *Banality of Good and Evil*, 49.

534. Heschel, *Aryan Jesus*, 1–27.

535. "The Old Testament did sanction slavery . . . And in the Gospels and Epistles, the institution is, to say the least, tolerated." See Fuller, "Letter from Richard Fuller," 3–4.

536. In some cases, Christians on opposing sides of the slavery debate appealed to the same *verses* of Scripture to support their respective positions.

537. Tertullian, *On Prescription of Heretics*, 43; Par. 1942–43; Par. 19.

538. The closest thing to an ancient Biblicist would probably be Irenaeus: "The entire Scriptures, the prophets, and the Gospels, can be clearly, unambiguously, and harmoniously understood by all, although all do not believe them." Irenaeus, *Against Heresies*, I.xxvii.2, http://www.newadvent.org/fathers/0103227.htm. But Irenaeus is here addressing the need for unity and continuity in Christian teaching and warning against esoteric (e.g., Gnostic) interpretations of Scripture. He also concedes, "parables admit of many interpretations"– which is precisely why great care and diligence is required of the interpreter (I.xxvii.3).

539. Augustine, *Confessions*, V.xiv.24, VI.iii.6.

540. Wright, *Simply Christian*, xii.

541. Warren, *Purpose Driven Life*, 31.

542. Gen 1:31.

543. In *The Closing of the American Mind*, philosopher Allan Bloom spoke of Scripture as the essential cultural underpinning of Western civilization: "In the United States, practically speaking, the Bible was the only common culture . . . the very model for a vision of the order of the whole of things, as well as the key to the rest of Western art, the greatest works of which were in one way or another responsive to the Bible" (58). Malcolm Muggeridge put it much more strongly in his 1985 speech, "The True Crisis of Our Time": "It was thus that our Western Civilization came into existence; deriving not from Darwin's *Origin of Species*, not from the *Communist Manifesto*, or even the American *Declaration of Independence*, but from the great drama of the Incarnation, as conveyed in the New Testament." Muggeridge warned that abandoning the Bible would be tantamount to abandoning the whole foundation and essence of Western civilization and history, which would, in turn, prove disastrous for the present. Muggeridge, "True Crisis."

544. Before Darwin, evolutionary theorists and geologists had been making advancements in determining the age of the earth and its life forms for quite some time, though they usually appealed to commonsense explanations rather than random variation and "natural selection." Pre-Socratic philosophers like Anaximander and Empedocles conceived of crude versions of evolutionary theory ("Evolution and Paleontology"). In *Dialogues*

Concerning Natural Religion, David Hume addressed how biological mechanisms adjust to one another in a "curious adapting of means to ends" that seems to dominate natural systems. Popkin and Stroll, *Philosophy*, 181.

545. Marty, *Great Schism*, 89. See also Lee, "Inherit the Myth," 348. As scholar David Bebbington explains, "many evangelicals had no qualms about evolution," even in the early 1920s. Bebbington, *Evangelicalism in Modern Britain*, 207.

546. Numbers, *Creationists*, 3–4.

547. In 1893, a Presbyterian minister named Charles Briggs lost his ordination for suggesting that Adam and Eve weren't literal historical figures. Krapohl and Lippy, *Evangelicals*, 29. Later, in the 1910s, a group of concerned fundamentalists formed the World Christian Fundamentals Association in order to combat the influence of evolution. Dorrien, *Remaking of Evangelical Theology*, 16.

548. Hodge, *What Is Darwinism?*, 45, 176–77. Hodge argued that since Darwinism couldn't be "recognized and authenticated in the Scriptures," it had to be rejected outright. Hodge, *Systematic Theology*, vol. 1, ch. 1, sec. 6. See also Hutchinson and Wolffe, *History of Global Evangelicalism*, 136.

549. As understood by B. B. Warfield, the "plenary inspiration" of the Bible means that every page of Scripture is equally authoritative and "free from error," "infallible" in what it teaches on all manner of subjects. Warfield, "Inspiration of the Bible," 614–40.

550. See Prov 3:34; 1 Pet 5:5; Matt 5:5; 20:16; Jas 4: 6–10; Luke 14:11, etc.

551. See Isa 29:16; 64:8; Job 10:8–12; Gen 2:7; Rom 9:20–21.

552. Barth, *Deliverance to the Captives*, 62. See also Augustine, *Confessions*, III.vi.11.

553. "'Do I not fill heaven and earth?' says the Lord." Jer 23:23–24.

554. Ps 139:7–8.

555. Mann, "Thirteenth Cone," 185.

556. John 4:24.

557. Numbers, *Creationists*, 272. Numbers is arguably the preeminent authority on the modern history of science in the West and especially the contemporary creationist/evolutionist debate.

558. The 1920s was the peak of the Fundamentalist-Modernist Controversy. Marsden, *Fundamentalism and American Culture*, 3. See also Bebbington, *Evangelicalism in Modern Britain*, 14.

559. Bebbington, *Evangelicalism in Modern Britain*, 207.

560. Darwin, "To Asa Gray. 22 May [1860]." Darwin was more militantly committed to materialism than to explicit atheism. See Gould, *Ever Since Darwin*, 25–27.

561. Hayden, "Darwin the Liberator." In the mid-1800s, scientists like Josiah Clark Nott and George Robins Gliddon were using skull comparisons to argue that each "race" had originated separately, a view known as polygenism.

562. Dobbs, "Darwin Seduced Asa Gray."

563. Beecher, *Evolution and Religion*, 93. See also Church and George, *Continuity and Discontinuity*, 313.

564. In his commentary on Peter Lombard's *Sentences*, Aquinas wrote, "With respect to the beginning of the world something pertains to the substance of faith, namely that the world began to be by creation, and all the saints agree in this. But how and in what order this was done pertains to faith only incidentally insofar as it is treated in scripture, the truth of which the saints save in the different explanations they offer." Quoted in McIrney, *Thomas Aquinas*, 91.

565. Woodrow, "Evolution," 301. Woodrow took it as "self-evident" that "under changing conditions the varieties best fitted to the new conditions would be most likely to survive" (296).

566. Woodrow, "Evolution," 288.

567. In the *Summa Theologica*, Thomas Aquinas makes careful distinctions between various types of causes: formal, material, and efficient causes; active causes (Iq104a1ans);

second causes (Iq116a2repobj1); mediate and intermediary causes (Iq103a6obj2); proximate and remote causes (Iq84a4ad3), none of which contradict the metaphysical claim that God is the first, final, and ultimate cause of all finite causes and effects (Iq44a1ans). An "intermediary" or "mediate" cause is the proximate, "particular" cause of something else (Iq103a6obj2–a7ans).

568. Aquinas, *Summa*, Iq103a6ans.

569. In his book *A Universe from Nothing*, Lawrence Krauss argues that the universe was birthed from nothing and required no divine intervention—though I'm still not sure Krauss knows what most people mean by the terms "nothing" and "physical law." Fellow atheist Jim Holt takes Krauss to task on this point, arguing that Krauss unwittingly appeals to a religious way of thinking about natural, physical laws—i.e., as divine dictates. "The [physical] laws have some sort of ontological power or clout that they can form the abyss, that it's pregnant with being." But as Holt points out, physical laws are nothing more than "generalized descriptions of patterns and regularities in the world." In other words, the laws of nature are derived from observable patterns and phenomena in the world. They don't exist prior to, above, or *outside* the world. Holt, "Why Does the Universe Exist?"

570. For example, see Aquinas, *Summa*, Iq103a7, Iq116a2–4.

571. Livingstone and Noll, "B. B. Warfield," 283–304. See also Livingstone, "Science, Region, and Religion," 26–29; Numbers, *Creationists*, 44; Lee, "Inherit the Myth," 347–82.

572. Chief among them was James Orr, an early proponent of "theistic evolution." McGrath, *Dawkins' God*, 117–18. George Frederick Wright, a fellow contributor to *The Fundamentals*, grew increasingly suspicious of evolution over the course of his career. Yet even Wright agreed with modern scientific estimates on the age of the earth. Numbers, *Creationists*, 21–38. See also Livingstone, "Science, Region, and Religion," 26.

573. Says historian Bruce Shelley: "Fundamentalism is usually dated from a series of twelve small books published from 1910 to 1915 containing articles and essays designed to defend fundamental Christian truths." Shelley notes that three million copies of the books were sent to missionaries, pastors, and theology students—all free of charge—in countries all over the world. (Shelley, *Plain Language*, 433.)

574. Calvin argued, "faith has its own peculiar way of assigning the whole credit for Creation to God." Calvin, *Institutes*, I.xvi.1. See also Noll, *Princeton Theology*, 297.

575. By the early 1900s, Warfield came to embrace the idea that God had directed evolution towards the eventual emergence of human beings. Livingstone, "Science, Region, and Religion," 27–29. According to historian of science Ronald L. Numbers, this was Warfield's "controlled naturalistic explanation of natural history," a history that probably included some form of evolution but ultimately depended on God's first act of creation and subsequent governance in directing the overall progress of history. Warfield believed God could have used a variety of means in exercising sovereign control over the development of the world through "divine providence." He was, however, critical of Christian ministers like Charles Briggs who seemed more confident in Darwin's explanation of evolution than the Bible. Numbers, *Creationists*, 29.

576. See Lev Shestov's 1935 address, "Kierkegaard and Dostoevsky."

577. Pinker and Harris argue that moral altruism can be explained without God. According to Pinker, "The essence of morality is the interchangeability of perspectives: the fact that as soon as I appeal to you to treat me in a certain way (to help me when I am in need, or not to hurt me for no reason), I have to be willing to apply the same standards to how I treat you, if I want you to take me seriously." Cited in Magee, "Belief in God Obsolete?" Harris agrees with Pinker's basic position. It is worth noting that some equally distinguished atheists disagree, including Caltech cosmologist Sean Carroll, who argues that morality is not, and cannot be, a part of science, since science deals only with empirical, observable reality: "If you have a dispute that cannot in principle be decided by recourse to observable facts about the world, your dispute is not one of science. . ." Harris defines "the good" and the "moral" as that which maximizes the "well-being of conscious

creatures," but Carroll sees such efforts as unavoidably unscientific: how do you design experiments that would yield *empirical* data revealing what constitutes a truly ethical act? See Carroll, "Can't Derive Ought from Is." Moreover, how can science precisely define "well-being" for any and all individual cases, except by resorting to a crude utilitarian mathematics? How do you extract moral judgments from purely scientific descriptions of the natural world and the manifold phenomena occurring therein? See Tallis, "Evolution Explain Our Behaviour?"

578. Matt 26:39.

579. Darwin, *Descent of Man*, 683.

580. Nietzsche, *Gay Science*, 168, emphasis mine.

581. This is especially true for certain naturalists who, by embracing scientism, deny the possibility of any transcendent purpose, will, personality, intentionality, or *super*natural reality outside the domain of empirically verifiability and falsifiability. See Krauss, *Universe from Nothing*, xii–xiii; and Dawkins, *Blind Watchmaker*, 29.

582. Gould, *Ever Since Darwin*, 24. Krauss, Dawkins, and Michael Shermer are popular proponents of reductive physicalism/naturalism.

583. One of the main reasons Charles Hodge thought natural evolution and Scripture were irreconcilable was that Darwinism seemed to exclude the possibility of divine interference in the "course of nature" or "events of history." Hodge, *What Is Darwinism?*, 45. The random aspect of biodiversification was also a sticking point for *The Fundamentals* contributor James Orr, who saw Darwinism and creationism as being otherwise compatible. McGrath, *Dawkins' God*, 117–18.

584. The theologian and geologist George Frederick Wright was one of the original contributors to *The Fundamentals*. Like fellow fundamentalist B. B. Warfield, Wright was comfortable interpreting the creation story of Genesis 1 non-literally in his younger years. Giberson and Collins, *Language of Science and Faith*, 173. Over time, Wright grew increasingly leery of Darwinism (as did Warfield). He worried that new interpretations of Darwin's ideas would effectively remove God from the "whole creative process." See Wright, "Passing of Evolution," 60–72; and Livingstone, *Darwin's Forgotten Defenders*, 146–54.

585. Especially Jesus' parable of the sower (see Mark 4:3–20; Matt 13:1–23; Luke 8:1–15), where the kingdom comes regardless of where the seeds are scattered.

586. The doctrines of the resurrection of the dead and final judgment of humanity are present in the earliest Christian creeds, summary statements that reflect and reinforce ancient Christian theological consensus. See Jenson, *Canon and Creed*, 43; Williams, *Retrieving the Tradition*, 28.

587. See Matt 19:28.

588. Aquinas, *Summa*, Iq103a2contra.

589. In his landmark, and often heretical, masterwork, *Systematic Theology*, Paul Tillich elaborates: "God does not exist. He is being-itself beyond essence and existence. Therefore, to argue that God exists is to deny him." Tillich, *Systematic Theology*, vol. 1, 205. And later: "It is as atheistic to affirm the existence of God as it is to deny it. God is being-itself, not *a* being" (237).

590. Lash, "Creation, Courtesy," 169. Lash explains that in the modern, post-Enlightenment West, "people are expected to speak as plainly and straightforwardly of *God* as of any other *object* of investigation." Which is a problem, since God is not an "object." In keeping with the basic insights of Augustine, Boethius, and Aquinas, modern theologian Paul Tillich describes God as the "ground of being," or "Being-Itself." Tillich, *Systematic Theology*, vol. 2, 8. See also Aquinas, *Summa*, Iq3a4ans–a6ans.

591. Williams, *On Christian Theology*, 187, emphasis mine.

592. See Carlson, *Indiscretion*, 155–89. As for Augustine, who was no doubt informed by his prolonged struggle and eventual disillusionment with Manichaeism, he had become adept at using non-spatial categories when speaking of immateriality. With the benefit of hindsight, Augustine's *Confessions* serves as a carefully constructed chronicle of his

protracted effort to overcome and displace the Manichean conceptual habits that he had previously embraced. "When I wanted to think of my God," Augustine writes, "I knew of no way of doing so except as a physical mass. Nor did I think anything existed which is not materia.l" Augustine, *Confessions*, V.ix.19–20). See also V.x.20–21, where Augustine confesses, "I could believe of him only what my vain imagination could picture."

593. Aquinas clarifies, "God is not in a *genus* as if He were a *species*." Aquinas, *Summa*, Iq3a5ans.

594. Traditionally, Christian theologians have understood God as "spiritual," meaning not physical or spatial in any way (which is why you don't gain weight all of the sudden when you receive the Holy Spirit). Augustine prefaces *De Trinitate* by comparing it to the teachings of certain anonymous adversaries of "crass spirit" and "crude mind" who imagine God in strictly corporeal terms (I.i.1). For Augustine, neither God nor the human soul exists in material, spatial dimensions. Augustine, *Confessions*, I.vi.6; V.ix.19–20; see also V.x.20–21. Similarly, Rowan Williams observes that as the angels are seated on either side of the empty tomb, "the cherubim flanking the ark defines a space where God would be *if God were anywhere*." Williams, *On Christian Theology*, 187, emphasis mine. See also John 4:24.

595. Stephen Jay Gould admitted as much in *Rock of Ages*, 41. See also Sterelny's *Dawkins vs. Gould*, 159.

596. Huxley, "Agnosticism [1889]," 209–62. See also Huxley and Huxley, *Life and Letters*, 314.

597. This is, among other things, what the philosopher and former atheist Antony Flew argued so eloquently in his essay "Theology and Falsification" (48–49). Flew eventually recanted his position and became a theist.

598. Rev 1:18; 21:6; 22:13.

599. See Matt 25:31: "When the Son of Man comes in his glory . . ."

600. See Wilson's *Heaven Misplaced*, 20–21.

601. Rev 21:4, NIV, emphasis mine.

602. See Rohr and Feister, *Jesus' Plan for a New World*, 3.

603. Miller, *King's Biblical Epic*, 182.

604. Rom 8:18.

605. Farrer, *Saving Belief*, 45–52.

606. Though a (single) predestinarian, Thomas Aquinas might have believed in some instance of "chance" within the created order. In refuting Empedocles, Aquinas offered the following: ". . . those things that happen by chance, happen only rarely; we know from experience, however, that harmony and usefulness are found in nature either at all times or at least for the most part." Aquinas, *On Truth*, q5a2. Such a concession would have infuriated John Calvin: "If *anything* is left to fortune [chance], the world is aimlessly whirled about . . ." Calvin, *Institutes*, I.xvi.8.

607. Though Calvin affirms the postlapsarian capacity for "free decision," he means the freedom to choose from a menu consisting only of wicked wants and evil desires. Put another way, we are not externally compelled to choose evil, but do so freely. Calvin, *Institutes*, II.ii.7. Some contemporary Calvinists understand the providential unfolding of history as God exerting power over human beings in a competition of wills. For instance, R. C. Sproul, who concedes that humans, like God, are free. If, however, our human freedom runs up against God's, then it is God who prevails. In other words, God's divine plans for his creation allow humans to function freely, but within the confines of those plans: "If God has no right of coercion, then he has no right of governing his creation." Sproul, *Chosen by God*, 42–43. In contrast, Aquinas didn't think of divine providence and human freedom as being in constant competition. *Summa*, 1q103a8. When God "moves" a free-willed, voluntary human being, "He does not deprive their actions of being voluntary: but rather is He the cause of this very thing in them; for He operates in each thing according to its own nature" (Iq83a1repobj3). God's will is exactly what allows human willing and

action to arise. Of course, the term "free will" is especially loaded nowadays. For those readers who are aware of current philosophical and neuroscientific debates regarding human agency and consciousness, let me be clear: I am not a substance dualist. I think consciousness and autonomy are natural, material, biological, emergent phenomenon in human beings—though I think it's flatfooted to dismiss conscious, "free-willed" selfhood as merely an "illusion." See Harris, *Waking Up*, 9.

608. Building on Aquinas, Farrer develops and explores the idea of "double agency." See Hebblethwaite and Henderson, *Divine Action*, 46–50.

609. Mark 9:31. See also Mark 8:31–32; Matt 10:32–34; 16:21–28; 20:19; 26:2: Luke 9:22–27; 18:31–34; John 12:23.

610. Buechner, *Magnificent Defeat*, 93

611. Luke 5:8.

612. Compare and contrast Luke 17:21 and 19:11–12.

613. Wright, *How God Became King*, 162.

614. Rohr and Feister, *Jesus' Plan for a New World*, 3.

615. In *Meno*, Plato exemplifies the Hellenistic understanding of learning as a kind of recognizing and remembering. http://classics.mit.edu/Plato/meno.html. See also Augustine, *Confessions*, X.x.17.

616. Rousseau, *On the Origin of Inequality*, 12–23.

617. McCabe, ""Original Sin," 177.

618. Col 3:4. See also Phil 2:15.

619. See Matt 25 and the Nicene Creed.

620. Rohr, *Eager to Love*, 209–16.

621. Rev 21:1.

622. Neuropsychologist Paul Broks explains that our thoughts, memories, and emotions are dispersed throughout the brain and do not converge at a single point. There is therefore no "cockpit of the soul" or "soul-pilot." Indeed, "The *self* is a *story*." Broks, *Into the Silent Land*, 41, emphasis mine. See also Flanagan, *Problem of the Soul*, xi, 162. Sam Harris agrees with Flanagan's basic insight: "There is no discrete self or ego living like a Minotaur in the labyrinth of the brain"—though I think Harris' description of the self/ego as an "illusion" is, at best, a sloppy oversimplification. Harris, *Waking Up*, 9. On this point, Flanagan and Harris echo the analysis of Ludwig Wittgenstein, Gilbert Ryle, and Daniel Dennett. The "self" is, at bottom, a bunch of sense data and perceptions pinging around in your brain, a steady stream of consciousness, a seemingly coherent first-person experience of emotions and thoughts that together delude you into thinking you have a "self"—or, more traditionally, a "soul." Which means all the great philosophers who spoke of the "self" as something "spiritual," autonomous, and transcendent—people like Plato, Descartes, Immanuel Kant, and Ralph Waldo Emerson—were wrong. Harris, Baggini, Flanagan, Dennett, and Metzinger, all worth reading, make similar criticisms of classical philosophy on this point, e.g., Metzinger, *Ego Tunnel*, 20, 130; Baggini, *Philosophy*, 83. But you're also gonna want to check out Wittgenstein, Malcolm Jeeves, Mortimer Adler, James Ross, Brian Leftow, Colin McGin, Ned Block, David Chalmers, and especially Austin Farrer.

623. This was Origen's doctrine of the pre-existence of the soul, which was explicitly rejected and anathematized by the Second Council of Constantinople (a.k.a. the Fifth Ecumenical Council) in 553 CE, long after being critiqued by the likes of Gregory of Nyssa. See "Anathemas Against Origen."

624. Olendzk, *Unlimiting Mind*, 131.

625. The fluidity of the "self" is artfully expressed in Buddha's statement, "This is not mine. This is not my self. This is not what I am." Albahari, "Nirvana and Ownerless Consciousness," 103.

626. Carr, *Shallows*, 18–24.

627. See the Buddha's statement, "*Self*, that which seems to those who love their *self* as their being, is *not* the eternal, the everlasting, the imperishable." Carus, *Gospel of Buddha*,

16, emphasis mine.

628. Harris, *Free Will*, 22.

629. In the U.S., "food deserts" are usually low-income urban areas that are lacking in whole food grocery stores. Consequently, local residents rely on local gas stations and quickie marts that stock mainly processed, sugar- and fat-laden foods. The problem is exacerbated by the fact that many low-income families do not own a car and are therefore dependent upon public transportation. Gallagher, "USDA Defines Food Deserts." See also Walker, "Disparities and Access."

630. As philosopher René Girard explains, "We desire what others desire because we imitate their desires." Quoted in Palaver, *René Girard's Mimetic Theory*, 265.

631. For example, Irenaeus, Gregory of Nyssa, and Aquinas. Regarding Irenaeus' thoughts on human development and initial immaturity. Corey, *Evolution and the Problem*, 179; Hamilton, *Understanding Philosophy*, 281. In chapters 28 and 29 of *De Opificio Hominis*, Gregory explicitly rejects Origen's idea of a pre-existent soul that is merely injected into a bodily shell at birth. Instead Gregory argues that the soul is manifested and displayed concomitantly as it is formed through one's natural human development in the world, "appearing at first somewhat obscurely, but afterwards increasing in radiance concurrently with the perfecting of the work." Gregory of Nyssa, *Sacred Writings*, 392.

632. 2 Cor 3:18, NIV, ESV.

633. See Rom 8:30.

634. Eastern Orthodox Christians trace the origin of the doctrine of *theosis* (a.k.a. divinization or deification) to Athanasius of Alexandria, who argued that God became human (incarnate in Jesus) so that humanity could become like God.

635. Van Biema, "Christians Wrong about Heaven."

636. Kierkegaard, *Papers and Journals*, 295.

637. Campolo, *It's Friday but Sunday's Comin'*, 10.

638. See Clay's succinct treatment of divine, eternal knowledge in the thought of Augustine and Boethius in "Augustinian Compatibilism," 92. Compare with Tillich, *Systematic Theology*, vol. 1, 274.

639. See Eph 3:9; Col 3:3. Compare with the apostle Paul's statement, "Therefore we do not lose heart. Though outwardly we are wasting away, yet inwardly we are being renewed day by day. For our light and momentary troubles are achieving for us an eternal glory that far outweighs them all. So we fix our eyes not on what is seen, but on what is unseen, since what is seen is temporary, but what is unseen is eternal" (2 Cor 4:16–18). Regarding the eventual disclosure and discovery of the "self," C. S. Lewis wrote, "Your real, new self (which is Christ's and also yours, and yours just because it is His) will not come as long as you're looking for it. It'll come when you are looking for Him [Christ]." Lewis, *Mere Christianity*, 226. See also Van Biema's interview with N. T. Wright, "Christians Wrong about Heaven."

640. Rev 2:17: "I will also give that person a white stone with a new name written on it, known only to the one who receives it."

641. John 10:10. See Blue Letter Bible's entry on *perissos*.

642. Tozer, *Pursuit of God*, 58.

643. According to Irenaeus, God created the first humans in a state of immaturity. Burns, *Theological Anthropology*, 3. See Lars Svendsen's brief explication of Irenaean theodicy in *A Philosophy of Evil*, 51.

644. Pannenberg, *Systematic Theology*, 640.

645. Phil 1:6, emphasis mine.

646. Rom 12:2.

647. Bebbington, *Evangelicalism in Modern Britain*, 14. See also N. T. Wright, interview. See also Dorrien, *Remaking of Evangelical Theology*, 16.

648. Postman, *Technopoly*, 14–15.

649. Geertz, *Interpretation Of Cultures*, 87–90.

650. Marsden, *Fundamentalism and American Culture*, 3.

651. Dorrien, *Remaking of Evangelical Theology*, 16.

652. Noll and Livingstone, "Biblical Inerrantist as Evolutionist," 283–304. By the 1920s, Bryan had come to view Darwinian evolution as "the only thing that has seriously menaced religion since the birth of Christ." Marsden, *Fundamentalism and American Culture*, 4.

653. Bryan and Bryan, *Memoirs*, 552–53. See also Kazin, *Godly Hero*, 140.

654. Larson, *Summer for the Gods*, 39.

655. The phrase "survival of the fittest" was original to Herbert Spencer, though Darwin eventually picked it up. See Spencer, *Principles of Biology*, 40. See also Darwin's letters to fellow biologist Alfred Russel Wallace, e.g., Letter 5140 (2 July 1866).

656. Kellogg, *Headquarter's Nights*, para. 28. Eugenicist Karl Pearson mirrors closely the comments made by German officers as recorded in Kellogg's book. Pearson, a contemporary of Kellogg, spoke of history as the "fiery crucible" out of which a finer, purer metal is produced: "History shows me one way, and one way only, in which a high state of civilization has been produced, namely, the struggle of race with race, and the survival of the physically and mentally fitter race. If you want to know whether the lower races of man can evolve a higher type, I fear the only course is to leave them to fight it out among themselves . . . I want you to see selection as something which renders the inexorable law of heredity a source of progress which produces the good through suffering, an infinitely greater good which far outbalances the very obvious pain and evil." Pearson, *Standpoint of Science*, 1–3.

657. Larson, *Evolution*, 212–17.

658. Mencken, *Mencken on Religion*, 197.

659. Larson, *Evolution*, 212–17.

660. Farrow, *Clarence Darrow*, 392.

661. Scopes Trial (1925).

662. Bebbington, *Evangelicalism in Modern Britain*, 12–13.

663. Dorrien, *Remaking of Evangelical Theology*, 16.

664. Dorrien, *Remaking of Evangelical Theology*, 17.

665. Williams, *God's Own Party*, 1–2.

666. See Schaeffer, *Christian Manifesto*, 24–30, 45–46, 70. Schaeffer's admonitions resonated with concerned Christian leaders of the day, helping fuel the emergence of the New Christian Right. Balmer, *Making of Evangelicalism*, 59–72. See also Taylor, *After God*, 2; LaHaye and Noebel, *Mind Siege*, 35–40; Douthat, *Bad Religion*, 131.

667. Some scholars point to the 1970s and 80s as the historical moment when dominionist theology emerged as a force to be reckoned with in American political life. See Sam Harris's (harsh) treatment in his *L.A. Times* article, "God's Dupes." For a brief, helpful, and nuanced overview of dominionism, see Robert Gagnon and Edith Humphrey's article, "Stop Calling Ted Cruz a Dominionist."

668. Col 2:15, ESV, emphasis mine.

669. See Kerr, *Christ, History and Apocalyptic*, 9–10.

670. Isa 53:3, ESV.

671. Stanley, *Global Diffusion of Evangelicalism*, 38.

672. See also Article XII: "We deny that Biblical infallibility and inerrancy are limited to spiritual, religious, or redemptive themes, exclusive of assertions in the fields of history and science. We further deny that scientific hypotheses about earth history may properly be used to overturn the teaching of Scripture on creation and the flood." Chicago Statement on Biblical Inerrancy.

673. Mohler, *Views on Biblical Inerrancy*, 51. Similarly, R. C. Sproul maintains the inerrancy and infallibility of all Scripture assertions, even with regard to matters of science and natural history. See Sproul, *Can I Trust the Bible?*, 36–38.

674. MacArthur, *Battle for the Beginning*, 17–18.

675. "You Can't Mix the Bible."

676. Pew Research Center, "Public's Views on Human Evolution."

677. In the tradition of the late Carl Henry, MacArthur is a prime example of an evangelical who is "staunchly committed to ideas" and interested in provoking "lasting intellectual renewal." Worthen, *Apostles of Reason*, 16–17.

678. Scopes Trial (1925). Bryan also concedes that specific, historical dates recorded in Scripture may not be exact. Like other evangelicals of his day, Bryan interpreted the seven "days" of creation in Genesis 1 as signifying long periods of time rather than literal, twenty-four-hour days. Numbers, *Creationists*, 58.

679. Cited in Lamoureux, *I Love Jesus*, 167.

680. Wright calls the creationism-evolution debate a "very America-specific issue." Wright, "America's Culture Wars."

681. Dawkins, *Greatest Show on Earth*, 147.

682. In his 1996 address to the Pontifical Academy of Sciences, Pope John Paul II stated, "Some new findings lead us toward the recognition of evolution as more than an hypothesis. In fact it is remarkable that this theory has had progressively greater influence on the spirit of researchers, following a series of discoveries in different scholarly disciplines. The convergence in the results of these independent studies—which was neither planned nor sought—constitutes in itself a significant argument in favor of the theory." John Paul II, "Address."

683. See 1 Cor 15. Jesus resurrection is the thematic center and theological lynchpin of Paul's letter to the Romans.

684. MLK accepted a modified form of Darwinian evolution. King, "Love in Action," 43. See also Carson, *Papers of Martin Luther King*, 154; and Chesterton, *Orthodoxy*, 30.

685. Numbers, *Creationists*, 24, emphasis mine. Wright was quoting the Westminster Confession of Faith.

686. Aquinas, *Selected Writings*, 91, emphasis mine.

687. See Article VI of the Church of England's Thirty-Nine Articles of Religion: "Holy Scripture containeth all things *necessary to salvation*: so that whatsoever is not read therein, nor may be proved thereby, is not to be required of any man, that it should be believed as an article of the Faith, or be thought requisite or necessary to salvation." Chapter 1, Section VII of the Westminster Confession of Faith reads: "All things in Scripture are not alike plain in themselves, nor alike clear unto all; yet *those things which are necessary to be known, believed, and observed, for salvation, are so clearly propounded and opened in some place of Scripture or other*, that not only the learned, but the unlearned, in a due use of the ordinary means [i.e. listening to sermons, individual or group study, etc.], may attain unto a sufficient understanding of them." A century before Westminster, Calvin said pretty much the same thing: "Scripture is the school of the Holy Spirit, in which, as nothing is omitted that is both necessary and useful to know, so nothing is taught but what is expedient [important] to know. Calvin, *Institutes*, III.xxi.3. Article V of the 1784 Articles of Religion of the Methodist Church, based on the Anglican Thirty-Nine Articles, reiterates the same basic point. United Methodist Church, "Articles of Religion." See also Turretin, *Doctrine of Scripture*, 167–94.

688. Bass, "Spiritual Amnesia?" Bass explains, "Thus we inhabit a post-traditional world—a world of broken memory—in which some tell history badly, others do not know it at all, and still others use history to manipulate people to their own ends."

689. Tweedy, "Theologians."

690. Quoted in Wilken, *Spirit of Early Christian Thought*, 26.

691. Evans, *Power of God's Names*, 42.

692. Gervais, "Invisible Babysitter."

693. Neither did Christopher Hitchens (*God Is Not Great*, 8).

694. Stedman, "What Oprah Gets Wrong," emphasis mine.

695. See Kant's description of "rational faith": "It is this rational faith which must also

be taken as the ground of every other faith, and even of every revelation. The *concept* of God, and even the conviction of His *existence* can be met only in reason, and cannot first come to us, either through inspiration or through tidings communicated to us, however great the authority behind them." Kant, *Religion and Rational Theology*, 14, emphasis mine.

696. For instance, Col 1:15 and Heb 1:3. See Williams, *On Christian Theology*, 97–99. Regarding Jesus' "finality," Paul Tillich describes Christ as the "decisive, fulfilling, unsurpassable revelation, that which is the criterion of all the others." Tillich, *Systematic Theology*, vol. 1, 133. See also Calvin, *Institutes*, I.xiii.2.

697. MacCulloch, *First Three Thousand Years*, 1.

698. See King, "Letter from a Birmingham City Jail," on the distinction between "I-it" and "I-Thou" relationships. King borrowed these categories from the famous Jewish philosopher Martin Buber.

699. Misener, "Why I Miss."

700. See the "Four Spiritual Laws" of Campus Crusade for Christ, as well as the accompanying instructions: http://www.crustore.org/fourlawseng.htm.

701. Wesley, *Works*, 513. For similar reasons, Watchman Nee noted, "Doctrinal and theological knowledge does not have that much usefulness. What is the use of mere mental knowledge of the Bible if the outward man [i.e., Rohr's 'false self'] remains unbroken?" Nee, *Release of the Spirit*, 21. Likewise, Charles Spurgeon warned, "It is a great mistake to fancy that to endorse sound doctrine is the same thing as possessing saving faith . . . I am not saved because I believe the Scriptures, or because I believe the doctrines of grace, but I am saved if I believe Christ; or, in other words, trust in him." Spurgeon, "Poor Man's Friend."

702. Tozer, *Knowledge of the Holy*, 6.

703. Staniloae, *Orthodox Dogmatic Theology*, 95.

704. Gregory of Nyssa, "On Virginity," 355.

705. Thus sayeth the psalmist. See also Isa 17:10; 26:4; 30:29; 44:8; Deut 32; Dan 2.

706. See Isa 66:13. Cf. Hos 11:3–4; 13:8; Deut 32; Isa 42:14; 49:15; Matt 23:37; Luke 15:8–10.

707. See Deut 4:24; Heb 12:29; 1 Tim 6:16.

708. From *Sayings of the Desert Fathers*, quoted in Ware, *Orthodox Way*, 133.

709. Bonhoeffer, *Christmas Sermons*, 153. See also Nicholas Lash's statement, "All language breaks, and fails, and crumbles, as we stammer our praise and adoration of the mystery of God." Lash, "Creation, Courtesy," 170.

710. I like Dumitru Staniloae's definition: "Theology is reflection upon the content of faith inherited from that witness and initial living out of revelation which we possess in the Scripture and in apostolic tradition. Its purpose is to make that content effective as a factor of salvation for every generation of believers." Staniloae, *Orthodox Dogmatic Theology*, 84.

711. Gould, *Rock of Ages*, 40.

712. See Frederick Copleston's comment, "The application of reason to theological data, in the sense of the data of revelation, is and remains theology: it does not become philosophy." Copleston, *History of Philosophy*, 18. See also Carl Henry's comment, "Revelation is mystery dispelled and conveys information about God and his purposes." Henry, *Confessions of a Theologian*, 73.

713. Kelly, *Early Christian Doctrines*, 42, 46.

714. Stott, *Cross of Christ*, 8–9.

715. See a recent flurry of books by pastors, theologians, and scholars including Baxter Kruger, John Piper, Derek Flood, Paul Young, N. T. Wright, D. A. Carson, and J. Denny Weaver.

716. 1 John 4:19.

717. The Christian conviction that humanity's saving relationship with God begins with divine initiative is shot through Roman Catholicism (especially Augustine), the Reformed tradition (especially Luther, Calvin, and Barth), and Eastern Orthodoxy. See

Krista Tippet's interview on *On Being* with Jaroslav Pelikan: "Our love to God . . . is always a response to a love that started with Him and ends in Him." Pelikan, "Need for Creeds."

718. See Coakley, *Powers and Submissions*, 84. The term "kneeling theology" is also Coakley's.

719. Romans 12:2

720. "Our language is remolded as we are," wrote the late theologian Colin Gunton, and this is especially important in the domain of theology. McGrath, *Theology*, 102.

721. The saying is widely attributed to O'Connor. Wood, *Christ-Haunted South*, 160.

722. See Gal 4:19: "Now that you know God—or rather are *known by* God . . ." Emphasis mine.

723. Ware, "Discovering the Inner Kingdom," 14.

724. John 15:15.

725. John 15:13.

726. As Etienne Gilson made clear, "We know of no system of Greek philosophy which reserved the name of God for a unique being, and made the whole system of the universe revolve round this single idea . . ." That includes even Aristotle. Gilson, *Spirit of Mediaeval Philosophy*, 43.

727. The exact quote reads, "I like mathematics because it is not human and has nothing in particular to do with this planet or the whole accidental universe—because, like Spinoza's God, it will not love us in return." Monk, *Bertrand Russell*, 248.

728. While influential evangelicals like Gordon Clark and Carl Henry were perhaps too eager to eliminate mystery from theological language; they were orthodox in their conviction that the Bible conveys effable content, a.k.a. reliably authoritative theological "data." See Copleston, *History of Philosophy*, 5–6; see also Aquinas, *Summa*, Iq1a2repobj2. For more on Clark's star student, Carl Henry, see Doyle, *Carl Henry*, 111. See also White's *What Is Truth?*, 188–90; and Henry's tome, *God, Revelation, and Authority*, vol. 2, 480–81 and vol. 3, 429–30.

729. Tozer, *Pursuit of God*, 4, emphasis mine.

730. Singh, *Reality and Religion*, 18–19.

731. 1 Tim 6:16.

732. Pack, "Prove the Bible's Authority," emphasis mine. See also Peter Enn's interview of Greg Boyd, who explains, "The reason these problems destroy the faith of so many today—as it did my own faith for a while—is because evangelicals today don't structure their faith the way they earliest Christians did." Ancient Christians didn't believe in Jesus because the Old Testament proved that he was the Son of God. Rather, they were convinced by Jesus' teaching, his authority, his love, his miraculous healings, the radicality of his witness, and (especially) by his resurrection. Then, once they had come to faith in Jesus, they looked for him in the pages of Scripture, in the Torah and the Prophets. Boyd, interview.

733. Calvin, *Institutes*, I.vii.1, emphasis mine.

734. Calvin, *Institutes*, I.vii.4–5; I.vii.1; viii.13. Though Calvin was an adamant critic of allegorical interpretation, he resembles Erasmus here. See Erasmus, "Correspondence," 239. See also Susan Schreiner, *Are You Alone Wise?*, 215.

735. Calvin, *Institutes*, I.vii.1, 4–5; x.2. See also Battles's "Introduction," li. For Calvin, the Bible remains inert, lest the reader be "inspired" by God to grasp its true meaning (I.x.2).

736. Calvin, *Institutes*, I.x.2. See also Battles's "Introduction," li.

737. Calvin, *Institutes*, I.x.2. See also Battles's "Introduction," li.

738. See Jas 2:19.

739. According to Calvin, one of the main hallmarks of spiritual regeneration is a personal awareness of being "nourished" by God's "fatherly care" and "kindness." See Calvin, *Institutes*, I.ii.1 (p. 41); I.v.8 60; I.xvi.5 (p. 204). See also Tillich's explication of Luther's doctrine of sola fide, summarized as follows: "Faith is receiving and only receiving." Tillich,

Systematic Theology, vol. 3, 135.

740. Jer 12:1. See also Ps 73.

741. Darwin, *Descent of Man*, 682.

742. American pastor John MacArthur makes the case that secularism renders morality impossible: "Having already rejected the God revealed in Scripture and embraced instead pure naturalistic materialism, the modern mind has no grounds whatsoever for holding to any ethical standard, no reason whatsoever for esteeming 'virtue' over 'vice', and no justification whatsoever for regarding human life as more valuable than any other form of life." MacArthur, *Think Biblically!*, 60.

743. Coulson, *Science and Christian Belief*, 20. Galileo warned against exalting Scripture as the final and encompassing authority on scientific knowledge: "I should think it would be the part of prudence not to permit anyone to usurp scriptural texts and force them in some way to maintain any physical conclusion to be true, when at some future time the sense and demonstrative or necessary reasons may show the contrary." Swindal and Gensler, eds., *Sheed and Ward Anthology*, 244.

744. As Daniel Kahneman observes in *Thinking Fast and Slow*, "We are prone to exaggerate the consistency and coherence of what we see" (114). See also Shermer, *Science Friction*, 189. Shermer's book harkens to Susanne Langer, who described how humans are capable of adapting to nearly any situation or context, with the notable exception of chaos: "Because his [*sic*] characteristic function and highest asset is conception, his greatest fright is to meet what he cannot construe." Langer, *Philosophy in a New Key*, 287. On the universal human phenomenon of meaning making and "metaphysical concern," see Geertz, *Interpretation of Cultures*, 102.

745. Geertz, *Interpretation of Cultures*, 89–91. Similarly, former Archbishop of Canterbury Rowan Williams describes the Christian religion as belonging to "the whole complex of human sign-making." Williams, *On Christian Theology*, 205.

746. See Hitchens's 2007 debate with Alister McGrath at Georgetown University, "Poison or Cure?"

747. See Fyodor Dostoyevsky's compelling portrayal of the dichotomy between justice and forgiveness through the character of Ivan in *Brothers Karamazov*, especially the chapter "Rebellion" (pp. 236–45).

748. Dawkins and Coyne, "Father George Coyne Interview," emphasis mine.

749. Eagleton, *Reason, Faith, and Revolution*, 7, emphasis mine.

750. By faith, Abraham was willing to sacrifice his own beloved son, Isaac. This is precisely what Kierkegaard found so perplexing, and what drove him to interrogate the nature of faith. Unlike a typical hero who's willing to make sacrifices for the sake of a good cause, Abraham was willing to do what made no earthly sense: "The hero I can *think* myself *into*, but not Abraham; when I reach that height I fall down since what I'm offered is a paradox." Kierkegaard, *Fear and Trembling*, 63.

751. Eph 2:8–9.

752. Bonhoeffer, *Act and Being*, 130–32. See also Matt 16:13–19.

753. Said H. Richard Niebuhr, "There is no continuous movement from an objective inquiry into the life of Jesus to a knowledge of him as the Christ who is our Lord. Only a decision of the self, a leap of faith, a *metanoia* or revolution of the mind can lead from observation to participation." Niebuhr, *Meaning of Revelation*, 43.

754. In the twentieth century, Alvin Plantinga, William Alston, Peter Kreeft, Richard Swinburne, Simone Weil, and others have provided compelling philosophical arguments for God's existence. In the ancient and medieval worlds, Anselm's ontological argument, the Kalām cosmological argument, Tertullian's *Credo quia absurdum*, and Aquinas' five ways were some of the more prevalent and influential theistic arguments. Today, Plantinga is probably the most widely respected and compelling proponent of logical arguments for God's existence. See Plantinga's *Faith and Rationality*.

755. Barth, "To Professor von Harnack," 183. "To equate revelation to any book, creed,

institution, dogma, practices religious institution, philosophy, emotional or ecstatic experience is, for Barth, to "rob revelation of content." Barth, *Göttingen Dogmatics*, 87.

756. Luke 10:22. See Athanasius, *On the Incarnation*, 18. See also Weinandy, *Athanasius*, 47, 36.

757. John 1:14. See F. F. Bruce's description of the meaning of Jesus' life, ministry, death, and resurrection in Bruce, *Are They Reliable?*, 2.

758. Kierkegaard, *Kierkegaard's Writings*, vol. 12, 11–12, 102, 113.

759. When Diogenes was purchased as a slave in Corinth, his owner asked him how he would like to be buried. "On my face," Diogenes answered. Then, when further clarification was requested, Diogenese continued, "Because, in a little while, everything will be turned upside down." Seddon, *Outline of Cynic Philosophy*, 69.

760. Chesterton, *St. Francis of Assisi*, 57.

761. Rohr, *Falling Upward*, xviii.

762. Martel, *Life of Pi*, 54.

763. Kerényi, *Gods of the Greeks*, 156–58.

764. Luke 23:34, ESV.

765. Endo, *Life of Jesus*, 173.

766. Updike, *Beauty of the Lillies*, 57.

767. Manning, *Relentless Tenderness of Jesus*, 145.

768. Coakley, "Rest on a Mistake?," 253.

769. Douglass, *Life and Times*, 276.

770. *Alcoholics Anonymous: Big Book*, 18–19, emphasis mine.

771. See Charles Williams's essay "The Way of Exchange," 122–31.

772. Heb 4:15.

773. Most notably, Slavoj Žižek, and Alain Badiou, whose *Saint Paul: The Foundation of Universalism* resources Christianity as an open "universal singularity" capable of transcending the boundaries of generational, cultural, ethnic, and class divisions. Badiou is adamantly opposed to the "process of fragmentation into closed identities" so endemic to (post-)modern political correctness, as well as the "culturalist and relativist ideology that accompanies this fragmentation" (10).

774. For a fascinating look at open universality in contemporary European philosophy, see Franke's "Cosmopolitan Conviviality," 30–49.

775. Kierkegaard, *Works of Love*, 77–78, emphasis mine.

776. Gal 3:28.

777. Rev 21:22.

778. See Zizek's commentary on tolerance in Mentan, *Decolonizing Democracy*, 50.

779. Williams, "Way of Exchange," 123.

780. Wagner, "Trial against Dylann Roof."

781. See Noam Chomsky's summation in "Burkini Bans, New Atheism."

782. 1 Cor 1:23–24.

783. Isa 53:3.

784. 1 Cor 1:25. Both the passage from Isaiah and 1 Corinthians are ESV.

785. Bonhoeffer, *Letters and Papers*, 169–70.

786. Matt 5:44, emphasis mine.

787. Rom 5:10.

788. Rom 5:10, emphasis mine; 9:3, ESV.

789. Dickens, *Christmas Carol*, 4.

790. See Emo Phillips's hilarious bit on religious sectarianism, "Best God Joke Ever."

791. When evaluating contemporary evangelicalism's preoccupation with the nuclear family, two important points are worth considering. First, for most of church history, the primary social structure has always been the household, not the prototypical family unit of the 1950s; second, Christians of old revered celibacy and virginity far more than procreation and/or the nuclear family. Voluntary celibacy was so prevalent in the early church

that the Roman emperor Diocletian made deliberate efforts to persecute, and ultimately martyr, Christian virgins. See Roberts, *Christian Mission*, 119–21, 124. See also the numerous accounts of virgin martyrs listed in Baronius' *Martyrologium Romanum*.

792. Thackeray, *Vanity Fair*, 359.

793. Updike, *Rabbit Is Rich*, 285.

794. Calvin, *Institutes*, I.xvii.10.

795. Hobbes, *Leviathan*, 89.

796. Jacobs, *Original Sin*, xii.

797. Bodhi, *In the Buddha's Words*, 46.

798. Miller, *Bhagavad-Gita*, 41.

799. Bodhi, *In the Buddha's Words*, 36–39.

800. Bodhi, *In the Buddha's Words*, 35–40.

801. Qur'an 12:53. http://quranexplorer.com/index/Sura_012_Yusuf_JOSEPH.aspx.

802. Eccl 7:20, NRSV. Note: the NIV, NASB, and ESV translations are no less cynical.

803. See Gen 3:16–19; Eph 2:1–10.

804. Calvin, *Institutes*, I.xi.4.

805. See Eliason, "Introduction," 14. See also Miller, "Errand into the Wilderness," 27–42.

806. Winthrop, "Model of Christian Charity," 19.

807. Eliason, "Introduction," 14; Raboteau, "African Americans, Exodus," 82–83. R. Marie Griffith explains how most Puritans saw America as a "divinely appointed refuge" for authentic Christians and an escape from the hollow idolatry of European society. Griffith, *American Religions*, 16.

808. Raboteau, "African Americans, Exodus," 83–84.

809. Bryson, "World Is a 'Mess.'"

810. Patton, "From Oprah to Chopra." See also Capretto, "Optimistic and Being Irrational."

811. There's a sizable amount of scholarship on the deleterious psychological effects of irrational and/or socially compelled optimism. According to Bohart and Greening, positive psychology often has a "dominant, separatist message" that can yield undesirable and unintended consequences. Bohart and Greening, "Humanistic Psychology," 81–82. In like manner, Barbara Held laments the "tyranny of the positive attitude," a problem that, she claims, dominates the contemporary American mindset. Held, "Tyranny of the Positive Attitude," 969, 986–87. See also Guignon, "Hermeneutics, Authenticity," 83–113; Snyder, "Future of Positive Psychology," 751–67; Larsen, "Turning Adversity to Advantage," 211–25; Chang, "Optimism and Pessimism," 127–45; Peterson, "Catastrophizing and Untimely Death," 127–30.

812. Chesterton, *Orthodoxy*, 8–9.

813. Mundell, "Brimming with Self-Esteem." According to researchers like San Diego State University psychologist Jean Twenge, prolonged efforts to boost self-esteem in children "may have created unrealistic expectations in today's youth, and their inflated self-esteem may lead to a sense of entitlement: 'I'm great, so I deserve great things.'" Radford, "Teen Self-Esteem."

814. Wiesel, *Night*, 8.

815. "Historical Estimates of World Population." Some estimate as many as sixty million people died as a direct result of WWII. National WWII Museum, "Research Starters: Deaths in World War II."

816. UNICEF, "12,000 Fewer Children Perish." According to Gary Haughen, poverty alleviation efforts over the last thrity-five years have successfully reduced the most extreme forms of poverty, i.e., those who live off of $1.25 a day or less. Haughen, *Locust Effect*, xiii. Whereas 50 percent of the planet lived in extreme poverty in 1980, that number has fallen to 15 percent. Similarly, while forty thousand kids died each day due to poverty in 1980, that number is now down to seventeen thousand. See Haughen, "Hidden Reason

for Poverty.""

817. Salomon, "Healthy Life Expectancy."

818. Bonhoeffer, *Letters and Papers*, 258.

819. Taubes, *Political Theology of Paul*, 75–76, emphasis mine.

820. John 1:10, KJV.

821. Merton, *Raids on the Unspeakable*, 72.

822. Psalm 34:18, NIV.

823. Bonhoeffer, *Christmas Sermons*, 22.

824. John 14:23, ESV.

825. Brennan and Charnetski, "Explanatory Style and Immunoglobulin," 251–55. See Raeikkoenen et al., "Effects of Optimism, Pessimism," 104–13. See also Taylor, "Psychological Resources, Positive Illusions," 99–109.

826. Ps 23:4, ESV, emphasis mine.

827. Barth, *Romans*, 40.

828. Giuliani, *A Centaur in Auschwitz*, 51.

829. Sontag, *As Consciousness Is Harnessed*, 408.

830. Lax, *Conversations with Woody Allen*, 362.

831. Butler et al., *Power of Religion*, 94.

832. Krauss, *Universe from Nothing*, 17. The broader point of Krauss's book is to overturn traditional theistic cosmological arguments for God's existence (e.g., the Kalām argument, Aquinas' "Five Ways," etc.). You can be the judge as to whether or not Krauss succeeds.

833. Dechesne et al., "Adjusting to Death," 727–37.

834. Sirach 40:2–5.

835. Solomon et al., *Worm at the Core*, especially the chapters entitled "Managing the Terror of Death" and "Literal Immortality."

836. Freud, *Totem and Taboo*, 76. Interestingly, the immortality of the soul was an ancient Greek concept, not a traditional tenet of Judaism or early Christianity. In substantial agreement with Gregory of Nyssa and the modern critical insights of Paul Tillich, Aquinas rejected depictions of the soul as an autonomous or pre-existent phantom, though he did argue for the soul's natural immortality. Likewise, Tillich dismissed Origenistic conceptions of a pre-existent soul. While Tillich rejected the immortality of the human soul in both its popular "superstitious" and "genuine Platonic" forms (*Systematic Theology*, vol. 1, 275), he correctly identified the immortality of the soul as a later Hellenistic addition to the Judeo-Christian thought-world.

837. Heb 2:15.

838. In 1 Cor 15:55–57, Paul proclaims Jesus' success in removing the "sting" of death.

839. Matt 20:18–19.

840. Heb 2:14–15.

841. Athanasius, *On the Incarnation*, 57.

842. Job 7:16.

843. Augustine, *Confessions*, V.xiv.23

844. Freud, *Moses and Monotheism*, 66. Paul Tillich made a similar point: "To elevate the dissected moments of time to infinite significance by demanding their endless reduplication is idolatry" and "identical with condemnation." Tillich, *Systematic Theology*, vol. 1, 275.

845. Ralkowski, *Louis C.K. and Philosophy*, 200.

846. Haidt, *Happiness Hypothesis*, 73–76.

847. McCabe, "Original Sin," 174–76.

848. Levi, *Reawakening*, 228.

849. King, "Stride Towards Freedom," 429.

850. King, "Letter from a Birmingham City Jail," 290.

851. Chesterton, *St. Francis of Assisi*, 12.

852. Niebuhr, *Man's Nature and His Communities*, 24.

853. Freud, *Totem and Taboo*, 72.

854. Augustine, *Confessions*, II.iv.9.

855. Augustine, *Confessions*, II.15–18.

856. Augustine, *Confessions*, II.iii.7.

857. Hitchens, *God Is Not Great*, 64.

858. Ps 51.

859. See Matt 25:31–46.

860. The passage continues, "For whoever does not love their brother and sister, whom they have seen, cannot love God, whom they have not seen (1 John 2:15)." See also Jesus' summary of the Law and Prophets in Matt 22:37–39: "'Love the Lord your God with all your heart and with all your soul and with all your mind.' This is the first and greatest commandment. And the second is like it: 'Love your neighbor as yourself.'"

861. Lewis, *Weight of Glory*, 46.

862. Gen 1:27, NRSV.

863. Ferreira, *Love's Grateful Striving*, 124–27.

864. Augustine, *On Nature and Grace*, 3.3, http://www.newadvent.org/fathers/1503.htm.

865. Augustine, *On Grace and Free Will*, 23.45. See also Pagels, *Adam, Eve*, 106–33.

866. Augustine's account of inherited guilt is universally rejected by the Eastern Orthodox Church as well as many modern-day Arminians.

867. Percy, *Lost in the Cosmos*, 152.

868. Blue Letter Bible, *chata'*.

869. Like fellow New Atheist Daniel Dennett, Sam Harris describes "free will" as an illusion. Harris, *Waking Up*, 9; see also Flanagan, *Problem of the Soul*, xi, 162. While conceding that aspects of subjective human experience defy current naturalistic explanation, even scientifically schooled defenders of property or phenomenological dualism like John Polkinghorne and Nancey Murphy affirm physicalist accounts of anthropology. According to Polkinghorne's "dual aspect monism," mind, soul, and body are different facets of the same fundamental reality. Polkinghorne, *Science and Christian Belief*, 21. Murphy describes the soul as a "functional capacity of a complex physical organism, rather than a separate spiritual essence that somehow inhabits a body." Murphy, "Human Nature," xiii.

870. See Pascal's *Pensées*, http://www.stat.ucla.edu/history/pascal_wager.pdf.

871. Gilbert, *Churchill: A Life*, 185.

872. Maisel, "God-Bug Syndrome."

873. The late literary critic René Girard made this point in his famous *Things Hidden* (141–23) and *Job: The Victim* (154–68).

874. See 1 Cor 6:20; 7:13; Heb 2:14–15; 1 John 3:8; 1 Pet 3:22.

875. Mark 10:45.

876. See Stephen Hawking's concise chapter on determinism, chaos, and predictability in *Brief Answers*, 87–99. See also Gleick's *Chaos*, 9–32, 241–72.

877. Augustine, *Confessions*, VII.iii.5, emphasis mine.

878. Sebastian Junger observes, "Humans don't mind hardship, in fact they thrive on it; what they mind is not feeling necessary." Junger, *Tribe*, xvii.

879. Aquinas, *Summa Theologiae: Gospel of Grace*, 2.

880. In particular, I'm referencing the writings of Black Elk, e.g., his famous statement, "Peace . . . comes within the souls of men when they realize their relationship, their oneness, with the universe and all its powers, and when they realize that at the center of the Universe dwells Wakan-Tanka, and that this center is really everywhere, it is within each of us." Black Elk, *Sacred Pipe*, 115.

881. See Lewis, *Abolition of Man*, 17–18; Rappaport, *Ritual and Religion*, 361–93. The *Tao Te Ching* defines the Tao as follows: "There is a thing inherent and natural, Which existed before heaven and earth. Motionless and fathomless, It stands alone and never

changes; It pervades everywhere and never becomes exhausted. It may be regarded as the Mother of the Universe. I do not know its name. If I am forced to give it a name, I call it Tao, and I name it as supreme." Quoted in Krejčí, *Before the European Challenge*, 228. See also Damascene, *Christ the Eternal Tao*, 1–35.

882. As Charles Williams argued, the great world religions are nearly unanimous in urging us to live up to our duty towards our neighbor. Williams, "Way of Exchange," 123–24.

883. Pascal, *Pensées*, 34. See also Kenny, *Rise of Modern Philosophy*, 56.

884. See Barth, *Romans*, 51.

885. Blumenthal, *Banality of Good and Evil*, 49.

886. Blumenthal, *Banality of Good and Evil*, 49.

887. Quoted in Langley, "Exploring Super-Villainy."

888. Klosterman, *Black Hat*, 1.

889. Following Socrates, most early Hellenistic theologians like Clement of Alexandria (150–215 CE), Origen (3rd century), and Athanasius assumed sin was a result of ignorance rather than intention. Ferguson, *Clement of Alexandria*, 152. In the *Summa*, Aquinas classifies sin as an "inordinate" act, as when a person freely chooses a lower over a higher good (I/IIq78a1ans). Following Pseudo-Dionysius, Aquinas insists that human beings only act in the interest of good: "for no one acts intending evil" (Iq103a8ans; I/IIq78a1repobj2). Just as all created things are naturally directed toward their own fulfillment, so too are rational creatures designed by God to desire and pursue the good of their own happiness (Iq2a1; Iq48a1ans; Iq103a8ans). See also Johnson, *Immoralists*, 193–95. See Plato, *Gorgias* 468b1–4; *Apology*, 28–32; *Meno*.

890. Merritt, "David Brooks on Character."

891. Isa 14:13–14, NIV.

892. See Augustine's commentary in *Confessions*, X.xxxvi.59.

893. Tolkien, *Fellowship of the Ring*, 410.

894. *Alcoholics Anonymous: The Big Book*, 60, emphasis mine.

895. 1 Pet 5:5 (ESV), Luke 1:51; cf. Prov 3:34; Jas 4:6.

896. Flint, *Cecil Rhodes*, 248–49.

897. Cited in Bruinius, *Better for All*, 190.

898. Lombardo, *Three Generations, No Imbeciles*, 26.

899. Griffin, ed., *Letters of Bertrand Russell*, 123. Infamously, Darrow wrote, "Chloroform unfit children. Show them the same mercy that is shown beasts that are no longer fit to live." Gorsuch, *Future of Assisted Suicide*, 35.

900. See Blumenthal's *Banality of Good and Evil*, 49, 339–41. Blumenthal references the famous (and controversial) Milgram Experiment to support his argument that evil is essential "banal." In the decades since WWII, various versions of the experiment have shown that most volunteer test subjects will administer lethal electric shocks to strangers when instructed to do so by a perceived authority figure in a laboratory setting. Renowned social psychologist and creator of the Stanford Prison Experiment, Philip Zimbardo, calls this general tendency the "Lucifer effect." See Zimbardo, *Lucifer Effect*, 229–57. See also McLeod, "Milgram Experiment."

901. Solzhenitsyn, *Gulag Archipelago Abridged*, 75.

902. Dostoyevsky, *Brothers Karamazov*, 164.

903. Martin, "Brother Christian's Testament."

904. 1 Tim 1:15.

905. Breton, *Nadja*, 160.

906. Dark, *Everyday Apocalypse*, 52–53.

907. Frost, "Once by the Pacific," cited in Gelpi, *Coherent Splendor*, 13.

908. My paraphrase. See Diogenes, *Lives of the Eminent Philosophers*, VI.32, 38, 41, 42, 76.

909. Selgin, *Confessions of a Left-Handed Man*, 180.

910. Mark 10:2.

911. Crossan, *Historical Jesus*, 72–88. See also Witherington, *Jesus Quest*, 58.

912. Matt 10:34.

913. 1 John 2:15.

914. Nietzsche, *Birth of Tragedy*, 23.

915. Luke 14:26.

916. Gen 6:6, ESV.

917. Goethe, *Faust*, 161.

918. Tolstoy, *Confession*, 35.

919. Wood, *Bertrand Russell*, 208.

920. Isa 24:1.

921. Marsden, *Understanding Fundamentalism*, 39–40, 158; Grenz, *Millennial Maze*, 14.

922. For a helpful overview of premillennial theology and the rapture, see Weber, "Dispensational Premillennialism." See also Magnum and Sweetnam's *Scofield Bible*, 71–89, 188–95. To be fair, Irenaeus, Cyprian, and Justin Martyr *might* have believed in some elements of premillennialism (for example, see Irenaeus' *Against Heresies*, V.29).

923. Grenz, *Millennial Maze*, 59–63.

924. The late theologian Amos Niven Wilder put it thus: "The one great and telling accusation made against the Christian religion in our modern period is that it is 'escapist' . . . that the Christian conviction of things not seen and the Resurrection hope means escapism, pie-in-the-sky, the opium of the people." Crossan, *Fragile Craft*, 38.

925. Blumhardt and his father, Johann, had an impact on the thought of influential theologians like Karl Barth, Dietrich Bonhoeffer, Jürgen Moltmann, and Jacques Ellul. Blumhardt and Blumhardt, *Thy Kingdom Come*, 29.

926. King, "Letter from a Birmingham Jail," 299.

927. Anderson, *Vision of the Disinherited*, 80.

928. Luke 12:49.

929. See "Suicide Statistics."

930. For more on the "disease of modernity" and "age of anxiety," see Hidaka, "Depression as a Disease," 205–14.

931. Bonhoeffer, *Letters and Papers*, 169–70, from a letter written to Eberhard Bethge on December 18, 1943.

932. Cone, "Lynching Tree."

933. Jer 1:11. See Morse, *Not Every Spirit*, 8.

934. Rilke, *Book of Hours*, 91.

935. Note: "worthy" and "deserving" are not the same thing. See Eph 2:8–9.

936. Col 1:19–20.

937. Following in Barth's footsteps, Hans Von Balthasar stated, "There is only the one world as it is"—a world created and loved by God, yet radically distinct from God's eternal being. Wigley, *Barth and Hans Urs Von Balthasar*, 38.

938. John 15:9.

939. Barth, "Ethics Today," 86.

940. John 3:16.

941. 2 Cor 5:19.

942. John 1:29.

943. 1 Tim 2:4, NRSV.

944. Barth, "Christian in Society, 1919," 46.

945. Matt 19:28; Eph 1:10. See also Dietrich Bonhoeffer's brief reflections on the recapitulation of all things. Bonhoeffer, *Letters and Papers*, 169–70.

946. Rev 21:22.

947. John 4:25.

948. Larson and Lowery, *1001 Quotations that Connect*, 194.

949. Isaac the Syrian, *Daily Readings*, 29.

950. Matt 16:25.

951. Wright, *Letters of John*, 20.

952. Augustine, *Confessions*, V.xiv.23.

953. The quote is attributed to Johanne Blumhardt (*Thy Kingdom Come*, 5).

954. Julian of Norwich, *Revelations of Divine Love*, 22.

955. Mahathera, *Buddha and His Teachings*, 397–98.

956. Rom 5:7.

957. Phil 1:23. Compare with 2 Cor 5:8: "We are of good courage, and we would rather be away from the body and at home with the Lord."

958. John 11:35.

959. Fronsdal, *Dhammapada*, 57.

960. Isa 53:3, ESV.

961. Luke 22:44.

962. Matt 26:39, ESV.

963. Augustine, *Expositions on the Psalms*, 37.6; 58.2, 6; 85.1; 93.18–19. See also Rom 5–6; Eph 1:22, 5:30; Col 1:18.

964. See especially Augustine's exposition of Ps 93. Boulding, *Expositions of the Psalms*, 394–97.

965. Rom 12:5; Col 1:18.

966. Calvin, *Institutes*, III.x.11.

967. Selderhuis and Huijgen, *Calvinus Pastor Ecclesiae*, 388. See also Ryken, "Union with Christ."

968. Damascene, *Christ the Eternal Tao*, 294.

969. In a sermon on the book of Acts, Calvin preached, "Truly we are united to Him, that He dwells in us in such a way that everything that belongs to Him is ours." Quoted in Wallace, *Calvin's Doctrine*, 15. See also Billings, *Calvin, Participation*, 17–22 Following in the general and established pattern of Reformed theology, Thomas Torrance wrote, "The Incarnation means that God Himself condescended to enter into our alienated human existence, to lay hold of it, to bind it in union with Himself; and the consummation of the Incarnation in the death and resurrection means that the Son of God died for all men, and so once and for all constituted men as men upon whom God had poured out His life and love, so that men are forever [*sic*] laid hold of by God and affirmed in their being as His creatures." Torrance, "Introduction," cxiii–cxiv. According to the fifth-century bishop Cyril of Alexandria, "He [Jesus] wears our own nature, refashioning it to his own life. And he himself is also in us, for we have all become partakers of Him, and have Him in ourselves through the Spirit. For this reason we have become partakers of the divine nature . . ." Cited in Keating, *Appropriation of Divine Life*, 8. Likewise, John of Damascus wrote of how Jesus' redemptive work restores and renews the image of God in those who believe: "For since He bestowed on us His own image and His own spirit and we did not keep them safe, He took Himself a share in our poor and weak nature, in order that He might cleanse us and make us incorruptible, and establish us once more as partakers of His divinity . . . let us apply our eyes and lips and brows and partake of the divine coal, in order that the fire of the longing, that is in us, with the additional heat derived from the coal may utterly consume our sins and illumine our hearts, and that we may be inflamed and deified by the participation in the divine fire . . . Participation is spoken of; for through it we partake of the divinity of Jesus. Communion, too, is spoken of, and it is an actual communion, because through it we have communion with Christ and share in His flesh and His divinity: yea, we have communion and are united with one another through it. For since we partake of one bread, we all become one body of Christ and one blood, and members one of another, being of one body with Christ." John of Damascus, *Exposition*, IV.13. In a similar vein, the late Orthodox theologian John Meyendorff summarized Maximus the Confessor's understanding of deification as "total participation in Christ Jesus." Fisk, *St. Gregory Palamas*,

39. Dimitru Staniloae, a twentieth-century contemporary of Meyendorff's, wrote, "The goal of Orthodox spirituality is the perfection of the believer by his union with Christ . . ." Staniloae, *Orthodox Spirituality*.

970. Augustine, *Tractate 21* (John 5:20–23). Aquinas followed suit: "The head and members are as one mystic person." Aquinas, *Summa*, IIIq48a2repobj1.

971. See Eph 2:8–9.

972. Augustine, *Confessions*, VIII.xi.27.

973. Matt 26:39, ESV.

974. Heb 2:17, emphasis mine.

975. Heb 4:15, emphasis mine.

976. Mark 4:31; 9:14–29, ESV.

977. Heb 4:16.

978. Heb 4:15.

979. See John 13:14; Matt 5: 38–42. Jesus' followers "shared everything they owned," until there were "no needy ones among them." Acts 4:32–36, 44–47.

980. Gal 6:2.

981. 1 Pet 2:24.

982. "He took our place and bore our sin." Stott, *Cross of Christ*, 6.

983. Heb 4:15.

984. 2 Cor 5:21, ESV. See also Stott, *Cross of Christ*, 9, 63.

985. See Olson, "'Judge Judged in Our Place.'"

986. Davies, "Limits of Language," 392, emphasis mine. Ironically, the doctrine of divine simplicity, as understood by Aquinas, is actually pretty complicated . . . and far beyond the scope of this book.

987. John 1:29; 14:6; 1 John 4:8.

988. 1 Tim 2:4. See also McDowell, *More Than a Carpenter*, 109–12.

989. See the soteriological language of exchange in 2 Cor 5:21: "God made him who knew no sin to be sin on our behalf so that we might become the righteousness of God in Him." See also Rom 3; 4:25; 5:6; Gal 3:10–13; and especially 1 Pet 3:18: "For Christ died for sins once for all, the righteous for the unrighteous, to bring you to God. He was put to death in the body but made alive by the Spirit."

990. Eph 6:12.

991. Williams, "Way of Exchange," 124, emphasis mine.

992. West, "Spiritual Blackout."

993. I borrowed most of the ideas presented in this section from Charles Williams's fabulous essay "The Way of Exchange" . . . though I should also point at that Williams borrowed many of his ideas from Antony of Egypt, Athanasius of Alexandria, Seraphim of Sarov, Paul, and others . . . which only goes to reinforce Williams's broader point about "living *from*" others.

994. See Matt 25:34; John 1:12, 17:22; Rom 8:14–17, 29; 2 Cor 8:9; Gal 3:29, 4:4–8; Eph 1:14; Col 1:2; 3:24; Heb 2:11; Jas 2:5; 1 Pet 1:4; 2 Pet 1:4.

995. John 15:9.

996. See the Nicene Creed, as well as Jesus' statement in John 10:30: "I and the Father are one."

997. Gal 2:20.

998. Or alternatively, "in him." Stott, "'In Christ.'" See also Canlis, "Best Description of Salvation."

999. Luke 9:23.

1000. Eph 4:22–24; Col 3:3–5; Rom 6:6. See Rohr, "What Is the False Self?"; and Manning, *Abba's Child*, 9.

1001. Rom 6:4, NRSV. See also Col 2:12.

1002. See Rom 12:1–2.

1003. Matt 11:30.

1004. John 19:30.

JUSTIN GUIDO ROSOLINO

IDIOT SOJOURNING SOUL

Bibliography

Aikin, Scott F. "So What if Horses Would Draw Horse Gods?" *Sophia*, 2015. http://www.academia.edu/797251/So_what_if_horses_would_draw_horse_gods.

Albahari, Miri. "Nirvana and Ownerless Consciousness." In *Self, No Self?: Perspectives from Analytical, Phenomenological, and Indian Traditions*, edited by Mark Siderits et al. Reprint ed. Oxford: Oxford University Press, 2011.

Alcoholics Anonymous: The Big Book. 4th ed. New York City: Alcoholics Anonymous World Services, 2001.

Allen, Ronald. "Between Text & Sermon: Philippians 2:1–11." *Interpretation* 61/1 (2007) 72–74.

"The Anathemas Against Origen." Fifth Ecumenical Council. In *Nicene and Post-Nicene Fathers*, 2nd ser., vol. 7, *The Seven Ecumenical Councils*, edited by Philip Schaff. http://www.ccel.org/ccel/schaff/npnf214.xii.ix.html.

Anderson, Robert Mapes. *Vision of the Disinherited: The Making of American Pentecostalism*. New York: Oxford University Press, 1979.

Ansbro, John J. *Martin Luther King, Jr: Nonviolent Strategies and Tactics for Social Change*. New York: Madison, 2000.

Aquinas, Thomas. *On Truth (De Veritate)*. Translated by Robert W. Mulligan. Chicago: Regnery, 1952. http://dhspriory.org/thomas/QDdeVer5.htm.

———. *The Summa Theologiæ of St. Thomas Aquinas*. Translated by the fathers of the English Dominican Province. 2nd ed. London: Burns, Oates and Washbourne, 1920. http://www.newadvent.org/summa/index.html.

———. *Summa Theologiae: Vol. 30, The Gospel of Grace: 1a2ae. 106–114*. Edited by Cornelius Ernst. New York: Cambridge University Press, 1972.

Armour, Ellen T. "Toward an Elemental Theology." In *Theology That Matters: Ecology, Economy, and God*, edited by Kathleen Darby Ray, 42–57. Minneapolis: Fortress, 2006.

Armstrong, Karen. *The Case for God*. New York: Anchor, 2009.

———. "Let's Revive the Golden Rule." TED talk, July 2009. https://www.ted.com/talks/karen_armstrong_let_s_revive_the_golden_rule.

Asad, Talal. *Formations of the Secular: Christianity, Islam, Modernity*. Stanford, CA: Stanford University Press, 2003.

Askew, Thomas A., and Richard V. Pierard. *The American Church Experience: A Concise History*. Eugene, OR: Wipf & Stock, 2008.

Aslan, Reza. *Zealot: The Life and Times of Jesus of Nazareth*, New York: Random House, 2013.

Ateek, Naim. "A Palestinian Perspective: The Bible and Liberation." In *Biblical Studies Alternatively*, edited by Susanne Scholz, 394–99. Upper Saddle River, NJ: Prentice Hall, 2003.

Athanasian Creed. https://reformed.org/documents/index.html?mainframe=https://reformed.org/documents/athanasian.html.

Athanasius. *Against the Heathen*. Translated by Archibald Robertson. In *Nicene and Post-Nicene Fathers*, 2nd ser., vol. 4, edited by Philip Schaff and Henry Wace. Buffalo, NY: Christian Literature, 1892. http://www.newadvent.org/fathers/2801.htm.

———. *On the Incarnation*. Crestwood, NY: St. Vladimir's Seminary Press, 1993.

———. *To Serapion on the Holy Spirit*. CreateSpace, 2014.

Auden, W. H. *Prose*. Vol. 2: *1939–1948*. Edited by Edward Mendelson. London: Faber and Faber, 2002.

Augsburg Confession. http://www.ccel.org/ccel/schaff/creeds3.iii.ii.html.

Augustine. *City of God*. http://www.newadvent.org/fathers/120115.htm.

———. *Confessions*. Translated by Henry Chadwick. New York: Oxford University Press, 1998.

———. *Contra Faustum*. http://www.newadvent.org/fathers/140612.htm.

———. "Exposition of Psalm 93." In *Expositions of the Psalms: 73–98*, translated by Maria Boulding, 394–97. The Works of Saint Augustine: A Translation for the 21st Century III/18. New York: New City, 2002.

———. *Expositions on the Psalms*. Translated by J. E. Tweed. In *Nicene and Post-Nicene Fathers*, 1st ser., vol. 8, edited by Philip Schaff. Buffalo, NY: Christian Literature, 1888. http://www.newadvent.org/fathers/1801.htm.

———. *On Grace and Free Will*. http://www.newadvent.org/fathers/1510.htm.

———. *On Nature and Grace*. http://www.newadvent.org/fathers/1503.htm.

———. *St. Augustine*. Vol. 1: *The Literal Meaning of Genesis*. Translated by John Hammond Taylor. Ancient Christian Writers. New York: Paulist, 1982.

———. *Sermon 272*. Translated by J. P. Migne. Quoted in *Eucharistic Theology*, by Joseph M. Powers, 20. New York: Seabury, 1967.

———. *Tractate 21* (John 5:20–23). http://www.newadvent.org/fathers/1701021.htm.

Badiou, Alain. *Saint Paul: The Foundation of Universalism (Cultural Memory in the Present)*. Translated by Ray Brassier. Stanford, CA: Stanford University Press, 2003.

Baggini, Julian. *Philosophy: All That Matters*. London: McGraw-Hill, 2012.

Bailey, Sarah Pulliam. "Why Some Fear This Election's Lasting Damage to American Christianity." *Washington Post*, November 9, 2016. https://www.washingtonpost.com/news/acts-of-faith/wp/2016/11/09/why-some-fear-this-elections-lasting-damage-to-american-christianity/?tid=ss_tw-amp&utm_term=.e54df5ed5ee1.

Bainton, Roland H. *Here I Stand: A Life of Martin Luther*. New York: Penguin, 1995.

Baird, Julia, and Hayley Gleeson. "'Submit to Your Husbands': Women Told to Endure Domestic Violence in the Name of God." *ABC Online*, January 23, 2018. http://www.abc.net.au/news/2017-07-18/domestic-violence-church-submit-to-husbands/8652028.

Ball, Philip. "The Trouble with Scientists: How One Psychologist Is Tackling Human Biases in Science." *Nautilus,* May 14, 2015. http://Nautilus.US/ISSUE/24/Error/The-Trouble-With-Scientists.

Balmer, Randall. *The Making of Evangelicalism: From Revivalism to Politics and Beyond.* Waco, TX: Baylor University Press, 2010.

———. *Redeemer: The Life of Jimmy Carter.* New York: Basic, 2014.

Bandstra, Barry L. *Reading the Old Testament: An Introduction to the Hebrew Bible.* 4th ed. Belmont, CA: Wadsworth, 2009.

Barna Group. "Barna Examines Trends in 14 Religious Factors over 20 Years (1991 to 2011)." July 25, 2011. https://www.barna.org/barna-update/faith-spirituality/504-barna-examines-trends-in-14-religious-factors-over-20-years-1991-to-2011.

Baronius, Caesar. *Martyrologium Romanum.* http://www.liturgialatina.org/martyrologium/15.htm.

Barth, Karl. "An Answer to Professor von Harnack's Open Letter." In *The Beginnings of Dialectic Theology,* vol. 1, edited by James McConkey Robinson, 175–85. Louisville: John Knox, 1968.

———. "Biblical Questions, Insights, and Vistas." 1920. In *The Word of God and Theology,* translated by Amy Marga, 71–100. New York: T. & T. Clark, 2011.

———. "The Christian in Society." 1919. In *The Word of God and Theology,* translated by Amy Marga, 31–70. New York: T. & T, Clark, 2011.

———. *Church Dogmatics.* Vol. 4, pt. 1: *The Doctrine of Reconciliation.* Edited by G. W. Bromiley and T. F. Torrance. New York: T. & T. Clark, 2004.

———. *Deliverance to the Captives.* Eugene, OR: Wipf & Stock, 1978.

———. "Fate and Idea in Theology." In *The Way of Theology in Karl Barth: Essays and Comments,* edited by H. Martin Rumscheidt, 25–62. Eugene, OR: Wipf & Stock, 1986.

———. *The Göttingen Dogmatics: Instructions in the Christian Religion.* Translated by G. W. Bromiley. Grand Rapids: Eerdmans, 1991.

———. "The Problem of Ethics Today." In *The Word of God and the Word of Man,* edited by Douglas Horton, 78–106. Gloucester, MA: Peter Smith, 1957.

———. "The Strange New World within the Bible." In *The Word of God and the Word of Man,* edited by Douglas Horton, 28–50. Gloucester, MA: Peter Smith, 1957.

Bass, Diana Butler. "Is Western Christianity Suffering from Spiritual Amnesia?" *Huffington Post,* May 25, 2011. http://www.huffingtonpost.com/diana-butler-bass/is-western-christianity-s_b_554231.html.453.

Battles, Ford Lewis. "Introduction." In *Institutes of the Christian Religion,* by John Calvin, edited by John T. McNeill and Ford Lewis Battles, xxix–lxxi. Philadelphia: Westminster, 1960.

Beaujon, Andrew. *Body Piercing Saved My Life: Inside the Phenomenon of Christian Rock.* Cambridge, MA: Da Capo, 2006.

Bebbington, David W. *Evangelicalism in Modern Britain: A History from the 1730s to the 1980s.* New York: Routledge, 2002.

Bellarmine, Robert. Letter to Foscarini, April 12, 1615. In *Modern History Sourcebook,* edited by Paul Halsall. Fordham University. http://sourcebooks.fordham.edu/mod/1615bellarmine-letter.asp.

Benestad, J. Brian, et al. *Five Views on the Church and Politics.* Edited by Stanley N. Gundry. Counterpoints: Bible and Theology. Grand Rapids: Zondervan, 2015.

Berger, Peter L. *The Desecularization of the World.* Grand Rapids: Eerdmans, 1999.

Berlin, Sir Isaiah. "Two Concepts of Liberty." In *Liberty: Incorporating Four Essays on Liberty,* edited by Henry Hardy, 166–217. 2nd ed. Oxford: Oxford University Press, 2013.

Berry, Susan. "Pope Benedict to Cuba: Marxism Doesn't Work." *Breitbart*, March 24, 2012. http://www.breitbart.com/Big-Government/2012/03/24/pope-benedict-to-cuba-marxism-doesnt-work.

Bhikkhu, Thanissaro, trans. "Cula-Saccaka Sutta: The Shorter Discourse to Saccaka (Majihima Nikaya 35)." *Access to Insight*, BCBS ed., 2012. https://www.accesstoinsight.org/tipitaka/mn/mn.035.than.html.

Billings, J. Todd. *Calvin, Participation, and the Gift: The Activity of Believers in Union with Christ.* New York: Oxford University Press, 2007.

Black Elk. *The Sacred Pipe.* Norman, OK: University of Oklahoma Press, 1989.

Blackwell, Albert L. *The Sacred in Music.* Louisville: John Knox, 1999.

Blake, Aaron. "Eric Holder: 'When They Go Low, We Kick Them. That's What This New Democratic Party Is About.'" *Washington Post*, October 10, 2018. https://www.washingtonpost.com/politics/2018/10/10/eric-holder-when-they-go-low-we-kick-them-thats-what-this-new-democratic-party-is-about/?noredirect=on&utm_term=.a628e900cd30.

Bloom, Allan. *The Closing of the American Mind.* New York: Simon & Schuster, 1987.

Bloomfield, Leonard, *Language.* New York: Rinehart & Winston, 1933.

Blumenthal, David. *The Banality of Good and Evil: Moral Lessons from the Shoah and Jewish Tradition.* Washington, DC: Georgetown University Press, 1999.

Blumhardt, Johann Christoph, and Christoph Frederich Blumhardt. *Thy Kingdom Come.* Edited by Vernard Eller. Grand Rapids: Eerdmans, 1980.

Bodhi, Bhikkhu, ed. *In the Buddha's Words: An Anthology of Discourses from the Pāli Canon.* Foreword by the Dalai Lama. Boston: Wisdom, 2005.

Boccaccini, Gabriele. *Beyond the Essene Hypothesis: The Parting of the Ways between Qumran and Enochic Judaism.* Grand Rapids: Eerdmans, 1988.

Bohart, Arthur C., and Thomas Greening. "Humanistic Psychology and Positive Psychology." *American Psychologist* 56/1 (2001) 81–82. http://dx.doi.org/10.1037/0003-066X.56.1.81.

Bonhoeffer, Dietrich. *Dietrich Bonhoeffer Works*, vol. 2: *Act and Being: Transcendental Philosophy and Ontology in Systematic Theology.* Edited by Wayne Whiston Floyd Jr. Minneapolis: Fortress, 1996.

———. *Dietrich Bonhoeffer Works*, vol. 6: *Ethics.* Edited by Clifford J. Green. Minneapolis: Fortress, 2008.

———. *Letters and Papers from Prison.* Edited by Eberhard Bethge. Enlarged ed. New York: Simon & Schuster, 1997.

Bovell, Carlos R., ed. *Interdisciplinary Perspectives on the Authority of Scripture: Historical, Biblical, and Theoretical Perspectives.* Eugene, OR: Pickwick, 2011.

Bowler, Peter J. *Evolution: The History of an Idea.* 3rd ed. Berkeley: University of California Press, 2003.

Boyd, Greg. "Greg Boyd on Doubt and the Christian Life—It's Unavoidable, Biblical, and Healthy." Interview by Peter Enns. *Patheos*, November 2, 2013. http://www.patheos.com/blogs/peterenns/2013/11/greg-boyd-on-doubt-and-the-christian-life-its-unavoidable-biblical-and-healthy/#ixzz37B5hE0S9.

Boyle, Alan. "Video Shows 'Scientist' in Congress Saying Evolution Is from 'Pit of Hell.'" *NBC News*, October 5, 2012. http://cosmiclog.nbcnews.com/_news/2012/10/05/14203607-video-shows-scientist-in-congress-saying-evolution-is-from-pit-of-hell.

Bremmer, Jan N. "Atheism in Antiquity." In *The Cambridge Companion to Atheism*, edited by Michael Martin, 11–26. Cambridge Companions to Philosophy. Cambridge: Cambridge University Press, 2006.

Brennan, Francis X., and Carl J. Charnetski. "Explanatory Style and Immunoglobulin A (IgA)." *Integrative Physiological and Behavioral Science* 35/4 (2000) 251–55.

Breton, André. *Nadja*. Translated by Richard Howard. New York: Grove, 1994.

Broks, Paul. *Into the Silent Land: Travels in Neuropsychology*. New York: Grove/Atlantic, 2003.

Brown, Greg. "Lord, I Have Made You a Place in My Heart." *The Poet Game*. Red House, 1994.

Brown, Warren, et al. *Scientific and Theological Portraits of Human Nature*. Minneapolis: Augsburg Fortress, 1998.

Bruce, F. F. "The Bible." In *The Origin of the Bible*, edited by Philip Wesley Comfort, 3–12. Carol Stream, IL: Tyndale, 2003.

———. *The New Testament Writings: Are They Reliable?* 6th ed. Downers Grove, IL: Intervarsity, 1981.

Brown, Harold P. J. "The Inerrancy and Infallibility of the Bible." In *The Origin of the Bible*, edited by Philip Wesley Comfort, 37–50. Carol Stream, IL: Tyndale, 2003.

Bruinius, Harry. *Better for All the World: The Secret History of Forced Sterilization and America's Quest for Racial Purity*. New York: Random House, 2007.

Bryan, William Jennings, and Mary Baird Bryan. *Memoirs of William Jennings Bryan*. Kessinger, 2010.

Buckley, Theodore Alous, ed. *The Catechism of the Council of Trent, Translated into English, with Notes*. London: Routledge, 1852.

Buechner, Frederick. *The Magnificent Defeat*. New York: HarperCollins. 1985.

Bultmann, Rudolph. *New Testament & Mythology*. Translated by Schubert M. Ogden. Minneapolis: Fortress, 1989.

Burns, J. Patout. *Theological Anthropology*. Philadelphia: Fortress, 1981.

Butler, Jon. "Enthusiasm Described and Decried: The Great Awakening as Interpretative Fiction." *Journal of American History* 69 (1982) 305–25.

Butler, Judith, et al. *The Power of Religion in the Public Sphere*. Edited by Eduardo Mendieta et al. New York: Columbia University Press. 2011.

Calvin, John. *Commentary on the Gospel According to John*. Vol. 1. Translated by William Pringle. https://www.ccel.org/ccel/calvin/calcom34.xi.viii.html.

———. *Institutes of the Christian Religion*. Edited by John T. McNeill and Ford Lewis Battles. Philadelphia: Westminster, 1960.

———. Prefatory Address to King Francis I of France. In *Institutes of the Christian Religion*, edited by John T. McNeill and Ford Lewis Battles, 9–32. Philadelphia: Westminster, 1960.

Campbell, Antony F., and Mark A. O'Brien. *Sources of the Pentateuch: Texts, Introductions, Annotations*. 2nd ed. Minneapolis: Augsburg Fortress, 2000.

Campolo, Tony. *It's Friday but Sunday's Comin'*. Nashville: Thomas Nelson, 2002.

Canlis, Julie. "The Bible's Best Description of Salvation Is a Phrase We Rarely Use." *Christianity Today*, January 29, 2019. https://www.christianitytoday.com/women/2019/january/bibles-best-description-salvation-is-phrase-we-rarely-use.html.

Capretto, Lisa. "The Difference between Being Optimistic and Being Irrational." *Huffington Post,* February 10, 2016. http://www.huffingtonpost.com/entry/optimism-vs-irrational-thinking_us_5696638de4bo86bc1cd5fffc.

Carlson, Julie, and Lori Fogleman. "Losing My Religion? No, Says Baylor Religion Survey." September 11, 2006. http://www.baylor.edu/mediacommunications/news.php?action=story&story=41678.

Carlson, Thomas A. *Indiscretion: Finitude and the Naming of God.* Chicago: University of Chicago Press, 1999.

Carr, Nicholas. *The Shallows: What the Internet Is Doing to Our Brains.* New York: Norton, 2011.

Carroll, Sean. "You Can't Derive Ought from Is." *Cosmic Variance* (blog), *Discover,* May 3, 2010. http://blogs.discovermagazine.com/cosmicvariance/2010/05/03/you-cant-derive-ought-from-is/#.VIEiWoi7l4I.

Carson, Clayborne, et al., eds. *The Papers of Martin Luther King, Jr.* Berkeley: University of California Press, 1992.

Carter, Warren. "The Gospel of Matthew." In *A Postcolonial Commentary on New Testament Writings,* edited by Fernando F. Segovia and R. S. Sugirtharajah, 69–104. London: T. & T. Clark, 2007.

———. *Matthew and Empire: Initial Explorations.* Harrisburg, PA: Trinity, 2001.

Carus, Paul. *The Gospel of Buddha.* Originally published 1894. CreateSpace, 2011.

Casiday, A. M. *Evagrius Ponticus.* Edited by Carol Harrison. New York: Routledge, 2006.

Cassin, Barbara, et al., eds. *Dictionary of Untranslatables: A Philosophical Lexicon.* Princeton, NJ: Princeton University Press, 2014.

Cassuto, Umberto. *The Documentary Hypothesis.* Jerusalem: Shalem, 2008.

Caussade, Jean Pierre de. *Abandonment to Divine Providence.* Translated by John Beevers. New York: Doubleday, 1975.

———. *The Joy of Full Surrender.* Translated by Hal M. Helms. Brewster, MA: Paraclete, 1986.

Cavanaugh, William. *Torture and Eucharist: Theology, Politics, and the Body of Christ.* Malden, MA: Blackwell, 1998.

Chafer, Lewis Sperry. *Systematic Theology.* Vol. 8. Dallas: Dallas Theological Seminary Press, 1948.

Chaffey, Tim, et al. *Demolishing Supposed Bible Contradictions.* Vol. 2. Green Forest, AZ: Master, 2012.

Chambers, Oswald. "The Baffling Call of God." In *My Utmost for His Highest.* https://utmost.org/classic/the-baffling-call-of-god-classic/.

———. "Let Us Keep to the Point." In *My Utmost for His Highest.* https://utmost.org/let-us-keep-to-the-point/.

———. "Repentance." In *My Utmost for His Highest.* http://utmost.org/repentance/.

Chan, Francis. *Crazy Love: Overwhelmed by a Relentless God.* Colorado Springs: David C. Cook, 2008.

Chang, Edward C., ed. *Optimism and Pessimism: Implications for Theory, Research, and Practice.* Washington, DC: American Psychological Association, 2001.

Chesterton, G. K. *A Miscellany of Men.* Norfolk, VA: IHS, 2004.

———. *Orthodoxy.* New York: Doubleday, 1990.

———. *St. Thomas Aquinas and St. Francis of Assisi.* San Francisco: Ignatius, 2002.

Chicago Statement on Biblical Inerrancy. 1978. http://www.reformed.org/documents/icbi.html.

Chomsky, Noam. "Burkini Bans, New Atheism and State Worship: Noam Chomsky on Religion in Politics." Interviewed by C. J. Polychroniou, August 31, 2016. https://chomsky.info/burkini-bans-new-atheism-and-state-worship-noam-chomsky-on-religion-in-politics/.

Chua, Amy, and Jed Lubenfeld. *The Triple Package: How Three Unlikely Traits Explain the Rise and Fall of Cultural Groups in America*. Penguin, New York: 2014.

Clay, Phillip. "Augustinian Compatibilism and the Doctrine of Election." In *Augustine and Philosophy*, edited by Phillip Cary et al., 79–102, Lanham, MD: Lexington, 2010.

Clement of Alexandria. *The Stromata*. In *The Ante-Nicene Fathers: Fathers of the Second Century*, vol. 2, edited by Alexander Roberts et al. Buffalo, NY: Christian Literature, 1885. http://www.newadvent.org/fathers/02107.htm.

Clement of Rome. *First Epistle of Clement to the Corinthians*. http://www.newadvent.org/fathers/1010.htm.

Clifford, William Kingdon, et al. *The Ethics of Belief*. Edited by A.J. Burger. Revised ed. CreateSpace, 2008.

Coakley, Sarah. "Does Kenosis Rest on a Mistake? Three Kenotic Models in Patristic Exegesis." In *Exploring Kenotic Christology: The Self-Emptying of God*, edited by C. Stephen Evans, 246–64. New York: Oxford University Press, 2006.

———. *Powers and Submissions: Spirituality, Philosophy and Gender*. Oxford: Blackwell, 2002.

Cohen, Leonard. *Beautiful Losers*. Toronto, Ontario: McClelland & Stewart, 2003.

Coleridge, Mark. "Life in the Crypt, or Why Bother with Biblical Studies?" In *Biblical Studies Alternatively: An Introductory Reader*, edited by Susanne Scholz, 12–21. Upper Saddle River, NJ: Prentice Hall, 2003.

Coleridge, Samuel Taylor. *Confessions of an Inquiring Spirit and Some Miscellaneous Pieces*. Lenox, MA: Hard, 2006.

Collinson, Patrick. *The Reformation: A History*. New York: Random House, 2006.

Comfort, Ray. "Answers to More Supposed Bible Contradictions." http://www.christiananswers.net/q-comfort/contradictions-bible.html.

Cone, James H. *A Black Theology of Liberation*. 20th anniversary ed. Maryknoll, NY: Orbis, 1990.

———. "Legacies of the Cross and the Lynching Tree." *Tikkun*, October 26, 2012. https://www.tikkun.org/newsite/legacies-of-the-cross-and-the-lynching-tree.

Coogan, Michael D. "The Great Gulf Between Scholars and the Pew." In *Biblical Studies Alternatively*, edited by Susanne Scholtz, 5–12. Upper Saddle River, NJ: Prentice Hall, 2003.

Coon, Lynda L. *Sacred Fictions: Holy Women and Hagiography in Late Antiquity*. Philadelphia: University of Pennsylvania Press, 1997.

Copleston, Frederick. *A History of Philosophy*. Vol. 2: *Medieval Philosophy: From Augustine to Duns Scotus*. New York: Doubleday, 1993.

Corcoran, Monica. "Katy Perry Kisses and Tells. "*Women's Health*, March 9, 2009. https://www.womenshealthmag.com/food/a19925692/katy-perry-interview/.

Corey, Michael Anthony. *Evolution and the Problem of Natural Evil*. Lanham, MD: University Press of America, 2000.

Corn, David. "Donald Trump Is Completely Obsessed with Revenge." *Mother Jones*, October 19, 2016. http://www.motherjones.com/politics/2016/10/donald-trump-obsessed-with-revenge.

Cornford, Francis MacDonald. "Preface." In the *Geneva Psalter*, translated by F. M. Cornford, 3.399c. New York: Oxford University Press, 1945.

Coulson, Charles A. *Science and Christian Belief.* London: Oxford University Press, 1955.

The Council of Trent: Canons and Decrees. Fourth Session, 1546. https://history.hanover. edu/courses/excerpts/111ct.html.

Cox, Daniel, et al. "Most Are Proud to Be American, Republicans More Likely to Engage in Patriotic Activities." Public Religion Research Institute, June 27, 2013. http://publicreligion.org/research/2013/06/july-2013-prri-rns/.

Crossan, John Dominic. *A Fragile Craft: The Work of Amos Niven Wilder.* Chicago: Scholars, 1981.

———. *The Historical Jesus: The Life of a Mediterranean Jewish Peasant.* Reprint ed. New York: HarperOne: 1993.

Crux. "Four Spiritual Laws." http://www.crustore.org/fourlawseng.htm.

Cyril of Jerusalem. "Catechetical Lecture 4.17." In *Catechetical Lectures (Cyril of Jerusalem)*, translated by Edwin Hamilton Gifford. http://www.newadvent.org/ fathers/310104.htm.

Cytowic, Richard. *The Man Who Tasted Shapes.* New York: MIT Press, 2003.

Dalrymple, Theodore. "What the New Atheists Don't See." *City Journal*, Autumn 2007. http://www.city-journal.org/html/17_4_oh_to_be.html.

Damascene, Hieromonk. *Christ the Eternal Tao.* Platina, CA: Valaam, 2012.

Dark, David. *Everyday Apocalypse: The Sacred Revealed in Radiohead, The Simpsons, and Other Pop Culture Icons.* Grand Rapids: Brazos, 2002.

Darwin, Charles. *The Descent of Man.* Edited by James Moore and Adrian Desmond. New York: Penguin, 2004.

———. "Letter 5140—Wallace, A. R. to Darwin, C. R., 2 July 1866." *Darwin Correspondence Project.* http://www.darwinproject.ac.uk/entry-5140—back-mark-5140.f5.

———. "To Asa Gray. 22 May [1860]." *Darwin Correspondence Project.* https://www. darwinproject.ac.uk/letter/DCP-LETT-2814.xml.

Davies, Brian. "The Limits of Language and the Notion of Analogy." In *The Oxford Handbook of Aquinas*, edited by Brian Davies and Eleonore Stump. New York: Oxford University Press, 2012.

Davis, Edward B. "That Isaac Newton's Mechanistic Cosmology Eliminated the Need for God." In *Galileo Goes to Jail (and Other Myths about Science and Religion)*, edited by Ronald L. Numbers, 115–22. Cambridge, MA: Harvard University Press, 2009.

Dawkins, Richard. *The Blind Watchmaker: Why the Evidence of Evolution Reveals a Universe without Design.* New York: Norton, 2006.

———. *The God Delusion.* New York: First Mariner, 2008.

———. *The Greatest Show on Earth: The Evidence for Evolution.* New York: Simon & Schuster, 2010.

———. Interview with Father George Coyne. Richard Dawkins Foundation for Reason and Science, December 9, 2008. https://www.youtube.com/ watch?v=pooZMfkSNxc.

Dechesne, Mark et al. "Adjusting to Death: The Effects of Self-Esteem and Mortality Salience on Well-Being, Growth Motivation, and Maladaptive Behavior." *Journal of Personality and Social Psychology* 84 (2003) 727–37.

Definition of the Council of Chalcedon https://reformed.org/documents/index. html?mainframe=https://reformed.org/documents/chalcedon.html.

DeHart, Paul. *Trial of the Witnesses: The Rise and Decline of Postliberal Theology.* Malden, MA: Wiley-Blackwell; 2006.

Desiderius, Erasmus. *The Correspondence of Erasmus.* Vol. 9 of *Collected Works of Erasmus.* Translated by R. A. B. Mynors. Toronto: University of Toronto Press, 1989.

———. "The Handbook of the Militant Christian." In *The Essential Erasmus,* edited by John Dolan, 24–93. New York: Continuum, 1990.

Dickens, Charles. *A Christmas Carol.* Edited by Stanley Applebaum. Mineola, NY: Dover, 1991.

The Didache. http://www.newadvent.org/fathers/0714.htm.

Dillard, Annie. *Teaching a Stone to Talk: Expeditions and Encounters.* New York: Harper & Row, 1982.

Dillenberger, John. "An Introduction to Martin Luther." In *Martin Luther: Selections from His Writings,* xi–xxxiii. New York: Doubleday, 1961.

Dobbs, David. How Charles Darwin Seduced Asa Gray. *Wired,* April 4, 2011. http:// www.wired.com/2011/04/how-charles-darwin-seduced-asa-gray/.

Dorrien, Gary. *The Remaking of Evangelical Theology.* Louisville: Westminster John Knox, 1998.

Dostoevsky, Fyodor. *The Brothers Karamazov.* Translated by Richard Pevear and Larissa Volokhonsky. New York: Farrar, Straus and Giroux, 2002.

Douglass, Frederick. *Life and Times of Frederick Douglass.* New York: Park, 1881.

Douthat, Ross. *Bad Religion: How We Became a Nation of Heretics.* New York: Free Press, 2012.

———. "Limbaugh Calls Pope's Teachings Marxist." Interview by Anderson Cooper. *CNN,* December 3. 2013. http://www.cnn.com/video/data/2.0/video/ bestoftv/2013/12/03/ac-marxist-pope.cnn.html.

Downing, Pamela A., et al. *The Linguistics of Literacy.* Philadelphia: John Benjamins, 1992.

Doyle, G. Wright. *Carl Henry, Theologian for All Seasons: An Introduction and Guide to Carl Henry's God, Revelation, and Authority.* Eugene, OR: Wipf & Stock, 2010.

Dube, Musa. *Postcolonial Feminist Interpretations of the Bible.* St. Louis: Chalice, 2000.

Dunn, James D. G. *The Epistles to the Colossians and to Philemon: A Commentary on the Greek Text.* Grand Rapids: Eerdmans, 1996.

Eagleton, Terry. *Reason, Faith, and Revolution: Reflections on the God Debate.* Terry Lectures Series. New Haven, CT: Yale University Press, 2010.

Easton, Burton Scott, trans. *The Apostolic Tradition of Hippolytus.* Cambridge: Cambridge University Press, 2014.

Eberling, Eric R. "Massachusetts Education Laws of 1642, 1647, and 1648." In *Historical Dictionary of American Education,* edited by Richard J. Altenbaugh, 225–26. Westport, CT: Greenwood, 1999.

Ehrenberg, John. *Civil Society: The Critical History of an Idea.* New York: New York University Press, 1999.

Ehrenreich, Barbara. *Nickel and Dimed: On (Not) Getting By in America,* New York: Henry Paperbacks, 2008.

Ehrman, Bart. *Did Jesus Exist?: The Historical Argument for Jesus of Nazareth.* New York: HarperCollins, 2012.

———. "How the Problem of Pain Ruined My Faith." https://www.beliefnet.com/columnists/blogalogue/2008/04/why-suffering-is-gods-problem.html.

———. *Lost Christianities: The Battles for Scripture and the Faiths We Never Knew.* Oxford: Oxford University Press, 2003.

———. *Misquoting Jesus: The Story Behind Who Changed the Bible and Why.* New York: HarperOne, 2005.

Eliason, Eric Alden. "Introduction." In *Mormons and Mormonism: An Introduction to an American World Religion*, edited by Eric A. Eliason, 1–22. Champaign: University of Illinois Press, 2001.

Eliot, T. S. *Murder in the Cathedral.* New York: Harcourt & Brace, 1963.

Endo, Shusaku. *A Life of Jesus.* Translated by Richard A. Schuchert. Mahwah, NJ: Paulist, 1978.

Enns, Peter. *Inspiration and Incarnation: Evangelicals and the Problem of the Old Testament.* Grand Rapids: Baker Academic, 2005.

Evangelicals in America, Greenberg Quinlan Rosner Research. *OMG! How Generation Y Is Redefining Faith in the iPod Era.* Reboot, April 2004. https://civicyouth.org/PopUps/OMG.pdf.

Evans, C. Stephen. "Introduction: Understanding Jesus the Christ as Human and Divine." In *Exploring Kenotic Christology: The Self-Emptying of God*, edited by C. Stephen Evans. New York: Oxford University Press, 2006.

———. "Seeing Ourselves in the Mirror of the Word." http://www.baylor.edu/content/services/document.php/174965.pdf.

Evans, Rachel Held. "Why Millennials Are Leaving the Church." *CNN Belief Blog*, July 27, 2013. http://religion.blogs.cnn.com/2013/07/27/why-millennials-are-leaving-the-church/?hpt=hp_c4.

Evans, Tony. *The Power of God's Names.* Eugene, OR: Harvest House, 2014.

"Evolution and Paleontology in the Ancient World." http://www.ucmp.berkeley.edu/history/ancient.html.

Farrer, Austin. *Saving Belief: A Discussion of Essentials.* London: Hodder, 1964.

Farrow, John A. *Clarence Darrow: Attorney for the Damned.* New York: Vintage, 2012.

Ferguson, John. *Clement of Alexandria.* Greece: Twayne, 1974.

Ferreira, M. Jamie. *Love's Grateful Striving: A Commentary on Kierkegaard's Works of Love.* New York: Oxford University Press, 2001.

Feuerbach, Ludwig. *The Essence of Christianity.* Translated by George Eliot. Amherst, NY: Prometheus, 1989,

Flew, Antony. "Theology and Falsification." In *Reason and Responsibility: Readings in Some Basic Problems of Philosophy*, edited by Joel Feinberg, 48–49. Belmont, CA: Dickenson, 1968.

Flint, John E. *Cecil Rhodes.* Boston: Little, Brown, 1974.

Foley, John Miles. *Homer's Traditional Art.* University Park: Pennsylvania State University Press, 1999.

Fonda, Jane. "Christianity Is My Spiritual Home." April 18, 2005. http://www.beliefnet.com/Faiths/2005/04/Christianity-Is-My-Spiritual-Home.aspx.

Force, James E. "The Newtonians and Deism." In *Essays on the Context, Nature, and Influence of Isaac Newton's Theology*, edited by James E. Force and Richard Henry Popkin, 43–73. Norwell, MA: Kluwer Academic, 1990.

Foucauld, Charles de. *Modern Spiritual Masters.* Maryknoll, NY: Orbis, 1999.

Foucault, Michel. *The Use of Pleasure.* New York: Parthenon, 1985.

Foxworthy, Jeff. "Jeff Foxworthy Hosts New Bible Show." Interview by Piers Morgan (transcript). *Piers Morgan Live*, August 21, 2012. http://transcripts.cnn.com/TRANSCRIPTS/1208/21/pmt.01.html.

Franke, William. "Cosmopolitan Conviviality and Negative Theology: Europe's Vocation to Universalism." *Journal of European Studies* 44/1 (2014) 30–49.

Franklin, Benjamin. "Articles of Belief and Acts of Religion." November 20, 1728. *Benjamin Franklin Papers*. http://franklinpapers.org/framedVolumes.jsp.

———. *Autobiography and Other Writings*. Cambridge: Riverside, 1771.

Frei, Hans. *The Identity of Jesus Christ*. Eugene, OR: Wipf & Stock, 1997.

———. *Types of Christian Theology*. Edited by George Hunsinger. Rev. ed. New Haven, CT: Yale University Press, 1994.

Freud, Sigmund. *The Future of an Illusion*. Translated by James Strachey. New York: Norton, 1961.

———. *Moses and Monotheism*. Translated by Katherine Jones. New York: Random House, 1939.

———. *Totem and Taboo*. Translated by James Strachey. New York: Norton, 1990.

Fronsdal, Gil, ed. *The Dhammapada: A New Translation of the Buddhist Classic with Annotations*. Boston: Shambhala, 2005.

Flanagan, Owen. *The Problem of the Soul: Two Visions of Mind and How to Reconcile Them*. New York: Basic, 2003.

Frost, Robert. "Once by the Pacific." Reproduced in *A Coherent Splendor: The American Poetic Renaissance, 1910–1950*, by Albert Gelpi. New York: Cambridge University Press, 1990.

Fuller, Richard. "The Letter from Richard Fuller to the Editor of *The Christian Reflector*." In *Domestic Slavery Considered as a Scriptural Institution*, 3–11. Boston: Gould, Kendall and Lincoln, 1845.

Fulton, Elaine, and Peter Webster. "Introduction: The Search for Authority in the Protestant Reformation." In *The Search for Authority in Reformation Europe*, edited by Helen L. Parish et al., 1–10. Farnham: Ashgate, 2014.

Gagnon, Robert, and Humphrey, Edith. "Stop Calling Ted Cruz a Dominionist." *Christianity Today*, April 2016. https://www.christianitytoday.com/ct/2016/april-web-only/stop-calling-ted-cruz-dominionist.html.

Galilee, Galileo. "Galileo to Castelli (21 December 1613)." In *The Galileo Affair: A Documentary History*, edited by Maurice A. Finocchiaro, 49–54. Los Angeles: University of California Press, 1989.

———. "Galileo's Considerations on the Copernican Opinion (1615)." In *The Galileo Affair: A Documentary History*, edited by Maurice A. Finocchiaro, 70–86. Los Angeles: University of California Press, 1989.

———. "Letter to the Grand Duchess Christina (1615)." In *Sources of The Making of the West*, by Katharine J. Lualdi, vol. 2, 43–46. 3rd ed. Boston: Bedford/St. Martin's, 2009, .

Gallagher, Mari. "USDA Defines Food Deserts." *Nutrition Digest* 38/2. http://americannutritionassociation.org/newsletter/usda-defines-food-deserts.

Gallup. "American Confidence in Organized Religion at All Time Low." http://www.gallup.com/poll/155690/confidence-organized-religion-low-point.aspx.

Gamble, Harry. *Books and Readers in the Early Church: A History of Early Christian Texts*. New Haven, CT: Yale University Press, 1997.

———. "The New Testament Canon: Recent Research and the Status Quaestionis." In *The Canon Debate*, edited by Lee Martin McDonald and James A. Sanders. Peabody, MA: Hendrickson, 2002.

Gandhi, Mahatma. *Gita the Mother*. Lahore, India: Free India, 1942.

Gathercole, Simon. *The Gospel of Judas: Rewriting Early Christianity*. Oxford: Oxford University Press, 2007.

Gaustad, Edwin, and Leigh Schmidt. *The Religious History of America: The Heart of the American Story from Colonial Times to Today*. Rev. ed. New York: HarperCollins, 2004.

Geertz, Clifford. *The Interpretation of Cultures*. New York: Basic, 1973.

Geisler, Norman. *When Critics Ask: A Popular Handbook on Bible Difficulties*. Grand Rapids: Baker, 1992.

Geisler, Norman, and Thomas Howe. *The Big Book of Bible Difficulties: Clear and Concise Answers from Genesis to Revelation*. Grand Rapids: Baker, 2008.

Gervais, Ricky. "Jesus Was My Invisible Babysitter." *Big*, February 26, 2009. https://bigthink.com/videos/jesus-was-my-invisible-babysitter.

Giberson, Karl. The Bible Is a Library, Not a Book. *Huffington Post*, October 15, 2011. http://www.huffingtonpost.com/karl-giberson-phd/the-bible-is-a-library-no_b_923690.html.

Giberson, Karl, and Francis Collins. *The Language of Science and Faith: Straight Answers to Genuine Questions*. Madison, WI: InterVarsity, 2011.

Gilbert, Martin. *Churchill: A Life*. New York: Holt, 1992.

Gilson, Etiene. *The Spirit of Mediaeval Philosophy*. Translated by A. H. C. Downs. Notre Dame, IN: University of Notre Dame Press, 1991.

Girard, René. *Job: The Victim of His People*. Stanford, CA: Stanford University Press, 1987.

———. *Things Hidden Since the Foundation of the World*. Translated by Stephen Bann and Michael Metteer. Stanford, CA: Stanford University Press, 1987.

Giuliani, Massimo. *A Centaur in Auschwitz: Reflections on Primo Levi's Thinking*. Lanham, MD: Lexington, 2003.

Gleick, James. *Chaos: Making a New Science*. New York: Penguin, 2008.

Goethe, Johann Wolfgang von. *Faust*. Translated by Walter Kaufmann. New York: Random House, 1990.

Goldenberg, Robert. Review of Daniel Boyarin's *Dying for God: Martyrdom and the Making of Christianity and Judaism*. *Jewish Quarterly Review*, n.s., 92/¾ (2002) 586–88.

Golem, Jessie. "I Was a Hardcore Christian, But This Is Why I Lost My Faith." *Huffington Post*, April 21, 2014. https://www.huffingtonpost.ca/jessie-golem/leaving-the-church_b_4816252.html.

Golitzin, Alexander. *Mystagogy: A Monastic Reading of Dionysius Areopagita*, edited by Bogdan G. Bucur. Collegeville, MN: Order of St. Benedict, 2013.

Gorsuch, Neil M. *The Future of Assisted Suicide and Euthanasia*. Princeton, NJ: Princeton University Press, 2006.

Gould, Stephen Jay. *Ever Since Darwin: Reflections in Natural History*. New York: Norton, 1977.

———. *Rocks of Ages: Science and Religion in the Fullness of Life*. New York: Ballatine, 2002.

————. *Time's Arrow, Time's Cycle: Myth and Metaphor in the Discover of Geological Time.* Cambridge, MA: Harvard University Press, 1987.

Graham, Lloyd M. *Deceptions and Myths of the Bible.* New York: Citadel, 1991.

Gregory, Caspar René. *Canon and Text of the New Testament.* Charleston, SC: Bibliolife, 2009.

Gregory of Nyssa. *De Opificio Hominis.* http://www.newadvent.org/fathers/2914.htm.

————. *On Virginity.* In *Nicene and Post-Nicene Fathers*, 2nd ser., vol. 5, *Gregory of Nyssa: Dogmatic Treatises*, edited by Philip Schaff. New York: Cosimo Classics, 2007.

————. *The Sacred Writings of Gregory of Nyssa.* Translated by Henry Austin Wilson. North Charleston, SC: Jazzybee, 2017.

Grenz, Stanly J. *The Millennial Maze: Sorting out Evangelical Options.* Madison, WI: InterVarsity, 1992.

Gribbin, John. *Science: A History, 1543–2001.* New York: Penguin, 2002.

Griffin, Nicholas, ed. *The Selected Letters of Bertrand Russell: The Private Years, 1884–1914.* New York; Routledge, 2002.

Grossman, Cathy Lynn. "Survey: 72% of Millennials 'more spiritual than religious.'" *USA Today*, October 14, 2010. http://usatoday30.usatoday.com/news/religion/2010-04-27-1Amillfaith27_ST_N.htm.

Guignon, C. Hermeneutics, Authenticity and the Aims of Psychology. *Journal of Theoretical and Philosophical Psychology* 22 (2002) 83–113.

Haanen, Jeff. "David Platt Wants You to Get Serious about Following Christ." *Christianity Today*, February 7, 2013. http://www.christianitytoday.com/ct/2013/february-web-only/david-platt-wants-you-to-get-serious-about-following-christ.html?paging=off.

Habermas, Jürgen. "An Awareness of What Is Missing." In *An Awareness of What Is Missing: Faith and Reason in a Post-Secular Age*, translated by Ciaran Cronin, 15–23. Cambridge: Polity, 2010.

————. *Religion and Rationality: Essays on Reason, God, and Modernity*, edited by E. Medieta. Cambridge, MA: MIT, 2002.

————. "Secularism's Crisis of Faith: Notes on Post-Secular Society." *New Perspectives Quarterly* 25 (2008) 17–29.

Haidt, Jonathan. *The Happiness Hypothesis: Finding Modern Truth in Ancient Wisdom.* New York: Basic, 2006.

Hallowell, Billy. "'I'm Not Christian': Pop Star Rejects Her Childhood Faith." *The Blaze*, December 31, 2013. https://www.theblaze.com/news/2013/12/31/im-not-a-christian-pop-star-katy-perry-rejects-her-childhood-faith-and-shares-her-current-views-on-theology.

Hamilton, Christopher. *Understanding Philosophy for AS Level.* Cheltenham, UK: Nelson Thomas, 2003.

Harris, Sam. *Free Will.* New York: Simon & Schuster, 2012.

————. "God's Dupes." *Sam Harris.org*, March 2007. https://samharris.org/gods-dupes/.

————. *Waking Up: A Guide to Spirituality Without Religion.* New York: Simon & Schuster, 2014.

Hatch, Nathan. *The Democratization of American Christianity.* New Haven, CT: Yale University Press, 1989.

Haughen, Gary. "The Hidden Reason for Poverty the World Needs to Address Now." TED Talk, March 2015. http://www.ted.com/talks/gary_haugen_the_hidden_reason_for_poverty_the_world_needs_to_address_now#t-264405.

———. *The Locust Effect: Why the End of Poverty Requires the End of Violence*. New York: Oxford University Press, 2014.

Hawking, Stephen. "The Beginning of Time." http://www.hawking.org.uk/the-beginning-of-time.html.

———. *Brief Answers to the Big Questions*. New York: Bantam, 2018.

———. *A Brief History of Time*. New York: Bantam, 1988.

Hayden, Thomas. "Darwin the Liberator: How Evolutionary Thought Undermined the Rationale for Slavery." *Washington Post*, February 15, 2009, BW03. http://www.washingtonpost.com/wp-dyn/content/story/2009/02/13/ST2009021302658.html?noredirect=on.

Hayford, Jack. *Rebuilding the Real You: The Definitive Guide to the Holy Spirit's Work in Your Life*. Lake Mary, FL: Charisma House, 2009.

Hebblethwaite, Brian, and Edward Henderson. *Divine Action: Studies Inspired by the Philosophical Theology of Austin Farrer*. Edinburgh: T. & T. Clark, 1990.

Hegel, Georg Wilhelm Friedrich. *Lectures on the Philosophy of Religion*. Vol. 1: *Introduction and the Concept of Religion*. Edited by Peter C. Hodgson. New York: Oxford University Press, 2007.

Held, Barbara S. "The Tyranny of the Positive Attitude in America: Observation and Speculation." *Journal of Clinical Psychology* 58/9 (2002) 969, 986–87.

Henry, Carl H. "The Authority of the Bible." In *The Origin of the Bible*, edited by Philip Wesley Comfort, 13–28. Carol Stream, IL: Tyndale House, 2003.

———. *Confessions of a Theologian*. Waco, TX: Word, 1986.

———. *God, Revelation, and Authority*. Wheaton, IL: Word, 1979.

Heschel, Susannah. *The Aryan Jesus: Christian Theologians and the Bible in Nazi Germany*. Princeton, NJ: Princeton University Press, 2010.

Hidaka, Brandon H. "Depression as a Disease of Modernity: Explanations for Increasing Prevalence. *Journal of Affective Disorders* 140/3 (2012) 205–14. https://www.ncbi.nlm.nih.gov/pmc/articles/PMC3330161/.

"Historical Estimates of World Population." https://www.census.gov/data/tables/time-series/demo/international-programs/historical-est-worldpop.html.

Hitchens, Christopher. *God Is Not Great: How Religion Spoils Everything*. New York: Twelve, 2009.

———. *The Portable Atheist: Essential Readings for the Nonbeliever*. Philadelphia, PA: Da Capo, 2007.

Hitchens, Christopher, and Alister McGrath. "Poison or Cure? Religious Belief in the Modern World." Georgetown University, October 11, 2007. http://hitchensdebates.blogspot.com/2011/10/hitchens-vs-mcgrath-georgetown.html.

Hochschild, Adam. *King Leopold's Ghost: A Story of Greed, Terror, and Heroism in Colonial Africa*. New York: Houghton Mifflin, 1999.

Hobbes, Thomas. *Leviathan: Revised Student Edition*. Edited by Richard Tuck. Cambridge: Cambridge University Press, 2003.

Hobbs, Kendall. "Why I Am No Longer a Christian: Ruminations on a Spiritual Journey out of and into the Material World. 2003. https://infidels.org/library/modern/testimonials/hobbs.html.

Hodge, Archibald Alexander, and Benjamin Breckinridge Warfield. "Inspiration." *Presbyterian Review* 2 (1881) 225–60.

Hodge, Charles. *Systematic Theology*. Vol. 1. https://www.ccel.org/ccel/hodge/theology1.html.

———. *Systematic Theology*. Vol. 3. New York: Scribner, 1874.

———. *What Is Darwinism?* New York: Scribner, Armstrong, 1874. Project Gutenberg. http://www.gutenberg.org/files/19192/19192.txt.

Holt, Jim. "Why Does the Universe Exist?" TED Talk, March 2014. https://www.ted.com/talks/jim_holt_why_does_the_universe_exist/transcript?language=en.

"How to Accept Jesus into Your Heart." http://www.wikihow.com/Accept-Jesus-Into-Your-Life.

Howell, Kenneth J. *Ignatius of Antioch & Polycarp of Smyrna: A New Translation and heological Commentary*. Rev. ed. Zanesville, OH: CH Resources, 2009.

Huckabee, Tyler. "The Evolving Faith of Lisa Gungor." *Relevant*, June 19, 2018. https://relevantmagazine.com/issues/issue-94/the-evolving-faith-of-lisa-gungor/.

Huizinga, Johan. *Erasmus and the Age of the Reformation*. New York: Harper, 1957.

Hume, David. *An Enquiry Concerning Human Understanding*. Section X. CreateSpace, 2017.

———. *The Natural History of Religion*. NuVision, 2007.

Hutchinson, Mark, and John Wolffe. *A Short History of Global Evangelicalism*. New York: Cambridge University Press, 2012.

Huxley, Thomas Henry. "Agnosticism" 1889. In *Collected Essays*, vol. 5, *Science and Christian Tradition*. New York: Appleton, 1902.

Huxley, Thomas Henry, and Leonard Huxley. *Life and Letters of Thomas Henry Huxley*. Vol. 1. New York: Cambridge University Press, 2011.

Idleman, Kyle. *Not a Fan: Becoming a Completely Committed Follower of Jesus*. Grand Rapids: Zondervan, 2011.

Ignatius of Antioch. *The Epistle of Ignatius to the Smyrnaeans*. http://www.newadvent.org/fathers/0109.htm. 1–6.

———. *Letter to the Ephesians*. http://www.newadvent.org/fathers/0104.htm.

Inskeep, Steve. "James Dobson Signs Off at Focus on the Family." Interview with Dan Gilgoff. *Morning Edition, NPR*, February 26, 2010. http://www.npr.org/templates/story/story.php?storyId=124105203.

Irenaeus. *Against Heresies*. http://www.newadvent.org/fathers/0103.htm.

Irons, Charles. *The Origins of Proslavery Christianity: White and Black Evangelicals in Colonial and Antebellum Virginia*. Chapel Hill: University of North Carolina Press, 2008.

Irvin, Dale T., and Scott W. Sunquist. *History of the World Christian Movement*. Vol. 1: *Earliest Christianity to 1453*. Maryknoll, NY: Orbis, 2001.

Isaac the Syrian. *Daily Readings with Isaac the Syrian*. Edited by A. M. Allchin. Springfield, IL: Templegate, 1989.

Isaacson, Walter. *Benjamin Franklin: An American Life*. New York: Simon & Schuster, 2003.

Jacobs, Alan. *Original Sin: A Cultural History*. New York: HarperOne, 2009.

Janz, Denis R., and Shirley E. Jordon. *Reformation Reader: Primary Texts with Introductions*. Minneapolis: Augsburg Fortress, 1999.

Jenkins, Philip. *The Lost History of Christianity: The Thousand-Year Golden Age of the Church in the Middle East, Africa, and Asia—and How It Died.* New York: HarperCollins, 2008.

———. *The New Faces of Christianity: Believing the Bible in the Global South.* New York: Oxford University Press, 2006.

Jenson, Robert W. *Canon and Creed.* Louisville: Westminster John Knox, 2010.

Jerome. *Against Helvidius (The Perpetual Virginity of Blessed Mary).* http://www.newadvent.org/fathers/3007.htm.

John of Damascus. *An Exposition of the Orthodox Faith.* Bk. 4, ch. 13. http://www.newadvent.org/fathers/33044.htm.

———. *St. John Damascene on Holy Images: Pros Tous Diaballontas tas Agias Eikonas.* Translated by Mary H. Allies. London: Thomas Baker, 1898.

John of the Cross. *John of the Cross: Selected Writings.* Edited by Kieran Kavanaugh. Mahwah, NJ: Paulist, 1987.

Johnson, Curtis N. *Socrates and the Immoralists.* Plymouth, UK: Lexington, 2008.

Jordan, David P. *The Revolutionary Career of Maximilien Robespierre.* Chicago: University of Chicago Press, 1985.

Julian of Norwich. *Revelations of Divine Love (Short Text and Long Text).* Translated by Elizabeth Spearing. New York: Penguin, 1998.

Junger, Sebastian. *Tribe: On Homecoming and Belonging.* New York: Hatchett, 2016.

Justin Martyr. *First Apology.* http://www.newadvent.org/fathers/0126.htm.

———. *Dialogue with Trypho, a Jew.* In *The Ante-Nicene Fathers: The Writings of the Fathers Down to A.D. 325,* vol. 1, *The Apostolic Fathers with Justin Martyr and Irenaeus),* edited by Rev. Alexander Roberts et al. New York: Cosimo, 2007.

Kahneman, Daniel. *Thinking Fast and Slow.* New York: Farrar, Straus and Giroux, 2011.

Kaiser, Walter C., et al. *Hard Sayings of the Bible.* Vol. 1. Downers Grove, IL: InterVarsity, 1996.

Kant, Immanuel. *Religion and Rational Theology.* Edited by Paul Guyer and Allen W. Wood. New York: Cambridge University Press, 2001.

Kasper, Walter. *Jesus the Christ.* New ed. New York: T. & T. Clark, 2011.

Kazin, Michael. *A Godly Hero: The Life of William Jennings Bryan.* New York: Random House, 2007.

Keating, Daniel A. *The Appropriation of Divine Life in Cyril of Alexandria.* New York: Oxford University Press, 2004.

Keeble, Brian, ed. *Every Man an Artist: Readings in the Traditional Philosophy of Art.* Bloomington, IN: World Wisdom, 2005.

Kellogg, Vernon. *Headquarter's Nights.* http://archive.org/stream/headquartersnighookell/headquartersnighookell_djvu.txt.

Kelly, J. N. D. *Early Christian Creeds.* London: Longman, 1972.

———. *Early Christian Doctrines.* Rev. ed. New York: HarperCollins, 1978.

Kelly-Gangi, Carol, ed. *Mother Theresa: Her Essential Wisdom.* New York: Fall River, 2006.

Kenny, Anthony. *The Rise of Modern Philosophy: A New History of Western Philosophy.* Vol. 3. New York: Oxford University Press, 2008.

Kerényi, Karl. *The Gods of the Greeks.* London: Thames and Hudson, 1951.

Kerr, Fergus. *Theology After Wittgenstein.* 2nd ed. London: SPCK, 1997.

Kerr, Nathan. *Christ, History and Apocalyptic: The Politics of Christian Mission.* Theopolitical Visions. Eugene, OR: Wipf & Stock, 2008.

Kidd, Thomas S. *The Great Awakening: The Roots of Evangelical Christianity in Colonial America*. New Haven, CT: Yale University Press, 2007.

Kierkegaard, Søren. *Fear and Trembling*, New York: Penguin, 2006.

———. *Concluding Unscientific Postscript to Philosophical Fragments*. Edited by Howard V. Hong and Edna H. Hong. Kierkegaard's Writings 12/1. Princeton, NJ: Princeton University Press, 1992.

———. *Papers and Journals: A Selection*. Edited by Alistair Hannay. New York: Penguin Classics, 1996.

———. *Philosophical Fragments*. London: Feather Trail, 2009.

———. *Works of Love*. Edited by Howard V. Hong and Edna H. Hong. Kierkegaard's Writings 16. Princeton, NJ: Princeton University Press, 1998.

Kilde, Jeanne Halgren. *When Church Became Theatre: The Transformation of Evangelical Architecture and Worship in Nineteenth-Century America*. New York: Oxford University Press, 2002.

King, Larry. Sam Brownback, Deepak Chopra, Dr. Barbara Forrest, John MacArthur, Dr. Jay Richards, Chris Shays. *Larry King Live*, CNN, August 23, 2005. http://transcripts.cnn.com/TRANSCRIPTS/0508/23/lkl.01.html.

King, Martin Luther. "An Experiment in Love." In *A Testament of Hope: The Essential Writings and Speeches of Martin Luther King, Jr.*, edited by James M. Washington, 16–20. Reprint ed. New York: HarperCollins, 1991.

———. "Faith in Man." Sermon. https://kinginstitute.stanford.edu/king-papers/documents/faith-man.

———. "Letter from a Birmingham City Jail." In *A Testament of Hope: The Essential Writings and Speeches of Martin Luther King, Jr.*, edited by James M. Washington, 289–302. Reprint ed. New York: HarperCollins, 1991.

———. "Love in Action." In *Strength to Love*, 31–42. Minneapolis: Fortress, 1981.

———. "Stride Towards Freedom." In *A Testament of Hope: The Essential Writings and Speeches of Martin Luther King, Jr.*, edited by James M. Washington, 417–90. Reprint ed. New York: HarperCollins, 1991.

———. *The Trumpet of Conscience*. Boston: Beacon, 2010.

———. "Walk for Freedom." In *A Testament of Hope: The Essential Writings and Speeches of Martin Luther King, Jr.*, edited by James M. Washington, 82–84. Reprint ed. New York: HarperCollins, 1991.

King, Ross. *Michelangelo and the Pope's Ceiling*. New York: Bloomsbery, 2003.

Kinnaman, David. "Lost and Found." Lecture. Nashville, October 23, 2012.

———. *You Lost Me: Why Young Christians Are Leaving Church . . . and Rethinking Faith*, Grand Rapids: Baker, 2011.

Kinnaman, David, and Gabe Lyons. *UnChristian*. Grand Rapids: Baker, 2007.

Klein, Linda Kay. *Pure: Inside the Evangelical Movement That Shamed a Generation of Young Women and How I Broke Free*. New York: Simon & Schuster, 2018.

Klosterman, Chuck. *I Wear the Black Hat: Grappling with Villains*. New York: Scribner, 2014.

———. *Sex, Drugs & Cocoa Puffs*. New York: Scribner, 2004.

Krapohl, Robert H., and Charles H. Lippy. *The Evangelicals: A Historical, Thematic, and Biographical Guide*. Westport, CT: Greenwood, 1999.

Krauss, Lawrence. "Ben Carson's Scientific Ignorance." *The New Yorker*, September 28, 2015. https://www.newyorker.com/news/news-desk/ben-carsons-scientific-ignorance.

———. *A Universe from Nothing: Why There Is Something Rather than Nothing.* New York: Simon & Schuster, 2012.

Krejčí, Jaroslav. *Before the European Challenge: The Great Civilizations of Asia and the Middle East.* Albany, NY: SUNY Press, 1990.

Laertius, Diogenes. *Diogenes Laertius.* Bks. 1–5. Translated by Robert Drew Hicks. Vol. 1 of *Lives of Eminent Philosophers.* Loeb Classical Library 184. CreateSpace, 2011.

LaHaye, Tim, and David Noebel. *Mind Siege: The Battle for Truth in the New Millennium.* Colorado Springs, CO: Word, 2000.

LaMott, Anne. *Traveling Mercies: Some Thoughts on Faith.* New York: Random House, 2000.

Lamoureux, Denis O. *I Love Jesus & I Accept Evolution.* Eugene, OR: Wipf & Stock, 2009.

Landy, Joshua, and Michael Saler. "Introduction: The Varieties of Modern Enchantment." In *The Re-Enchantment of the World: Secular Magic in a Rational Age,* edited by Landy and Saler, 1–14. California: Stanford University Press, 2009.

Langer, Susanne. *Philosophy in a New Key.* 3rd ed. Cambridge, MA: Harvard University Press, 1996.

Langley, Travis. "Necessary Evil Documentary: Exploring Super-Villainy." *Beyond Heroes and Villains* (blog), *Psychology Today,* October 22, 2013. http://www.psychologytoday.com/blog/beyond-heroes-and-villains/201310/necessary-evil-documentary-exploring-super-villainy.

Larsen, Jeff T., et al. "Turning Adversity to Advantage: On the Virtues of the Coactivation of Positive and Negative Emotions." In *A Psychology of Human Strengths: Fundamental Questions and Future Directions for a Positive Psychology,* edited by Lisa G. Aspinwall and Urusula M. Staudinger, 211–25. Washington, DC: American Psychological Association, 2013.

Larson, Craig Brian, and Brian Lowery, eds. *1001 Quotations that Connect: Timeless Wisdom for Preaching, Teaching, and Writing.* Grand Rapids: Zondervan, 2009.

Larson, Edward J. *Evolution: The Remarkable History of a Scientific Theory.* New York: Modern Library, 2004.

———. *Summer for the Gods: The Scopes Trial and America's Continuing Debate over Science and Religion.* New York: Basic, 2008.

Lash, Nicholas. "Considering the Trinity." *Modern Theology* 2/3 (1986) 169–284.

———. "Creation, Courtesy and Contemplation." In *The Beginning and the End of 'Religion',* 164–82. New York: Cambridge University Press, 1996.

———. "Ideology, Metaphor, and Analogy." In *Theology on the Way to Emmaus,* 95–119. Eugene, OR: Wipf & Stock, 1986.

———. "'Son of God': Reflections on a Metaphor." In *Theology on the Way to Emmaus,* 158–66. Eugene, OR: Wipf & Stock, 1986.

Lax, Eric. *Conversations with Woody Allen: His Films, the Movies, and Moviemaking.* New York: Knopf, 2009.

Lee, Kevin P. "Inherit the Myth: How William Jennings Bryan's Struggle with Social Darwinism and Legal Formalism Demythologize the Scopes Monkey Trial." *Campbell University of Law Review* 33 (2004) 347–82. http://scholarship.law.campbell.edu/cgi/viewcontent.cgi?article=1040&context=fac_sw.

L'Engle, Madeleine. *The Rock That Is Higher: Story as Truth.* Writers' Palette. Colorado Springs, CO: WaterBrook, 2002.

Levi, Primo. *The Reawakening*. Translated by Stuart Woolf. New York: Simon & Schuster, 1995.

Levine, Amy-Jill. "Introduction." In *The Historical Jesus in Context*. Princeton Readings in Religions. Princeton, NJ: Princeton University Press, 2006.

Lewis, C. S. *The Abolition of Man*. New York: HarperCollins, 1974.

———. "Introduction (On the Reading of Old Books)." In *St. Athanasius: On the Incarnation*, 3–10. Crestwood, NY: St. Vladimir's Seminary Press, 1993.

———. *Mere Christianity*. Nashville: Broadman & Holman Reference, 1999.

———. *Reflections on the Psalms*. New York: Harvest, 1958.

———. *Surprised by Joy: The Shape of My Early Life*. 1st ed. Orlando, FL: Harcourt, Brace, Jovanovich, 1955.

———. *The Weight of Glory*. New York: HarperOne, 2009.

Lewis, W. H., ed. *Letters of C. S. Lewis*. New York: Harcourt, Brace, 1966.

Leibniz, Gottfried. *The Oxford Handbook of Philosophy of Religion*. Edited by William J. Wainwright. New York: Oxford University Press, 2005, 285.

Lincoln, Abraham. "Second Inaugural Address." March 4, 1865. Http://www.bartleby.com/124/pres32.html.

Lindberg, Carter. *The European Reformations*. Malden, MA: Blackwell, 1996.

Little, Jane. "Media Coverage of Religion." *C-Span*, January 9, 2014. http://www.c-span.org/video/?317096-1/media-coverage-religion.

Livingstone, E. A. *The Concise Oxford Dictionary of the Christian Church*. New York: Oxford University Press, 2006.

Livingstone, David N. *Darwin's Forgotten Defenders*. Grand Rapids: Eerdmans, 1987.

———. "Science, Region, and Religion: The Reception of Darwinism and Princeton, Belfast, and Edinburgh. In *Disseminating Darwinism: The Role of Place, Race, Religion, and Gender*, edited by Ronald L. Numbers and John Stenhouse, 7–38. Cambridge: Cambridge University Press, 2001.

Livingstone, David N., and Mark A. Noll. "B. B. Warfield (1851–1921): A Biblical Inerrantist as Evolutionist." *ISIS: A Journal of the History of Science* 91/2 (2000) 283–304.

Lombardo, Paul. *Three Generations, No Imbeciles: Eugenics, the Supreme Court, and Buck v. Bell*. Baltimore: Johns Hopkins University Press, 2008.

Loomba, Ania. *Colonialism/Postcolonialism*. New York: Routledge, 2005.

Louis C. K. "My Life Is Really Evil." September 12, 2010. https://www.youtube.com/watch?v=lC4FnfNKwUo.

Luther, Martin. *On the Freedom of a Christian: With Related Texts*, edited by Tryntje Helfferich. Indianapolis, IN: Hackett, 2013.

———. "To the Christian Nobility of the German Nation." In *Three Treatises to the Christian Nobility of the German Nation*, translated by Charles M. Jacobs. Minneapolis: Fortress, 1970.

Lyons, Eric. "The Myth of 'Factual' Bible Contradictions." *Apologetics Press*, 2003. http://www.apologeticspress.org/apcontent.aspx?category=6&article=40.

MacArthur, John. *The Battle For The Beginning: Creation, Evolution, and the Bible*. Nashville: Thomas Nelson, 2001.

———. "God's Warriors: Fighters for Faith." Interview by Larry King. *Larry King Live*, CNN, March 11, 2003. http://www.cnn.com/TRANSCRIPTS/0303/11/lkl.00.html.

———. "How to Study Your Bible." *Grace to You.* http://www.gty.org/resources/positions/p16/how-to-study-your-bible.

———. *Think Biblically!: Recovering a Christian Worldview.* Wheaton, IL: Crossway, 2003.

MacCulloch, Diarmaid. *Christianity: The First Three Thousand Years.* Reprint. New York: Penguin, 2011.

MacDonald, George. *Donal Grant.* New York: Routledge, 1883.

MacDowell, Josh. *The Bible Handbook of Difficult Verses: A Complete Guide to Answering the Tough Questions.* Eugene, OR: Harvest House, 2013.

Magee, Michael D. "Does Science Make Belief in God Obsolete?" *Academia*, July 16, 2008, 16. https://www.academia.edu/16141148/Does_science_make_belief_in_God_obsolete.

Machen, John Gresham. *Christianity and Liberalism.* Grand Rapids: Eerdmans, 2009.

Mahathera, Narada, ed. *The Buddha and His Teachings.* Mumbai, India: Jaico, 2006.

Maisel, Eric R. "The God-Bug Syndrome." *Rethinking Mental Health* (blog), *Psychology Today*, September 27, 2012. https://www.psychologytoday.com/us/blog/rethinking-mental-health/201209/the-god-bug-syndrome.

Mann, Neil. "The Thirteenth Cone." In *W. B. Yeats's A Vision: Explications and Contexts*, edited by Neil Mann et al. Clemson, SC: Clemson University Digital Press, 2012.

Mannion, Gerard, and Eduardus Van der Borght, eds. *John Calvin's Ecclesiology: Ecumenical Perspectives.* New York: T. & T. Clark, 2011.

Manning, Brennan. *Abba's Child: The Cry of the Heart for Intimate Belonging.* Colorado Springs: NavPress, 2002.

———. *The Relentless Tenderness of Jesus.* Grand Rapids: Baker, 2005.

Marsden, George. *Fundamentalism and American Culture.* New ed. New York: Oxford University Press, 2006.

———. *Understanding Fundamentalism and Evangelicalism.* Grand Rapids: Eerdmans, 1990.

Martel, Yann. *Life of Pi.* New York: Houghton Mifflin, 2001.

Martin, Fthr. James. "Brother Christian's Testament." *America Magazine*, November 14, 2015. https://www.americamagazine.org/content/all-things/dom-christians-testament.

Marty, Martin. *Martin Luther: A Life.* New York: Penguin, 2004.

———. *The Modern Schism: Three Paths to the Secular.* Eugene, OR: Wipf & Stock, 2012.

Marx, Karl. *A Contribution to the Critique of Hegel's 'Philosophy of Right'.* Cambridge Studies in the History and Theory of Politics. New York: Cambridge University Press, 1982.

Mayer, John. "Stop This Train." Track 7 on *Continuum*. Columbia, 2006.

McBride, Jennifer. *The Church for the World: A Theology of Public Witness.* New York: Oxford, 2012.

McCabe, Herbert. "Original Sin." In *God Still Matters*. London: Continuum, 2005.

McClymond, Michael J. *Familiar Stranger: An Introduction to Jesus of Nazareth.* Grand Rapids: Eerdmans, 2004.

McCormick, Neil. "Tom Petty: A Rock Star for the Ages." *The Telegraph*, June 16, 2012. http://www.telegraph.co.uk/culture/music/rockandpopfeatures/9334051/Tom-Petty-a-rock-star-for-the-ages.html.

McDowell, Josh. *More Than a Carpenter.* Wheaton, IL: Tyndale, 1987.

McEvoy, Marc. "Interview: John Green." *Sydney Morning Herald*, January 21, 2012. https://www.smh.com.au/entertainment/books/interview-john-green-20120119-1q71w.html.

McGaughy, Lane, et al. *The Authentic Letters of Paul: a New Reading of Paul's Rhetoric and Meaning*. Ebook. Salem, OR: Polebridge, 2010.

McGrath, Alister E. *Dawkins' God: From The Selfish Gene to The God Delusion*. 2nd ed. Malden, MA: Wiley-Blackwell, 2015.

———. *Theology: The Basic Readings*. Malden, MA: Blackwell, 2008.

McGuckin, John Anthony. *The Westminster Handbook to Patristic Theology*. Louisville: Westminster John Knox, 2004.

McIrney, Ralph, ed. *Thomas Aquinas: Selected Writings*. 3rd ed. New York: Penguin, 1999.

McLeod, Saul. "The Milgram Shock Experiment." *Simply Psychology*, 2017. http://www.simplypsychology.org/milgram.html.

Meeks, Wayne A. "A Nazi New Testament Professor Reads His Bible: The Strange Case of Gerhard Kittel." In *The Idea of Biblical Interpretation: Essays in Honor of James L. Kugel*, edited by Hindy Najman and Judith H. Newman. Leiden: Brill, 2004.

Meier, John. *A Marginal Jew: Re-Thinking the Historical Jesus*. Vol. 2: *Mentor, Message, Miracles*. New York: Doubleday, 1994.

Mencken, H. L. *H.L. Mencken on Religion*. Edited by S. T. Joshi. Amherst, NY: Prometheus, 2002.

Mentan, Tatah. *Decolonizing Democracy from Western Cognitive Imperialism*. Mankon, Bamenda, Cameroon: Langaa RPCIGP, 2015.

Mercadante, Linda. "Good News about the 'Spiritual but Not Religious.'" *CNN Belief Blog*, February 22, 2014. http://religion.blogs.cnn.com/2014/02/22/good-news-about-the-spiritual-but-not-religious/.

Merrick, J. and Stephen M. Garrett. "Introduction: On Debating Inerrancy." In *Five Views on Biblical Inerrancy*. Ebook. Counterpoints: Bible and Theology. Grand Rapids: Zondervan, 2013.

Merritt, Jonathan. "David Brooks on Character, Sin, and Rumors about His Religious Journey." *Washington Post*, May 1, 2015. https://www.washingtonpost.com/national/religion/qand038a-david-brooks-on-character-sin-and-rumors-about-his-religious-journey/2015/05/01/dd4203a6-f046-11e4-8050-839e9234b303_story.html?utm_term=.33aab911ddfb.

Merton, Thomas. *New Seeds of Contemplation*. New York: New Directions, 2007.

———. *Raids on the Unspeakable*. New York: New Directions, 1966.

Metzinger, Thomas. *The Ego Tunnel*. Philadelphia: Basic, 2010.

Meyendorff, John. *St. Gregory Palamas and Orthodox Spirituality*. Translated by Adele Fisk. Crestwood, NY: St. Vladimir's Seminary Press, 1974.

Milavec, Aaron. *The Didache: Faith, Hope, & Life of the Earliest Christian Communities, 50–70 C.E.* Mahwah, NJ: Newman, 2003.

Milbank, John, and Slavoj Zizek. *The Monstrosity of Christ: Paradox or Dialectic?* Edited by Creston Davis. Cambridge, MA: MIT Press, 2009.

Milburn, Robert. *Early Christian Art and Architecture*. Berkeley: University of California Press, 1988.

Miller, Barbara Stoler, trans. "Krishna's Council in Time of War (The Second Teaching: Philosophy and Spiritual Discipline)." In *The Bhagavad-Gita*, 62. New York: Random House, 2004.

Miller, Keith D. *Martin Luther King's Biblical Epic: His Final, Great Speech.* Jackson: University of Mississippi Press, 2012.

Miller, Perry. "Errand into the Wilderness." In *American Religious History*, edited by Amanda Porterfield, 27–42. Malden, MA: Blackwell, 2002.

Milson, Andrew J., et al., eds. "John Cotton, c.1641, Spiritual Milk for American Babes Drawn Out of the Breasts of Both Testaments for Their Soul's Nourishment." In *Readings in American Educational Thought: From Puritanism to Progressivism*, 1. Information Age, 2004.

Misener, Jessica, Why I Miss Being a Born Again Christian." *Buzzfeed*, May 21, 2014. http://www.buzzfeed.com/jessicamisener/why-i-miss-being-a-born-again-christian.

Mitchell, Margaret M. *Paul, the Corinthians and the Birth of Christian Hermeneutics.* New York: Cambridge University Press, 2010, p.3.

Moffett, Samuel. *A History of Christianity in Asia: Beginnings to 1500.* Maryknoll, NY: Orbis, 1998.

Mohler, Albert. "When the Bible Speaks, God Speaks: The Classic Doctrine of Biblical Inerrancy." In *Five Views on Biblical Inerrancy* Ebook. Counterpoints: Bible and Theology. Grand Rapids: Zondervan, 2013.

Moltmann, Jürgen, ed. "Eberhard Jüngel." In *How I Have Changed: Reflections on Thirty Years of Theology*, 3–12. Harrisburg, PA: Trinity, 1998.

Monk, Ray. *Bertrand Russell: The Spirit of Solitude, 1872–1921.* New York: Free Press, 1996.

Monro, D. B. *The Modes of Ancient Greek Music.* Oxford: Clarendon, 1894.

Morrill, Bruce T. "Christ's Sacramental Presence in the Eucharist: A Biblical-Pneumatological Approach to the Mystery of Faith." *American Theological Inquiry* 4/2 (2011) 3–25.

Morse, Christopher. *Not Every Spirit: A Dogmatics of Christian Disbelief.* New York: T. & T. Clark, 1994.

Muggeridge, Malcolm. "The True Crisis of Our Time." 1985. https://smbtv.org/resources-links/muggeridge-true-crisis-audio-transcript.

Mundell, E. J. "U.S. Teens Brimming with Self-Esteem." *U.S. News and World Report*, November 12, 2008. http://health.usnews.com/health-news/family-health/brain-and-behavior/articles/2008/11/12/us-teens-brimming-with-self-esteem.

Muñoz, Vincent Phillip. *God and the Founders: Madison, Washington, and Jefferson.* New York: Cambridge University Press, 2009.

Murphy, Nancey. "Human Nature: Historical, Scientific, and Religious Issues." In *Whatever Happened to the Soul? Scientific and Theological Portraits of Human Nature*, edited by Warren Brown et al. Minneapolis: Augsburg Fortress, 1998.

Murphy-O'Connor, Jerome. *Paul: A Critical Life.* Rev. ed. Oxford: Oxford University Press, 1998.

Murray, Andrew. *Absolute Surrender.* CreateSpace, 2017.

Murray, Douglas. "Atheists vs. Dawkins: My Fellow Atheists, It's Time We Admitted that Religion Has Some Points in Its Favour." *Spectator*, February 2013. http://www.spectator.co.uk/features/8839081/call-off-the-faith-wars/.

National WWII Museum. "Research Starters: Worldwide Deaths in World War II. "https://www.nationalww2museum.org/students-teachers/student-resources/research-starters/research-starters-worldwide-deaths-world-war.

Nee, Watchman. *The Release of the Spirit.* New York: Christian Fellowship, 2000.

Nichols, James Hastings. *Corporate Worship in the Reformed Tradition*. Philadelphia: Westminster, 1968.

Niebuhr, H. Richard. *The Meaning of Revelation*. Louisville: Westminster John Knox, 2006.

Niebuhr, Reinhold. *Man's Nature and His Communities*. New York: Scribner, 1965.

Nietzsche, Friedrich. *The Birth of Tragedy and the Case of Wagner*. New York: Vintage, 1967.

———. *The Gay Science*. Edited by Walter Kaufmann. New York: Vintage, 1974.

———. *On the Genealogy of Morals and Ecce Homo*. Edited by Walter Kaufman. New York: Vintage, 1989.

Nineham, Dennis. "Epilogue." In *The Myth of God Incarnate*, edited by John Hick. Louisville: Westminster, 1977.

Noll. Mark A. "Common Sense Traditions and American Evangelical Thought." *American Quarterly* 37/2 (1985) 216–38. doi:10.2307/2712899.

———. *The Old Religion in a New World: The History of North American Christianity*. Grand Rapids, MI: Wm. B. Eerdmans, 2002.

———. *The Princeton Theology, 1812–1921: Scripture, Science, and Theological Method from Archibald Alexander to Benjamin Warfield*. Grand Rapids: Baker, 2001.

———. *The Scandal of the Evangelical Mind*. Grand Rapids, MI: Wm. B. Eerdmans, 1995.

———. *Turning Points: Decisive Moments in the History of Christianity*. 2nd ed. Grand Rapids: Baker Academic, 2000.

Nouwen, Henri. *With Open Hands*. Notre Dame, IN: Ave Maria, 1995.

Numbers, Ronald L. *The Creationists: From Scientific Creationism to Intelligent Design*. Expanded ed. Los Angeles: University of California Press, 2006.

Oberman, Heiko A. *Luther: Man Between God and the Devil*. Translated by Eileen Walliser-Schwarzbart. New Haven, CT: Yale University Press, 2006.

Oberst, Conor. "Let's Not Shit Ourselves (To Love and to Be Loved)." Track 13 on *Lifted or The Story Is in the Soil, Keep Your Ear to the Ground*. Saddle Creek 2002.

Olendzk, Andrew. *Unlimiting Mind: The Radically Experiential Psychology of Buddhism*. Somerville, MA: Wisdom, 2010.

Olenick, Richard P., et al. *The Mechanical Universe: Introduction to Mechanics and Heat*. Cambridge: Cambridge University Press, 2007.

Olson, David. *The World on Paper: The Conceptual and Cognitive Implications of Writing and Reading*. Cambridge: Cambridge University Press, 1994.

Olson, Jeannine E. *Calvin and Social Welfare: Deacons and the Bourse Française*. Cranberry, NJ: Associated University Presses, 1989.

Olson, Roger E. "The 'Judge Judged in Our Place': Substitutionary Atonement Reclaimed." *Patheos,* January 10, 2019. https://www.patheos.com/blogs/rogereolson/2019/01/the-judge-judged-in-our-place-substitutionary-atonement-reclaimed/.

———. *The Mosaic of Christian Belief: Twenty Centuries of Unity and Diversity*. Downers Grove, IL: InterVarsity, 2002.

Origen. *Contra Celsum*. Translated by Frederick Crombie. In *Ante-Nicene Fathers*, vol. 4, edited by Alexander Roberts et al.. Buffalo, NY: Christian Literature, 1885. http://www.newadvent.org/fathers/04163.htm.

Otto, Rudolf. *The Idea of the Holy*. Translated by John W. Harvey. New York: Oxford University Press, 1958.

Pack, David C. "You Can Prove the Bible's Authority!" May 31, 2013. http://realtruth. org/articles/130429-001.html.

Packer, J. I. "The Inspiration of the Bible." In *The Origin of the Bible*, edited by Philip Wesley Comfort, 29–36. Carol Stream, IL: Tyndale, 2003.

Padilla, Steve. "More Fuel for Faith-vs.-Science Debate." *Los Angeles Times*, May 24, 2008. https://www.latimes.com/archives/la-xpm-2008-may-24-me-beliefs24-story.html.

Pagels, Elaine. *Adam, Eve, and the Serpent: Sex and Politics in Early Christianity.* New York: Random House, 1989.

Palaver, Wolfgang. *René Girard's Mimetic Theory.* East Lansing: Michigan State University Press, 2013.

Pannenberg, Wolfhart. *Systematic Theology.* Vol. 3. Translated by G. W. Bromiley. Gottingen: Vanderhoeck & Ruprecht, 1993.

Parish, Helen L. *A Short History of the Reformation.* New York: I. B. Tauris, 2018.

Pascal, Blaise. *Pensées.* Translated by A. J. Krailsheimer. New York: Penguin, 1995.

———. *Pensées.* Translated by John Warrington. http://www.stat.ucla.edu/history/ pascal_wager.pdf.

Patton, Alison. "From Oprah to Chopra: Is All This Positive Thinking Really Making Us Feel Better?" *Huffington Post*, March 15, 2013. http://www.huffingtonpost.com/ alison-patton/from-oprah-to-chopra-is-a_b_2441855.html.

Patte, Daniel. *Religious Dimensions of Biblical Texts.* Atlanta: Scholars, 1990.

Patterson, Stephen. *The God of Jesus: The Historical Jesus and the Search for Meaning.* Harrisburg, PA: Trinity, 1998.

Pearson, Karl. *National Life from the Standpoint of Science.* London: A. & C. Black, 1905. https://archive.org/details/nationallifefromoopearrich/page/n8.

Pelikan, Jaroslav. *The Christian Tradition: A History of the Development of Doctrine.* Vol. 1: *The Emergence of the Catholic Tradition (100–600).* Chicago: University of Chicago Press, 1975.

———. *Jesus Through the Centuries: His Place in the History of Culture.* New Haven, CT: Yale University Press, 1985.

———. "The Need for Creeds." Interview by Krista Tippet. *On Being*, September 19, 2003. https://onbeing.org/programs/jaroslav-pelikan-the-need-for-creeds/.

Percy, Walker. *Lost in the Cosmos: The Last Self-Help Book.* New York: Farrar, Straus and Giroux, 1983.

———. *Love in the Ruins.* New York: Picador, 1971.

———. *Signposts from a Strange Land.* New York: Farrar, Straus and Giroux, 1991.

Perrin, Joseph-Marie, and Gustave Thibon. *Simone Weil as We Knew Her.* New York: Routledge, 2003.

Peterson, Christopher, et al. "Catastrophizing and Untimely Death." *Psychological Science* 9 (1998) 127–30.

Pew Research Center. "America's Changing Religious Landscape." Pew Forum, May 12, 2015. http://www.pewforum.org/2015/05/12/americas-changing-religious-landscape/.

———. "The Changing Religious Composition of the U.S." Chapter 1 of *America's Changing Religious Landscape.* Pew Forum, May 12, 2015. https://www.pewforum. org/2015/05/12/chapter-1-the-changing-religious-composition-of-the-u-s/.

———. "'Nones' on the Rise." Pew Forum, October 9, 2012. https://www.pewforum. org/2012/10/09/nones-on-the-rise/.

———. "Public's Views on Human Evolution." Pew Forum, December 30, 2013. https://www.pewforum.org/2013/12/30/publics-views-on-human-evolution/.

———. "Section 6: Religion and Social Values." June 4, 2012. http://www.people-press. org/2012/06/04/section-6-religion-and-social-values/.

Phillips, Emo. "The Best God Joke Ever—and It's Mine!" *The Guardian*, September 29, 2005. https://www.theguardian.com/stage/2005/sep/29/comedy.religion.

Phillipson, Nicholas. *Adam Smith: An Enlightened Life*. New Haven, CT: Yale University Press. 2010.

Piper, John. *Future Grace*. Colorado Springs: Multnomah, 1995.

Plantinga, Alvin, and Nicholas Wolterstorff. *Faith And Rationality: Reason and Belief in God*. Notre Dame, IN: University of Notre Dame Press, 1984.

Plato. *Apology*. Translated by Benjamin Jowett. Internet Classics Archive. http://classics. mit.edu/Plato/apology.html.

———. *Gorgias*. Translated by Benjamin Jowett. Internet Classics Archive. http:// classics.mit.edu/Plato/gorgias.html.

———. *Meno*. Translated by Benjamin Jowett. Internet Classics Archive. http://classics. mit.edu/Plato/meno.html.

———. *Republic*. Translated by Benjamin Jowett. Internet Classics Archive. http:// classics.mit.edu/Plato/republic.8.vii.html.

Platt, David. *Radical*. Colorado Springs: Multnomah, 2010.

Polkinghorne, John. *Science and Christian Belief: Theological Reflections of a Bottom-Up Thinker*. New York: Sheldon, 1994.

Pope Benedict XVI. *Caritas in Veritate*. http://www.vatican.va/holy_father/benedict_ xvi/encyclicals/documents/hf_ben-xvi_enc_20090629_caritas-in-veritate_ en.html—_edn61.

Pope Boniface VIII. *Unam Sanctum*. 1302. Medieval Sourcebook. https://sourcebooks. fordham.edu/source/b8-unam.asp.

Pope Francis. *Evangelii Gaudium*. http://www.vatican.va/holy_father/francesco/apost_ exhortations/documents/papa-francesco_esortazione-ap_20131124_evangelii- gaudium_en.html—No_to_the_new_idolatry_of_money.

Pope John Paul II. *Address to Pontifical Academy of Sciences*. 1996. http://www.ewtn. com/library/papaldoc/jp961022.htm—return.

———. *Ut Unum Sint* "On Commitment to Ecumenism." 1995. http://www.vatican. va/holy_father/john_paul_ii/encyclicals/documents/hf_jp-ii_enc_25051995_ut- unum-sint_en.html#-B.

"Pope's Address to Popular Movements." *Zenit*, July 9, 2015. http://www.zenit.org/en/ articles/pope-s-address-to-popular-movements.

Popkin, Richard Henry, and Avrum Stroll. *Philosophy*. Reprint ed. Burlington, MA: Elsevier, 2007.

Porter, Stanley E. *Reading the Gospels Today*. Grand Rapids: Eerdmans, 2004.

Postman, Neil. *Technopoly: The Surrender of Culture to Technology*. New York: Vintage, 1993.

"Progressive." *Merriam-Webster Dictionary*. https://www.merriam-webster.com/ dictionary/progressive.

Prothero, Stephen. *American Jesus: How the Son of God Became a National Icon*. New York: Farrar, Straus and Giroux, 2003.

Raboteau, Alan J. "African Americans, Exodus, and the American Israel." In *Religion and American Culture: A Reader*, edited by David Hackett, 73–88. New York: Routledge, 2003.

———. *Slave Religion: The Invisible Institution in the Antebellum South.* New York: Oxford University Press, 2004.

Radford, Benjamin. "Teen Self-Esteem May Be Too High." *LiveScience*, December 5, 2008. http://www.livescience.com/3111-teen-esteem-high.html.

Raeikkoenen, Katri, et al. "Effects of Optimism, Pessimism, and Trait Anxiety on Ambulatory Blood Pressure and Mood During Everyday Life." *Journal of Personality and Social Psychology* 76 (1999) 104–13.

Ralkowski, Mark. *Louis C.K. and Philosophy: You Don't Get to Be Bored.* Chicago: Open Court, 2016.

Rappaport, Roy A. *Ritual and Religion in the Making of Humanity.* Cambridge Studies in Social and Cultural Anthropology. New York: Cambridge University Press, 2004.

Ricoeur, Paul. "Toward a Hermeneutic of the Idea of Revelation." In *Essays on Biblical Interpretation*, edited by L. S. Mudge, 73–118. Minneapolis: Fortress, 1980.

Rilke, Rainer Maria. *Rilke's Book of Hours: Love Poems to God.* Translated by Anita Barrows and Joanna Macy. New York: Riverhead, 1996.

Roberts, Alexander, et al., eds. *The Ante-Nicene Fathers: The Writings of the Fathers Down to A.D. 325.* Vol. 1: *The Apostolic Fathers with Justin Martyr and Irenaeus.* Edited by Alexander Roberts et al. New York: Cosimo, 2007.

Roberts, Dana L. *Christian Mission: How Christianity Became a World Religion.* Malden, MA: Wiley-Blackwell, 2009.

Robertson, Edwin, ed. *Dietrich Bonhoeffer's Christmas Sermons.* Translated by Edwin Robertson. Grand Rapids: Zondervan, 2005.

Rohane, Kyle. "Are Pastors Discarding the 'Evangelical' Label?" *Christianity Today*, November 21, 2016. http://www.christianitytoday.com/pastors/2016/november-web-exclusives/are-evangelical-pastors-discarding-evangelical-label.html.

Rohr, Richard. *Eager to Love: The Alternative Way of Francis of Assisi.* Cincinnati: Franciscan, 2014.

———. *Falling Upward: A Spirituality for the Two Halves of Life.* San Francisco: Jossey-Bass, 2011.

———. *Immortal Diamond: The Search for Our True Self.* San Francisco: Jossey-Bass, 2013.

———. "What Is the False Self?" Center for Action and Contemplation. August 7, 2017. https://cac.org/what-is-the-false-self-2017-08-07/.

Rohr, Richard, and John Bookser Feister. *Jesus' Plan for a New World: The Sermon on the Mount.* Cincinnati: St. Anthony Messenger, 1996.

Rothstein, Richard. *The Color of Law: A Forgotten History of How Our Government Segregated America.* New York: Norton, 2018.

Rousseau, Jean-Jacques. *Discourse on the Origin of Inequality.* New York: Classic Books America, 2009.

Rowling, J. K. *Harry Potter and the Sorcerer's Stone.* New York: Scholastic, 1998.

Russell, Bertrand. *Mysticism and Logic and Other Essays.* Ebook. Project Gutenberg. https://www.gutenberg.org/files/25447/25447-h/25447-h.htm.

Rutledge, Fleming. *The Crucifixion: Understanding the Death of Jesus Christ.* Grand Rapids: Eerdmans, 2015.

Ryken, Philip. "Liberal Arts in the New Jerusalem." In *Liberal Arts for the Christian Life*, edited by Jeffrey C. Davis and Philip G. Ryken, 293–302. Wheaton, IL: Crossway, 2012.

———. "Union with Christ: A Matter of Spiritual Life and Death." Ligonier, Oct ober 8, 2014. https://www.ligonier.org/blog/union-christ-matter-spiritual-life-and-death/.

Saad, Lydia. "Three in Four in U.S. Still See the Bible as Word of God." Gallup, July 12, 2012. http://www.gallup.com/poll/170834/three-four-bible-word-god.aspx.

Sabatier, Paul. *Life of St. Francis of Assisi*. Translated by Louise Seymour Houghton. CreateSpace, 2016.

Salomon, Joshua A. "Healthy Life Expectancy for 187 Countries, 1990–2010: A Systematic Analysis for the Global Burden Disease Study 2010." *The Lancet* 380/9859 (December 15, 2012) 2144–62. http://www.thelancet.com/journals/lancet/article/PIIS0140-6736%2812%2961690-0/abstract.

Schaeffer, Francis. *A Christian Manifesto*. Rev. ed. Wheaton, IL: Crossway, 1982.

Scholz, Susanne. "Preface." In *Biblical Studies Alternatively: An Introductory Reader*, edited by Susanne Scholz, xiii–xvii. Upper Saddle River, NJ: Prentice Hall, 2003.

Schreiner, Susan. *Are You Alone Wise?: The Search for Certainty in the Early Modern Era*. New York: Oxford University Press, 2011.

Schultz, Thom. "The Rise of the 'Done with Church' Population." *Churchleaders. com*, February 23, 2018. http://www.churchleaders.com/outreach-missions/outreach-missions-articles/177144-thom-schultz-rise-of-the-done-with-church-population.html#.VJYhLsnbVEJ.facebook.

The Scopes Trial (1925). University of Minnesota Law Library, Clarence Darrow Digital Collection. http://moses.law.umn.edu/darrow/trials.php?tid=7.

Second Helvetic Confession. http://www.ccel.org/ccel/schaff/creeds1.ix.ii.v.html.

"Secular." *Lexico*. https://www.lexico.com/en/definition/secular.

Seddon, Keith, ed. *An Outline of Cynic Philosophy: Antisthenes of Athens and Diogenes of Sinope in Diogenes Laertius*. Translated by C. D. Yonge. Morrisville, NC: Lulu, 2008.

Segovia, Fernando. *Decolonizing Biblical Studies: A View from the Margins*. New York: Orbis, 2000.

———. "Postcolonial Criticism and the Gospel of Matthew." In *Methods for Matthew*, edited by Mark Allan Powell, 194–238. New York: Cambridge University Press, 2009.

Selderhuis, Herman J., and Arnold Huijgen, eds. *Calvinus Pastor Ecclesiae: Papers of the Eleventh International Congress on Calvin Research*. Göttingen: Vandenhoeck & Ruprecht. 2016.

Selgin, Peter. *Confessions of a Left-Handed Man*. Iowa City: University of Iowa Press, 2011.

Seligman, Martin E. P. *Authentic Happiness: Using the New Positive Psychology to Realize Your Potential for Lasting Fulfillment*. New York: Atria, 2013.

Seller, Patricia. "Ted Turner at 75." *Fortune*, November 19, 2013. http://fortune.com/2013/11/19/ted-turner-at-75/.

Senn, Frank C. *Christian Liturgy: Catholic and Evangelical*. Minneapolis: Fortress, 1997.

Shelley, Bruce L. *Church History in Plain Language*. Dallas: Word, 1995.

Shermer, Michael. *The Believing Brain: From Ghosts and Gods to Politics and Conspiracies—How We Construct Beliefs and Reinforce Them as Truths.* New York: Times, 2011.

———. *Science Friction: Where the Known Meets the Unknown.* New York: Holt, 2005.

Shestov, Lev. *Athens and Jerusalem.* Edited by Ramona Fotiade. 2nd ed. Athens: Ohio University Press, 2016.

Shestov, Lev. "Kierkegaard and Dostoevsky." Lecture. Academy of Philosophy and Religion, Paris, 1935. http://shestov.phonoarchive.org/sk/sk_01.html.

Simon, Paul. "Slip Slidin' Away." Track 1 on *Greatest Hits, Etc.* Columbia, 1977.

Shuler, Bill. "Anne Rice Quits Christianity—10 Thoughts on Jesus and the Church." *Fox News Network,* August 8, 2010. http://www.foxnews.com/opinion/2010/08/08/rev-shuler-anne-rice-christianity-quit-christ-pharisees-god-love-forgiveness.html.

Singh, Sadhu Sundar. *Reality and Religion: Meditations on God, Man and Nature.* London: MacMillan, 1924.

Smith, Christian. *The Bible Made Impossible: Why Biblicism Is Not a Truly Evangelical Reading of Scripture.* Grand Rapids: Brazos, 2011.

Smith, Christian, et al. "Roundtable on the Sociology of Religion: Twenty-Three Theses on the Status of Religion in American Sociology—a Mellon Working Group Reflection." *Journal of the American Academy of Religion* 81/4 (2013) 903–38.

Smith, Gregory A., and Jessica Martinez. "How the Faithful Voted: A Preliminary 2016 Analysis." Pew Research Center, November 9, 2016. http://www.pewresearch.org/fact-tank/2016/11/09/how-the-faithful-voted-a-preliminary-2016-analysis/.

Smith, James K. A. *You Are What You Love: The Spiritual Power of Habit.* Grand Rapids: Brazos, 2016.

Smith, Ted A. *The New Measures: A Theological History of Democratic Practice.* New York: Cambridge University Press, 2007.

Snyder, C. R., et al. "The Future of Positive Psychology: A Declaration of Independence." In *Handbook of Positive Psychology,* edited by C. R. Snyder and S. J. Lopez, 751–67. New York: Oxford University Press, 2002.

Solomon, Sheldon, et al. *The Worm at the Core: On the Role of Death in Life.* New York: Random House, 2016.

Solzhenitsyn, Aleksandr. *The Gulag Archipelago Abridged: An Experiment in Literary Investigation.* New York: Harper Collins, 2007.

Sontag, Susan. *As Consciousness Is Harnessed to Flesh: Journals and Notebooks, 1964–1980,* edited by David Rieff. New York: Farrar, Strauss and Giroux, 2012.

Southern Baptist Convention. "Resolution on Abortion." St. Louis, Missouri, 1971. http://www.sbc.net/resolutions/13.

Spencer, Herbert. *The Principles of Biology of 1864.* Vol. 1. Charleston, SC: BiblioLife, 2009.

Sproul, R. C. *Can I Trust the Bible? Crucial Questions.* Lake Mary, FL: Reformation Trust, 2009.

———. *Chosen by God.* Wheaton, IL: Tyndale, 1986.

Spurgeon, Charles. "The Poor Man's Friend: A Sermon (No. 1037)." http://www.blueletterbible.org/commentaries/comm_view.cfm?AuthorID=10&contentID=3677&commInfo=16&topic=Sermons&ar=Mar_9_29.

Staniloae, Dumitru. *Orthodox Dogmatic Theology: The Experience of God.* Vol. 1: *Revelation and Knowledge of the Triune God.* Brookline, MA: Holy Cross Orthodox, 2005.

———. *Orthodox Spirituality: A Practical Guide for the Faithful and a Definitive Manual for the Scholar.* Translated by Archimandrite Jerome (Newville). Ebook. South Canaan, PA: St. Tikhon's Seminary Press, 2013.

Stanley, Brian. *The Global Diffusion of Evangelicalism: The Age of Billy Graham and John Stott.* History of Evangelicalism, People, Movements and Ideas in the English-Speaking World. Downers Grove, IL: InterVarsity, 2013.

Stanley, Charles. *The Spirit-Filled Life: Discover the Joy of Surrendering to the Holy Spirit.* Nashville: Thomas Nelson, 2014.

Stark, Rodney. "Epidemics, Network, and the Rise of Christianity." *Semeia* 56 (1992) 164–65.

Stedman, Chris. "What Oprah Gets Wrong about Atheism." *CNN Belief Blog*, October 16, 2013. http://religion.blogs.cnn.com/2013/10/16/what-oprah-gets-wrong-about-atheism/Opinion.

Steinmetz, David C. "The Superiority of Pre-Critical Exegesis." In *The Theological Interpretation of Scripture: Classic and Contemporary Readings*, edited by Stephen E. Fowl, 26–38. Malden, MA: Wiley-Blackwell, 1997.

———. "Why the Reformers Read the Fathers." *Christianity Today*, October 1, 2003. http://www.christianitytoday.com/ch/2003/issue80/5.10.html.

Sterelny, Kim. *Dawkins vs. Gould: Survival of the Fittest.* Cambridge: Icon, 2007.

Stevenson, Tyler Wigg. *Brand Jesus: Christianity in a Consumerist Age.* Ebook. New York: Seabury, 2007.

Stott, John. *The Cross of Christ.* Downers Grove, IL: InterVarsity, 2006.

———. "'In Christ': The Meaning and Implications of the Gospel of Jesus Christ." C. S. Lewis Institute, July 15, 2013. http://www.cslewisinstitute.org/In_Christ_page1.

Strobel, Lee. *The Case for Christianity Answer Book.* Grand Rapids: Zondervan, 2014.

Sugirtharajah, R. S. "Postcolonial Notes on the King James Bible." In *The King James Bible after Four Hundred Years: Literary, Linguistic, and Cultural Influences*, edited by Hannibal Hamlin and Norman W. Jones, 146–63. New York: Cambridge, 2010.

"Suicide Statistics." American Foundation for Suicide Prevention. https://afsp.org/about-suicide/suicide-statistics/.

Sullivan, John Jeremiah. "Upon This Rock." In *Pulphead: Essays.* New York: Farrar, Strauss and Giroux, 2011.

"Super." *Latdict: Latin Dictionary and Grammar Resource.* http://www.latin-dictionary.net/search/latin/super.

Svendsen, Lars. *A Philosophy of Evil.* Translated by Kerri Pierce. Dalkey Archive, 2010.

Sweetnam, Mark S., and R. Todd Mangum. *The Scofield Bible: Its History and Impact on the Evangelical Church.* Colorado Springs, CO: InterVarsity, 2009.

Swift, Art. "Americans' Trust in Mass Media Sinks to New Low." Gallup, September 14, 2016. https://news.gallup.com/poll/195542/americans-trust-mass-media-sinks-new-low.aspx.

Swindal, James C., and Harry J. Gensler, eds. *The Sheed and Ward Anthology of Catholic Philosophy.* New York: Rowman & Littlefield, 2005.

Sydow, Momme von. "Charles Darwin: a Christian Undermining Christianity? On Self-Undermining Dynamics of Ideas Between Belief and Science." In *Science and*

Beliefs: From Natural Philosophy to Natural Science, 1700–1900, edited by David M. Knight and Matthew D. Eddy, 141–56. Burlington: Ashgate, 2005.

Tallis, Raymond. "Does Evolution Explain Our Behaviour?" *On the Human*, National Humanities Center, September 28, 2009. http://nationalhumanitiescenter.org/on-the-human/2009/09/does-evolution-explain-our-behaviour/.

Taubes, Jacob. *The Political Theology of Paul*. Translated by Dana Hollander. Stanford, CA: Stanford University Press, 2004.

Taylor, Charles. *A Secular Age*. Cambridge, MA: Belknap, 2007.

Taylor, Derrick Bryson. "Oprah Admits the World Is a 'Mess.'" *Essence*, August 24, 2011. http://www.essence.com/2011/08/24/oprah-admits-the-world-is-a-mess/.

Taylor, John. *Bible Contradictions?* Lulu, 2012.

Taylor, Mark C. *After God*. Chicago: University of Chicago Press, 2009.

Taylor, Shelley E., et al. "Psychological Resources, Positive Illusions, and Health." *American Psychologist* 55 (2000) 99–109.

Tertullian. *Against Praxeas*. http://www.newadvent.org/fathers/0317.htm.

Thackeray, William Makepeace. *Vanity Fair*. Ware, Hertfordshire: Wordsworth Editions Limited, 1998.

Thejanlynn. "Notes from Q." *The View From Her* (blog), May 3, 2010. https://theviewfromher.com/2010/05/03/notes-from-q/.

Thirty-Nine Articles of Relgion. http://anglicansonline.org/basics/thirty-nine_articles.html.

"This Pig Wants to Party: Maurice Sendak's Latest." *Fresh Air*, NPR, September 20, 2011. http://www.npr.org/2011/09/20/140435330/this-pig-wants-to-party-maurice-sendaks-latest.

Thompson, Augustine. *Francis of Assisi: A New Biography*. Ithaca, NY: Cornell University Press, 2012.

Tillich, Paul. *Systematic Theology*. 3 vols. Chicago: University of Chicago, 1967.

———. "Two Types of Philosophy of Religion." In *Theology of Culture*, edited by Robert Kimball. New York: Oxford University Press, 1964.

Tippett, Krista. "Moral Man and Immoral Society: Rediscovering Reinhold Niebuhr." Interview with Paul Elie, Jean Bethke Elshtain, and Robin Lovin. *On Being*, October 25, 2007. https://onbeing.org/programs/paul-elie-jean-bethke-elshtain-and-robin-lovin-moral-man-and-immoral-society-rediscovering-reinhold-niebuhr/.

Tolkien, J. R. R. *The Fellowship of the Ring: Being the First Part of The Lord of the Rings*. New York: Random House, 1986.

Tolstoy, Leo. *A Confession*. Translated by Aylmer Maude. Dover Books on Western Philosophy. Mineola, NY: Dover, 2005.

Torrance, Thomas F. *Incarnation: The Person and Life of Christ*. Edited by Robert T. Walker. Downers Grove, IL: InterVarsity, 2008.

———. "Introduction." In *The School of Faith: The Catechisms of the Reformed Church*, cxiii–cxiv. Eugene, OR: Wipf & Stock, 1996.

Tozer, A. W. *The Knowledge of the Holy*. New York: HarperCollins, 1961.

———. *The Pursuit of God*. Edited by James L. Snyder. Ventura, CA: Regal, 2013.

Tracy, James D. *Erasmus of the Low Countries*. Berkeley, CA: University of California Press, 1996.

"Trump Off Camera: The Man Behind the 'In-Your-Face Provocateur.'" *Fresh Air*, NPR, August 23, 2016. http://www.npr.org/2016/08/23/491037719/trump-off-camera-the-man-behind-the-in-your-face-provocateur.

"Trump Warns GOPers: 'Anybody Who Hits Me, We're Gonna Hit 10 Times Harder.'" *Fox News Insider*, November 3, 2015. http://insider.foxnews.com/2015/11/03/donald-trump-warns-republican-candidates-about-using-negative-ads-against-him.

Turretin, Francis. *The Doctrine of Scripture (Locus 2 of Institutio Theologiae Elencticae)*, edited by John W. Beardslee III. Grand Rapids: Baker, 1981.

Tweedy, Jeff, et al. "Theologians." Track 10 on *A Ghost Is Born*. Nonesuch, 2004.

Twelve Steps and Twelve Traditions. 14th ed. New York: Alcoholics Anonymous, 2004.

Tyrrell, George. *Christianity at the Cross-Roads*. London: Longmans, Green, 1910.

Tyson, Neil deGrasse. "The Perimeter of Ignorance." *Natural History*, November 2005. https://www.haydenplanetarium.org/tyson/essays/2005-11-the-perimeter-of-ignorance.php.

UNICEF. "12,000 Fewer Children Perish Daily in 2010 than in 1990." http://www.unicefusa.org/news/releases/unicef-believes-in-zero.html.

United Methodist Church. *The Articles of Religion of the Methodist Church*. 1784. http://www.umc.org/what-we-believe/the-articles-of-religion-of-the-methodist-church.

Updike, John. *In the Beauty of the Lillies*. 3rd ed. New York: Random House, 2013.

———. *Rabbit Is Rich*. New York: Random House, 1981.

———. *Rabbit Redux*. New York: Random House, 1999.

Van Biema, David. "Christians Wrong About Heaven, Says Bishop." *Time*, February 7, 2008. http://www.time.com/time/world/article/0,8599,1710844,00.html.

Veyne, Paul. *Did the Greeks Believe in Their Myths?: An Essay on the Constitutive Imagination*. Translated by Paula Wissing. Chicago: University of Chicago Press, 1988.

Viola, Frank. *Beyond Bible Study: Finding Jesus Christ in Scripture*. 2007. http://www.ptmin.org/beyond.pdf.

Vitali, Ali. "Melania Stumps for Donald Trump: 'He Will Punch Back 10 Times Harder.'" *NBC News*, April 4, 2016. http://www.nbcnews.com/politics/2016-election/melania-stumps-donald-trump-he-will-punch-back-10-times-n550641.

Voltaire. *OEuvres Complètes De Voltaire: Commentaires Sur Corneille Appendice*. Paris: Garnier Frères, 1880.

Wagner, Meg. "As Trial Against Dylann Roof Begins, Families of Charleston Church Shooting Victims Still Show Mercy." *New York Daily News*, November 3, 2016. https://www.nydailynews.com/news/national/s-church-shooting-victims-families-forgive-dylann-roof-article-1.2855446.

Waligore, Joseph. "The Piety of the English Deists." *Intellectual History Review* 22/2 (2012) 181–97.

Walker, Renee E., et al. "Disparities and Access to Healthy Food in the United States: A Review of Food Deserts Literature." *Health & Place* 16 (2010) 876–84. http://www.rootcausecoalition.org/wp-content/uploads/2017/07/Disparities-and-access-to-healthy-food-in-the-United-States-A-review-of-food-deserts-literature.pdf.

Wallis, Jim. *God's Politics: Why the Right Gets It Wrong and the Left Doesn't Get It*. New York: HarperCollins: 2005.

Bibliography

Wallace, Ronald S. *Calvin's Doctrine of the Christian Life*. Eugene, OR: Wipf & Stock, 1997.

Ward, Benedicta, ed. *The Desert Fathers: Sayings of the Early Christian Monks*. New York: Penguin, 2003.

Ware, Kallistos. "Discovering the Inner Kingdom." Transcribed by Parker Hasler and Reijo Oksanen. Torrance, CA: Oakwood, 1997. http://www.prayerofheart.com/docs/Kallistos Prayer of the Heart-6.pdf.

————. *The Orthodox Way*. Rev. ed. Crestwood, NY: St. Vladimir's Seminary Press, 1979.

Warfield, Benjamin Breckinridge. *The Inspiration and Authority of the Bible*. Phillipsburg, NJ: Presbyterian and Reformed, 1948.

————. "The Inspiration of the Bible: A Lecture." *Bibliotheca Sacra* 51 (1894) 614–40.

————. *Revelation and Inspiration*. New York: Oxford, 1927.

Warren, Jonathan. "The Theology of Michael Ramsey for Today." *Anglican Pastor*, July 9, 2014. http://anglicanpastor.com/the-theology-of-michael-ramsey-for-today/.

Warren, Rick. Interview by Piers Morgan. *Piers Morgan Live*, December 6, 2013. http://transcripts.cnn.com/TRANSCRIPTS/1312/06/pmt.01.html.

————. *The Purpose Driven Life: What on Earth Am I Here For?* Grand Rapids: Zondervan, 2011.

Warren, Rick, et al. "The Cost of Freedom: How Disagreement Makes Us Civil." Co-sponsored by Torrey Honors Institute and the Biola University Center for Christian Thought, April 30, 2015. https://www.youtube.com/watch?v=XNDQj8QK8Zc.

Weber, Max. "Science as a Vocation." In *Max Weber: Essays in Sociology*, edited by H. H. Gerth and C. Wright Mills. New York: Oxford University Press, 1946.

Weber, Timothy. "Dispensational Premillennialism: The Dispensationalist Era." *Christianity Today* 61, 1999. https://www.christianitytoday.com/history/issues/issue-61/dispensational-premillennialism-dispensationalist-era.html.

Weil, Simone. *Letter to a Priest*. New York: Penguin, 2003.

————. *Simone Weil: An Anthology*. Edited by Siân Miles. New York: Grove, 1986.

————. *Waiting on God*. Translated by Emma Craufurd. New York: Routledge, 2009.

Weinandy, Thomas Gerard. *Athanasius: A Theological Introduction*. Burlington, VT: Ashgate, 2007.

Wesley, John. "I Felt My Heart Strangely Warmed." In *Journal of John Wesley*. http://www.ccel.org/ccel/wesley/journal.vi.ii.xvi.html.

————. *The Works of the Rev. John Wesley*. Vol. 8. 1st American ed. New York: J. & J. Harper, 1827.

West, Cornel. "Spiritual Blackout, Imperial Meltdown, Prophetic Fightback." Harvard convocation address, September 8, 2017. Transcript. https://hds.harvard.edu/news/2017/09/08/transcript-cornel-wests-2017-convocation-address#.

Westerkamp, Marilyn J. *Women and Religion in Early America, 1600–1850: The Puritan and Evangelical Traditions*. New York: Routledge, 1999.

Westfall, Richard S. *Never at Rest: A Biography of Isaac Newton*. New York: Cambridge University Press, 1983.

Westminster Confession of Faith. http://www.ccel.org/ccel/schaff/creeds3.iv.xvii.ii.html.

White, James Emery. *A Traveler's Guide to the Kingdom: Journeying Through the Christian Life*. Downers Grove, IL: InterVarsity, 2012.

————. *What Is Truth?: A Comparative Study of the Positions of Cornelius Van Til, Francis Schaeffer, Carl F. H. Henry, Donald Bloesch, Millard Erickson.* Eugene, OR: Wipf & Stock, 2006.

Wood, Ralph. *Flannery O'Connor and the Christ-Haunted South.* Grand Rapids: Eerdmans, 2004.

Wuthnow, Robert. *After the Baby Boomers: How Twenty- and Thirty-Somethings Are Shaping the Future of American Religion.* Princeton, NJ: Princeton University Press, 2010.

————. "Small Groups Forge New Notions of Community and the Sacred." *Christian Century* 110/35 (1993) 1239–40.

Wiesel, Elie. *Night.* Translated by Marion Wiesel. New York: Hill and Wang, 2006.

Wigley, Stephen. *Karl Barth and Hans Urs Von Balthasar: A Critical Engagement.* London: T. & T. Clark, 2007.

Williams, Charles. "The Way of Exchange." In *Selected Writings*, edited by Anne Ridler, 122–31. London: Oxford University Press, 1961.

Williams, Daniel H. *Evangelicals and Tradition: The Formative Influence of the Early Church.* Grand Rapids: Baker Academic, 2005.

————. *Retrieving the Tradition and Renewing Evangelicalism: A Primer for Suspicious Protestants.* Grand Rapids: Eerdmans, 1999.

Williams, Daniel K. *God's Own Party: The Making of the Christian Right.* New York: Oxford University Press, 2010.

Williams, Rowan. *Dostoevsky: Language, Faith, and Fiction.* The Making of the Christian Imagination. Waco, TX: Baylor University Press, 2008.

————. *On Christian Theology.* Malden, MA: Blackwell, 2000.

Wilson, Douglas. *Heaven Misplaced: Christ's Kingdom on Earth.* Moscow, ID: Canon, 2008.

Winter, Bruce. "Acts and Food Shortages." In *The Book of Acts in Its Graeco-Roman Setting*, edited by David W. J. Gill and Conrad Gempf. Grand Rapids: Eerdmans, 1994.

Winthrop, John. "A Model of Christian Charity." In *American Religions: A Documentary History*, edited by R. Marie Griffith, 16–18, New York: Oxford University Press, 2008.

Witherington, Ben. *The Jesus Quest: The Third Search for the Jew of Nazareth.* Downers Grove, IL: InterVarsity, 1997.

Wittgenstein, Ludwig. *Tractatus Logico-Philosophicus.* Translated by D. F. Pears and B. F. McGuinness. New York: Routledge, 2001.

Wood, Alan. *Bertrand Russell, the Passionate Sceptic.* New York: Routledge, 2013.

Woodrow, James. Evolution. In *American Religions: A Documentary History*, edited by R. Marie Griffith, 284–300. New York: Oxford University Press, 2008.

Woolfolk, R. L. "The Power of Negative Thinking: Truth, Melancholia, and the Tragic Sense of Life." *Journal of Theoretical and Philosophical Psychology* 22/1 (2002) 19–27.

Worthen, Molly. *Apostles of Reason: The Crisis of Authority in American Evangelicalism.* New York: Oxford University Press, 2013.

Wright, George Frederick. "The Passing of Evolution." In *The Fundamentals: A Testimony to the Truth*, vol. 4, edited by Reuben A. Torrey, and Amzi C. Dixon, 60–72. Ages Digital Library Reference. http://ntslibrary.com/PDF%20Books%20II/Torrey%20-%20The%20Fundamentals%204.pdf.

―――. "Professor Wright and Some of His Critics." *Bibliotheca Sacra* 42 (1885) 352.

Wright, N. T. *How God Became King: The Forgotten Story of the Gospels.* New York: HarperCollins, 2012.

―――. *The Letters of John.* N. T. Wright for Everyone Bible Study Guides. Downers Grove, IL: InterVarsity, 2012.

―――. "N. T. Wright and Pete Enns: America's Culture Wars." Interview by Peter Enns, *BioLogos,* January 16, 2013. https://biologos.org/resources/americas-culture-wars-with-n-t-wright-and-pete-enns.

―――. *Simply Christian: Why Christianity Makes Sense.* New York: HarperCollins, 2006.

Yeats, William Butler. "The Second Coming." In *The Collected Works of W. B. Yeats,* vol. 1, *The Poems,* edited by Richard J. Finneran. 2nd ed. New York: Scribner, 1997.

"You Can't Mix the Bible and Evolution." *Wretched,* February 5, 2013. https://www.youtube.com/watch?v=smIJoj_BECo.

"Your Word Is Truth." Evangelicals and Catholics Together, August 2002. https://www.firstthings.com/article/2002/08/your-word-is-truth.

Zacharias, Ravi. *Jesus Among Other Gods: The Absolute Claims of the Christian Message.* Nashville: Thomas Nelson, 2000.

Zimbardo, Philip. *The Lucifer Effect: Understanding How Good People Turn Evil.* New York: Random House, 2007.

Zizek, Slavoj. *The Puppet and the Dwarf: The Perverse Core of Christianity.* Cambridge, MA: MIT Press, 2003.

Made in the USA
Middletown, DE
20 February 2020